Sociology
Since Midcentury

ESSAYS IN THEORY CUMULATION

Sociology Since Midcentury

ESSAYS IN THEORY CUMULATION

Randall Collins

Department of Sociology
University of Virginia
Charlottesville, Virginia

ACADEMIC PRESS
A Subsidiary of Harcourt Brace Jovanovich, Publishers
New York   London   Toronto   Sydney   San Francisco

ACADEMIC PRESS, INC.
111 Fifth Avenue, New York, New York 10003

United Kingdom Edition published by
ACADEMIC PRESS, INC. (LONDON) LTD.
24/28 Oval Road, London NW1 7DX

Library of Congress Cataloging in Publication Data

Collins, Randall, Date.
    Sociology since midcentury.

    Includes index.
    1. Sociology--History--20th century. I. Title.
HM19.C642   301'.9'04   81-13034
ISBN 0-12-181340-1   AACR2

PRINTED IN THE UNITED STATES OF AMERICA

81 82 83 84   9 8 7 6 5 4 3 2 1

Contents

___I___
The Advance of Historical Sociology

II
Structuralism and Conflict

III
Sociology of Education: The Cutting Edge

IV
Breakthroughs in Microsociology

V
The Old Guard and the New

Preface

This book is a collection of pieces written over the past 10 years. Some originated as review essays on significant books or careers in sociology; others are new essays on various important theorists whose work I have never formally reviewed. Together they should give a fair sampling of the major intellectual developments in sociology of the last few decades. There may be some important things that I have missed, but enough is included, I hope, to prove my point: that sociology has moved into a new phase, beyond the orthodoxies that characterized the middle of the twentieth century.

In my opinion, writings on the history of sociology should be forward looking. Rather than viewing the past, they should help us select what we can from it to mold the future. All of the essays I have written on other sociologist's works are slanted in that direction. My emphasis may therefore differ from the original authors' intentions. I am not sure, for example, that Lévi-Strauss would accept all of my interpretations of his work, but that is secondary compared to the potential use that we might make today of some of his earlier ideas. All too often the best parts of sociological theory do not cumulate precisely because they are buried among tangential issues debated by historically oriented commentators. I offer this account of the recent history of sociology not as an end in itself, but as a guide to our own future.

Also included in this book are some theories of my own, together with empirical evidence from which, in several cases, they have been inducted. These develop some of the themes that are found in the works of other theorists, or present rival models. The topics treated include a macrohistorical theory of geopolitics, intended somewhat as an alternative to the Wallerstein economic theory of world-systems. At the opposite end of the spectrum, there will also be found here a microtheory, based on the results of ethnomethodology and on Goffman's interaction ritual, which I suggest provides a basis for linking up to and reconstructing macrosociological theories. In between, I deal with structuralism, ritual violence and solidarity, and the symbolic economy of culture. These help fill in the middle ground between the very large and the very small in time and space. Out of such themes, I would argue, will be produced the more sophisticated sociology of the future.

I am indebted to Norbert Wiley and to many others for their comments on various drafts of these chapters.

Introduction

The theme of this book is quickly stated. There is a sociology beyond the orthodoxies of midcentury. This may sound akin to announcing that there is life after death. The question in both cases, of course, is: of what kind?

Midcentury sociology was dominated by a set of theoretical positions. The main pretender to being a general theory was functionalism, the strongest of the various abstract classificatory schemes that had emerged since the 1930s. For social change, the preference was an ethnocentric evolutionist developmentalism. On the microlevel, there was the narrow positivism of social behaviorism, or the "loyal opposition" of symbolic interactionism with its antideterminist emphasis on the emergence and negotiatedness of behavior and on the definition of the situation.

All this has changed radically in the last decade and a half. One obvious development is the upsurge of antipositivism. There has been an explicit reaction against rigidly statistical sociology, and against the "black box" agnosticism of social behaviorism. There has been a widespread rejection of the idea of science itself. This has been abetted, rather ironically, by the rise of an empirical sociology of science, of which Thomas Kuhn has been the most famous representative. To be sure, positivism is still with us. But it has nothing like the theoretical prestige it once had, when even rather ascientific functionalists gave ritual obeisance to it, and Talcott Parsons used to call his theoretical analysis an empirical exercise. Positivist sociology now constitutes only another enclave within the field of contending schools. Its most specialized statistical and mathematical forms have grown increasingly isolated from the rest of sociology, although there are some important exceptions like Harrison White's blockmodeling, which have managed to tie in with current theoretical concerns. Another, separate positivist enclave has recently come on the scene as well. This is sociobiology, which is reminiscent of a much older, turn-of-the century positivism, and sometimes of its racist and sexist overtones as well.

But these are sidelights to the more prominent theoretical developments of recent years. Among the most obvious of these is the upsurge of Marxism. As a sociological theory, Marxism has virtually come back from the dead, and not only because of a shift in the political winds since the virulent anticommunism of the 1950s. For Marxism had virtually given up the ghost as an avowedly economic sociology, seemingly frightened off by the inexplicable survival of twentieth-century capitalism and by the repressive political regimes of the socialist states. But post-midcentury Marxism has come back from the philosophical and humanistic enclave in which it made its last-ditch defense a few years ago, and has again claimed empirical relevance for the processes of politics and economics, class struggle and world upheaval.

Post-midcentury sociology has also been a golden age for historical and macrocomparative sociology generally. Some of this has been Marxist in theme, some Weberian, some avowedly eclectic. All versions have shown a willingness to drastically revise received positons, and the result has been a quantum leap forward in our macrotheories. The resonances among the various historical sociologies, moreover, promise a much more powerful macroparadigm in the making.

At the same time, we have seen the emergence of much more sophisticated microsociologies. From an influx of phenomenology, and from the detailed study of fact-to-face situations, have emerged ethnomethodology, cognitive sociology, and a variety of contending theoretical positions. The area is still in ferment, but a key difference from earlier intepretive and situational sociology is the combination of philosophically sophisticated theorizing, with a new research technology of audio and videotape recordings. Microsociology now goes on at a level of precision and at a theoretical depth that has never before been achieved, and if the results are still up in the air, this is because the theoretical and empirical opportunities are just beginning to be opened up.

Somewhere between or across the micro- and macrolevels has come another influential development, the siren spell of structuralism. Its proponents come in several varieties. One version emphasizes the macrostructural reality of social networks, and presses toward a highly empirical and even mathematical form of analysis. An opposing version emphasizes a purely mental form of structure, and rejects positivism in favor of the decoding of cultural texts. This latter version meets on common ground with the more static Husserlian versions of phenomenology. The most famous of all structuralists, Lévi-Strauss, has somewhat clouded people's perceptions of structuralism by shifting from an early macro network-oriented structuralism to a later mentalist structuralism. I think more and more that there is a significant structuralist opening, but I would judge that the early Lévi Strauss was closer to it than most of the European structuralism that has developed subsequently.

I am not primarily concerned here, however, with history told just for the sake of the story. This book uses intellectual history as the occasion for reflecting on what theory and research has accomplished, and on what it suggests as further paths forward. Part of the book consists of my own efforts to carry certain lines of analysis further. This is not strictly a history of recent sociology, then, but everything in it, historical pieces included, is intended to be an essay in theory cumulation. Indeed, everything worthwhile in a science (if I may use that unpopular word once again) should be. For the key to a science is not any particular research method, nor a type of mathematical formalization. Science is above all the successful effort at cumulation. In this sense, a good deal of nonquantitative sociology is more scientific than statistical exercises that do their best to ignore everything that went before.

There is much recent sociology that I have not attempted to cover. I have said nothing about the Frankfurt School and post-Frankfurt German sociology. Its Hegelianizing and Diltheyizing of sociology does not impress me as very significant for explanatory advance. Neither is the recent Weberianizing of Marxism that has gone on in Europe. Abstract arguments regarding the autonomy of the state may be a breakthrough from the point of view of a dogmatic Marxist, but they say little that a Weberian does not already know. Similarly, little of value seems to have come out of French structuralist Marxism. The most significant omission in this book, from my viewpoint, is James O'Conner's theory of the fiscal crisis of the state. Though cast too much in terms of a polemic and a case study of a particular time and place, the underlying theory is a significant revision of Marxism, and indeed of the relationships between economics and sociology. For it points to the state itself as itself a crucial *economic* actor and consumer, not something outside the economy that either reacts to it or, given sufficient "autonomy," regulates it.

The borderline between economics and sociology is being significantly crossed now, and in both directions. Economics itself, despite its current popularity for business and government careers, is in a theoretical crisis. Conventional economics is unable to deal with the dynamic issues: the combination of stagnation and inflation that has characterized western economies in recent years; the determinants of economic inequality; the trends of economic development and failures of development. The basic analytical tools of economics are no doubt at fault, above all the market equilibrium model and the utilitarian calculus underlying it. Sociology, I would suggest, offers a way out. It has begun to develop nonutilitarian exchange models. The early Lévi-Strauss gives one aspect of this, with his emphasis on ceremonial exchanges and on the shape of the alliance network that results from them. The conventional economic exchange model concerns itself only with prices and quantities of goods produced and exchanged, and ignores the pattern of *who* will exchange with *whom;* the sociological exchange model is good precisely for showing how structures of exchange emerge and how they change through the dynamics of alliance networks themselves. These exchange structures constitute the organization of society, including the organization of its economic units, and the sociological model builds up such macrostructures out of the empirically real microexchanges. Bourdieu's effort to create a theory of "cultural capitalism" crosses the borderline neatly to the domain that economists have ignored: the innumerable small exchanges of human communication that make up the microdetail of stratified human society. My own micro–macro argument regarding chains of interaction rituals is another effort to fit together the pieces of the puzzle. It has not all come together yet, but I think the new integration of economics and sociology will be a major development of the end of the twentieth century.

Another significant direction in which we are moving is toward a theory of the state. The major themes, I would claim, are a revival of a long-submerged Weberian point: the primacy of international dynamics among states, and, hence, the importance of geographical position and of war. The theory of the state may well turn out to be in large part a theory of geopolitics. Theda Skocpol has taken the theory of revolutions a major step forward by demonstrating the connections of war with revolution, both as a crucial cause of the breakdown of the old regime, and in the consolidation of the revolutionary regime. By an even more international strategy of analysis, Reinhard Bendix has produced an intellectual revolution in what used to be ethnocentrically and unhistorically called "modernization." I suggest that a general theory of geopolitics, including "internal geopolitics" as well as the more conventional external sort, may indeed give us the key to both domestic shifts in political power, and to the configuration of international dominance.

Wallerstein agrees with this emphasis on the international perspective, but gives the economic dimension priority over the military and political. Wallerstein's is an effort to reconstruct the cyclical dynamics of the Marxian business cycle, with its revolutionary culmination, but on the vastly enlarged time span of the world scale. Wallerstein's massive project of historical sociology is no more than half finished, and it will continue to provide a lively and fruitful contention of opposing positions in the next decades. A grand theory of the world-system should have taken form by the end of the twentieth century. We shall see on this ground which of the two great macrotraditions, those of Weber and of Marx, has had to incorporate the most from the other.

The sections of this book are organized as follows. We begin with a treatment of the major historical and comparative sociologies, the traditions of Marx and Weber with their subsequent transformations. Then comes a section on structuralism. It presents my own idiosyncratic version of it, to be sure. Above all, this is the modern continuation of the Durkheim–Mauss school of thought. Other ramifications of these ideas are also found elsewhere in this book, such as in their obvious influences on Bourdieu, and their not so obvious but equally strong influence on Erving Goffman. I include here a piece of mine presenting a theory of violence. This attempts to demonstrate, among other things, that a Durkheimian theory need not leave us with a naively benign view, but can explain the darkest side of human society.

The sociology of education merits a heading for a peculiar reason. There is usually a particular research specialty in each decade that is central for advances in theory. I think the sociology of education has played this role recently. Part of the interest in education came originally from an earlier research concern of the 1950s and 1960s, the emphasis on studies of social mobility. Mobility was seen, in an older paradigm, as the key to a modern achievement-based society, and to its political stability. Social mobility research came to concentrate heavily on educational attainment, as apparently the most important determinant of careers—at least, it was the most important variable that could be easily measured. The subsequent revolution in the sociology of education, then, has been a rejection of meritocratic and technocratic views of modern society. In their place we have gotten a breakthrough understanding of the cultural code underlying class stratification, and both Weberian and Marxian efforts to build alternative theories of the prominence of education in modern stratification. I include here an ongoing effort of my own to catch the long-term historical dynamics of cultural credential systems, and their linkages with political and economic development and crisis.

The section on mircosociology is not comprehensive. It does make a special effort to do justice to Erving Goffman. The more we look at his work, in my opinion, the more he emerges as the leading figure in the microsociology of our times. I would certainly do more with the phenomenologists and ethomethodologists in a full-fledged history. Especially interesting is their philosophical background, stretching back to the philosophical revolutions of the early twentieth century, and beyond them to the mathematical revolution of the previous century. The old self-assured positivism broke down first in the foundations of mathematics, producing the waring schools of formalists and intuitionists. The rumour of this controversy has rippled through adjacent fields ever since, at the leisure pace of intellectual transmission, and has become incorporated into microsociology in our own post-midcentury generation. This deserves much more than a cursory historical treatment. I do try to illustrate a bit of the kind of ethnomethodology that ought to be better known, however, by discussing some of the notable results of the research revolution produced by the introduction of the cassette tape recorder. Recent microsociology, far from being a loosely interpretative philosophy, is the new ultra-empiricism, which undercuts the claims of more conventional quantitative research to get at the true empirical reality of society. The section concludes with my own essay which tries to draw out the theoretical consequences of these breakthroughs in microsociology.

The final section is a miscellany on various positions of which I am by and large not very fond. It is at least a token effort to give the devil his due, and to sketch some of the intellectual history of rival positions. There is no specific section on conflict theory, although it is obviously my favorite. This is because it pops up everywhere, on all levels and in different substantive topics.

My basic claim is that we are living in a major intellectual era for sociology. This is not always easy to see, especially if one is a participant in the day-by-day routines of intellectual life. But intellectual developments move relatively slowly. Truly major advances may take as much as a generation by the time they are made, consolidated, and widely recognized. This is why a long-term historical stockkeeping is so important for seeing what is happening right now.

A level of theoretical sophistication was reached in sociology in the generation of the beginning of the twentieth century. This is why we consider it the period of our classics: Weber, Durkheim, the Cooley-Mead-Thomas complex of ideas, as well as Simmel, Michels, Sorel, and others. The creative development of most of these positions was largely interrupted in the next generation. Instead of further advances along the lines of classic theory, we had mainly their epigones, reiterating the older positions, or debating their philosophical premises. Methodology and metatheory took the place of explanatory theory. It fits this pattern that midcentury sociology was dominated by the nonexplanatory classification schemes and teleological justification of the functionalists, by the loose interpretative stance of the symbolic interactionists, and by an atheroretical statistical positivism.

The power of post-midcentury sociology has been that it has recovered the theoretical impulse that characterized the classics. Part of this is due to a renewed link that we have forged between theory and research. It has not come about under anyone's preconceived methodological canons: Neither the historical works of our new golden age of historical sociology, nor the tape-recording studies of the ethnomethodologists, would have come about if sociologists took all their research inspiration from methods textbooks. But even conventional quantitative sociology has made considerable strides. In the last decade, statistical work is not solely pursued for its technical virtuosity, and does not only present purely descriptive materials; a significant fraction of it is now oriented toward testing explanatory theories. Probably the general popularity of Marxism or of some version of conflict theory among younger researchers is responsible for this; for these are the types of theory that now intrude into what was once the province of a bland functionalism.

To a considerable degree, political shifts seem responsible for the long-term shifts in sociology's development. Midcentury politics, from the Nazi triumph in Germany on through the height of the Cold War, had debilitating effects on social theory. Both Marxism and its Weberian and idealist alternatives, which had existed in a fruitful tension at the turn of the century, were driven out of Germany by the fascists. The U.S. settled into an antiextremist (and intellectually, this meant especially anticommunist) posture which made sociologists deal with stratification—in my opinion, the very core topic of our field—in the most gingerly middle-of-the-road terms. The alliance of functionalism and hyperpositivism was the result, with the role of opposition taken by a politically harmless symbolic interactionism, which rejected any kind of structural theory and hence was impotent to deal with stratification or with macropatterns. Post-war European intellectuals did not help this situation much, as their engagé Marxism and antipositivism merely presented the opposite side of the coin, and generated no explanatory sociology.

The political shift of the 1960s, with rebelliousness against orthodoxy apparent within both Cold War blocs, struck a crucial blow for intellectual liberation. The upsurge of Marxism in sociology has been obvious, and so has the influx of antipositivist phenomenology and other philosophical sociologies. The intellectual significance, though, has come not because we have substituted one orthodoxy for another, but because the openness of intellectual contention has risen again back to the level of the early twentieth century. Alternative positions are being fought over on both micro- and macrolevels. The classics are now revived in a fruitful way and made the bases for further developments, precisely because the contenders of today need to make use of all the intellectual resources they can get. The Marxisms of the last decade have suddenly become much less orthodox than any in the previous few generations, and it is this willingness to change the paradigm that accounts for Marxism's new *intellectual* appeal. In conjunction with this, Weberian sociology is forging ahead, turning Weber's leads into specific theories, and incorporating many more angles from Marxism as well as from other positions than previously.

The tension of political positions seems to be a sine qua non for an advance in sociological theory. The predominance of *any* political faction, left, right, or center, results in an intellectual orthodoxy which is the end of creativity. To be sure, this is not all that has contributed to our current intellectual surge. The steady accumulation of empirical results in midcentury, atheoretical though so much of it was, provided a significant base on which reawakened interests in general explanatory theory could build. A few sociologists have always done good work combining theory and empiricism, enabling empirical research traditions to cumulate as well as theoretical ones. These chains of results may move slowly and unspectacularly, but they are an important element in the progress toward a powerful sociological science. We are fortunate that the political controversies of today do not simply become translated immediately into the realm of sociological ideas, but mingle with and vitalize some mature research traditions.

To be sure, there is plenty of political polemicizing that goes on in sociology today, plenty of specialized methodological pronouncements, plenty of detailed research that seems to go nowhere, and of metatheorizing that links up with nothing in the real social world. The intellectual community, seen from close up and with eye to the ground level, usually appears contentious, confusing, repetitious, going nowhere, and accomplishing little. This is the way things always look if one cannot see the core theoretical issues, and what is happening to them. That is why it is essential to back off and look down on this planet like viewing an intellectual newsreel of the entire century. The larger pattern is there, if you want to see it. Better yet: it is a pattern waiting to be extended, by those who are willing to work at it.

I

The Advance of Historical Sociology

The Empirical Validity of
the Conflict Tradition*

The history of sociology remains alive in a peculiar sense not found in other disciplines. The classic sociologists are studied today, not for their purely historical interest, but because in important respects we have not yet gone beyond them. In relation to major figures like Marx and Weber (and others), we are like the scholars of the Rennaissance rediscovering the Greeks—not that we seem destined never to move past them, but that we have yet to move through them in their full depth. Add to this the clash of self-definitions that characterizes contemporary sociology, and we see another reason why sociology's classics should be brought into contention. Different figures are favored and their different facets turned toward the modern eye, depending on current interests in social criticism and social reconstruction, historicist interpretation, epistemological argument, justification for research techniques, or the construction of an explanatory science.

I am concerned here with the last: the prospects of sociology as a science, that is to say a system of causal generalizations borne out by

* Originally published in *Theory and Society* 1974, 1: 147–178. Copyright 1974 Elsevier Scientific Publishing Company, Amsterdam.

empirical test. The ideal has sustained considerable attack, above all on epistemological grounds. But most of this battle has been fought out over programmatic and methodological claims; critiques of the *possibility* of scientific sociology would look rather different directed against an existing set of empirically validated generalizations.

My claim is that sociology does contain a solid core of explanatory principles, but they are not to be found in the places where they are most often sought. The scientific tradition in sociology has usually been considered to be the positivist tradition, especially its organic side from Comte through Durkheim to contemporary functionalists. The failure of this tradition to produce much more than acausal categorizations and postfacto justifications of dominant institutions has been a major reason for the declining prestige of the scientific ideal. Another version of positivism has given science a bad name by stressing raw induction and purely technical canons of data gathering, again without producing serious generalizations. Other versions of sociology—the interpretive social psychologies and philosophies, along with sociological historicism and various forms of political activism—have, of course, rejected the aim of producing a sociological science.

But these contending positions do not exhaust the field. There is another line of development, interrelated with some of the preceding, but cutting a distinctive path of its own: conflict theory. It is a distinctive tradition in that it proceeds along a certain line of insight worn steadily deeper over time; it is a scientific tradition, both in that the ideal of social science was developed within it, and in that we may draw from it a consistent network of causal generalizations of considerable empirical power.

The basic stance of conflict theory was taken by Machiavelli. Its fundamental element is a capacity for naturalistic realism, for sustained periods of intellectual detachment from the rhetoric of popular controversy. People follow their own interests; success breeds honor; power breeds ambition; morality is based on violence, but works best by deception, espcially through the deliberate staging of dramatic gestures; mass support is useful in the struggle of elites, and can be manipulated by show, especially of the externals of religion. This line of analysis was advanced by Marx's sociology, which specifies the conditions shaping interests and conflicts, describes the resources that enable particular interests to dominate, and generalizes about the relationship between the ideological surface of public consciousness and the real events below. Parallel developments were made by the realism of modern historiography, by the German theorists of *realpolitik* and of the conquest theory of the state. A sophisticated synthesis of these lines of thought with elements of Marxian sociology was accomplished by Max Weber, and applied to more limited topics of modern politics by Robert Michels and his successors.

This constitutes the main line of conflict theory on the macrolevel. There is also a development on the microlevel, a tradition of tell-it-like-it-is in private life that extends from Schopenhauer through Nietzsche to Freud. Here again we find explanation in terms of amoral self-interest, with morality interpreted as the effect of external social pressures, and an interplay between a surface of deceptive ideals and an underworld of real interests. Standing somewhere between macro- and microlevels is Georges Sorel, with his recognition of the interrelations of violence and moral solidarity, of the ideological surface and the realm of real satisfactions. Darwin is in the background for all of the later nineteenth-century conflict theory. It reflects not so much his evolutionism as his picture of man as an animal in a situation of biological struggle upon which civilization is only a veneer.

What I am interested in here is an abstraction from the whole body of their work: what this tradition has accomplished in the way of explanatory generalizations borne out by empirical research. The most important figures of the conflict tradition are very famous; their thought pulled together many strands, and they have contributed to many different lines of subsequent development. Some of these lines—especially those that have recently been prominent—have obscured the aspect of their thought that I wish to concentrate upon. I am not necessarily concerned here with their philosophies or methodological orientations, nor with the total body of their substantive theories, but only with what we can take from them that will bear fruit in subsequent research.

Above all, I wish to put to one side the political positions of these thinkers and the political interpretations that have been placed upon them. The importance of such detachment is especially clear in the case of Weber. Weber has been taken up by liberal anti-Marxists and presented first as a one-sided idealist who gave a religious explanation of capitalism and a legitimist interpretation of politics; then as a multicausal pluralist who invalidates any emphasis on class influences, and above all as the proponent of a doctrine of value neutrality that justifies obliviousness to conceptual and methodological choices which can make seemingly objective research into covert propaganda for particular value positions. Thus Weber has been made into both an idealist and a positivist, and the object of polemical attack by the philosophical Left in contemporary sociology.

As a result, Weber's most significant work remains obscured. His early work on the Protestant Ethic is only a fragment of his full analysis of the preconditions for capitalism. Throughout his main writings, Weber develops a complex and sophisticated version of the conflicting interests, material resources, and organization forms that make up the stuff of history. Religious ideas play an important part, not as incursions from a transcendent realm, nor yet as unmediated reflections of a class structure. With his good command of historical detail, Weber shows ideals as created by religious practitioners and sustained by religious organizations and explores their affinity with the interests of various classes and status groups and their use as weapons in struggles for political control. In stratification, organizations, and elsewhere, far from being the proponent of idealized abstractions, Weber provides some of our sharpest insights into the process of conflict and the weapons of domination.

It has been the political interests of both liberals and radicals that has obscured Weber's main accomplishments for so long; the history of the reception of his own work is one of the strongest arguments for Weber's conception of scholarly detachment. For it should be noted: Weber's doctrine of value neutrality is no naïve shutting of the eyes to the sources of hidden value bias. It is, on the contrary, a deliberate choice in favor of a difficult form of self-discipline, a continual effort to rise above political factions and toward the maximally powerful line of scholarly explanation. The orientation of conflict theory facilitates this, as it emphasis on the nature of conflicting factions warns the analyst against being caught in their self serving argumentation. The strategy does not preclude taking sides at some point, but it calls for every effort to do this in full consciousness, while preserving a separate realm of scholarship whose standards are not those of the world of politics.

The same applies to Marx. I am concerned here with his sociology, not his political philosophy, nor with the aspects of his economic system that seem to be molded by the historical aspirations of his era. I do not claim to be inclusive, nor am I interested here in arguments as to what is the authentic Marxism. My criterion is purely pragmatic: to pick out those theoretical generalizations that can explain the evidence and lead to even more powerful conceptual refinements. Hence I deliberately emphasize the broadly materialistic stance that flows so naturally from Marx, but give this a sociological focus rather than identifying it with the system of economic evolution presented in *Capital*. The most fruitful explanatory principles are those that give the conditions for class consciousness and political mobilization, with their implications for explaining organized conflict and dominance in all spheres. This kind of pragmatism about sociological ideas from the past is the most appropriate epistemological method for conflict theory; truth is always historically situated, and advances by continual reformulations, as thinkers strive for maximal explanatory coherence of ideas and evidence. Conflict theory can recognize that the existence of an intellectual community with sufficient autonomy from external pressures to carry this on depends on particular historical circumstances; as long as we have those conditions, there is nothing contradictory about making use of them to further the development of the most detached and coherent theory possible.

My aim, then, has been to take up the universal side of Machiavelli, rather than his schemes for the Florentine state; the leading insights of Nietzsche and Freud, without their biologism and their sexism. Conflict theory is Machiavelli without the Prince; Marx without Hegel; Darwin without Spencer; Weber without idealism; Freud without Victorianism—better yet, Freud restored to his Nietzschean historical premises. With sufficient detachment, the main line of explanatory accomplishment in sociology should come into view.

My contention is that conflict theory has been vindicated by empirical evidence to an extent approached by no other sociological theory. This involves understanding several things. First, that the body of conflict theory does contain a network of causal, testable explanatory generalizations, although they must often be abstracted from specific historical discussions, and above all, from the political and philosophical polemics that have obscured them. Second, that there is a fair amount of sociological research, on both contemporary and historical materials, that bears out the main propositions of conflict theory, and enables us to add refinements to them. Again, one must abstract out the relevance of this research, for it is seldom presented as explicitly bearing on conflict theory—or for that matter, on any explanatory generalizations at all. This is particularly true of research on stratification, which has been primarily descriptive and its larger relevance has usually been taken in terms of social problems or ideological controversies.

The task now is to put together the pieces, to treat the evidence as it bears on explicitly formulated conflict theory, and thus to recognize where we stand. Sociology has accomplished a good deal more than is usually recognized. It is the prominence of the acausal abstractions of functionalism and of interpretive social psychologies that give such a widespread impression that sociology has no real explanatory power. The materials of stratification and of organizations do fall into a fair degree of order around the propositions of conflict theory, and there is little within the scope of sociology that cannot be treated as a variant

on stratification and/or organizational principles. The evidence is not
as precise as one might wish, but the overall pattern is clearly there;
and after all, it is the broad coherence of theory and research that is the
basic criterion of validity. The theoretical obliviousness of ultra-
positivist methodologists and of the more solipsistic ethnomethodologists alike is nothing more than polemical defense of overspecializa-
tion; the only path toward a science, and the only way of resolving
methodological ambiguities, is to see specific researches in the context
of the largest possible system of generalizations. Conflict theory hardly
provides a complete science, but it is firmly on the path toward one.
Theory building in a science is always a dialectic between gathering
evidence and conceptual organization; in the history of conflict sociology, these poles have been pulled rather far apart, but the underlying
connections are nevertheless strong. The important task now is to
recognize them. The evidence we have now, for all its imperfections,
supports more than a program.

OUTPOSTS OF A NATURALISTIC REALISM

The dominant forms of thought about the social world have been
idealistic throughout most of history. Religion was the mode of legit-
imizing the state and stratification in most societies until the modern
era, and even the more rationalistic systems that emerged from time to
time—those of Plato and Aristotle, for example—legitimized some
ideal form of social structure on the basis of transcendent forms. The
emergence of a realistic conflict theory thus required special conditions, especially a situation of sustained political struggle among interests of approximately equal strength, so that no single legitimization
could claim undisputed reality. Thus we find brief outcroppings of
naturalistic realism in the most conflictful periods of ancient civilization.

In China, the long period of warring states preceding the Han
dynasty produced a variety of intellectual factions, among them the
followers of Mo Ti (ca. 400 B.C.), who taught a doctrine not unlike
Hobbes: that self-interested conflict was the natural state, and only
complete obedience to a ruler who set all standards of truth and
morality could bring social order. In India, the period during which the
ancient tribal republics were giving way to a series of petty kingdoms
and to the rigidification of the caste system produced a variety of
heterodox reactions: these ranged from asceticism and mysticism to
materialist cynicism, and Gautama Buddha himself (ca. 560–480 B.C.)

taught that the world as ordinarily experienced is nothing but conflict among creatures following their sensual appetites. In Greece, the chaotic period of democratization and balance of power among warring city–states saw the doctrine of Heraclitus (ca. 500 B.C.) whose cryptic pronouncements included the doctrine that strife is the basis of all things; and of the Sophists, who taught that standards of truth and morality are socially created by self-interested parties. In the fourth century B.C., these efforts at realism crystallized in Epicureanism, which incorporated the atomic theory of matter to argue against the existence of gods and sought happiness in a kind of anarchist intentional community.

These insights into the world of material conflict led to no sustained explanatory analysis. For the most part, although existing doctrines of religious legitimation were rejected, recognition of social conflict was only a stepping stone to a new practical solution. The Mohists became a quasi-military sect; the Buddhists' cynicism was simply the counterpart of a thorough-going mystical rejection of the world; the Sophists were content to teach rhetorical tactics; and the Epicureans, for all their espousal of the major scientific achievement of ancient society, became a conservative and antiintellectual sect. What was necessary to produce a conflict theory was not only a detached realism, but also an effort at systematic generalizations, and an effort to test generalizations against a range of empirical evidence. The third of these conditions had to await modern times; the second—the effort at stating general laws—was found primarily among the idealists. The doctrines of Plato, Pythagoras, Plotinus, Hermes, and Aristotle (the last incorporating material science in a position subordinate to ideal forms) carried the intellectual field, and all but oblivated the more realistic insights of their opponents for future generations.

KAUTILYA, THUCYDIDES, MACHIAVELLI

The most explicit and secularized expositions of social conflict came from three men whose careers were in the heart of political struggle: one of them a successful revolutionist, the other two ending up as exiles. Kautilya (ca. 320 B.C.), living at the end of the period of intensive doctrinal struggle in north India, engineered a coup d'etat to bring Chandragupta Maurya to the Nanda throne, and, as his chief minister, directed the policy of war and alliance that produced the Maurya empire—the only state of premodern times to conquer all of India. Kautilya's *Arthashastra*, like Machiavelli's *The Prince*, is designed to

express the principles of realistic statecraft. Its tone is completely
secular and pragmatic, recognizing military force as the sine qua non
of the state, and recommending rational calculation of strengths in
deciding on wars and alliances, tactics of trickery and stirring up dissension among enemies, and a system of spies for domestic order.
Nothing is ever at rest, asserts Kautilya, and the power of a state is
always increasing or decreasing; he details a dynamic policy to ensure
military expansion. Yet the *Arthashastra* falls short of a scientific
treatise. It is a handbook for a king, and its great length includes an entire legal and administrative system, ranging from marriage customs to
taxation; the doctrines of political conflict are put only in the form of
tactical admonitions, without historical examples or any effort at empirical explanation. It falls short, as well, of the major insight of
modern conflict theory: the importance of ideological superstructure as
a weapon in conflict—the religious legitimation whose manipulation
Machiavelli was to stress. Kautilya's tone, indeed, is on a level of
cynical realism scarcely approached since.

Thucydides (ca. 456–396 B.C.) was an Athenian general put in command of an expedition early in the Peloponnesian war (431–404 B.C.);
the expedition ended in disaster, and Thucydides went into exile rather
than face the wrath of Athenian democracy. In a position of enforced
detachment, he wrote a history of the war based on his observations
and interviews on both sides of the conflict. The result founded the discipline of serious historiography. Thucydides is the first historian to be
concerned about his sources, and to make efforts to check them from
alternative accounts; in his work, too, the usual allusions to divine intervention, to omens and portents, are completely missing. History for
the first time reveals what a thoroughly secular and realistic account of
the world looks like; even the distortions of patriotism are strained out
in Thucydides' detachment from his city's losing cause. The world that
is revealed is one of conflict and brute force. Athenian imperialism is
taken for what it is, and its leaders put aside moralizing to justify it in
terms of *realpolitik*. The class struggles within the city—states, the realities of slavery, the maneuvering of political factions, the intolerance
of the victors toward their opponents, are displayed without disguise.
With Thucydides begins a line of development whose importance for
conflict theory cannot be overestimated: the discipline of realistic
history writing itself. For history is largely a record of conflict of a very
un-ideal sort, and it is out of familiarity with serious historiography
that most of the modern conflict theorists have drawn their insights.
Thucydides, moreover, is the one exemplar of ancient realism whose
works came down to the modern era as an accepted classic; Hobbes'

first work was a translation of the *Peloponnesian War*, and it is from its realism that Hegel and Marx apparently drew their insights into the conflicts of ancient Greece.

Machiavelli (1469–1527) was another individual who danced precariously on the chopping block of history. As a youth, he lived through the popular uprising led by the fanatical monk, Savonarola, which overthrew the rule of the Medicis in Florence and established the Florentine republic. In 1498, after the fall and execution of Savonarola, Machiavelli served as secretary of state for the new government, in charge of military reforms as well as foreign diplomacy. Thus he had firsthand dealings with the Borgias, the most worldly and corrupt of the Renaissance popes, with the shifting alliances in a period of foreign invasion and domestic Italian rivalries, as well as with popular revolts and internal coups in his native city. In 1512, the Florentine republic was overthrown and the Medicis returned to power; Machiavelli was tortured and then exiled. *The Prince* (1513), his immediate response to this change of fortune, was both the distillation of his experiences and an effort (which proved unsuccessful) to offer his services to the new Medici power. This work, together with his later ones, which included a history of Florence, expressed a realistic insight into the mechanisms of power and conflict to a degree not seen for two thousand years. His historical work, together with that of his countryman Guiciardini, began the modern tradition of realistic historiography; in its pages, the class conflicts of Florence were laid bare for all who wished to see. Yet this beginning was not followed up. Machiavelli's attack on the conventional religious pieties concerning statecraft brought him only infamy; his analysis of the mechanisms of conflict was too tightly interwoven with his political advice to be easily separable. For Machiavelli was not yet in the scientific tradition; for him the world was a matter of *Fortuna* and *virtu*, not of explanatory principles and empirical evidence. The transformation of realistic insight into conflict theory awaited the work of Hobbes and the post-Reformation free thinkers.

HOBBES AND VOLTAIRE

Hobbes (1588–1679) and Voltaire (1694–1778) are important figures in the conflict tradition, not so much because of the actual content of their doctrines about conflict, but because they established a tradition of naturalistic social realism within the emerging ideal of science. Personally, their lives show a similar pattern with that of other thinkers who had the necessary detachment to understand conflict. Both of them were exiles: Hobbes, an aging tutor attached to a royalist family during the English civil war, published his *Leviathan* (1651) while at the exiled court of Charles II; Voltaire, exiled to England as a young man (1726–28) over a personal quarrel with an aristocrat, returned to publish his *Lettres Philosophiques sur les Anglais* (1734), the subversiveness of which banished him from Paris again for most of the rest of his long life. Their political aims were similar only in a common opposition to the existing state of affairs; Hobbes put forth his arguments against the libertarian doctrines that led to civil war; Voltaire attacked religious superstition and aristocratic privilege in the name of tolerance. Their crucial point of agreement was in removing religious justifications as a basis for understanding the state, although they did this in the context of different political opponents and allies—Hobbes' position deriving from his conservative attachments in a civil war where the rebels were religious fanatics, Voltaire's from a parvenu's antagonism to traditionalistic elites, and his hope of preferment by the rationalist bureaucracies of the new absolutist monarchs.

For different political reasons, both men drew the intellectual battle lines at science versus religion. Hobbes was already a follower of Galileo and an acquaintance of Descartes before the outbreak of Civil War in 1640; political events motivated him to produce a thoroughly materialistic social philosophy to counter the religious, moralistic, and legalistic doctrines of the rebels. Thus the immortal soul and the kingdom of heaven are irrelevant in a material world, where worldly power alone rules; morality is reduced to obedience to social conventions, and these in turn are nothing if not upheld by the state. The state is organized violence, and that is its basis for keeping order; laws are upheld only because the state controls violence, and cannot be a basis for it. Material interest in individual self-preservation is the basic driving force; good and evil are reduced to appetite and aversion—reward and punishment. Hobbes' analytical notion of a state of nature in which there is conflict of all against all is taken to be the logical consequence of these axioms; the resulting contract which produces order by providing absolute obedience to a sovereign who controls violence is Hobbes' doctrinal conclusion, justifying royal absolutism.

What was important about Hobbes' doctrine was not this conclusion, which in fact drew very little assent, even from royalists (who preferred the cloak of religious legitimacy to this strange new justification). For despite much vilification on this score and for his atheism, Hobbes succeeded in popularizing the doctrine that scientific method and materialism apply to society as well as elsewhere. For the most part, they were watered down to eliminate the conflict elements; in the hands of Locke, the material interests of different individuals are seen as adjustable through a common interest in upholding private property, and the social contract becomes a benign agreement. The recognition of stark political violence underlying the state was muted; Hobbes' axiom-following political man was transformed into the utilitarians' economic man.

Hobbes' political conclusions had little importance for conflict theory, and his immediate followers took something of a detour from the path of social realism. For, if Hobbes formulated the ideal of social science, the victorious British liberals who appropriated this ideal made it into another doctrine which served to protect privileged interests and hide the harsh realities of social conflict. In the hands of Locke and his utilitarian successors, Hobbes' conflictful materialism became utopian positivism. The label emerges later, but the doctrine appears here. From Locke onwards, culminating in the economics of Adam Smith, the rationalist reformism of Bentham and John Stuart Mill, the evolutionism of Spencer, and eventually the associationist and behaviorist psychologies, the ideal of scientific materialism is taken to imply peaceful progress in a world of mutually self-adjusting individuals. The sharp teeth of Hobbes' realism were hidden by a superficial smile.

Voltaire, a rebel of a later generation and from a more autocratic state than the one that succeeded Hobbes, illustrates the ambivalence of the conflict tradition in the eighteenth century. For although he is the archenemy of superstition and pretense, he believes that victory is so close that his criticisms become muted in an appreciation of the coming rational order. His jokes and slogans keep the spirit of atheism alive, and with it, the recognition of the arbitrariness of traditional stratification, but he feels it necessary in his later works to support a rationalistic deism to replace the old dogmas. He writes world history as a record of quarrels and follies, but he cannot resist the urge to propagandize for a long-term evolution that is about to usher in the Age of Reason. The presence of England on the European scene gives him an ideal society whose internal conflicts are invisible to him; along with the doctrines of Newton, Voltaire popularizes Locke's positivism. It is only one step further to the *philosophes*, to Turgot and Condorcet, with their claims that science shows an evolution of reason, manifested alike in technology and in social progress, that inevitably (and without conflict) brings with it the better age of the future. The militant atheism of the seventeenth century underground was gradually becoming transformed into the bourgeois rationalism of the nineteenth.

The ideal of social science as it emerged in the seventeenth century contained the fundamentals of conflict theory. As long as religion was a powerful enemy, the connection was maintained. As modern states and political factions began to provide for their own secular justification, however, the cutting edge of science towards a realistic view of social conflict was blunted; the ideal (if not the substance) of science became subverted into a screen to hide social conflicts. The thinkers of the French Revolution, where science became the slogan of a victorious faction, contribute nothing to conflict theory; their successors, Saint-Simon and Comte, establish the theories of technocracy, social organicism, and benign evolutionism that have made up the positivist tradition in sociology ever since.

Yet, an iconoclastic cutting edge remained sheathed within the scientific tradition. Behind the liberal economists lurked Hobbes's doctrine of conflict and the violence of the state; behind Saint-Simonian evolutionism lurked Voltaire's religious iconoclasm. Karl Marx, in synthesizing these traditions, was to gather them together at their roots.

THE MARXIAN SYNTHESIS

It is a commonplace that Marx integrated British economics, French history, and German philosophy. What these labels conceal, however, are much wider traditions; Marx pushed through to the underlying conflict theories in each of them. (He also incorporated elements that are not part of the conflict tradition.) The English economists exemplified by Ricardo, for example, were but the forward edge of the entire movement of liberal rationalism, with its faith in science and its belief in the rational calculability of individual motives. In the early nineteenth century, it still carried the critical, anti-Establishment tone of bourgeois radicalism. And more importantly—for this utilitarian thought was even then turning into an Establishment ideology of its own (or at best a genteel reformism)—it carried beneath its surface the realistic insights of Hobbes and the unguarded class interests of Locke. It is from this that Marx acquired a full-blown materialism, and a model of society proceeding entirely from the pursuit of individual self-interest. In the background is Hobbes' bold assertion of the fundamentality of conflict, and of the violence upholding the state. From Locke comes the revelation that the basic purpose of the state is to uphold property, as well as the labor theory of value. And from Adam Smith himself proceeds the implicit contradiction within an economic system: Smith's self-adjusting market moves men and resources inevitably in a chase for profits as long as supply and demand are out of balance, until a profit-free equilibrium is reached. It only remains to show that the empirical existence of long-term stratification and economic growth implies terrible convulsions within this system.

The French historians who influenced Marx are usually taken to be the bourgeois radicals, Thierry and Guizot. Behind them stood the whole evolutionist tendency of the late Enlightenment, which was made immediately relevant by Saint-Simon's claims for industrialism as the underlying reality of the post-1789 era. And one stage behind this was a more radical note, the attack by Voltaire and the freethinkers on religious superstition; Marx's own father was an ardent Voltairian. The theme of science versus the supernatural was to be brought up to date in Marx's hands as economics versus ideology.

German philosophy means above all Hegel, whose idea of the movement of the spirit into greater and greater self-consciousness Marx was to stand on its feet as the historical dialectics culminating in communism. It is striking, however, how explicitly Marx's conflict theory is expressed already in Hegel. The *Phenomenology of the Spirit* (1807), takes the pattern of world history to be reflected in the history of philosophy, but Hegel's mode of exposition is remarkably Marxian. The initial problem of Greek philosophy, Hegel asserts, can be found in the conflict of slave and master; successive philosophical systems are seen as different mental maneuvers in that conflict, producing a series of one-sided views, which are finally united in Hegel's own philosophy. Ideas are seen as reflecting the social conditions of each historical epoch, although for Hegel this contributed to an idealist conclusion because ideas were finally revealed to be the underlying reality of the entire world. In Hegel's dialectic, history moves by conflict, by ironical reversal, by the extension of each phase into an extreme at which it breaks, and although his references are most often to the history of ideas, he is well aware that history itself is a record of violence and bloodshed. "History [is] the slaughter bench at which the happiness of peoples, the wisdom of States, and the virtue of individuals have been victimized [Hegel, 1957:365]"—although the end of history justifies its sacrifices, Hegel is one of the first great realists of the ordinary experience of human events.

How did Hegel attain this insight? The man did not stand alone, nor was he merely reacting to Kant, Fichte, and Schelling. German philosophy is a gloss on a larger movement of scholarship: the rise of modern historiography. Philosophy was not the only subject which came alive in the refurbished German universities of the turn of the nineteenth century. The study of classical languages, the history of law, political and religious history were undergoing the quantum leap that constitutes the beginning of critical modern historical scholarship.[1] Hegel was the philosopher who took fullest advantage of this movement, and as always, the revelation of an even mildly informed historical view was of the enormous importance of conflict, the violence and ironic deflections of human aims, the sense of larger forces beyond the ken of the ideas that accompanied them. Hegel is of the same milieu as Niebuhr and von Ranke with their effort to tell history as it really happened. In the German tradition, then, Marx is heir to the emerging discipline of historical realism; his own mentors—David Strauss and Bruno Bauer—were historical scholars who unmasked Biblical Christianity precisely in their capacity as critical researchers in religious history.

What, then, does Marx represent for the development of conflict theory? He brought together for the first time the major sources of the conflict tradition: the revelations of historical scholarship, the effort at a materialist theory of society, the iconoclasm of the freethinkers. Along with this, he incorporated elements that have proven misleading. He was too willing to accept the closed economic system of the utilitarian positivists, too sanguine about some historically inevitable version of Saint-Simon's industrial utopia, too wedded to secularized equivalents of Hegel's spiritual trends. Marx's work as a whole is multisided, and subsequent traditions have emphasized quite different implications, including a version of positivist scientism, an economic evolutionism, and most recently a realistic version of idealist philosophy. My intention is to pick out another theme: the implications of Marx's work as the first comprehensive expression of a scientific conflict sociology.

This means emphasizing, in a broad sense, Marx's materialism, and his positive orientation towards science in general, and putting aside highly abstract dialectics. The basic premise is that sociological explanation is grounded in the physical world. It is the action of human bodies in space and the material things amid which they move that are the basic elements of explanation; all else is to be related to these. This

---

[1] Underlying the sudden outpouring of ceativity in the German universities, especially in the period 1780–1820, was a structural change. The philosophical faculty, previously only an undergraduate preparation for the higher faculties of theology, medicine, and law, struggled for and finally achieved upgrading to advanced status. The battle centered on the effort to show that preparatory fields could become subjects of scholarship, with the field of classical studies leading the way; the classics seminars at Göttingen and Halle in the late eighteenth century set the model for critical historical method in other fields.

is the Hobbesian program again, in which laws are understood in terms of the process of enforcement, and the state in the threat of violence. What Marx added, of course, is a special emphasis on the principles of economics. But even more important for sociological explanation are two other implications of the materialist principle: first, that human action depends on its material setting, and on the material resources available; second, that motivation is to be understood in terms of the material desires of human bodies. Marx couched this primarily in terms of the need to stay alive as prerequisite to everything else, the fundamentality of the economic system in society and of the individual's place in it as the source of his most basic outlook. This principle is capable of further extension, however; maneuvering for physical dominance, for emotional satisfaction, and for sexual pleasure all fall within its purview, when understood as behavior of an organism. On this abstract level, the materialist principles are general and programmatic, directing us toward the sources of explanation. More specific applications give the conditions for various empirical outcomes.[2]

Property and the State

The crucial characteristic of any society, Marx asserted, is its form of property; and the crucial determinant of any individual's behavior is the individual's relation to property. Marx thus characterized ancient Mediterranean societies in terms of slavery, feudal societies in terms of landed estates with attached laborers, capitalist society in terms of industrial equipment. From these proceed the distinctive interests and

---

[2] It should be noted that this broad conception of materialism is not equivalent to vulgar positivism, with its claim that only material *objects* exist and that all ideas are impressions of them. Marx himself emphasized (in *Theses on Feuerbach*), rather, that it is human beings as *material subjects* who do thinking—a formulation that enables us to recognize the crucial importance of the material world as a setting for thought, while also keeping conscious thought as an *activity* with a crucial part to play in the material world. This is an especially appropriate viewpoint for a conflict sociology, with its emphasis on active, self-interested maneuvers in the world, in which mental action plays a crucial part, while yet constrained by the material conditions that surround it. The idealist versions of Marxism which have become popular in the mid-twentieth century are reactions against a rigidly evolutionist economic interpretation of Marx, one that has proven an embarrassment both as a predictive instrument and as a favorite viewpoint of bureaucratic Communist Party interests. A broader materialism, which takes into account the conscious material actor and does not limit the material world to economic system, is a more fruitful path for recovering the sociological contributions of Marx.

cultures of slave-owners and slaves, lords and serfs, capitalists and workers. There are other property relationships as well; one might be outside the prevailing ones, such as freemen in slave societies, urban groups in feudal societies, petit bourgeoisie who work their own property in industrial societies. There are also usually *several* kinds of property in any society. Marx's interest in picking out the principal form of property was to explain the predominant form of *political* action, but this need not detain us from examining the full implications of the analysis. Nor are we limited to the few historical types Marx stressed, as any empirical society is amenable to the same principles. These have three specifiable components.

Property Is Upheld by the Violence of the State

It is for this reason that property classes are involved in politics. Control over material goods and human labor (which is either a direct form or an indirect result of property) is based upon violent threat, whether administered personally, by the army or by the police. The state, as the organization of violence, is the necessary prop under every property system. Marxian analysis has usually emphasized the causal link from economic interest to political action; this was bolstered by the corollary emphasis on technology as setting the conditions for the type of property system possible. But there is another direction of causality implied, which is of immense importance: The conditions of political organization (i.e., the organization of violence) directly control the form of property. The connection of property with state violence is reciprocal, and material conditions can be invoked in both spheres to explain causal processes in each direction.

I have stressed an implication that is somewhat contrary to many of Marx's own assertions. Marx was at pains, in *The German Ideology* and elsewhere, to attack the idealist notion of the state as a manifestation of *Geist,* of the people, or an abstract ideal of justice, and to contrast this ideologizing with the real world of economic goods over which men struggled. And since his major scientific effort was to create a comprehensive economic theory, he tended to stress economic dynamics above all else. But the same logic tends to uncover a realm of the state that is engaged in actual material activity: guarding property, arresting thieves, issuing money, regulating transactions, and the like. It is not a great shift from Marx's own formulations to regard the state, in these material activities, as part of the relations of production, and to see them in reciprocal interplay with the specific technology involved in the means of production (Althusser, 1971:123–173). It does go beyond Marx to give political factors a crucial place in determining important variations in the economic system, even *within* a given type of technology; but as we shall see, this is a realistic and important implication. It helps us to understand the very existence of the twentieth-century communist revolutions, and it provides the embryo of a theory for the shaping of all aspects of earning a living—the system of credit, the media of exchange, the boundaries of occupational positions—by political power.

Property Is the Basis of Class Divisions

What people do and think always takes place in a physical world in which they must assure their physical survival. Making a living is the one unavoidable necessity, even if this is done indirectly by attaching oneself to others who provide sustenance. Thus, one's relationship to property—which for Marx summarized the whole complex of earning a living—is the most important thing in one's life, and it takes up the biggest portion of one's time as well. By a complex of influences, it shapes class cultures:[3] the characteristic outlooks of persons who spend major portions of their lives at particular tasks, with their peculiar worries and insecurities, their particular personal associations, their particular kinds of consumption and leisure. Moreover, since property is inherently connected with state violence, it implicitly invokes threat, domination and conflict. The experiences of different social classes are different not only because their daily lives are different, but because cross-class encounters involve the inherent antagonism of those who can successfully call on state violence to back them up, as opposed to those who are dominated by such threats.

This confrontation is more explicit between slave owners and slaves, lords and serfs, than between employer and employee, and these historical variants add degrees of specificity to the kinds of class cultures found in each case. The general principle also holds: cultural differences not only proceed from differences in livelihood but also take an important part of their content from the implicit amount of conflict in the dominance relationships in that sphere. This is the basis of a conflict theory of stratification.

---

[3] Again we discover that Marx's model has implications, in this case in terms of individual social psychology, which have sociological value outside of the context of his original formulation on the level of the economic system.

Property Divisions Are the Basis of Political Action

Property creates political interests as part of the ongoing process by which it is upheld. Thus, political attitudes and behavior are predictable from class divisions. The analysis may be refined as far as one wishes. There are as many economically motivated political factions in a particular society as there are discernible kinds of property. There is also a further level of political analysis: Within the *general* interest of a class in upholding a particular form of property (or other economic arrangement), individuals struggle for state influence on behalf of themselves alone—for franchises, land-grants, monopolies, gifts, exemptions. For Marx himself, the problem of predicting political alliances among different property sectors, as well as the transition points between classwide political action and individual self-seeking within an economic class, was solved by concentrating on periods of economic crisis and transition from one system to another. For the short run of everyday politics, Marx's own theory was underdetermined, and he himself analyzed particular historical events with retrospective rather than predictive clarity. This is not entirely necessary, for there are additional principles buried in Marx's work and obscured by his concentration on economics which go some way toward the necessary specificity.

Material Conditions Determine Mobilization of Interests

Material conditions determine the degree to which class interests are effectively brought into action. Property relationships thus not only shape political interests, but also determine the degree to which men may participate in the struggle to control the state. In Marx's own work, this principle is expressed in two places: in the *Communist Manifesto*, the famous phrase about capitalism producing its own gravediggers follows a discussion of the factory system as bringing the workers together to organize with the full weight of numbers; in the *Eighteenth Brumaire*, Marx explains the lack of effective political participation of the peasantry by their ecological dispersion, which results in their having no more organizational unity than "potatoes in a sack [Marx, 1963]." Social ecology, conditions of transportation, and the effects of property systems and disposable wealth are all crucial conditions that determine which interests win out to what degree. Small elites can control large numerical majorities precisely because of the unequal distribution of facilities for mobilization. Marx tended to focus on the major economic changes which brought about periods of revolutionary mobilization, but the principle has much wider applicability in the explanation of politics, and does not depend for its validity on a doctrine of economic evolution. By implication, the principle of mobilization also serves to refine the theory of stratification by showing the processes through which conditions of social ecology and communication affect class outlooks. This leads to another principle.

Material Means of Mental Production
Determine Consciousness

The dominant ideas of an historical period are those of the dominant class, Marx asserted in *The German Ideology,* because they control the means of mental production. This introduces an intervening variable between property itself and the ideological superstructure; although the theory was not explicitly worked out on this point, in principle it allows for considerable refinements in the way the means of mental production are organized, and hence in the varieties of consciousness. The theory of mental production applies to two different areas. It is an extension of the theory of interest mobilization, specifying another set of material resources—writing materials, printing presses, wealth to pay for secretaries, teachers, publicists, priests, entertainers, and so on—which, when unequally distributed, result in the formulation of the ideas that dominate public discourse, official definitions of reality. It also has implications for the theory of class cultures taken in themselves: Those classes that have the greatest control of the means of mental production are correspondingly cultured, in the popular sense of the term, whereas those with little such control are less intellectual, less taken up in playing with symbols.

Marx presents us with principles that can be formulated sharply enough so that we may fruitfully compare them with the empirical evidence accumulated since Marx's day. To do so is to recognize how serious a start upon a scientific sociology is provided by conflict theory at this stage of formulation; even where the principles have been modified, the direction of movement proves that it is on the right track.

Property Upheld by State

This principle implies a theory of wealth: Variations in the conditions of political organization have corresponding systems of property distribution. This is the line of analysis taken by Lenski; in his model, the technology of material production (and certain other resources and conditions affecting political–military mobilization) determines both the sheer amount of wealth in a society and its distribution via intervening effects on the organization of the state (Lenski, 1966). The theory is successfully tested by Lenski on a broad set of societal types covering all of world history, and has been borne out by contemporary cross-national comparisons (Cutright, 1967). This is a striking achievement, above all, since it is the *only* theory of the distribution of wealth which has proven successful by empirical test. The various functional theories of wealth, for all the argument that has surrounded them (e.g., the Davis–Moore–Tumin debate) have yet to be even formulated in sufficiently causal terms to bear testing; nor has neoclassical economics produced any general theory of the distribution of wealth.[4]

By extension, not only property but other distributive features of economic life are influenced by the organization of political power. This approach has not yet culminated in explicit hypotheses relating particular political variables to particular features of economic life, but there are moves in this direction. Occupational position is being dereified, understood as a sphere of action that may be divided up more narrowly or combined with other actions and hedged with varying degrees of tenure (Stinchcombe, 1965:162–63). Just where occupational boundaries are drawn (and with them their corresponding controls over remuneration, possibilities of promotion, and degree of monopolization over recruitment procedures) depends on maneuverings which are ultimately backed up by the law (i.e., the coercive threat of the state). The theory of professions—where political enfranchisement is particularly obvious—is moving in this direction (Friedson, 1970).

It is also worth noting that conflict theory has issued explicit propositions in the area of crime which recognize the political-power–property-defense connection (Quinney, 1970); it only remains to cast

---

[4] In fact, the Davis–Moore theory, carried to its logical conclusions, does not imply any inequality at all, but the reverse; since it envisions a market for talent flowing to the socially most desirable services, it falls prey to an implication that was explicit in Adam Smith: that the flow of labor supply to areas of greatest demand would tend to produce equality of all wages. (Thomas, 1956) This paradoxical result actually leads to a new application of the Davis–Moore type of theory, although in a different sense than originally intended: if the pure tendency of the market is toward equality, then inequalities must indicate areas of *constraint* on the market—which again tends to emphasize the importance of political power in shaping the property and occupational system, as suggested below.

this model in a sufficiently historical and comparative form to provide a firm empirical test of its power.

Property and Class Cultures

In a general sense, Marx's principle that the means of earning a living determine cultural distinctions has been overwhelmingly borne out by the evidence. Community studies, whether sympathetic to Marx or not, have inevitably (and sometimes inadvertently) turned out to be descriptions of stratification among occupational levels. Survey studies have proven occupational class to be the most ubiquitous of all independent variables, predicting political attitudes and participation, personal associations, marriage, childrearing practices, work attitudes, career patterns, leisure activities, consumption styles, sexual behavior—the list is endless.

In a more specific sense, however, the Marxian formulation is inaccurate. For the strongest break between categories of the variable are between white-collar and blue-collar classes, even though a great deal of the former are on the *property-less* side of the dividing line proposed by Marx (Glen and Alston, 1968; Kahl, 1957). The principle required reformulation; this was done by Dahrendorf, who proposed distinctions of power, between order givers and order takers, as the most general determinant of class cultures, and property ownership as an historically specific form of power relation.[5] This accounts for the modern blue-collar–white-collar line, for analogous cultural distinctions in socialist societies, for the dominant-class orientation of management even where separated from ownership, as well as for the tendency for similar splits in outlook to appear between leaders and followers within voluntary associations.

In this form, the conflict principle of stratification is strongly buttressed by empirical evidence. But the general form is capable of much further specification to account for various forms of power relationship—for the difference between the upper class, whose face-to-face encounters consist almost entirely of giving orders, and the middle class, who experience both giving orders (to some) and taking orders

---

[5] (Dahrendorf, 1959) It should be stressed, however, that property distinctions *also* exist in modern societies, and continue to influence political attitudes above all; this is important for the difference between socialist and capitalist societies, a difference which Dahrendorf was at pains to obliterate in the *applications* of his theory to contemporary issues.

(from others); for differences in ethos between more independent and more centrally controlled occupations and between occupations experiencing varying degrees of explicit control and the different kinds of sanctions applied. Many of the empirical variations may doubtless fall into this conceptual order (Kohn and Schooler, 1969).

It remains the case that occupational variables are not the only ones which affect attitudes and behaviors: education, sex, age, ethnicity, religion, parental background, personal associations also have their effects. The theory of stratification must have many causal links; but the multiple variables can be integrated around common principles of conflict theory. Many of these variables are themselves indirect transmitters of occupational class cultures; influences of parents, spouse, and acquaintances add further occupational variables to the individual's own, whether to reinforce it or dilute it. Other variables represent nonoccupational influences. In both cases, the shaping of individual cultures is very much in the realm of the conditions formulated under the principles of mobilization and of mental production.

Class Divisions and Political Action

The Marxian principle (especially as reinterpreted by Dahrendorf, to account for white-collar–blue-collar distinction) has had considerable success in survey research on political behavior (Korpi, 1971; Lipset, 1960:230–278). Other variables affect political behavior as well; but to understand that this principle is part of a set of principles goes some distance towards accounting for this—above all, the principle of mobilization of interests helps account for much political behavior not in keeping with the class model.[6]

Another source of validation comes from comparative–historical approaches. Barrington Moore has demonstrated the success of a refined application of the principle of property interest in determining the structural form of the state (Moore, 1966). Focusing on the period of commercialized agriculture which precedes industrialization, Moore proposes that class interests vis-à-vis opposing forces determine political orientation; the peasants, landowning aristocracy, bourgeoisie, industrial workers, and government bureaucracy are characterized in

---

[6] It should be apparent that this principle does not stand or fall on predictions of revolutions; that involves not only class attitudes, but also their mobilization, and above all the military weakness of the state. Marx, in another part of his overall system, attempted to tie all of these to an *economic* model predicting economic crises, but that is beside the *sociological* point presented here.

terms of their preference for democracy, fascism, or communism as means of enhancing their economic positions. The particular mode of agricultural property, in turn, is a crucial variable specifying the orientation of the aristocracy (the most mobilized class of the period); from this, and from historical violence which forcibly removes particular classes from the lineup of contenders, Moore is able to explain the main historical divergences of the modern period. The analysis is bolstered by Stinchcombe's independent comparison of the political tendencies of various agricultural property arangements, which arrives at similar conclusions (Stinchcombe, 1961). The extension of this mode of analysis to the constellation of class interests upholding the entire range of variations in political structures, in view of this success, is quite plausible.

Resources for Interest Mobilization

The principle that power is proportional to the degree of mobilization of interests has recently received a number of applications. Mann shows that the evidence supports the view that it is not only the higher classes who keep the modern working class from defending its political interests, but also its lesser command of the resources of mobilization (Mann, 1970); Pinard, that the capacity for concerted political action depends on organizational ties on the informal level (Pinard, 1968); Burstein and Portes, that class consciousness depends on class community structure as well as work relations (Burstein, 1972; Portes, 1071); Domhoff, on the national level, and Perrucci and Pilisuk, on the community level, give descriptive evidence of the ties of intercom munication that are correlated with effective power (Domhoff, 1967; Perrucci and Pilisuk, 1970); Lieberson explains areas of elite control in government policy in terms of their sole mobilization of interests in those areas (Lieberson, 1971). The interaction of material interests with the resources mobilizing such interests begins to introduce some theoretical order into the overly descriptive and polemical area of the study of political influence.

The principle of mobilization also adds further specification to the process by which class cultures are shaped. Gans, on the basis of an empirical summary, demonstrates that a crucial distinction between working-class and middle-class culture is in the degree of localization and personalization of world views, which in turn rests on the actual conditions of work participation in networks of communication; similar principles account for the outlook of highly localized peasants in traditional rural society (Gans, 1962). Analogous principles may be extended to account for the ultracosmopolitanism of the most highly mobilized occupations, such as professions oriented towards national networks.

Means of Mental Production

This principle was formulated originally on the political level, and although systematic comparative tests are lacking, there are several studies of the mass media which describe the mechanisms by which class interests affect public reality by affecting the material means of its production (Breed, 1955; Tuchman, 1972). Education has also been shown to reflect the resources and cultural stances of dominant classes (Bourdieu, 1970; Collins, 1971a). Such analyses explicitly introduce intervening variables into the process of cultural production, which point the way toward a theory of variations in the superstructure; and they add refinements to the stratification model, by showing how cultural selection, the process by which occupational careers are mediated, is itself the product of interest groups and their unequal resources for producing culture. More remotely, the means of intellectual production are being analyzed in the relatively autonomous communities of natural science, where studies have shown the importance of the struggle for advancement in the context of variations in the availability of positions and research equipment, and in the number of rivals (Ben–David and Collins, 1966; Hagstrom, 1960 and 1971); these variables explain both the ethos of particular intellectual disciplines and the innovativeness and some of the directions of scientific ideas.

The most far-reaching extension of the principle of the means of mental production has occurred in the study of organizations. Michels' *Political Parties* (1911) was among the first works to show not only the existence of internal conflicts of interest within voluntary organizations, but also a principle that accounts for the outcomes of such conflicts: Power is proportional to a faction's control over the technical means of administration, not only as it provides for the superior intercommunication (i.e., mobilization) of that group, but also as means of controlling the information upon which opponents operate. Subsequent studies in this tradition have borne out the importance of variations on this dimension (Lipset, Trow, and Coleman, 1956; Selznick, 1949 and 1952). The same general principle emerges in the studies of Crozier, who finds that organizational power goes to those groups that preserve autonomous control over areas of uncertainty, which they alone can

define to the rest of the organization (Crozier, 1964); a similar principle
has been borne out by Wilensky (Wilensky, 1956). It reappears again in
comparative studies of the conditions which enable an occupational
group to achieve monopolistic control over its own recruitment, work
practices and advancement (i.e., to professionalize) (Wilensky, 1964).
Much of the area of organizations is thus unified around a set of variations on the principle that power is proportional to control over the
material means of defining the cognitive reality within which other organizational members act.

The Marxian synthesis of conflict theory traditions is unques-
tionably—if retrospectively—the take-off point for a sociology with empirical scope and explanatory success. Its flaws came largely from
elements extraneous to the conflict tradition, above all from its overly
evolutionist treatment of the economy, and from its idealized conception of a final historical stage. Yet even within its own bounds, Marxian
sociology left major areas of omission. The next major step towards filling them in was taken by Weber.

WEBER AND GERMAN HISTORICAL SOCIOLOGY

Marxian thought remained in the underground through most of the
nineteenth century, and began to receive sustained intellectual attention only in the 1890s, in the controversy over Marxian economics and
the related issue of revisionism that followed from the adoption of
Marxism as the official doctrine of the German Social Democratic
Party. Weber, as an academic economist and a member of the reformist
Verein für Sozialpolitik, was one of the first generation of nonsocialist
intellectuals to become aware of Marx's accomplishments, and to take
account of them in his own work. There were, of course, other important influences on his thought. There were the doctrines of neo-Kantian
idealism, which Weber made the basis of his methodology, and which
have given the impression to readers who know little of Weber first-
hand besides his methodological essays that Weber was primaily an
idealist. More importantly, Weber was at the heart of the German historicist tradition, the part that emphasized cold-blooded understanding
of the role of violent conflict in world history. The tradition of critical
realism in history that we already found in Hegel's background had
made tremendous advances during the century in recovering ancient
and non-European history; one difference between Marx and Weber,
accordingly, was that the latter knew a great deal more history than the
former, and was in a position to formulate principles with a good deal

more scope and precision. The German economic tradition in which Weber worked, moreover, followed historical rather than the classical (Ricardian) lines taken up by Marx; where Marx emphasized the laws of the market and fell back on technological development as the principal exogenous determinant of change, Weber stressed the organizational arrangements that underlay the rise of a market in specific historical periods. (Weber, in other words, was an institutional economist, of the sort represented in the United States by Veblen and Commons.) More generally, the German tradition of histiography was oriented towards conflict, but along military rather than economic lines; this was reflected in contemporary sociology in the conflict theories of Gumplowitz, Ratzenhofer, and Oppenheimer, with their special emphasis on conquest in the origins of the state, and in the theory of geopolitics put forward by Ratzel. Not least was the influence of the political doctrine of realpolitik a revival of Machiavellian realism fostered by Bismark and transmitted to Weber by personal experience and by observation of his father's parliamentary career.

Weber, then, was in an auspicious position to develop the conflict tradition through his acquaintance with Marxism, his thorough exposure to indigenous German conflict theories, and his broad knowledge of the accomplishments of mature historiography. For my purposes here, I shall not even attempt to sketch his overall position (which was primarily concerned with world economic history), but only to deal with those propositions that Weber adds to the conflict theory which first came to maturity with Marx. This means ignoring Weber's historicism—his expressed limitation of generalizations to aid in the analysis of unique historical sequences. But we are not bound by this aspect of Weber, any more than we are by Marx's economic evolutionism; once we take the step of formulating Weber's principles more sharply than he did himself, and comparing them with Weber's own evidence and with subsequent research, it is apparent that Weber achieved a second stage of synthesis in the conflict tradition.

Weber's Congruence with Marxian Sociology

It should be noted first that Weber's sociology not only accords with, but also builds upon Marxian fundamentals. The primacy of self-interested conflict, the importance of material conditions, the effects of interests on ideology, the existence of economic class struggle—all of these are found in Weber. Indeed, Weber gives an even sharper formulation of economic conflict, pointing out conflicting class interests in the credit and commodity markets as well as the labor market; as Wiley points out, these help us understand class conflict in historical contexts, where it is usually glossed over by the more conventional emphasis on worker–employer conflict alone (Wiley, 1967). The principles of property interacting with the state, of interest mobilization, and of the means of mental production are illuminated by Weber's work; his contributions to conflict theory may be understood as amplifying them in regard to the technical conditions of violence and of administrative organization, to internal conflict within organizations, as well as adding another principle that we may refer to as the means of emotional production, which subsumes the contributions Weber made under the labels of "legitimacy" and "status groups," and in his sociology of religion.

Means of Violence and Its Administration

Weber was highly aware of the role of military force in history, and his theory of political organization proposes a set of conditions under which it takes different forms (Weber, 1968: Part II, Chapter 9–16). There is an inherent struggle for power wherever coercion is involved. Hence states are unified or break apart depending on the technical means available for keeping administrative control over the organization of violence. Coercive power is maintained by a network of mutual threats among the bearers of arms, and the control goes to whoever can control the network of surveillance through which this operates, and the sources of military supply.

Weber's model of bureaucratic and patrimonial organization gives the main variations in technical resources and their political results. There is the military technology itself: Weapons such as firearms, which must be centrally supplied and administered, favor a unified organization, whereas weapons such as those of self-equipped knights foster decentralization. Technology of transportation and communication determines the extent to which centralized control over supplies may be maintained. Literacy and the material resources for written records—the availability of paper, files, writing implements of varying degrees of cumbersomeness—affect the ease of centralized administration, and hence the size of the geographical area that can be controlled. The availability of literate administrators has a similar effect. The mode of household organization also affects the problem of control: The key to the patrimonial type is the billeting of troops in the personal household of leaders, caring for them from a common larder, and thus making no distinction between personal and public relationships; the accompanying structural tendency is for superiors to lose control whenever their subordinates must administer a distant territory, especially when they appropriate land there to support themselves. Bureaucratic organization is an effort to counter this tendency; in addition to the technical resources noted above, it depends on a system of recruitment from outside of household and family ties. Universal churches have been important politically because they provide just such a form of organization, and governments of any degree of bureaucratization have depended on this form—initially by directly using the priests as administrators, later by wholesale imitation of church organization through a secular bureaucracy.[7]

Organizational Power Struggles

Weber explicitly saw organizations as sites of conflict. The tendency of subalterns to assert their autonomy whenever distance permitted was the main theme of patrimonial regimes; a parallel struggle goes on in bureaucracies due to the control by subordinates over the administrative machinery. (Weber's protegé Robert Michels provided a fairly straightforward application of this principle to modern parties, and Weber's own writings on modern politics emphasize similar observations.) As Roth points out, Weber's use of ideal types implies that bureaucracy is only one of several strategies employed in struggles for control; personalistic (patrimonial) networks of individual loyalties remain part of the structure within formally bureaucratic organizations because of their utility in the ongoing struggle (Roth, 1968). The history of organizational theory since Weber has thus included much rediscovery of insights already formulated by Weber.

This is made explicit in Etzioni's theroy of organizational control, which summarizes evidence showing that coercion, material rewards, and normative control—applications of Weber's party, class, and status dimensions—each have their distinctive consequences for compliance, and hence for the kinds of tasks that can be achieved with them (Etzioni, 1961). Etzioni's synthesis draws on a great deal of organizational research from Mayo and Barnard onwards, which reveals organizations to be sites of continual maneuvering for control, even though these studies have tended to be interpreted within the frame-

---

[7] These principles have been applied to various historical contexts by Bendix, 1964; Roth, 1968; and Wertheim, 1968.

work of managerial ideologies that obscure their relevance for conflict theory.[8] But some studies have gradually brought about the explicit recognition of conflict as a major determinant of organizational phenomena (Crozier, 1964; Dalton, 1959; Gouldner, 1954). Together with the advances in formulating explanatory principles mentioned above (as extensions of the principle of the means of mental production), this work adds up to a fairly refined and empirically well-grounded conflict theory of organizations.

The Means of Emotional Production

Weber is best known for a series of contributions that apparently break the Marxian mold. These include the importance of status groups—the dimension of stratification into communities distinguished by life style and ranked by prestige, communities that are built up over and above class lines, sometimes cutting across them; the importance of religion in setting personal attitudes and social change; the importance of legitimacy as the basis of stable political order. These are indeed important and original contributions by Weber, but they remain within the conflict tradition, and supplement rather than negate the model of conflict over material goals and through material resources. To make this clear, I have reformulated the underlying principle under the term, *the control of the means of emotional production:* the conditions in the material world whereby individuals are influenced to experience emotions, especially social solidarity, fear, awe, or a sense of purpose. The implication is that these are resources to be used in conflicts (for the goals of power and wealth as well as for emotional gratification), and that the control of these means is itself affected by the distribution of resources resulting from other forms of conflict.

Weber made a discovery analogous to those of Durkheim and Freud (and above all Nietzsche, on whom he drew), when he recognized that people have emotional desires and susceptibilities, and that these are crucial for their social lives. Weber saw that particular conditions excite emotional dynamics, above all, conditions of conflict, deprivation, and threat on one hand, and on the other, ceremonies and displays that arouse emotions and resolve them into feelings of solidarity and awe. Manipulation of the settings of such face-to-face encounters is the

---

[8] Carey, 1967, shows that the so-called "Hawthorne effect" is a myth, and that the original evidence shows that material incentives, not good "human relations," were the effective variables in boosting production.

basis of religion. Weber does not reduce religion to economic interests, although he shows that social classes have their typical religious propensities (Weber, 1968:468–486); rather, it is to be understood as a distinctive area of emotional gratification, and the product of a distinctive group, the priests. With his sense of the internal conflicts of organizations, Weber recognizes religious developments as proceeding from the interests of religious elites themselves in struggling for dominance both vis-a-vis each other (in which the outcomes are influenced by the material conditions of church organization, analogous to the principles of political struggle), and in relation to the public and to the state, which makes use of religion in its own struggles.

Weber's underlying theory of status groups is that the means of emotional production affect the organization of interest groups as communities and serve as resources in social conflict. The means of emotional production include the ecological conditions and material resources that bring people together for emotional encounters, the material resources for putting on ceremonial display, and the resources to communicate and monopolize accumulated techniques for emotional manipulation. Control over these resources means control over people's physical mobility, and over the stage settings on which they meet. Analogous to what has been said above regarding the means of intellectual production, the means of emotional production determine (a) the formation of groups with varying degrees of internal solidarity; and (b) the domination of the ceremonial standards of some groups over others, due to their greater resources for putting on emotionally compelling displays, and thus creating an order of prestige. Such communities can be based upon economic classes, and this occurs to the extent that the distribution of the means of emotional production coincides with class lines. But since ecological propinquity and standards of communication (a common language and symbolic tradition) are important means of emotional production, migration or conquest by cultural aliens produces community splits which may cross economic lines, and whose immediately determining variables are in the distribution of the means of emotional production rather than in economics per se. Such cultural solidarities, which are now to be called ethnic groups, in turn produce continuing conflicts over political and economic goals, and further reinforce lines of cultural distinction. In The Religion of India above all, Weber lays down the fundamentals of a theory of cultural stratification, upon which the variations of caste, feudal estate, educationocracy, or modern high society may be seen as the results of different distributions of the resources for producing status solidarity and domination.

The theory of legitimacy should be read in this light. Empirically,

Weber's concept of traditional legitimacy refers to the uses that governments historically have made of religious ceremony in order to manipulate emotional support; rational–legal legitimacy is an appeal to
secular ceremonial equivalents. The *goals* of politics remain the struggle for material advantage and power; legitimacy refers to another set
of *techniques* to be manipulated in this struggle. The same applies
within organizations; Etzioni's (1961) category of normative control
refers to the manipulation of particular kinds of techniques for emotional solidarity. Goffman (1959) who builds his original model of
"frontstage" ceremony and "backstage" solidarity upon the same empirical results of industrial relations research, can be seen as specifying
some of the mechanisms by which the production of emotional effects
is achieved.

Many of Weber's theoretical propositions have been tested by empirical evidence inadvertently rather than consciously and deliberately. The area of organizations has been ordered, however, around his
underlying model of conflict and control under different conditions of
administrative and technological resources and means of emotional
manipulation. The area of ethnic and other kinds of status communities has been well described in research, but has only recently
begun to be subjected to comparative analysis aimed at testing causal
propositions. Bonacich (1972, 1973) formulates principles based upon
comparative evidence which bear out the thrust of the above argument,
with special emphasis on the types of economic conflicts that sustain
ethnic antagonisms. Weber's political sociology has only slowly
emerged into broader understanding. Cast in more explicit form, and
seen in conjunction with the principles established in the Marxian synthesis, we can find in Weber the development of conflict theory to a
considerable level of sophistication.

CONCLUSION

The conflict tradition does not end with Max Weber, but there is
room for only the barest sketch of subsequent or even contemporary
developments. We have already covered many of the followups of the
Marx–Weber line of conflict sociology. Among these, there is the important line of influence in which Michels served as the link between
Weber's historical theory of organizational politics and the organizational studies of the 1940–1960s. Studies of stratification, although
often pursued with naive theoretical categories, have gradually accumulated a gread deal of evidence bolstering and refining the classical principles explained above; and some work especially since the

time of C. Wright Mills (but not necessarily influenced by him) has made a conscious effort to build on classical theory.

Some other lines of conflict theory must at least be mentioned. The social-psychological tradition of conflict theory originating with Schopenhauer and Nietzsche, of course, has Freud as its most famous representative. This level of analysis, despite various theoretical attempts, has not yet been convincingly related to the organizational/stratification level outlined above, nor has it had as much empirical support. But this social-psychological conflict tradition continues to have great potential importance. It holds out the promise of a model for the shaping of the individual psyche by the emotional and symbolic interchanges involved in struggles for interpersonal advantage to replace the artificially one-sided and relatively static models of psychological learning theory. Its premises move toward replacing adult-centered socialization theory with a two-sided view of age conflict under conditions of unequal resources. And when cast in an explicitly historical form, its insights into sexual repression become the basis of a comparative theory of sexual stratification (Collins, 1971b).

Many other interesting figures have been slighted in this brief history. Some, like Simmel and Pareto, appear isolated from the main stream, as they subordinated their insights about conflict to principles which led in quite different directions: neo-Kantian idealism and liberal positivism respectively. Others, like Sorel, came closer to the main line, above all, in Sorel's emphasis that conflict is *the* basis of moral solidarity, a point which resonates with Weber's understanding of group ceremony as the basis of legitimacy and solidarity *precisely* in situations of conflict and domination. From here, the possibility exists for appropriating the main achievements of the Durkheimian tradition—the understanding of the ceremonial bases of social reality-constructing—into a comprehensive conflict theory.

For the arena encompassed by conflict theory is not only the moments of obvious strife in society, but also the systematic explanation of the entire social structure. The central focus is on the organization of material arrangements into a system of power that divides society into interest groups struggling for control. Such material conditions operate not only through the sphere of economic production, but also directly condition the mobilization of interest groups for political action, as well as the production of ideas and of emotional ties. We need no longer rest with an abstract assertion of the determination of structure by contending interests with varying material resources; refined principles of conflict theory explain specific outcomes in all areas of society.

Wallerstein's World-System

The success of Immanuel Wallerstein testifies to the strategic place of sociology among the disciplines. No one but a sociologist would have attempted what Wallerstein is in the process of accomplishing. The roots of his massive project, *The Modern World-System*, are in other disciplines, in economics and in history. But what Wallerstein has done with their leads is distinctively his own, and distinctively sociological.

Marxian economists since the time of Lenin and Luxembourg have shifted their focus of attention from the internal to the international arena. It was apparent that the internal crises of capitalism were capable of being circumvented by being exported abroad, although in the long run it was expected that the dynamics of imperialism would produce its own crises. More recently, dependency theorists such as André Gunder Frank have shifted the emphasis, not to what imperialism does for the metropolis, but to the way in which it has not only shaped but also created underdevelopment. Frank, Furtado, and others developed their arguments primarily from Latin America. Wallerstein generalized the argument, pushing it backward in time and outward in space, to argue that capitalism has always and necessarily been an international phenomenon, and that its very origins, as well as its crises, have depended on the way that it has shaped the stratification of the world.

Wallerstein's project would not have been possible, however, without the massive work done by historians, especially of the French *Annales* school. In fact, the subject of the first volume of *The Modern World-System* coincides in time with that of the masterwork of that historical school, Fernand Braudel's *The Mediterranean and the Mediterranean World in the Age of Philip II* (1972). Wallerstein's debts to Braudel are substantial. Braudel's is the epitome of comprehensive history, uniting the details of economic life with the history of the climate and the contours of geography, and setting political and military events against this background. All this represents the kinds of materials, worked up by historians, which Wallerstein uses for his synthesis. Even more centrally, Wallerstein takes from Braudel the very conception of a world-system. For Braudel's great theme was to show that the Mediterranean must be treated as a total unit. It was a system, not in the abstract and teleological sense of the sociological functionalists, but in its physical reality: goods, ships, people, and money flowed around it in regular patterns, and its fundamental history consisted in the establishing of such patterns, their disruption, and their shifts to new locations. In a sense, Wallerstein simply generalized this to a larger frame. Even a specific key to Wallerstein's account of the capitalist takeoff, the wage–price gap of the sixteenth century, is argued already in Braudel.

Nevertheless, Wallerstein's work stands out beyond its various ingredients. For the magnificent piece of historical synthesis that it is, its greatest value is as a work of theory construction. No historian could have written it. For historiography, even when it rises above the closely defended boundaries of specialists, is intensely antitheoretical. It has its long-standing issues, but these are always of a concrete nature (was there a rising bourgeoisie? a crisis of the gentry? etc.). Its professional ethos is against generalization and abstraction. This is history's Achilles heel, for all explanations, even very concrete ones, rest on some causal dynamism that is assumed to be true. With their fetish for the concrete, historians are never able to test, or usually even to formulate, their own underlying explanatory apparatus. It remains for the outsider, usually a sociologist, to lay bare the skeleton beneath the skin. It is at this surgical work that Wallerstein, like Max Weber in his day, excels.

Much of Wallerstein's theory hinges upon the concept of a world-system. *World* here is not to be taken literally. It means not the whole globe, but a world-in-itself, a set of societies that are linked together, so that none is a self-subsistent entity, although together, for all intents and purposes, they are. Wallerstein's main point is that societies are almost never self-subsistent, although at some times in history certain tribal societies may have been. Among world-systems, he recognizes two main types: "world-empires," which are sets of societies tied together by a dominating state which extracts economic tribute from the others; and "world-economies", which are characterized by a multiplicity of political units, and which are tied together by warfare and by economic exchange. There is also a third possible type, a socialist world-government, which does not exist, although it may in the future. Given his world-system perspective, Wallerstein doubts that there truly are socialist economies in the twentieth century, but only socialist-controlled states within the capitalist world-economy.

The distinction among Wallerstein's two main types is schematic and not entirely worked out. Thus he can speak of medieval Europe as being neither a world-empire nor a world-economy, but only a "civilization" (1974:36), by which he seems to mean it had the cultural unity of the Christian church, although culture per se he considers a peripheral phenomenon. I think the confusion comes because Wallerstein sometimes defines a world-economy only in political terms (any set of nonisolated societies that is not dominated by a single state is a world-economy; 1974:348) whereas often in practice he sems to have economic criteria in mind (e.g., he speaks of there being a medieval world-economy in Northern Italy, another in the Neverthelands and Northern Germany; 1974:36–37). Obviously there can be various sorts of nonlocalized systems that are not empires; some could be organized as economies, whereas others interact only militarily or culturally. By the same logic, the distinction between world-empires and world-economies is a relative one; for empires both grow and fragment over time. Hence the same territory can sometimes be a world-empire, sometimes a political plurality, and of the latter, sometimes a genuine economic network as well.

The crucial distinction for the purposes of Wallerstein's theory is between situations in which a conquest state dominates the economy by taking tribute, and those in which no state is strong enough to do so. For an imperial state, like Chine or Rome, limits the autonomous development of the economy. State officials are supreme and need make no concessions to low-status mercantile groups; nor, in the absence of military competition among states, is there an incentive to rationalize the state apparatus and its economic policy. On this point, Wallerstein (1974:60) not only follows but also quotes Max Weber (1974:60). On the other hand, competition among states means that they must make concessions to mercantile and financial interests. Early European capitalists thus were able to move their sites of operations to the most favorable places, while the expense of constant warfare gave the princes a necessary incentive to give them concessions.

The sheer pluralism of political power, then, is a crucial element in economic growth. Further, within a world-economy some states are stronger than others, politically and economically. This gives us a division into core, semiperiphery, periphery, and external area. The composition of the core has shifted historically and Wallerstein suggests that there is a built-in circulation of elites in the world-system (1974:350).

The advantages of the core states are several. They are able to militarily and economically dominate the periphery, thus creating an international division among different types of labor systems. Forced labor on the periphery builds up wealth for the core. This is crucial for several reasons. It enables the core states to have a free and relatively well-paid labor force, thus reducing the amount of costly class warfare internally and providing a mass consumer market for economic products. Core states tend to become cumulatively richer.

A core position also enables the state to escape the vicious cycle that tends to undermine state finances. States attempting to build up their military strength need officials to collect taxes and money to pay mercenaries. In the past, the venality of offices (especially tax-collection offices) was typically used to raise money. But the more offices that were sold to the rich nobility, the less the tax revenue collected for the state itself. If the prince squeezed those below, it set off a chain reaction, increasing the likelihood of expensive peasant revolts against the exactions of the officeholders. States could only get ahead of this cycle if they could increase their income and confidence faster than their expenditures and resistance. The core states, by exploiting the periphery, could do this, enabling them to reduce their financial reliance upon the sale of offices, and in effect reversing the whole cycle. Thus over time the fate of different states became more widely divergent, depending on whether they were caught in this vicious cycle or circumvented it. Those that failed to do so (like Poland) tended to fall into the periphery and themselves became exploited.

Absolute leadership within the world-economy, however, was not necessarily the most advantageous position. Spain and France, as the two largest states of the sixteenth century, were caught in ruinous wars against each other. Spain in particular had the burden of excessive advantages, which tempted it into the expensive but unattainable ambition of becoming a world-empire. England, with lower military expenses and fewer foreign possessions, emerged economically and politically sounder, ready to dominate the next phase of world geographical expansion. Wallerstein (1974:296) goes so far as to suggest that France's success in achieving military unification at the end of the medieval period was in the long-run a disadvantage, and that a weaker state in a smaller territory of northern France would have turned to bourgeois rather than aristocratic interests and could have led the industrial revolution instead of England.

The foregoing constitutes Wallerstein's most explicit theorizing about the origins of economic growth. Despite the historical detail with which he cloaks it, it is a very abstract model. In essence, too much political domination stifles economic development; a modest and relative domination within a pluralist international political situation fosters it. But is this latter enough to account for the capitalist takeoff? Implicitly, Wallerstein seems to recognize that there must be other, more specific mechanisms, and hence he provides two more specialized hypotheses.

One comes in his discussion of the transition from the medieval to the early modern European economy. He describes medieval Europe as going through an up-and-down cycle, with a phase of growth in economic production, cultivated territory, and population from about 1150 to 1300 A.D., followed by a phase of decline in all of these from 1300 to 1450. Why did the medieval crisis occur, and why did a capitalist world-economy emerge from it? Wallerstein reviews various explanations of the crisis and finally decides upon a combination of all three. There was a long-term economic cycle, in which the population had expanded up to the limits made possible by existing productive technology and even beyond, and hence had to undergo contraction. There was a secular trend, in which the feudal mode of surplus appropriation eventually came to place such heavy burdens upon the peasantry that no more could be squeezed out, with the result of ruinous warfare and demographic collapse. And there was a shift in climate that reduced the productivity of the soil and increased vulnerability to epidemics. As the result of the conjuncture of these three factors, there was not only a medieval crisis, but also a crisis of such magnitude that Europe was prodded into escape by an entirely new route—the geographical expansion and the creation of a capitalist world-economy (1974:37).

This argument, taken as a whole, is rather hard to believe. Wallerstein lapses into teleology when he assumes that Europe's problems were such that they required a solution of this magnitude. For there is no reason why societies must solve their problems; history is full of failures to do so. There is no inherent reason, in Wallerstein's argument here, why the transformation should have begun, instead of a continuing stagnation. His invocation of a cyclical imagery does not help, for he presents no real evidence to prove that there are cycles in the pre-medieval economy, nor any mechanism for why *this* kind of society should recover from its downturn. Nor is his claim of a conjuncture of three different factors entirely convincing. In effect, he has reviewed three different hypotheses about the medieval crisis, and unable to decide among them, declares that they are all true. Yet the climatological argument, for example, is probably not valid, since the same climatological changes in other parts of the world (e.g. Japan) had quite different effects. Similarly, the argument regarding the limits of technology is unconvincing; in both China and Europe the medieval period was one of continuous technological innovation, and this innovation continued in Europe right on through the economic downturn of the 1300s and 1400s.

Wallerstein on the very beginnings of the European takeoff, then, is not in one of his strong suits. I will suggest in the following that he has only a partial theory of the factors involved in the rise of capitalism, and that his sounder, political model of the world-economy needs to be supplemented with a better theory applicable to the changes of the Middle Ages.

Wallerstein has yet one more specific mechanism for the capitalist takeoff. This one is located in the sixteenth century. He adopts the explanation, put forward by Earl Hamilton and defended by Fernand Braudel, that the influx of bullion from the New World created a price inflation while wages lagged behind. This wage lag enabled Europe to live beyond its savings, and hence to generate the expansion of productivity and trade that began real economic growth. Wallerstein manages at least implicitly to tie this to his abstract theory. For it was geographical expansion that brought about the influx of money. The creation of a world-system on a new scale, by incorporating a new periphery in the Americas, was directly behind the specific mechanism of economic accumulation. Taken together with Wallerstein's more structural model of the importance of military pluralism and the core–periphery relation, we can see that the geographical relations among states as they shift over time set the basic dynamics of economic development.

Once the capitalist world-system is fully launched, its nature, according to Wallerstein and his collaborators (Research Working Group, 1979), is inherently cyclical. The cycles are analogous to the periodic crises of Marxian economics, except that in Marx their periodicity is about 10 years, in Wallerstein on the order of a century. Wallerstein's cyclical dynamics, of course, unlike Marx's, are inherently transnational.

Core societies have high-skill, high-wage economies of production; peripheral societies have low-skill, low-wage economies. Prosperity in the core societies depends upon their ability to exploit the low-wage periphery, and also upon the effective demand for high-priced goods which their own labor force provides. An expansionary cycle (A phase) begins when the demand for high-wage goods (e.g. manufactured products) is greater than its supply, and the demand for low-wage goods (e.g. raw materials) is also greater than its supply. Hence the core societies expand their economic tentacles into new regions of the globe. This results in an increased flow of goods from the periphery, which in turn expands production of high-priced goods in the core, although at a slower rate.

The turning point comes when the supply of goods from the periphery exceeds demand. Foreign expansion slows down, because it is no longer profitable. This causes core production to stagnate. But this downturn period is also fruitful for the long-term growth of the world-economy. During this time, capital becomes more centralized, preparing the way for a new expansion. The accumulation of capital is not just an originating process preceding the rise of capitalism, but a continuous and recurrent process through each trough of the cycle. Also during the time of stagnation, unemployment and other economic miseries for the working class in the core causes an upsurge of class struggle. The result is to force some redistribution of income. This increases demand for goods, setting the expansion cycle in motion once again.

Wallerstein and his colleagues propose that there is a double cycle ($A_1-B_1-A_2-B_2$). The first cycle of the pair has a milder downturn than the second; at the end of the pair of cycles, there is an especially great crash, in which low-wage production not only stagnates but also contracts, and high-wage production (which is always more elastic) takes a very sharp drop.

The political side of this cycle is not only that class conflict increases during the downturn phases, but also that rivalry between cores states erupts into especially severe warfare at those times. The hegemony of one particular core state over the others, though, shifts only over an *entire* double cycle, making up 100 years or more. A new power emerges during the A_1 phase, comes to predominance through B_1, reaches its height in A_2, and declines in B_2. The shift of hegemony from one core state to another is not accidental, but is tied to economic advantages. A state becomes hegemonic when its production, commerce, and finance exceed those of other states; hence, it can invest in the military force that enables it to dominate the international arena. But such hegemony always slips away. Ultimately it depends upon a technological edge and upon relatively low internal costs of maintaining order. In order to keep class conflict within bounds, increasing concessions must be made to the workers. These concessions raise the costs of production. Since technology always diffuses elsewhere by imitation, another state with lower initial labor costs can seize the edge.

There is thus a continuous movement in and out of the core, and also in and out of the semiperiphery. Although the total productivity of the world-system as a whole is not fixed, there seem to be a limited number of slots in each sector: As some societies move up into the semiperiphery, others move down and or out. Wallerstein (1980) instances Sweden, Prussia, and the British American colonies as moving up in the 1600–1750 period; Spain, Portugal, and to a lesser extent northern Italy and the Rhineland as moving down.

Wallerstein has framed all of modern history, and hence the four volumes of his half-completed series, The Modern World-System, in terms of successive cycles. Volume I describes the initial takeoff of the capitalist world-economy from 1450 to its final crash around 1620–1640, as well as a brief analysis of the medieval cycle that was a prelude to it. Volume II takes us from the crisis of the 1600s to another turning point around 1750. The projected Volume III deals with the growth of industrial capital during 1750–1917; Volume IV with the truly global situation that has emerged since 1917 and in which we find ourselves today (Wallerstein, 1979). On the political side, these can be regarded as a succession of four hegemonies: Spain in the first period, The Netherlands in the second, Britain in the third, and the United States in the fourth (Research Working Group, 1979).

This dating of the cycles, and the analysis of the mechanisms that produce them, is of course still quite tentative within Wallerstein's project. The series of economic data put forward in its support are not all consistent, and the dates of alleged political hegemonies are even less precise. On the theoretical side, one important difficulty is in fitting together cycles of varying lengths. The most formally argued model for cycles (Research Working Group, 1979) is that of double pairs $(A_1–B_1–A_2–B_2)$ covering about 100–125 years total. (This is somewhat longer than a pair of Kondratieff cycles, conventionally dated at 40–70 years each.) Within each double pair, there are two phases of expansion and two of contraction, with the last being especially severe. But Wallerstein also appears to tie his analysis into the long cycles or logistics of some 300–500 years each that have been proposed for the period since the beginning of the medieval economic growth around 900–1000 A.D. Thus of the first two volumes of The Modern World-System, the first as a whole is regarded as an up-phase (1450–1620/1640), the second as a long down-phase (1600–1750). This would make 1750–1917 another long up-phase, 1917–? a down-phase—obviously, in the very long run sense, with most of our history from 1917 to the present apparently prosperous, but actually the transition for a great downturn to come. (There is some evidence, short-term as it may be, that, at least for the U.S., an economic turning point may have been reached around 1970.)

At a minimum, we must say that the long-term cyclical model has not been worked out. Wallerstein et al. have proposed a mechanism for why there should be ups and downs *within* the 100–125 years double cycle, but not for why each of these long units should itself alternatively be up or down. Perhaps this latter characterization is destined to slip out of the model. For Wallerstein does not contemplate that cycles of either kind will go on forever. For one thing, the evidence suggests that cycles have been growing shorter, presumably because the mobility of capital around the world has accelerated. Even more importantly, there are certain secular trends that have inherent limits. These are the trends to include a greater percentage of the world area in the capitalist world-economy, a greater percentage of personal incomes in the form of wages for labor, and a greater percentage of capital in the form of machinery. Once the reserves of unexploited land, labor, and nonmechanized production have dried up, the core states will no longer be able to expand into a new periphery. The basic mechanism of capitalist growth will have disappeared. Class conflict at a high level of mobilization will become unavoidable throughout the world. The system will only be able to survive this final crisis by transforming itself into something entirely new—presumably a socialist world-government.

Wallerstein's projection of the future ending of capitalist cycles expresses the Marxian revolutionary hope in a new form. In effect, his theory outline proposes to put the entire Marxian dynamic on a new foundation. Not all aspects of the model are convincing, however. The secular trends upon which the future transformation is based do not seem inevitable. The drawing of the total world labor force into an urban type of wage labor would not necessarily lead to unified pro-socialist class action. A high degree of labor mobilization can just as well lead to a proliferation of self-interested enclaves, a variety of unions, professions, and bureaucratic niches competing against one another for their own advantage. The example of modern core societies like the U.S. certainly shows this pattern. A similar problem applies to earlier periods. Wallerstein asserts that core societies in all historical eras tend to decline eventually because of concessions made in class conflicts. But it isn't clear why the working class should always win important gains. The evidence that this has usually happened is not at all convincing, and certainly the pattern is not a uniform one.

On the other hand, one can think of other mechanisms producing economic crises besides this one. For example, in the twentieth century, one mechanism has been the Keynesian problem of technological unemployment and insufficient demand. The solution to this adopted in the U.S. has been to expand a bureaucratic sinecure sector, although this displaces the strains elsewhere (Collins, 1979). It contributes to inflationary pressures in the monetary system, such that the price inflation of the sixteenth century, of which Wallerstein makes so much, appears mild compared to the much more rapid inflation of the twentieth century. A further strain occurs within the surrogate currency by means of which sinecures and occupational monopolies are legitimated: the production of educational credentials. These are promulgated under a technocratic ideology, which threatens to break down under the pressure of inflationary devaluation of credentials as they become overplentiful.

This invokes an arena of cultural production which Wallerstein, sticking closer to Marx than to Weber, does not wish to give much of a role. Yet a number of weaknesses in Wallerstein's model stem from this omission. Class conflict, I have argued, does not necessarily lead to unified working-class gains, precisely because the degree of unity or fragmentation of the working class is determined by cultural factors. It is the distribution of culture, both informally and in credentialled forms, that has produced splits among salaried (long-contract) and wage-paid (short-contract) workers, and that has made possible the organization of work monopolies (the professions) and bureaucratic sinecures.

To invoke the production and consumption of culture, however, points to a mechanism beyond the capitalist economy. It implies that the capitalist era shows some of the same dynamics as noncapitalist ones, that the European Middle Ages, for instance, went through a cycle that is fundamentally similar to subsequent cycles. Generally speaking, Wallerstein wishes to deny this. In his theory, the dynamics of capitalist eras should be specifically capitalist. But on the other hand, he invokes not only a specific capitalist cycle (the double Kondratieff model), but also long cycles—and of the latter, there are only two well-known instances, the most sharply delineated of which in fact is the precapitalist, medieval one. Wallerstein thus leaves open the possibility of unifying his model of capitalist dynamics with a noncapitalist model. But these latter dynamics may be heavily cultural. As I have argued elsewhere ("Crises and Declines in Credential Systems," in this volume) it is possible to show that the medieval cycle is in important respects one in which the expansion and overexpansion of cultural production—in this case, the organization of the medieval church—plays a key role.

To invoke such a culture-producing organization would also enable us to fill in one of the remaining gaps in Wallerstein's model. As I have argued above, his account of why the capitalist takeoff began at all is incomplete. What Wallerstein leaves out are the organizational forms within which capitalism could emerge—the legal and financial systems within which property, labor, and credit could be reliably and rationally contracted for. These forms, as Weber (1961; cf. Collins, 1980) argued, ultimately depended upon the organization of the church, which in turn provided the foundation for the bureaucratic state. This level of analysis Wallerstein tends to take for granted, while at the same time dismissing its long-term cause, the church, as essentially unimportant because it is essentially ideological. This is a mistake. What is most important about religion is not its beliefs, but its real organizational forms enacted by the body of priests and monks. The church is a material institution like any other, and its property and its economic consumption—and for the medieval period its innovative economic productivity (as well as its cultural productivity)—are key elements in the pattern that made possible the birth of capitalism.

I am suggesting, then, that Wallerstein's model would be made stronger if its Marxian dynamics were still further integrated with the Weberian tradition. In a sense, of course, Wallerstein has already produced a transformation of Marx in a Weberian direction. This is not the Weber who emphasizes cultural factors, but the political Weber, the Weber who shows the importance of the territorial state and its underpinnings. Wallerstein's main model of the capitalist takeoff, incomplete though it may be, concentrates on the important element of military pluralism versus military empires; and the really novel dynamics of his model of capitalist crises hinges on the geographical core–periphery relation. Wallerstein's strength, then, is essentially geopolitical.

What is unique about Wallerstein's approach, compared to more conventional geopolitics, is that he is able to show how military relations in space have *economic* effects. Conventional geopolitics, on the other hand, is concerned only with explaining the shifting powers of states themselves. A synthesis of the two approaches should be mutually beneficial. Wallerstein's model tells us of at least one crucial determinant of long-run political power; the state itself is an economic consumer, and its military strength depends upon the armies it can finance. In the other direction, Wallerstein's model would fill in some of its explanatory gaps if it were tied to a systematic theory of geopolitical factors (such as the sheer physical relations among heartland territories and natural barriers), which could predict the expansion and contraction of states over time ("Long-Term Social Change and the Territorial Power of States," in this volume).

On numerous fronts, then, Wallerstein's theory makes contact with the very issues upon which the Weberian tradition has something to offer. Where Wallerstein lacks predictive power, Weberian theories of culture-based organization and of the military state propose definite explanatory mechanisms. Whether Wallerstein himself is likely to take advantage of these theoretical complementarities, of course, is not known. Neither is it truly important. For the future advance of a sociology of world history, it is significant only that the opportunities are there. If the data will support such a synthesis, it will doubtless be produced somewhere in our intellectual field.

The impressive thing about Wallerstein's work, then, is not only what it has accomplished, but also what it promises. Wallerstein himself promises yet another two (or more) full volumes of The Modern World-System. By the time they are ready, a decade or more from now, they will doubtless show further advances in theory building. Whether they can truly reconstruct the Marxian edifice in all respects remains to be seen. At the same time, Wallerstein's work motivates and leads the rest of the field toward greater achievements. The progress of The Modern World-System promises to mark sociology's coming of age.

The Chain of Modernization*

The last decade and a half has been a golden age of comparative-historical sociology. Reinhard Bendix's *Kings or People* (1978) is among the latest in a series of major comparative and historical studies, alongside Gerhard Lanski's *Power and Privilege* (1966), Barrington Moore's *Social Origins of Dictatorship and Democracy* (1966), Immanuel Wallerstein's *The Modern World-System* (1974, 1980), Perry Anderson's *Lineages of the Absolutist State* (1974), Theda Skocpol's *States and Social Revolutions* (1979) and a series of works by Charles Tilly *et. al.* (1967, 1975, 1978). Bendix explicitly sets himself in opposition to the more prominent explanations of political structures in terms of the organization of the material economy. He sets out to vindicate the proposition that politics is autonomously determined by ideas and by external, international events. On the last point, of course, he is not so far away from Wallerstein's (and Braudel's) internationalism, but Bendix and Wallerstein are not really interested in explaining the same thing: Wallerstein tries to explain the capitalist takeoff; Bendix the political fortunes of five great states.

* Originally published in *Journal for the Scientific Study of Religion*, 1979, *18*. Copyright 1979 by Society for Scientific Study of Religion.

Bendix's volume is of monumental size (some 300,000 words), and like Wallerstein's, handsomely illustrated with historical woodcuts, paintings, and photographs. Emulation among publishers, it seems, as well as among scholars, has had good effects on the quality of these publications. *Kings or People* is in one sense a series of monographs, each a substantial history of a state from its first ancestors to its most recent form: England from 40 A.D. onward, France from 1100, Germany from 700, Russia from 800, and Japan from 600 A.D. Enormous amounts of factual material are packed in on government structures, wars, populations, education, religion, popular culture, and the ideas of intellectuals. Bendix's well-organized writing makes all this come across clearly, sometimes even vividly, as in the final dramatic chapter on Russia.

What seems strange, though, in a book written by a sociologist, is an almost complete lack of familiar sociological theories or concepts. Bendix, the dean of American Weber scholars, scarcely betrays a Weberian note. On first glance, one might think this the work of a pure historian (except that dealing with such a breadth of materials would be professional heresy). Nevertheless, although Bendix does often revel in pure historical tale-telling, there is a theoretical theme. It is sociological, and it is Bendix's own. Briefly put, it is a theory of modernization.

Modernization is thoroughly relative, Bendix holds; it is not a transition all states have made along one road from "tradition" to "modernity." It is a process by which follower states emulate a "reference society" that they feel is ahead of them, especially due to their military inferiority. Each one takes up from the last, blending their own domestic traditions with reforms imported from abroad, so that each new stage of "modernization" is different from the last.

The important materials to pay attention to are wars and armies, since these determine external fortunes, and the cultural media, which provide the images and feelings about things abroad by which domestic political movements of emulation are stirred up. The uniqueness of Bendix's work is to provide this kind of documentation. He describes the numbers and organization of aristocrats and government officials, the history of state revenues and the strains caused by wars and by increasingly large-standing armies. But he also gives us the numbers of schools and students, of newspapers and books; he reviews what is said in the popular press as well as by intellectuals.

England is the first modern state, by virtue of two consequences of its foreign affairs of the 1500s. Militarily powerful Spain was its reference society, at first in a positive sense, then in a negative one. The war between England and Spain, fueled by the struggle of Protestant Reformation versus Catholic Counter-Reformation, and culminating in the attempted Spanish invasion in 1588, mobilized the English people into a national identity around the Crown. But the financial costs of England's military defenses brought a struggle over the taxation powers of the Crown, and this culminated in the shift of the new national power to the Parliament. Thus external struggles both created nationalism and weakened the King, transferring power to the leaders of the people.

France, in turn, attempted to build up a powerful military machine and an absolutist government. Its internal critics looked first to England, but the real crisis came with the American War of Independence. France made a military alliance with the colonists, with the consequences of both mobilizing French public opinion in favor of democratic ideals, and putting financial strains on the French king. The two of these together led directly to the French Revolution.

Germany, and especially its best-organized military sector, Prussia, was caught in the same dynamic. Seeking to modernize militarily, states like Prussia emulated the French culture and state organization. But France was often a military enemy, and the upshot of its Revolution was the Napoleonic Wars, which conquered Germany. In these circumstances, France became a negative ideal, and England could be taken as a more conservative form of modern state to be emulated. Popular German nationalism emerged in the revolt against Napoleon, and the conservative style of German parliamentarism came from its very limited success in undermining the King's power and from its conservatively chosen role modeling.

Japan and Russia modernized as the result of further military threat and cultural emulation. The Japanese responded to the U.S. naval expedition in 1853 by a domestic revolution which created a modern mass army and deliberately chose the Prussian constitution as its political structure. Russia began deliberately emulating Western (especially French) styles and bureaucratic organization in the early 1700s as part of its expanding military posture. Serfdom was finally abolished in the aftermath of Russia's defeat in the Crimean War, and local representative institutions were established to aid in creating a modern state administration in the absence of local government administrators. There was a long series of partial efforts to import modern institutions from Western European reference societies, before the financial strains and military defeats of World War I destroyed the Czarist regime and brought the Communist modernizers to power. The revolutionary tradition from France, and the underground tradition of failed German revolution (Marx) ultimately proved to be the victorious foreign imports in Russia rather than the more conservative models imported earlier in partial form.

The theory is an original and striking one, and Bendix documents his case convincingly. The theory tells us that the major political changes have occurred because of international military dynamics; states which are strong enough to fight back against strong enemies have had to mobilize their populations, both for increasingly larger armed forces and to pay for increasingly expensive wars. Thus the shift "from kings to people" is a long-term military dynamic. The points at which states *fail* in this international competition are even more crucial: Partial, *financial* failures especially set the stage for democratizing revolutions. More complete military defeats also open the way to change, although apparently with less favorable consequences for representative institutions (i.e., Germany, Russia—I would put Japan and Germany after 1945, though, as exceptions to this principle). In either case, the foreign reference societies affect what model is chosen after such an upheaval.

The limitations of Bendix's argument, for me, are primarily in its historicist mode of presentation. Bendix provides very little systematic theorizing or summary above the level of concrete examples; the theoretical model I have given is culled from the book, but is nowhere laid out in one place. If it had been argued more formally, it might have given stronger answers to why the experiences of different states have consisted of quite different variants on mass-mobilized politics: England's rather successful expansion of representative institutions, France's continuing series of revolts and revolutions, Russia's despotic forced mobilization, Germany and Japan's relative authoritarianism. Bendix attributes the differences to the cultural traditions of each society.

I do not find this entirely convincing. Traditions can change or stop being relevent; Germany and Japan, after the military and economic reconstructions of 1945, for example, seem to have broken into a new political pattern. Just what the really operative bases of the earlier, long-term political histories were, in any case, would benefit from systematic explanation. The external military–cultural dynamic seems just as much in evidence throughout history as it is post-1600 A.D., and it may well be that a tradition is only a gloss on what such exigencies make it worthwhile for political actors to retain at any moment in time. I also have my doubts about the wisdom of limiting relevance of economic processes down to the exigencies of government finance. Theories like Barrington Moore's (1966) about the political consequences of the different ways aristocrats can relate to capitalist agriculture can fill in a gap that Bendix leaves in explaining why the shift from kings to people sometimes results in democracy, sometimes in fascism or communism.

Its limitations notwithstanding, Bendix's work marks a major advance in the theory of the state and its changes. Above all, the model of an international chain of emulation is an important step. It has already begun to have its intellectual effects.

Geopolitics and Revolution*

Part of the recent onsurge in comparative–historical sociology has been a revival of Marxian sociology. It has also been a time of upheaval in Marxian thought. Increasingly, the borderlines between Marxian and non-Marxian theory have been crossed. Theda Skocpol's *States and Social Revolutions* (1979) exemplifies all of these phenomena. As a result, it is the best book that has ever been written on revolutions, and a major step forward in political theory.

One of the striking features of Skocpol's book is the way she reverses some long-standing Marxian ideas. Revolutions are not caused, she asserts, by economic contradictions bursting through the bonds of existing political relations, and revolutionary agents are not rising social classes. New economic organization and classes are likely to appear after and as the result of successful revolutionary transformations. Thus the French revolution cleared the way for large-scale markets and bourgeois classes to appear in the nineteenth century; the Russian and Chinese revolutions created the possibility of a socialist

* Originally published in *Theory and Society* 1980, 9. Copyright 1980 Elsevier Scientific Publishing Company, Amsterdam.

organization of industry, not as an anomalous skipping of stages, but as the natural course of such events.

The main causes and consequences of revolutions are not economic at all, but political. But the dynamic is not ideological, nor is it the volition of revolutionaries. Here Skocpol takes to an extreme the trend within current Marxist thought to give a degree of autonomy to the state. Where structuralist Marxists like Poulantzas see the state as capable of mediating among social classes in order to uphold the economic system as a whole, Skocpol points out that the state has interests of its own. These interests are above all international: Political chiefs are concerned about international prestige and related military security and power. This affects their internal policies as well, for they must compete with other social classes, especially the economically dominant ones, for economic surplus to put to use in paying their military bills. Indeed, the administrative apparatus of the state grew up as little more than a device for supporting armies and navies, later increasingly for supporting itself.

This is an important formulation. Although Skocpol does not say it in so many words, the members of the state constitute a social class. They represent a distinctive way of making a living: by military and administrative appropriation. Empirically realistic class-conflict schemes are suddenly clarified once we realize this.

If the state is basically military, then we have the starting point for a new theory of revolutions. Revolutions are not possible as long as the military apparatus of the state holds together. Hence the most basic condition is the breakup of armies and internal forces of domination. Other theories about the motivation of rebels by long-standing grievances, relative deprivation, or cultural strain, or about the availability of resources for organizing revolts, cannot be adequate explanations, since they miss the most basic feature of revolutions. What then causes military breakdowns? The causes are above all international. The competitive dynamism of the European state system lies behind the three great revolutions Skocpol discusses. France, Russia, and China were all potential Great Powers, overextended or poorly organized for military relations. Their efforts to keep up with or defend themselves against more powerful states brought fiscal crises and downright disintegration of the coercive apparatus. Moreover, if one could see the revolutionary crisis coming long before the event, it was because international emulation had been going on for a long time. As in Reinhard Bendix's model, which Skocpol cites, modernization is always historically relative, and it is a process of external emulation based on military motives. Since state rulers are the most internationally oriented people in their realms, they themselves are the transmission belts for foreign standards, and thus tend to seal their own fates.

For revolutions to be truly major, though, the military breakdown must be combined with internal pressures, especially a mass movement from below. Thus Skocpol notes several different types of revolutions. First are the classic cases, her primary subject; cases in which there is not only a political but also a social transformation, and in which these changes are accompanied by class upheaval. These class upheavals, in France, Russia, and China, were peasant rebellions. The other types of revolution are: the early European, liberal revolutions like the English revolution of the seventeenth century; and the nation-building revolutions of modern times in the Third World.

Skocpol uses a number of these other cases to demonstrate the importance of her external-plus-internal conjuncture in France, Russia, and China. Thus England and Prussia had political revolutions, triggered by foreign-based fiscal strains or military defeats, but not social revolutions, because in neither England nor Prussia was the crisis from above accompanied by a peasant revolt from below. Similarly, the Meiji restoration in Japan was the result of a purely military crisis, with no internal revolt. In France, China, and Russia, there were long-standing problems of the rural economy, exacerbated by short-term strains of crop failure or war; revolts were fostered by autocratic reform efforts from above. In a combination of themes from Barrington Moore and Alexis de Tocqueville, Skocpol points to the transformation of rural property relations, the removal of day-to-day aristocratic supervision of the peasants, and government encouragement of collective rural organization for administrative purposes, as factors which organized the peasant potential for revolt. Her comparisons do good service here. In England, for example, the clergy were under local aristocratic patronage, whereas in France they were centrally appointed; thus in the former case local leadership was united around the aristocracy, whereas in the latter there was a structural split that facilitated antiaristocratic revolt. France and Russia had somewhat similar rural structures; China was closer to the English model of local gentry control of the economy, and hence the social part of the Chinese revolution was delayed several decades until the communists had reorganized the peasantry.

One of Skocpol's major contributions comes at the point where most theories of revolution have ended. She asks: Why is revolutionary reconstruction possible after the initial breakdown? Natural history accounts of revolutions never raise the question at all, nor do motivational or conflict resource theories, which apply only to the initial phase. Yet there is no intrinsic reason why the state should re-emerge, and in a more centralized and strengthened form at that. The people's alleged weariness with revolutionary ardors need not lead to a Thermidorian reaction, unless there is some process that keeps the state from fragmenting into smaller parts, or becoming subject to foreign conquest—all of which have been real occurences at other times in history. The overthrow of previous Chinese dynasties, for example, has often given rise to warlord periods far longer than the 35 years it took to consolidate the revolution of 1911.

The logic of Skocpol's argument is that the structural forces behind the major social revolutions are above all in the military apparatus and its international relations. The long-term cause of the military breakdown was an unsuccessful effort to expand military capacity, and hence internal structures of domination and surplus extraction. The orientation of personnel within the state was to move further in this direction, and improved administrative organization and physical facilities were not only planned but also at least partially constructed. The conflicts of the revolutionary period did not displace these goals, but revolved around struggles over who was to bear the short-term costs of the failure to achieve them. The leaders of the revolutions were not a new class rising with a new economy, but the aspiring administrators produced by previous reforms, and deriving from the core provinces where the state was strongest. As the revolution removed the more parasitical elements of the privileged classes, and settled the more ephemeral grievances of the populace, the cadres of the expanding state were left at the center of the stage.

Thus, although the great revolutions were beset with long struggles with anarchical elements, counterrevolutihnary forces, regional warlords, or foreign intervention, these violent aftermaths actually contributed to the consolidation of the state. The revolutionary parties had the opportunity to create new armies, based on bureaucratic principles and purged of the patrimonial inefficiencies of the old forces, and out of their success arose the new structure and the legitimating ethos of the centralized state. For France, says Skocpol (p. 186), the outbreak of war in 1792 and the accompanying fear of counterrevolution, was as important as the conjuncture of 1789 in determining the course of the revolution. In Russia, where the peasants' revolt turned toward anarchistic decentralization, the civil war was the key to recentralization by pulling the peasants back into the reconstituted army. Here, the industrial and railroad-building policies of the Czarist regime, motivated by strategic considerations, had a crucial payoff. The industrial workers, though a small part of the labor force, were a key support for the revolutionary consolidation because their livelihood depended upon maintaining a large-scale devision of labor. The railroad and tele-graph workers, who depended even more immediately upon centraliza-tion, played a key part in the movement of troops along interior lines which provided the physical basis of reconstituting state control. Again, China is a mixed case, lacking extensive physical and adminis-trative apparatus for centralization. But its interregnum was drawn to a close precisely because of the Japanese invasion, which made China's military fate depend upon the multiple international forces of World War II. Eventually the communist cadres, the heirs of the old imperial career tradition in the core provinces, were able to defeat the peripher-ally based Kuomintang in the race to fill the vacuum left by the Jap-anese defeat.

Skocpol's overall theory is particularly interesting because it is capable of some far-reaching extensions. If the causes of revolutionary crises and consolidation are military, then we should be able to gener-alize about the long-term conditions under which revolutions happen. Skocpol's main cases fit very strikingly into a geopolitical model I have proposed elsewhere (Collins, 1978; reprinted in this book as "Long-term Social Change and the Territorial Power of States,") to account for long-term shifts in the territorial power of states. The first two vari-ables in that model are territorial resource advantage (wealthiest and most populous states expand) and marchland advantage (states with enemies on the fewest fronts expand). Pre-revolutionary France, Russia, and China each had divergent values on these two key vari-ables. Each state was among the largest of its time; but each had gotten into a negative position on the marchland variable. France had the largest population and the largest army in Europe, but had strained its resources atempting to be both the major land power on the Continent and England's rival as a naval power. Moreover, France's continental wars, ranging from the Netherlands to Italy, had long since reached a stalemate; and the eighteenth century saw the loss of her Indian and Canadian colonies, with only an expensive victory by her American allies in 1777–1783 as compensation. Similarly, Russia in the late nine-teenth century had expanded beyond her huge capacities, capping its centuries-old drive into Eastern Europe and Turkestan with an overex-pansion to the Pacific, where Japan inflicted the defeat in 1905 that set off the prelude to revolution. China in the nineteenth century faced col-onial incursions all along its coast, followed by ruinously expensive in-ternal revolts, while attempting to maintain an empire stretching from Tibet to Vietnam to Korea.

Thus the military strains that produce revolution seem to follow from a mixture of favorable and unfavorable geopolitical factors: the favorable one luring a state into overexpansion, while the unfavorable one (which indeed may be created by the physical contours of that overexpansion) ensuring that military defeat and/or fiscal strain will follow. In the long run, then, all large states in a militarily competitive world are threatened with revolution, unless they can arrest their expansive tendencies at a geographically defensible point.

What about the internal component of a revolutionary conjuncture? Is not this the result of a separate set of factors, so that although military strains may occur, the result may be no more than a political rather than a social revolution? This may turn out to be so. Nevertheless, it is worth exploring the possibility that internal class upheavals are explainable as a condition of *internal geopolitics*. This is an unfamiliar notion, but Skocpol's analysis is very suggestive in this direction. What is so refreshing in her exposition is that there is nothing abstract or obfuscating about her concepts of political relations. We get a strong sense of how these consist of people spread out across a landscape, linked or not by roads, postal carriers, and railways; of groups assembling once a week in the parish church, or split up in isolated estates under the watchful eyes of supervisors.

The long-run principles here are not very formalized, but as a lead it is worth noting that the histories of rural property relations are most usefully seen as sets of variations on the geographical dispersion of different social classes. The English enclosure movements probably had their greatest political effects because they physically removed the peasantry, while leaving the aristocrats esconsed in the countryside (but also assembling annually in London); in France, the removal process was the reverse, the peasants becoming more locally entrenched and the aristocrats more absentee, thus opening the way to peasant revolt. Or in China, we can see the geographical weakness of the Kuomintang by its ability to collect taxes directly only in the coastal cities, relying on warlord intemediaries elsewhere. For an earlier period, the physical placement of aristocrats' lands—scattered or geographically consolidated—and of government administrators was a key to the physical control of internal territory by various classes. Thus, although we have scarcely begun to think of a theory of internal geopolitics, it should be possible to formulate some long-term principles that mesh with those of external politics, and add up to a full-fledged explanatory model.

At this point it is important to consider the limits that Skocpol has placed on her analysis. For several reasons, she confines it to the French, Russian, and Chinese revolutions. She excepts cases like seventeenth century England, or nineteenth century Prussia or Japan, from her theory because they did not undergo social as well as political transformations; in fact, precisely for this reason she is able to use them as test cases, and thus to show how the military crisis must be combined with an internal mass revolt if a social revolution is to follow. But this is really only a form of exposition. A theory of revolutions should be a theory of the conditions for various kinds of revolutions, and Skocpol herself has stated some of the key determinants of the variations just mentioned. The same approach can be taken to her remarks on another set of revolutions, which acutally combined external and internal factors in a fashion rather like her classical cases. These are such twentieth century revolutions as those in Yugoslavia, Algeria, Vietnam, Cuba, and parts of Africa. These do not fit the classic model, she says, because the crises of France, Russia, and China took place in wealthy and politically ambitious agrarian states which were never colonially subjugated. In contrast, the Third World revolutions took place following crises in colonial or post-colonial dependency relations which were breaking up because of shifts in Great Power relations. This may be so. But I would prefer to see the modification as an elaboration rather than a limitation on a successful theory. In this light, a rather powerful geopolitical theory of many varieties of revolutions should be coming into focus.

Skocpol's work sets me to reflecting backward in history as well. For there are a number of other revolutions that may well fit this kind of theory. The revolutions in the city–states of ancient Greece and Italy, for example, had their bases in shifting forms of military mobilization, and occured at times of rapid change in external relations. There are the civic revolutions of the High Middle Ages and the Renaissance, and the sixteenth century Dutch revolution in its war of independence against Spain—the first of the great anticolonial revolutions, and of the modern liberal revolutions as well. The consequences of these for the legal bases of property relations were so significant that Max Weber (1951:62) declared that they determined the destiny of the Occident.

Long-Term Social Change and the Territorial Power of States*

The state consists ultimately of military control over a territory. As Weber (1968:901–902) remarked, the intensity of this control has many variations, and the borders of the territory may not be sharply defined or reliably defended. But some degree of effective military control, based upon at least some well-guarded locations, is the key to all the other features of a state.

What determines the extent of states? From this perspective, the determinants are of two sorts: the organizational resources that make up the bases of military power, and the territorial configurations in which this power is exercised.

1. Among the organizational bases of the military are the type of
   a. weapons and military structure;
   b. economy; and
   c. administrative resources, which include both the technology

* Portions of this article were originally published in Louis Kriesberg (Ed.), *Research in Social Movements, Conflicts, and Change*, vol. 1, 1978. Copyright 1978 by JAI Press.

of administration and cultural resources in the form of
religion and ethnicity.
2. Among the territorial configurations we must consider
    a. heartlands;
    b. barriers; and
    c. the external relationships among heartlands and the states
       that are built upon them.

The organizational and territorial variables interact; both types
must enter the analysis to explain and predict which states will be large
or small, strong or weak. Moreover a glance at the historical record
shows that state boundaries are seldom stable over long periods of
time, but expand and contract, combine and fragment. These changes
have been the normal condition of states for most of human history.
What appears to be stable from a short-term perspective—within the
human generation or two that makes up a contemporary viewpoint on
political events—can usually be seen in an overview of long-term history, as a temporary balance-point in some larger dynamics. An explanatory theory, then, must be a dynamic one. It must aim to explain
the pattern of movement of state boundaries; and the variables that can
account for these will also account for their times of stability. In effect,
this comes down to accounting for the incidence and outcome of wars.
      Since the processes involved are dynamic ones, it is important for
a theory not only to display the crucial variables and the direction of
operation but also to indicate the length of time involved in each of
these processes. Most of these time periods are relatively long; certain
configurations of variables may take as many as 10 to 30 generations to
work themselves out. The time-laws that follow are an effort to provide
at least an outline of this aspect of the theory. They are no more than
crude approximations at this point; they could hardly as yet be more,
given the multicausal nature of the processes involved, and the resulting complexity of the comparative historical analysis.
      The point is worth some elaboration. The major theories of long-
term social change have usually taken the entire society as their unit,
and have asserted that societies move through a predictable series of
changes from a given starting point. This is the case both of linear evolutionary models (e.g., Comte, Spencer, Marx, Parsons), and of cyclical
models (e.g., Ibn Khaldun, Spengler, Sorokin, Toynbee). The nature of
the stages and of the mechanisms of change vary from theory to theory.
But the focus of each theory on a single sequence of changes means that
each, in effect, is a monocausal theory. Which is to say, side-variations
from the main line of change may be recognized by the theorist, but

they are regarded simply as empirical details for which a general theory is unnecessary.

In my view, a single-factor theory is inadequate to anything but the most selective version of world history. When we examine the organizational processes (Collins, 1975: 470–523; 348–402) that actually produce various aspects of culture, the economy and its related stratification forms, and the different types and expanses of the state, there is no reason to expect that all of these should necessarily change together in a common sequence. The historical evidence suggests the same conclusion: Eras of cultural innovation need not correspond to the height of state power, or even necessarily to a given phase in the history of states.[1] The variables that determine cultural productivity, in other words, are more specific than at the level of the entire society, and are not necessarily the same variables that affect the state. Similarly, economic prosperity, although likely to be high in a strong state, is not necessarily confined to such states,[2] nor is a highly advanced economy necessarily characteristic of strong states.[3]

In other words, cultural, economic, and political histories, although affecting each other, are determined by their own sets of variables; each requires its own theory. But to separate these realms means that we cannot fall back on the mixture of examples from different realms that have commonly been used to bolster either a sequence of stages of successively increasing social power or complexity, or a rise-and-fall model of improvement and decline. To explain any one of these realms, such as the state, we are obliged to look for much more specific patterns in it. The unit of analysis becomes much more defined; we are no longer looking for whatever pieces of history might have once been grouped together as aspects of a civilization,[4] but for an explanation of as much of the variations in the territorial powers of states as we possibly can. We have taken on an empirically more definite task. And although this may be more demanding in terms of

---

[1] The great Roman literary period, for example, is at the time of the initial transition from Republic to Empire; the first great artistic period of China is in the period of dissolution following the downfall of the Han empire. Rome lacks a great philosophical period entirely; and so on.

[2] For example, the prosperous Switzerland of today is not a strong state.

[3] Their prosperity may simply be based on the predatory success of the military state itself, as in the case of early modern Spain, and many other examples in world history.

[4] As Spengler or Toynbee did by focussing on the connection between cultural events that took place in quite different territorial states, or as the evolutionary theorists did with "levels" of culture from disparate parts of the world.

complexity of causal conditions, it has a corresponding payoff in the confidence with which we may be able to treat conclusions. The mono-sequence theories, in effect, reduce their conceptual apparatus to a level at which they are hard to prove wrong. One selects those pieces of evidence that can be arranged in order of increasing social productivity or scientific rationality or social differentiation—or in an order of rise-and-fall. The small number of categories predetermines that almost everything can be classified into the scheme. To escape tautology, it is necessary to focus on those aspects where empirical evidence itself makes a difference for the theory. To delineate *time periods* for such sequences would be the main path available to them to show their pre-dictive power, and by the same token their testability.[5]

The same applies to the analysis of empirically more definite units, the territories of states. If one can show not only that certain variables determine state boundaries, but also that they do so in particular time periods, the empirical validity of the theory would be greatly en-hanced.[6] So would its practical utility, insofar as such a theory would have contemporary application in making predictions.

In what follows, I suggest some general principles determining the territorial power of states, first on the internal organizational side, and then on their territorial configurations and external relationships. I place greatest emphasis on the external patterns; partly because these have been relatively neglected in the sociological analysis (although certainly not in the historiography) of states, and partly because I believe that these have an overriding influence in what is nevertheless a multicausal situation. These principles of external relations are largely inductive, derived above all from the analysis of historical atlases in conjunction with topographic maps, supplemented by nar-rative histories. I have confined my primary source of data to the boundaries of civilized states (states based on some degree of literate administration) in the geographical areas of China, the Middle East, and Europe. In time periods, this gives us China from approximately

---

[5] These theories are not all valueless in this respect. Toynbee (1954:234–295) in par-ticular provides detailed information and makes the effort to establish the time laws of specific political sequences.

[6] This is true both in a general methodological sense, and in a more specific strategy of theory construction. For to show that political processes work themselves out in a given amount of time, for example a given number of human generations, would open the way to a connection between the microevents of human lifetimes that make up the fundamental empirical substance of our discipline, and the compacted summaries that we conceptualize as world history. To draw the connection, even sketchily and in principle, enables us to bolster the probability of our macroexplanations by their plausibility in terms of what we know of the microprocesses that must take them up.

1000 B.C. onward, the Middle East from approximately 3000 B.C., and Europe from approximately 1000 B.C. (more recently in the northern part). Although these time periods as we ordinarily judge them appear enormous, for an analysis of the changing boundaries of states and considering the length of the processes involved, the number of cases is not overwhelming.[7]

THE ORGANIZATIONAL BASES OF MILITARY POWER

Weapons and Military Structure

In another place (Collins, 1975: 356–363), I have described three sets of variations in military organization: whether weapons are expensive or cheap, and individually or group operated; whether the army is supplied individually, by group foraging, by monetary systems, or by centralized administration; and whether the conquered territory is administered by a system of booty, feudal land-grants, garrisons, or centralized civilian-run taxation. These three sets of variables all affect the degree of centralized control of a state internally. But they also affect its external boundaries, because they affect the cohesion of the state, and hence its relative external strength and its susceptibility to conquest. The extremely weak forms (cheap, individually-operated weapons, self-supplied troops, booty systems of rewards) cannot create strong and lasting states (as illustrated by the short-term empires of the Huns and other nomads). At the other end, expensive group-operated weapons (as in modern mechanized warfare), combined with centralized supplies and taxation, help keep the state together, and ensure that its conquests are likely to be more permanent.

But these military structures in themselves do not determine the size of the state. The Huns and other nomad empires have been very large, and some modern military states are quite small. Nor is state stability necessarily predicted by these variables, except at the extreme

---

[7] Sources for the material cited in the following, unless otherwise noted, are under appropriately dated maps in McEvedy (1961, 1967, 1972). Herrmann (1966), Shepherd (1964), Toynbee and Myers (1959), and Bartholomew (1954), with additional narrative accounts in Eberhard (1969), McNeill (1963, 1964), and Toynbee (1954:234–295). I deal only with the contiguous territories of the European states, neglecting their overseas empires. The latter would provide additional material for analysis, as would the territorial states of North and South America (both Mexican and Andean, and the European colonial states), and of India, Africa, and Southeast Asia. I have focused on the European, Middle Eastern, and Chinese materials only because they are more accessible through first-rate historical atlases.

weak end of the continuum. States with quite centralized military organization nevertheless may be vulnerable to external conquest due to
geopolitical configurations. Conversely, some of the moderately weak
forms (such as landed feudalism of individually-armed knights) have
characterized states that have held stable external boundaries over
long periods of time; for example, the Sassinid Persian empire lasted on
this basis from approximately 200–600 A.D.

Economy

The major historical differences in types of productive economies
are background determinants of the weapons and supply systems that
make up the immediate bases of states. The main economic types are
hunting-and-gathering, fishing, primitive and advanced horticultural,
pastoral, trading, agrarian, and industrial, plus various mixtures
among these (Collins, 1975; 355–356; Lenski, 1970). Only the more productive economies can have highly centralized supply systems and very
expensive large-scale weapons. Also more productive economies have
proportionately greater surplus for investment in war equipment,
larger populations, and greater proportions of the population freed for
military action. Thus the more productive economies usually result in a
military advantage over less productive ones. But this is not so absolute
a determinant as one might think; if it were, the main pattern of history
would simply be the conquest of less productive economies by more
productive ones. The opposite also happens: the so-called barbarian
conquests that have been important phases in all parts of the world.
These are possible because weapons selectively diffuse, and the economic basis of a productively less advanced society can be provided by
warfare itself—its economy may become a predatory one. Again,
whether such a predatory state can defeat an economically more productive one depends especially upon external (geopolitical) configurations.

Administrative Resources

How the state is administered is another set of background variables determining the type of military structure, by affecting how
troops are organized and conquered territories controlled. I have discussed elsewhere (Collins, 1975; 364–380) the cultural and technical
resources involved in creating a bureaucratic or merely patrimonial
(personal, household-based) administration. Most important histor-

ically have been a literate priesthood and universalistic religion as bases for initially creating a bureaucracy; out of this, secular administration and legitimacy might emerge.

A related factor that bears elaboration is ethnicity. This means a common culture that when reflected upon (e.g., in situations of conflict with people of another culture) can become a self-conscious ethnic identity. A common culture is made up especially of a common language and religion (as well as by style of art, entertainment, and consumption). It is solidified by literacy, because it creates a repository of major cultural works, and often by furthering a specialized linguistic identity through a unique form of script. Such a cultural identity is important as an administrative resource because it facilitates communications and hence organization. Commonly where a single ethnic culture is lacking, political and organizational factions form along the cultural divide. The fact that symbolic communications are also procedures for practical inclusion and exclusion means that they tend to mobilize emotional identifications, and thus transform the struggle for power into moral or prestige issues.

An important question for the theory of the state, then, is to what degree an ethnic identity is established within a given territory. This is a rather underdeveloped area in sociological theory. I would suggest that the success of the state itself in maintaining long-term control over a territory is crucial. For in a situation without any political controls, small groups that may inhabit territory quite close to each other often seem to move in the direction of increasing cultural polarization. The most diverse sets of languages, for example, are found among the indigenous hunting-and-gathoring and primitive horticultural tribes of the Americas or of New Guinea. A shift towards linguistic uniformity seems to go along with increasing size of states and intensity of internal administration. But a short-lived state is unlikely to have much effect in creating a stable ethnic identity; a series of shifting conquest empires over a territory is likely to foster continual cultural change, and leave a complex pattern of cultural enclaves, rather than to create an ethnic identity.

The relationship, then, is a circular one. The longer a state controls an area, the more likely an ethnic identity is to emerge; and the stronger the ethnic identity, the more likely the state is to be strongly administered, and to quickly expel outside conquerors by mobilizing a nativist reaction.[8] This formulation is not *logically* circular (a vicious

---

[8] Egypt and China, areas whose relatively isolated geographical boundaries have fostered long-term cultural identities, have had the most persistent propensities to nativist reactions against outside conquerors. Also, modern industrial bureaucracies

circle), but only *empirically* so. The relationship between the variables occurs over time, and we can attempt to specify the number of generations of stable state control it takes to establish an ethnic identity of varying degrees of potency. The amount of time it takes to establish a distinct language is one important clue. For example, although northern France and Germany were unified in the Frankish and Carolingian empires from the 500s through the early 800s A.D., by 1200 the difference between the French and German languages already approximated twentieth-century differences. This line of investigation needs to be taken much further. I can only mention it here, but it deserves a prominent place in the set of interacting variables that should ultimately make up a predictive model of the power of states.

TERRITORIAL CONFIGURATIONS

The main emphasis of this paper is to shift the focus of attention to the external relations of states. In this light, the physical territories upon which military control is exerted are crucial determinants of the possibilities of state power.

Heartlands

A heartland is a territory with some geographical unity that makes it much more easily and uniformly accessible to military control from within it than from any point outside (Stinchombe, 1968: 216–230). The Hungarian basin in eastern Europe is a good example of a nearly closed heartland, ringed almost completely by mountains. Egypt is another naturally closed heartland, unified by the natural transportation system of the Nile, and separated by desert to the east, west, and south, and by the Mediterranean to the north. The degree to which territories are closed off as natural heartlands varies around the globe. Thus one key variable in the stability and size of states is the extent to which closed heartlands exist on the territory they attempt to control. Closed river valleys, islands without significant internal barriers, and peninsulas are the most naturally closed heartlands, open plains are the least closed.

---

seem especially hard to conquer for any length of time, because of the intensity of national identity, which is itself a product of the internal cultural mobilization brought about by bureaucratization and by a high degree of literacy generally.

Heartlands are the basic units of geopolitics. As we shall see, the external configurations among them are crucial for the ebb and flow of military struggles to extend state boundaries. The first step is to establish military control over an entire heartland. This in turn has an economic precondition. Usually at least the level of advanced horticultural technology is necessary for this degree of organization in the simplest heartland, a river valley. In larger plains areas, agrarian technology, or at least some diffusion of agrarian techniques is necessary. Heartlands differ as well in the type of economy most suited for each. Therefore broad differences in cultural style (ethnic differences) emerge among territories most amenable to pastoral, horticultural, agrarian, or commercial-trading economies; and these will become stabilized into strong ethnic identities if the degree of military stability permits.

Barriers

The boundaries of closed heartlands are set by natural barriers. These are also politically important in those more ambiguous geographical cases where closed heartlands do not exist. Rivers are rarely strong barriers; although they may be seized upon by diplomats in negotiating frontiers, this is usually a sign of ambiguous heartland boundaries or an unsettled military situation. For a river valley is usually a natural transportation unit. Thus China has usually been unified around the common valley of the Hwang Ho and the Yangtze rivers; France around the common valley of the Seine and the upper Loire. The attempt of France to push its border to the Rhine has usually failed because both sides of the valley are a natural unit, most easily held by the Germans.

Seas and large lakes are more definite boundaries. But they may also serve as transportation channels for maritime warfare. In the case of some Mediterranean empires, the waterways have been the key to political unity.

Mountains are a more important barrier, and we find states have often bordered at the Pyrenees, the Alps, the Himalayas, the Andes. But if the heartland on one side of a mountain range is much bigger and richer than the other side, or otherwise militarily disproportionate, the territory immediately beyond the mountains is likely to be controlled as well (as we see in the case of the Urals, Rockies, Appalachians, and Carpathians in modern times, and the usual historical relationship between the dominant Persian plateau and the Mesopotamian lowlands beyond the Zagros range).

The most significant natural barriers are lands that are absolutely inhospitable, such as deserts and jungles. These can support such small populations, and can cover such large expanses, that military threats cannot be stably mounted either in or across them. But even here an advanced military technology such as mechanization may make inroads.

In short, natural barriers in themselves are rarely absolute determinants of state boundaries, but must be seen in combination with the technology of military transportation, the size and economies of the heartlands on either side, and the dynamics of the external relations among the states surrounding them. In a full-fledged explanatory model, we should have to establish some degrees of difficulty of access across barriers, and add this into the total picture of dynamic military factors.

We come now to the crux of this theoretical sketch: the geographical configurations among states. All of the previously mentioned factors operate within this matrix. I suggest seven main geopolitical principles.

1. Territorial Resource Advantages

States based upon the largest and wealthiest heartlands tend to dominate the smaller and poorer ones, all else being equal. The larger a heartland, the larger its population, for a given level of productive technology. Considering this variable alone, then, the largest among a given set of states will be able to field the largest army, and thus tend to conquer or dominate the smaller states. Similarly, a territory which is rich in fertile land, mineral deposits, or other natural wealth will be able to field a larger proportion of its population, and to equip its army better than its poorer rivals.

There are many instances of this phenomenon. At any given moment in history, the larger states tend to dominate the smaller. This is especially apparent during a period of cumulative expansion. Rome, the largest city in Italy in the fourth century B.C.,[9] absorbed its smaller rivals one by one, and thus fielded an increasingly larger army in each

---

[9] The population of 10,000 attained by Rome soon after 400 B.C. (McEvedy 1967:54) remains a puzzle, considering the economic backwardness of the area; most plausibly, the pressures of the Celts and Etruscans had motivated this clustering as a means of defense. By the first century A.D., the Roman army had grown to 260,000 (McEvedy 1967: 76).

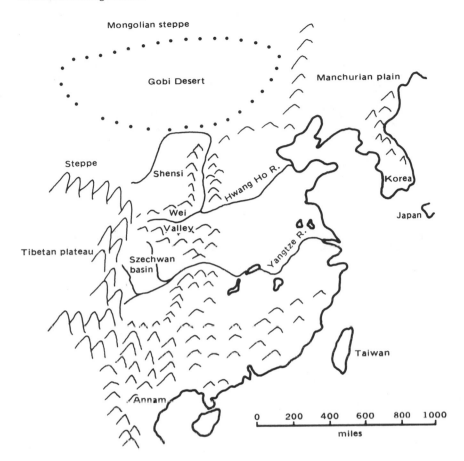

Figure 1. China.

campaign. Athens, the richest of the Greek cities of the fifth century B.C., had the largest navy, and grew increasingly powerful while its victories increased its levies upon the conquered states of Greece. The same pattern is undoubtedly found in the expansive period of every empire, at least once successful conquest is under way. And the very existence of any government depends upon a local application of this principle: The central state is held together because it usually can draw upon more troops and equipment than any segment of the population that might rise in opposition.

This factor can be a dynamic one. The Warring States period in ancient China (ca. 800–200 B.C.) was brought to an end after the state of Ch'in, one of the seven major rivals for domination, expanded into the

Figure 2. Middle East, North Africa, and Europe.

adjacent virgin territory of the Szechwan basin (see Figure 1); within four generations, Ch'in's population gave it military superiority over all rivals (especially the other marchland states). In Europe, Spain was the dominant imperial power in the sixteenth century A.D., when its revenues were perhaps three times that of its nearest rival, France; in the eighteenth century, France took the leading military part as its revenues topped the list, and Spain fell to about one-quarter of France's level (McEvedy, 1972:38,58). In the Second World War, the economic resources of the U.S., Britain, and the U.S.S.R. favored military predominance over Germany, Italy, and Japan (Liddell-Hart, 1971:16–24).

Yet clearly this principle has limitations. Empires not only expand, but also contract; cumulative growth of resources may give way to cumulative decline; and sometimes the larger and richer states are beaten or even conquered by the smaller and poorer ones. In other words, multiple causality holds; the resources of a given territory are only one variable among several. It is these other determinants that facilitate cumulative processes, and also turn them in a negative direction.

2. Marchland Advantage

Marchland states have a power advantage over more centrally located states. That is, of a group of contiguous states on the same level of military organization, those on the edge of the group tend to have an advantage over the others. Marchland states are the first to break free from an empire, the longest to hold out against an empire, and most importantly, the principal creators of conquest states.

The marchland principle may be shown in the rise of almost all the great states and empires.[10] In China, there were seven major periods of unification following periods when multiple states existed in China. Of these, the first two unifying states (Chou ca. 1000 B.C.; Ch'in in 221 B.C., followed in 206 B.C. by Han in an internal dynastic succession) conquered the others (downstream in the Hwang Ho and Yangtze River valleys) from a home base in the Wei valley, which is a long, narrow river valley to the extreme west of this fertile cultivated area. Subsequent periods of disintegration were ended by Sui in 589 A.D. (followed by T'ang in 618 in an internal succession) which had conquered first the north from this same western Wei base; and then by the Sung in 960, again from a base in the north, progressively mopping up the fragmented states of the south. The Sung state became divided by conquest of its northern half by a series of Manchurian peoples who had acquired Chinese civilization, including the use of Chinese administrators, which is to say by a new marchland to the northeast. The reunification of China was finally reaccomplished by the spread of civilized techniques to the Mongols, who constituted yet another marchland at the northern rear of their predecessors. This unified state eventually passed into indigenous Chinese control (the Ming dynasty). Another nomadic people, the Manchus, had now become civilized in the Manchurian marchland, and conquered the Ming in 1644, after intervening in a dispute over dynastic succession. After European incursions from the sea had weakened central control, and Japanese invasions (beginning in Manchuria/Korea in 1895, extending to all of lowland China by 1940) had destroyed all established government, the Communist regime reestablished unity by a conquest emanating from its base in Shensi, a marchland on the edge of the desert in the far northwest (an extension of the earlier Wei valley marchland from which the first two unifica-

---

10 For the following examples, see Figures 1 and 2.

tions proceeded). Of the seven unifiers, then, all were marchland states operating against a divided interior (although this is least clear in the case of the Sung—the weakest unifier). Moreover, it appears that the beginnings of disintegration ending the centralized periods usually came from the revolt or external conquest of the peripheral provinces, especially in these same northern frontiers.

In the ancient Middle East, we find another succession of marchland conquerors. The miltiple city–states of early Egypt and Mesopotamia were first unified, in each case, by peripheral up-river cities (Thebes in Egypt, Akkad in Mesopotamia). Succeeding empires also tend to be marchlands: the Hittites and the Hyksos, expanding briefly from Anatolia; the Assyrians, from the mountains of Armenia in the north of the Mesopotamian valley; the Arameans, from the edges of the Arabian desert to the south; the Babylonians expanding into Syria from the far southeast of Mesopotamia; the Medes and then the Persians from the hitherto uncivilized Iranian plateau to the east.

The spread of civilization to the Mediterranean further exemplifies the marchland advantage. Greece was civilized in a politically decentralized form; unification was first established by the late-civilizing, peripheral state to its north in Macedonia. Alexander took the marchland position of Greece as a whole as a base from which to conquer the entire Middle East as far as the Indus valley, although the unity of the empire lasted only during his brief lifetime. The spread of civilization to Italy and North Africa (present-day Tunisia) outflanked these territories with yet another pair of marchland states, Carthage and (after various complexities to be considered below) Rome; and Rome played the role of the marchland to the eastern Mediterranean as a whole. Later, the Islamic empire conquered all of the southern Mediterranean and the Middle East from a base in western Arabia, peripheral to the stalemates of the contending states to the north.

With the spread of civilized military organization to northern Europe, a new series of marchlands emerged. The initial unification of Romanized Gaul and adjacent Rheinland Germany was carried out by the Franks, the first of the German tribal confederations in the area to adopt the administrative advantages of Christianity, and the group which held the marchland position at the far north of this territory. With the spread of civilized organization eastwards in Europe, however, the Frankish empire (which had expanded into the Carolingian empire centered on Germany and Italy), lost its marchland position and became outflanked by strong states on both sides, eventually disintegrating. For a time, the marchland advantage in eastern Europe lay on the edges of the Baltic; Lithuania and then Poland enjoyed periods of imperial hegemony over the eastern plains in the fourteenth and fifteenth centuries A.D., due to their position without enemies to the rear; and Sweden briefly succeeded to this position when it became strongly organized in the early seventeenth century and placed the continental Baltic states in a weak central position. Russia was unified in the sixteenth century by the principality of Moscow, the far northeast frontier (facing the remnants of the Mongols on the steppe), which conquered the half-dozen Russian states caught between it and Poland, then proceeded to take advantage of Poland's interior position. And in the seventeenth and eighteenth centuries, with Poland turned into a stalemated central zone by Swedish and Russian pressures, Prussia, the easternmost of the hundreds of German states, acted the part of a marchland state for Germany as a whole; with no effective enemy to the rear, Prussia turned its military force to the west and south and eventually unified all of Germany. Similarly, Italy was eventually unified in the nineteenth century by Savoy, a principality in the far northwest of Italian-speaking territories in the lower reaches of the Alps. Other states enjoying the marchland advantage were Spain, after its unification in the late fifteenth century, which enabled it to play an imperial role in Europe in the sixteenth and even seventeenth centuries, especially vis-à-vis centrally located Italy; and Austria, which benefited in the eighteenth century from the fragmentation of central Germany to its rear in the west, so it could play marchland to the states left by the declining Polish and Ottoman empires in the east.[11]

Wherein does the advantage of the marchland consist? I believe that the principal advantage is in having significant enemies on only one front. The advantage is thus a relative one, intimately connected with the disadvantage of centrally-located rivals which have several fronts to contend with. There are alternative possible explanations. One might say that the marchland army is tougher, because it is on the periphery of civilized states; it has become tough by fighting the barbarians beyond, or it carries over some barbarian toughness within itself due to its recent conversion to civilization. But there are a number of considerations that suggest this explanation is incorrect. Barbarians are not intrinsically superior militarily to move civilized states, even if they are, in many cases, more warlike on an individual basis. The illiterate Gauls were certainly more ferocious and belligerent individually than the Romans, but the latter conquered them easily with their superior organization, numbers, and equipment. Alexander's Greeks

---

[11] There is another way to demonstrate the power of marchlands: At any moment in time during a period of disunity, the marchlands states are likely to be the largest.

considered their Persian opponents effeminate soldiers, and despised the vast Persian superiority in numbers, although in point of time the Persians had become literate somewhat later than the Greeks. Examples might be multiplied; in general, it may be said that where a civilized state lacks the disadvantage of a multifront configuration (including civil war), it is usually superior to barbarians. Barbarian successes are usually cases of marchland advantages on their side, and they always, I believe, are bolstered by a rough equality on the organizational side due to the diffusion of key organizational techniques from the central civilizations. The point is bolstered by a number of instances in which the marchland advantage holds, in which none of the states involved can be considered more barbarian than the others: the unification of Italy by Savoy, of Germany by Prussia, of Russia by Moscow are cases in point.

Furthermore, there are cases of marchland states which derive their strength, not because they border upon barbarian territory, but because they back up against natural barriers. The strong territorial position of Burgundy, with its back to the Alps, enabled it to hold out against French unification for many centuries, despite its disadvantage in the number of troops it could field from its hilly territory. Its advantage even fostered attempts at Burgundian imperialism. Once it expanded beyond its mountainous base, however, by its drive to the low countries on the North Sea, it entered the fragment-producing central position among major states. The same might be said of Austria, in an analogous position on the east of the Alps: it could easily establish and maintain independence from the German Empire, and was able to carve out a domain in eastern Europe; but when it expanded far enough to the north to encroach on the central fragments of Germany, it entered the realm of stalemate that spelled the death of empire.

The marchland principle, although simple to apply in many instances, nevertheless contains a number of complexities. We have seen from the examples of Burgundy and Austria that there can be "internal marchlands" based upon relatively compact natural barriers such as a mountain range. Near to the barrier, the marchland advantage is strong, but largely for defensive purposes. As such a state expands away from its "back wall," it may enter a central position in a field of forces, within which its advantage disappears. Our examples suggest another type of internal marchland as well, exemplified by the case of Prussia in relation to Germany, or of Savoy in relation to Italy. It is because Poland was neutralized by enemies to the north and east that Prussia became free to assume the role of a marchland vis-à-vis Germany to its own south and west; similar considerations neutralizing

France to its west at the end of the Napoleonic wars gave Savoy its chance to play marchland to the fragmented petty state of Italy. The existence of internal marchlands, then, can fluctuate. In general, I would propose that such marchland advantages are shorter-lasting and less extensive in the impetus they give to territorial acquisition than pure "external marchlands."[12]

Even genuinely peripheral marchlands are subject to change. We have seen that the spread of civilized organization has turned one-time marchlands into interior states, as new marchlands grew up beyond them. We find this process in China, in which in succession, marchland advantage passes from (a) the Wei valley; to (b) Manchuria, Mongolia, and Shensi; and finally in a sense to (c) Japan. It also appears in the diffusion of civilization from the Middle East river valleys, first to their outlying cities; then to their peripheral highlands; then to the eastern Mediterranean littoral, which in turn becomes outflanked by the western Mediterranean; then outflanked by the Arabs in the south and the Teutons in the north; and eventually by marchlands to the far north, first in the Baltic and then the north of Russia.

Marchlands are relative in still another sense: relative to the technologies of military transportation and supply. The advantage of "no enemies to the rear" depends upon what kind of territory is militarily accessible to a given technology. Mountains have become much less inaccessible since the introduction of bureaucratic supply systems and then mechanized transportation, and the advantage of mountain retreats like Burgundy and Austria have disappeared. Nevertheless, independent—if not threatening—states remain in Switzerland and elsewhere, as testimony to some remaining degree of invulnerability of such geopolitical positions. Sea power makes states accessible to attack that previously enjoyed an inpregnable rear on the water. (Thus Japan forfeited its marchland position vis-à-vis China in the twentieth century by a naval confrontation on different fronts with the U.S. and Britain.) Modern air power might be considered to virtually eliminate the relevance of the marchland principle, since all territories now become accessible to each other. But this conclusion seems to go too far. Although the geopolitics of air warfare remain to be even crudely sketched out, the evidence of twentieth century wars (especially the experience of Germany) suggests that contiguity by land remains a crucial determinant of states' powers, and that contact by sea operates with only some

---

[12] Thus the Prussian conquest of Germany produced only 75 years of unification (1870–1945); and Savoy itself, although providing the basis for the Italian monarchy, was eventually incorporated into France.

diminished degree of the land-contiguity effects. The differences in the expense of military supplies and occupation by these different routes suggests why this gradient would apply. Air contact would have a still smaller effect in the ability to hold territory. Some of these considerations are amplified in the final section of this paper, in which the contemporary applications of geopolitical principles are suggested.

3. Balances of Power

A balance of power exists when two or more states confront one another with relatively equal positional or other advantages. I am using the term broadly here, to include not only a simple two-sided balance, but also various types of complex multisided situations. The more complex the situation, the more contending parties, the less necessary it is for all or even a few of the states to be equally balanced in power resources. Nor should one assume that a balance of power implies stability. In fact, it is usually a dynamic situation, and typical long-term trends shift balances of power in various directions, changing both the numbers and the relative powers of the states involved.

A. SIMPLE, STABLE BALANCE OF POWER FOSTERS BUFFER STATES AROUND BARRIERS

Where a pair of strong states exist on opposite sides of a natural land barrier (especially high mountains), the border is likely to be stable. There is also likely to be a stable buffer state (or possibly several) in the barrier region.

A prime historical example can be found in the mountainous area roughly designated at Armenia: the area at the meeting-place of the Mesopotamian valley to the south, the Persian plateau to the east, and the Anatolian plateau to the west; and extending northward between the Black Sea and the Caspian sea to the Caucasus mountains. This area is contiguous to the major states and empires of the historical Middle East but it has been the site of independent states almost continually since it was first civilized in the second millenium B.C. The empires of the Assyrians, Babylonians, Medes, and Persians rarely penetrated this territory. Ironically, the Assyrian state first originated in the southern part of this mountainous area; but as soon as the Assyrian Empire was established and its base moved down into Syria and Mesopotamia, the highlands became independent again. This area was one of the few to hold out during the height of the Roman Empire, because it was subsidized as a buffer on the natural borders of Rome to the West and the Parthian–Persian empires to the south and east. The Islamic conquest in its first flush of expansion unified this area into its empire briefly, but with the revival of the Byzantine empire to the west and the gradual weakening of the Caliphate, the Armenia–Caucasus states quickly regained independence. The last independent states in this area disappear only in the eighteenth century, with the expansion of bureaucratic states in both Turkey and Russia.

Other examples suggest that even modern bureaucratic control does not necessarily eliminate buffer states. Thus there are several tiny independent states in Europe of this sort: Andorra in the Pyrenees barrier between France and Spain; Monaco in the mountain barrier between France and Italy; Luxemburg in the hilly region between France, Germany, and Belgium. Belgium itself bears out the description of a buffer state, but that it is marked off by no sharp natural barriers, and its independence may be explained by the more general process of fragmentation considered below.[13]

B. A MULTISIDED BALANCE OF POWER FRAGMENTS THE INTERIOR STATES

The mechanism in the case of buffer states is an aspect of a more general one. The presence of mountain barriers simply makes the intervening states especially stable, since the boundaries of the contending large states tend to be stable. The mechanism is this: When strong states surround an intervening territory, if they cannot immediately conquer it, they tend to subsidize small states within it adjacent to themselves to keep it independent of their opponents. Moreover, the interior territory is likely to be difficult to conquer in the first place because of the presence of strong enemies intervening from the other side. Or repeated conquests of the middle by various of the outside states tend to repeatedly absorb and release different slices of the middle, leaving an uneven pattern inside. Thus over a period of time, the number of interior states tends to grow continuously larger. Another way of describing the situation is that the larger, stronger states are likely to be on the margins. Put this way, we see that the balance of

---

[13] In the Far East, an independent buffer state may be illustrated by Korea, in the mountainous peninsula between China and Japan. It has been the object of their attempts at conquest since Han times in the case of China, and since the 1500s in the case of Japan; to defeat the invasion of the 1590s, the Chinese intervened as allies of the Koreans, just as they did in 1950 to turn back the Japan-based American armies. Korea has historically been divided into three fragments. Thus the current north–south split is not unnatural, and may not even be the result ultimately of the Communist–capitalist confrontation, although it bears its emblems upon the surface.

power principle simply shows the obverse of the dynamics of the marchland principle.

The process is clearly illustrated by the disunified periods of Chinese history. During the Warring States period (ca. 770–220 B.C.) after the disintegration of the Chou dynasty, the initial pattern of fragmentation soon formed itself into a struggle between two large states, to the north and south of the Hwang Ho river. But the showdown war between these two major contenders (538–506 B.C.) resulted in their mutual exhaustion, and this was followed by a second period of disintegration. The number of states in the middle increased once more; and the process was aided by the diffusion of civilization to outlying areas, which tended to transform the two major states into interior states, themselves subject to fragmentation.

In the second period of disunity (ca 220–590 A.D.) following the fall of the Han dynasty, China again at first divided into northern and southern states, plus the third of the "Three Kingdoms" in the Szechwan basin to the southwest. These three were temporarily reduced again to two, but a stalemate between them resulted in a process of fragmentation that eventually led to 16 independent states.

The third period of disunity (ca 900–960 A.D.) after the fall of the T'ang also went through a cycle of an initial splitting off of the northern border provinces; then followed a succession of northern dynasties while the southern interior fragmented into some ten states.[14]

In the ancient Middle East, there were a series of clearly separated

---

[14] We may note that extreme south China, although very hilly, has never been politically fragmented, but has always formed part of a large southern state south of the Yangtze. This is because the south has never been a buffer zone between major states; to the southwest, the jungle and the edge of the Tibetan mountains has supported only small, noncivilized tribes which have constituted no military threat, and the coastal kingdoms which sprang up from time to time in Annam (Vietnam) were too minor and too distant to create a balance of power. In the far north, there are no natural defensive barriers; the arable plain simply turns into steppe suitable only for grazing, and hence the habitat of nomads. The Chinese states of the late Warring States period created artificial barriers by building walls; but these could only be borders, since unlike mountains they provide no territory for a buffer state. Once diffusion of military and organizational technology built up the strength of the nomads, the last millenium and a half of Chinese history has tended to involve a two-state confrontation between nomads and Chinese: sometimes located outside the walls versus inside the walls, and sometimes with nomadic conquest of the northern river valley (Hwang Ho) balanced against Chinese control of the Yangtze and the south. This situation has not produced a fragmentation of northern China, because it is a simple rather than a multiple balance of power; without natural barriers to the north, buffer states could not arise. The Chinese evidence thus suggests the importance of a multisided balance of power for setting the dynamics of fragmentation into operation.

natural heartlands. Strong states arising in Egypt, Mesopotamia (or its outliers on the Persian plateau), and Anatolia tended to either conquer or fragment the intervening area of Syria (which I am defining broadly to include the area around Palestine), especially in the period 1700–700 B.C. There was no possibility of a strong state emerging from this intervening area; the Hebrew Empire under David and Solomon (ca. 975–925 B.C.) was short-lived, and held sway only among the small states of Syria itself.[15] From time to time one of the major contending states would mount an empire over most of the others, swallowing up the middle fragments as well. But the Assyrian, Median, Babylonian, Persian, and Macedonian empires all tended to be relatively short-lived (for reasons, see #5 below), and subsequent to each one the renewed independence of each major heartland would result in the resurgance of fragmentary interior states. But as civilization spread to the west, the fragmented interior shifted as well, to center on Asia Minor. This fragmentation was finally reduced only with the Roman conquest which took all the heartlands bordering the Mediterranean, and the rise of Parthian power in the compact area of Persia/Mesopotamia, leaving only the Armenian buffer states between.

In European history, we find the process of fragmentation of the middle most notably in the German empire (originally the Carolingian Empire established ca. 800 A.D., and re-established after dynastic splits around 1000 A.D.). With the rise of strong states in eastern Europe, however, and a north-south battle for sovereignty between Pope and Emperor, the Empire in Germany and Italy fragmented into numerous small states. This process brought about the eventual independence of Switzerland, which previously—as in Roman times—was a province of the unified empire. Thus we see that the natural barriers, even very high mountains, are not by themselves sufficient for independence, but only as activated by a balance of power around them.[16]

The modern fragmentation of the Balkans derives from the same process. The strong empire of the Ottomans unified this area during the fifteenth to eighteenth centuries; the fragmented zone was further north

---

[15] It is ironic that this area should give rise to the militant monotheism of the Hebrew war god, since it had no real chance of universal conquest. This only became a real possibility when this monotheism diffused to the marchlands of Arabia, to emerge in the form of Islam.

[16] Similarly, the Pyrenees become a crucial dividing line only with the consolidation of the French and Spanish states; as late as 1200 A.D., the coastal areas around Barcelona in Spain were united with the coastal area of southern France as a separate state.

in southern Russia and Germany. The rise of the unified Russian state, plus pressure from the emerging empire of Austria-Hungary, (and in the nineteenth century, sea-borne military pressure from England) led to a Turkish withdrawal that none of the contending European states would let the others use to their exclusive advantage.

By the same principle, the current division of Germany into East and West seems natural; it is the central area between the capitalist Atlantic alliance to the west and the Russian communist sphere of influence in the east. The quasi-independence of Yugoslavia and Albania, states which constitute the same central buffer zone further south-east, may be explained in the same fashion.

C. LONG–TERM TRENDS AND CRUCIAL TURNING POINTS

The foregoing suggest the need for long-term principles, since none of these cases are stable. The principles of marchland advantage and of fragmentation of the middle not only are parts of the same process, but at the extreme, they produce military imbalance such that conquest of the small by the large is inevitable. Thus after the various fragmentations of China follow reunifying conquests; and the fragmented periods of the Middle East and Mediterranean heartlands have been overcome by the unifying empires of the Assyrians, Persians, Macedonians, and Romans. The process does not stop there; the unified empires themselves have subsequently collapsed, sometimes by internal splits (the causes of which are suggested in principle # 5), sometimes by the growth of additional civilized heartlands outflanking them (principle # 7).

It is little help to assert that history is a cyclical rise and fall, however, without some determining detail of when and where each of these will happen. What are the time laws of these processes? Unfortunately, there is no simple numerical pattern. In China, the unified periods have lasted approximately 250, 400, 300, 160, and 600 years, and the periods of disunity approximately 600, 400, 60, and 160 years.[17] In the Middle East and Europe, the process is more complicated to assess because of a continuous extension of the number of heartlands with civilized states upon them. In the ancient Middle East there were six periods of hegemony by a single state in the large, isolated river-valleys, those in Mesopotamia lasting 100 years each, those in Egypt

---

[17] I am counting from the Mongol conquest of the Southern Sung through the fall of the Manchus as one relatively unified period, since the changes of dynasties were relatively quickly accomplished, and not preceded by any prolonged split into rival states.

lasting about 700, 300, and 800 years. This was followed by a period of general dissolution throughout Mesopotamia and its outliers lasting some 1000 years, while civilization expanded into adjacent areas of the eastern Mediterranean and Persia. The next wave of Middle Eastern empires (none of which covers all the civilized areas) lasted approximately 150, 50, and 200 years each.[18] With the rise of Rome, the situation became more complex; it held hegemony around the entire Mediterranean for some 500 years (ignoring its own civil wars, none of which were very long—mostly one to two years, with the longest of up to 20 years of intermittent fighting. Simultaneously, the ancient Mesopotamian and Persian heartlands formed a separate empire of their own, lasting (with the succession of different dynasties) some 700 years. After this, east and west (or southeast and northwest) diverged. The splitting off of the Eastern Roman empire created a more pluralistic situation in the Middle East. Islam unified the area south of Anatolia and along the southern shore of the Mediterranean as far west as Spain for about 100 years; the next really large unifying empire, the Ottomans (whose boundaries, however, were more European and Mediterranean than strictly Middle-Eastern), had general multiheartland hegemony for some 300 years. In Europe, the largest empires never covered more than a small subset of the total heartlands,[19] and even the periods of merely predominating international influence by separate states (Spain, France, England, Germany) were relatively short, rarely lasting as long as two centuries. Periods of relative and partial unification, then, lasted approximately 700, 100, 100, 100, 300, 800, 150, 200, 50, 500, 700, 100, and 300 years. Counting the periods of dissolution, one would estimate 1000, 100, 200, and then 1500 years in the West, 700 in the East.

The lack of simple temporal pattern is not surprising, when we consider that it is a multifactor situation. Time laws are not likely to be manifested in a simple surface pattern if there are several independent variables involved; the pattern would be in derivative functions of these quantities, not these quantities themselves. What can we say, then, as a first approximation? First, balance of power processes are relatively long-term, compared to a single human lifetime. Even the

---

[18] I count the first Persian empire and its brief Macedonian successor as a single unit, as there is no period of dissolution in between them; the Macedonian empire scarcely deserves to be considered an independent unit given its duration of less than 30 years.

[19] The very largest, the Napoleonic and the Nazi, each lasted less than ten years, which suggests that stable control was never actually reached.

shortest periods of unification (or using the weaker criterion for modern European history, for multiheartland influence) are on the order of 100–160 years, while the longest are 600–700 years. Periods of dissolution range from 60 years at the shortest (that between the T'ang and Sung dynasties in China), but more commonly at least 100 years, with a maximum of up to 1000–1500 years. Geopolitical processes, in other words, do not seem to depend much on the policies of particular individuals, or even the conscious mood of an entire cultural era. If one generation fails to react to the opportunities or pressures of the time, some of the generations over a period of centuries are almost certain to do so.

There also seem to be crucial turning points in these long-term processes. In the Warring States period of ancient China, the early fragmentation into dozens of states had been reduced in about 250 years to a showdown between major states in the north and south. But neither was able to decisively crush the other, and their stalemate ushered in a second phase of fragmentation of the middle territory (especially through the disintegration of the northern state, which held the Hwang Ho valley, and the rise of new marchlands around them through the spread of civilization). The example suggests a general principle: Once the impetus flows decisively to reduce the number of states to two large contenders, it becomes crucial that one should win out and establish total unification. If not, the process is likely to flow in the opposite direction. In the case of ancient China, this second phase took some 280 years, at the end of which a second reduction in the number of contenders took place.

A similar pattern may be found in the period of the Three Kingdoms that followed the dissolution of the Han empire. After 60 years, the three contenders were reduced to two and the northern of these apparently won a decisive victory. But in the process it had to call in the aid of barbarian tribes from the northern steppe, who quickly (within 35 years—one adult generation) fragmented the empire into as many as 16 states, and this period of fragmentation took 265 years to reunify. Again, the crucial turning point was missed, as the apparent victory of the northern kingdom was actually a weak victory through coalition.

D. MILITARY FEROCIOUSNESS INCREASES NEAR CRUCIAL TURNING POINTS

A corollary of this last principle concerns the manner in which wars are carried out. Ferociousness increases as the number of major states diminishes and complete unification seems possible.[20] Con-

---

[20] I owe this principle to Toynbee (1954:270–272, 287–288).

versely, in highly fragmented periods, there is a tone of chivalry, of warfare treated as a game. This gentlemanly mildness is found during the midst of the Warring States period in China, as well as in the European Middle Ages, and in modern European history during the complex and inconclusive dynastic wars of the 1700s.[21] Towards the end of the Warring States period in China, the severity of warfare greatly increased, especially on the part of the principal unifying state of Ch'in. We find the same ferociousness on the part of the Mongols (who would pile up huge mounds of heads of their victims) during their phase of initial conquests, a ferociousness that was not matched during their subsequent regime (at least in China, as witnessed for example by Marco Polo). Similarly, the Assyrians, the first state to unify all of the Middle East after 1000 years of fragmentation, were regarded as by far the most ferocious armies known to the peoples of the time, much more ferocious then their Persian successors, whose task of conquest had been made much easier. This principle also explains the extreme treatment of the Romans to defeated Carthage, their crucial rival in the western Mediterranean; after this victory, the fragmented states of the eastern Mediterranean were easy pickings, and the level of ferociousness of combat and its aftermath sharply declined.

Apparently, the parties sense when they near a crucial turning point, and increase their efforts accordingly: fighting to annihilation, sparing no captives, plowing captured cities into the ground, attempting to dramatize the extent of their determination and their power.[22] This process occurs even if the contest ends in a stalemate, or if the apparent opportunities for total conquest do not turn out to be as extensive as they seem. Thus the ferociousness of the Peloponnesian war, which was the showdown conflict in Athens' attempt to unify Greece for the first time, was regarded as unprecedented at the time; but the result was an Athenian defeat and a protracted stalemate. In modern Europe, the ferociousness of the Nazi regime, with its concentration camps and extermination programs (matched to some extent by similar policies on the Russian side of the long-disputed territory of eastern Europe), may be seen as an example of a similar dynamic, as the long-standing fragmentation of eastern Europe seemed to be entering a showdown between two major powers. A similar dynamic seems in-

---

[21] Chivalry in the narrower sense is usually associated with the technology of individually-armed knights. but the chivalrous style was found in ancient China, without this mode of weaponry; and it was found in a different version in the etiquette of the "parade ground" armies of Europe in the 1600s and 1700s. Thus the geopolitical pattern seems to be primary.

[22] For a more limited formulation, see "Three Faces of Cruelty," in this volume.

volved in the threats of nuclear warfare made by the U.S. and the
U.S.S.R. in the period of heady expansion into apparent world-domina-
tion that followed after the collapse of all the other world powers in
World War II.

4. Stalemates and Power Vacuums

The expansion of conquering states is often attributed to their
superior qualities. Historians speak of the "efficiency" and "energy" of
the early Romans, and of their loss of these qualities after their successful empire turned them "soft." I would suggest, however, that a
conquering people is not successful because they are especially hungry;
after all, most peoples at any given time are have-nots. Nor need we
leave these qualities without explanation by attributing them to "national genius." Rather, the most spectacularly expansive states usually
intrude into a power vacuum. The geopolitical opportunities for a state
in a favored position give it the military confidence and enthusiasm to
make it fight well, helping build up a string of victories and more confidence and enthusiasm. On the negative side of the same process, there
is a progressive lack of courage and energy among the rival states with
poorer geopolitical positions.

Power vacuums are an extreme form of geopolitical advantage.
Such a vacuum arises especially where major contending states are exhausted after a severe but stalemated struggle. The rise of Rome was
based on its position between two stalemated balances of power in the
western Mediterranean, and its position to profit from a third stalemate
in the East. Initially, Rome was simply part of an intermediate territory
between two great conflicts: between the Etruscans and the Gauls in
northern Italy, and between the Greek colonies and Carthage in Sicily
to the south. Rome's position was originally quite weak. They were
dominated by the Etruscans in the seventh and sixth centuries B.C., and
even sacked by the Gauls around 400 B.C. But the Etruscans and Gauls
fought each other to a standstill, creating a protective barrier to the
north; while to the south, a similar situation repeated itself as the
Greek colons led by Syracuse fought inconclusively for some 250 years
with Carthage over control of Sicily. During the latter part of these
stalemates, Rome unified the small states and tribes of mountainous
central Italy between the two fronts, and in the third century B.C., took
advantage of the general exhaustion of the major powers to north and
then south to conquer all of them. Once the western Mediterranean
area was unified, the stalemated balance of power in the eastern
Mediterranean among the successor states of the Persian–Macedonian

empires offered yet another power vacuum, into which Rome's expansion as a marchland state was eventually regarded as unstoppable by all parties involved.[23]

The analogy is bolstered by the meteoric rise of other empires. The Islamic empire developed in a similar fashion. Its background was the long-standing conflict between the eastern Roman Empire and Persian empire along their border in Syria, to the north of the Arabian peninsula. I shall suggest in principle 5b that the no-intervening-heartland rule precluded further possibilities of conquest beyond this line by either side. But the major states severely weakened themselves by attempting just that (see principle 5a) in the early 600s A.D. Internal dynastic conflicts in Persia and then Byzantium tempted the one to intervene in setting a puppet on the other's throne, and in the ensuing wars the entire coast from Syria to Egypt changed hands rapidly several times. It was precisely during these years of upheaval and weakness that a militant universal religion was organizing on the trade routes of the nearby Arabian marchland, to go into military expansion into the disputed territory in 634, just five years after a short-lived Persian conquest of the coast had collapsed. The religious movement thus expressed the geopolitical optimism of the marchland people towards a bordering political vacuum, and its success in gaining coverts and allies was the resulting cumulative process.[24]

There are a number of other examples. I will mention only one: the unification of Greece for the first time in its military history, carried out by the Macedonians in 352–338 B.C. This was another case of marchland expansion, which took place after the exhaustion of the Athenian and Spartan coalition in the stage of extreme ferociousness characteristic of a showdown period.

The time periods involved in a power vacuum can be quite long, in terms of active human lifetimes. For the Romans, the stalemates among its Italian neighbors lasted some 250 years, during the end of which it made its first consolidation of power; and it took 70 years of fighting to defeat Carthage, and another 80 years to benefit from the balance of power in the East. Islam arose in the context of 30 years of unstable warfare between rivals (which had earlier been stalemated along this

---

[23] Thus the King of Pergamum (western Asia Minor) simply willed his state to Rome in 133 B.C. as a deathbed bow to the inevitable.

[24] The Arabs of Mecca–Medina were actually in something like Rome's position between *two* stalemated conflicts; for in the south, there was a long-standing stalemate between the much earlier civilized states of Yemen and Abyssinia; and Yemen (on the Arabian peninsula, as Abyssinia was not) fell immediately to the Islamic conquest.

same front for the preceding 600 years), and its conquests expanded for some 80 years. The long-standing division of Greece among small city–states was first reduced when Athens took command of a unified Greek resistance and counterattack against the Persians throughout some 60 years; this culminated in 30 years of showdown war with the Spartan coalition that arose to resist the Athenian league; and Macedon's unification came at the end of the stalemated 60 years following the end of the Peloponnesian War. Overall, the periods of preceding stalemates may go back many centuries, although usually entering an acute phase of 30–60 years that creates the severe power vacuum; taking advantage of this may take anywhere from 15 to 120 years, depending on the amount of territory open to be conquered. The length of these periods themselves shows that the factors involved are not psychological, but structural.

5. Overexpansion and Disintegration

The disintegration of states is not merely produced by an inferior position in a balance of power. A state may be clearly strongest, without effective rivals, but its own activities towards its periphery may result in a fatal strain.

A. OVEREXPANSION BEYOND THE RESOURCES OF A HEARTLAND OR EMPIRE RESULTS IN DISINTEGRATION, EITHER OF THE PARTICULAR REGIME OR OF THE STATE TERRITORY ITSELF

The beginning of the downfall of virtually every strong Chinese empire was a military defeat on a far distant frontier, or a revolt of troops or supply workers in such a project of distant conquest. The distant enemies were not usually powerfully organized rival states, but simply tribal forces which were too far removed from populous Chinese territory for effective Chinese operation, while the local forces had no such disadvantage. Sometimes even an over-costly victory could have the same result. Note that the results could either by a dynastic change leaving the state intact; or the beginnings of breakdown of central control. The first is illustrated in the replacement of the unifying Ch'in dynasty, after only 15 years of rule, by the initially less expansive Han in 206 B.C.: and again in a similar replacement of the unifying Sui, after only 31 years, by another regime which began more modestly, in T'ang in 618 A.D. In its more extreme form, a long period of military strain due to ambitions or distant frontiers was the cause of revolts which spelled the end of the unified state of the late Han, the late T'ang, and the Sung, of the Mongols' conquest state, as well as the Ming and the Manchu regimes.

For the West, I will mention only a few modern examples. Both the Nazis' and Napoleon's empires fell after a string of victories over adjacent states, because both extended their lines to Russia and North Africa. The Czarist regime in Russia fell in the early twentieth century after some 400 years of successful expansion within its natural heartland; but prior to World War I it extended not only into Poland in the west, but also across Siberia to the Pacific. The defeat in 1905 of Russia by the Japanese in Manchuria (a neighboring heartland for Japan, but a very distant one for Russia) began the military and political strain that eventually culminated in Russian military disintegration in World War I, and the resulting downfall of the regime.

The fact that domestic revolution is thus brought about by distant military defeat is not surprising. Since the basis of the state is military power, any serious blow to this power results in a loss of control, not only on the periphery, but possibly also at the seat of government. Thus not only these earlier changes of regime, but also most modern popular revolutions have been made possible by defeat in war which destroyed the coercive apparatus of the state, but happened to leave the defeated territory unoccupied by the conqueror: the modern Communist revolutions in Russia and China were of this sort, as was the Paris commune of 1871.[25]

B. THE NO–INTERVENING HEARTLAND RULE

What precisely comprises overexpansion? The most important constraint seems to be: *control over territories beyond the heartlands adjacent to a state's own base is extremely difficult, and tends to disintegrate rapidly.* Successful empires have all conquered heartlands contiguous to their home territory. The principle is easiest to see in the negative cases where it is violated. The initial Islamic Caliphate conquered all the territory from Persia in the east, across North Africa to Spain in the west, while its administrative center was in Syria and then Mesopotamia. The Caliphate soon (within 40 years) began to lose control over the extreme west, beginning with Spain, and then over each successive North African province as far as Egypt. Since Islam was not a sea power, Spain had to be administered across the distance of some

---

[25] In a more extended sense, the financial exhaustion of the French crown before 1789, and of the English before 1640, were not only the precipitating factors leading to their revolutions; they were themselves debts due to wars which did not pay their own way.

four intervening heartlands. This apparently was too much of a strain upon controls, and the breakoff of the farthest heartland set in motion a wave of disintegration that eventually washed back to the central base itself.

By contrast, the Roman Empire was a sea power, and its conquests of all the heartlands surrounding the Mediterranean were thus contiguous to its home territory. By the same token, the Roman conquest could never be carried inland from coastal Syria into Mesopotamia, or from western Asia Minor to eastern Anatolia, and most of its major defeats (such as those of Julian, which spelled the end of the pagan reaction against Christianity) were the result of efforts on this front. The same can be said of the significance of the Rhine frontier, the site of Rome's other major defeats. Whereas Gaul was contiguous to Italy, Germany was not, and efforts to control past this intervening heartland were failures.[26]

C. UNIVERSAL RELIGIONS AND IDEOLOGIES FOLLOW THE NO–INTERVENING–HEARTLAND RULE

A final corollary concerns the cultural sphere. *Universal religions and their secular equivalents provide prolonged unification only of adjacent heartlands, and disintegrate into heterodoxies as military unity disintegrates.*

Religions are useful for mobilizing troops and for administration. The case of Islam shows how a geopolitical power vacuum can foster the rise of a universal religion to take advantage of it. Christianity was crucial in transforming German tribal coalitions (especially that of the Franks) into literately-administered kingdoms; in Asia the military power of the Mongols and Tibetans was organized by the importation of Buddhism, that of the Turks (another group of central Asia nomads) by Islam. The "barbarian" conquerors of China always organized a religious–administrative base (often by importing Confucianism) before their conquests.

Religions have thus been crucial for conquest states. But their ideological content has not overruled basic geopolitical possibilities. Universal religions imply a potential world unity, and sometimes their adherents have attempted to establish just such a dominion. But even conquests organized as religious movements, when they have violated the no-intervening-heartland rule, have been subject to political disunity. On the religious side, this has been expressed in the form of religi-

---

[26] Britain is an apparent exception to this rule. But this territory was sparsely inhabited at the time; it was also the weakest part of the empire, and the first to be lost.

ous heresy. Thus the split of Spain from the Baghdad Caliphate took place under the form of theological dispute concerning the succession from Mohammed, and further fragmentation of Islam in North Africa and Egypt in the West, and in Persia in the East, took the form of the Sunni–Shi'a heresy dispute. In Christianity, the split of the church into East (Greek) and West (Roman Papacy) followed the fall of the western Roman empire to the Germans. Later the Protestant Reformation occurred as the German empire uniting Germany and Italy disintegrated, and northern and southern Europe became decisively organized by national states.

In general, religions and other universal ideologies follow geopolitical lines, not vice versa.

6. Imperialism Follows Unification

Despite the dangers of strain upon their resources, states often seem compelled to expand up to and even beyond their limits. The dynamics of this process may be laid bare in examining what happens when a state finally unifies a territory which has experienced long-standing fragmentation, especially a single natural heartland. In general, *immediately following the unification of its heartland, a state embarks upon conquest of adjacent territories.*

In China, the unifying Ch'in and Sui regimes both embarked on external conquest of neighboring territories; so did their successors Han and T'ang, but only after several generations had passed and internal control was consolidated. The unifying Sung immediately embarked on conquest into the northern steppe, with disastrous consequences; and the early Ming and Manchu states also underwent early expansion far from the central heartland, although generally curbing these efforts as soon as strains appeared. The mechanism for such imperialism was clearly not immediate external threat or even serious territorial advantage, for in China's case, the fertile territory was already in the heartland, and conquests were rather gratuitously directed at outlying areas such as Korea, Annam (Vietnam), and central Asia.

In the Middle East, the first unifying states in the Mesopotamian river valley immediately spread outwards beyond the heartland. Macedonia unified Greece and immediately (Alexander being the next generation after Philip, the unifier) embarked on a plan of world conquest, aimed at the Persian empire and beyond. In Europe there are many instances of this process in comparative recent times. Spain became unified only around 1500 A.D., and rapidly embarked on international conquest: not only in the Americas, but also in Italy and the

Netherlands. France finally expelled the English from its western territories in the 1450s, and ended the independence of Burgundy in 1477; by the 1490s it had embarked upon the attempted conquest of Italy—efforts which went on until the time of Napoleon. Russia was gradually unified in the fifteenth and sixteenth centuries, and continued its expansion for the next several centuries into the ethnically alien territories of eastern Europe, central Asia, and Siberia. The United States entered into overseas conquest after its civil war, although after a gap of 30 years. A similar time period is found in the case of modern Germany, which unified after many centuries of fragmentation in 1870, and then pursued an aggressive foreign policy around the turn of the century, culminating in the Nazi attempt at total European conquest in the 1930s. The time principle involved covers a relatively long period; "immediate" expansion can be within the next 30 years, and may go on for many centuries (as in the case of Russia) if successes permit.

Why does this process occur? A powerful explanation would no doubt tie these external policies to the internal dynamics of political control. Certainly in all of the more decentralized weapons systems, the only way a state can be kept together is by continual warfare (Collins 1975:359–360). But many of the above examples involve quite centralized modern weapons systems. Another possibility is that of the predatory state, living off of the fruits of its conquests. If so, the political leaders usually operate more upon impulse than calculation, for many states (e.g., various Chinese dynasties) have fallen by attempted conquests of comparatively valueless territories. What seems most likely to be operating is a political analogue of the predatory pattern: not that the material gains of conquest are crucial, but that the psychological mood, the energy dynamics discussed under principle # 4, are strongly desired by leaders of newly unified states in order to consolidate their positions. In many cases, they attempt to generate this energy without the benefit of an external power vacuum. It is in this sense, among others, that power corrupts, and absolute power corrupts absolutely.

7. Partial Diffusion and External Proletariats

Military and economic technology diffuses rapidly to less civilized territories adjacent to dominant heartlands, resulting in outlying population growth and periodic barbarian invasions.

Cross-cutting all of these processes is another, extremely noticeable at certain points in history. The number of civilized or at least militarily potent areas does not stay constant. New heartlands tend to appear on the periphery. These do not spring up all at once; what is called "barbarism" is an intervening stage before full literate state organization, but more militarily organized than isolated precivilized tribes. Such "external proletariats," in Toynbee's metaphor, develop because technology diffuses partially rather than as an entire system. Knowledge and possession of weapons diffuses especially fast, as do some economic techniques (such as iron-working). Trade relations between civilized and peripheral areas create a symbiotic division of labor among them, preserving rather than undermining the cultural and political distinctiveness of the periphery. Even warfare carried by the civilized states towards the exterior, or raids in the opposite direction, lead to the diffusion of weapons.[27] Through these processes, scattered tribes become barbarian military coalitions. Their military importance grows as technological diffusion and other effects of civilized contact produce population growth. Often this leads to various pressures and conflicts among the different barbarian groups themselves causing them to jostle each other into enforced migrations, such as those that eventually brought the invasion of the western Roman empire. The population may even build up to levels far beyond what the local economic resources can support, forcing a shift towards a predatory symbiosis with the civilized areas.[28]

The growth of barbarian military power is typically fostered by balance-of-power tactics on the part of the civilized states. China, Persia, and Rome all subsidized some of their barbarian neighbors against the others. The next step, incorporating barbarian troops into the civilized border armies, eventually transformed the former borders into interior areas, outflanked by new marchlands. With this change, the

---

[27] Thus the spread of American weapons to the Vietnamese guerillas was not an isolated or an ironic phenomenon, but the typical historical pattern of contact between forces on different technological levels.

[28] Such population growth does not inevitably happen. An alternate pattern is that contact between a more isolated population and a more cosmopolitan one brings about population reduction through epidemics. The isolated populations in particular are unlikely to have developed widespread immunities. Sometimes this has decimated primitive and advanced horticultural populations (such as the American Indians and some of the Oceanic peoples). At other times, it has been the nomadic barbarians who are the more immune; it has been suggested, for example, that the Black Plague which killed one-third of Europeans in the fourteenth century was brought by the population movements ensuing from the Mongol conquests of the previous century (McNeill 1964:8–9). One cannot rule out the possibility, though, that resistance to disease is a psychosocial phenomenon, and is especially low among demoralized conquered peoples whose organizational resources for defense are enormously outweighed by the aliens'.

energy dynamics shifted toward the marchland advantage, and together with external population pressures, usually led to unsupportable pressure upon the civilized state. Thus China has been increasingly dominated by its northern barbarians during the last 1500 years; even though they have usually been quickly assimilated into the much larger native population, and sometimes overthrown by nativist reactions (like those which overthrew the Mongols and the Manchus). Each successive outpouring of nomadic conquerers from the steppe, however, has left a population vacuum in which a new population could eventually build up, resulting in a new barbarian threat.

In the Middle East, this diffusion pattern produced a long series of major conquests, including several groups entering the Iranian plateau, several outpourings of Arabs from the desert, and several waves of Turks from central Asia. In Europe, there was the succession of barbarian waves of Greeks, Gauls, Germans, and most recently Scandinavians.

Eventually we may be able to estimate some time principles of population growth among external proletariats, and of rates of diffusion of military technology, and thus account for the periodicity of barbarian invasions. My efforts so far show no simple pattern in the spacing of such outbursts. But a simple numerical pattern would indicate a single causal sequence, whereas it is clear that the processes involved are multicausal. Not only do several factors affect barbarian mobilization, but the external relationships among the civilized states interact with them into an overall geopolitical matrix. This brings us to a more general conclusion regarding time laws. The processes that we can measure—the numbers and extents of states, the periods of time over which they exist, the timing and intensity of barbarian irruptions—are affected by the whole series of causal conditions that I have summarized. The ideal of a more precise and hence more explicitly predictive theory depends upon developing a complex formula for their interaction.

CONCLUSION

This analysis could proceed much further. More evidence could be offered, and the hypotheses and their ramifications could be tested through more systematic comparisons. Composite quantitative principles in the form of time laws are still only a goal. But the major difficulty in this area is less the testing of hypotheses than formulating workable units of analysis that can marshall the evidence, however crudely. This is difficult because concepts provide the basic focus of our attention, but existing ones are usually awkward, and the work of analysis forces one to develop new concepts in midstream.

Nevertheless, preceding the general hypotheses and their corollaries, concerning external relations of states, strike me as being on the way to a good approximation of a successful explanatory model. It still remains to tie together the variables (weapons and military organization, economy, administrative resources) affecting the internal organization of the state, to show where they add additional predictive power in the multicausal composite of external factors. Conversely, it remains to show the ramifications of external geopolitics for internal processes of domestic politics, economic change, and stratification. And finally, there are possible analogues to be explored between geopolitical principles and explanatory principles within other structures of competition, such as intellectual fields.

As a way of assessing their utility, let us review the geopolitical principles with brief comments on their application to the immediate world situation.

1. *Territorial resource advantage:* The current world military influence of the U.S. and the U.S.S.R. follow from this principle.

2. *Marchland advantage:* With the military recuperation of China, and the multiple fronts that result from the use of naval and air power by the major states, none holds the marchland advantage. Thus the shift in the situation from immediately after World War II, when the U.S. and the U.S.S.R. held this advantage as well.

3. *Balance of Power:* The major dynamic here, the fragmentation of the middle territories, seems to have begun again after World War II between the American and Russian lines. In long-term trends, we seem to have just passed a crucial turning-point when the number of contending states was reduced briefly to two; the failure of either to secure hegemony now seems to put us in the reverse phase of the cycle, and the prospects are for its continuation for another 100 years at least—conceivably as long as the next 500 years or more. By the same token, the ferociousness peak seems to have been around the second World War and just thereafter, especially with the total-war tactics of extermination bombing. Possibly the atrocities of the Vietnam war are the end phase of this mood of showdown struggle for world hegemony.

4. *Stalemates and power vacuums:* Clearly no major power vacuum exists now on the world scale. In the historical analogue, this could have come about if the U.S. and the U.S.S.R. had proceeded to all-out nuclear way; the result would have been a power vacuum into which peripheral states might have expanded into world domination.

5. *Overextension and disintegration:* The political difficulties of the nationalist faction in the U.S. seem to be the result of the military strains of overextension into distant wars. This is a comparatively mild price being paid, illustrating the point that state leaders can choose between persistence in an extreme policy, and its diminution; just how severe the domestic consequences will be depends upon which choice is made.

The no-intervening-heartland rule was not directly violated by the U.S. involvement in Korea and Vietnam. But in each case there was an enormous transportation difficulty, not shared by the opposing forces; and intermediate staging areas (such as Japan in the case of the Korean war) might provide part of the strain of such wars.

A clear illustration of the fact that ideologies follow geopolitical lines is the breakup of international Communism into competing national factions. The Chinese and Russian ideological lines, and other variants such as Titoism, are precise analogues to religious heresies produced by geopolitical strains.

6. *Imperialism follows unification:* We seem to be witnessing this principle in India, where the largest state has been pursuing an aggressive foreign policy and absorbing its small neighboring states ever since it became an independent state after World War II (and the first highly unified state on the subcontinent in its history). It is another logical extrapolation that if a true (i.e., military) unity were to be established in Europe, we would witness its subsequent military aggression as well. And in Africa, where existing state boundaries are ethnically arbitrary carryovers from colonial days, we may expect a long series of wars following the eventual decolonization of the extreme south. (In this conflict, the long-run prognosis would be to expect the greatest success from the territorially richest marchland states: notably South Africa itself).

7. *Partial diffusion and external proletariats:* In a general sense, the entire Third World is in exactly the position of the "barbarians" beyond the frontiers of the major historical civilizations. The advanced military and communications technology has diffused much faster than the full economic and cultural structure; the population pressures have also been building up. But this does not in itself mean an inevitably successful conquest by this "external proletariat." The world as a whole is a complex balance of powers now; only a stalemate of conflict leading to military exhaustion by the major powers (such as a nuclear war) would clearly shift the balance to the advantage of new predatory states on the periphery.

II

Structuralism and Conflict

Lévi-Strauss's Structural History

Structuralism is often regarded as ahistorical, a search for the fundamental categories and processes of a universal human mind. This may be increasingly true of the later work of Lévi-Strauss, from *The Savage Mind* onward into the *Mythologiques* series. We find there delineated a sort of pan-mind, working through but not encompassed within specific individuals. It is a code of opposites and mediators, and it is deciphered as a total system: One explicates particular myths by looking at other myths, from distinctive as well as similar cultures. Individual action seems to disappear in this scheme.

This mentalism which is so prominent in the later Lévi-Strauss, and so heavily emphasized by his commentators, is nevertheless not what is most of value in structuralism, nor in the works of Lévi-Strauss himself. The controversies around structuralism have concentrated on its alleged idealism and on its denigration of the empirical world. Lévi-Strauss appears to have made anthropology and sociology into interpretive disciplines, in which the task is to make sense of things, not to explain them determinatively. But whose sense is it, the tribal member or the outside observer's? In response to criticism, Lévi-Strauss declares that it does not matter. "For if the final aim of anthropology is to con-

tribute to a better knowledge of objectified thought and its mechanisms, it is in the last resort immaterial whether in this book the
thought processes of the South American Indians take shape through
the medium of my thoughts, or whether mine take place through the
medium of theirs [1969:13]." The human mind is everywhere, but it
operates by a secret code which requires our efforts at intepretation.

Lévi-Strauss thus appears to be part of the tide of antipositivism
and aestheticism of recent years. Clearly he has talent in a literary vein.
His writing weaves in and out among vivid and exotic details, returning
just in time with an abstract generalization to spice the empirical stew.
He avoids any plodding organization of his books, but gives them a
structural backbone by imaginative devices of his own creation. He
will go so far as to orchestrate his materials, calling their chapters
"overture," andante," "third variation," and so forth.

The result is a unique reading experience. But the *Mythologiques*
series does not seem to go anywhere. The later volumes do not add
much to the former, and the charm wears off as one realizes that we
are not going to get anything more but variations on what has already
been rather tentatively shown. In an unkind mood, one is tempted to
conclude that Lévi-Strauss himself indulges in the same occultist
pattern-seeking as the nonscientific "savage mind" of his books. There
is, after all, a difference between making a meaningful interpretation
of the world (which is what astrology does), and showing not just a
meaningful story but a determinative explanation of why something
happens rather than something else. Reading Lévi-Strauss on myths,
one has no idea that the tribes might have fought over what interpretations would prevail, or that ideas can be manufactured as ideology,
used for Goffmanian stage-setting and for domination by impression
management. This criticism might seem unfair to Lévi-Strauss, in that
he seems to be declaring that the universal human mind works like the
"savage mind," not like the scientific ideal; one mood of recent sociology, of course, is to declare that science itself is a myth, and that we too
are constructing reality, imposing our interpretations on the world.

Nevertheless, Lévi-Strauss himself is no relativist, although the recent moods of the intellectual field may have pulled him more and
more in that direction. He likes to speak of "axiomatic" systems; certainly his work has none of the animus against mathematics of current
phenomenological sociologies. Recall that André Weil, one of the
world's great mathematicians, wrote a brief appendix to *The Elementary Structures of Kinship*. Recall too that Piaget (1970), who uses
similar concepts of structural transformations in his analyses of child
mental development, wrote a book about structuralism in all the dif-

ferent social sciences, organized as a series of elaborations upon the mathematical theory of groups. Lévi-Strauss himself is fond of using scientific analogies: Even in the later part of the *Mythologiques* series he likens codes to electronic transmission on amplitude or frequency modulations (1968/1978:21). Even more concretely, he suggests that the mental codes are not only similar to arrangements of chromosomes, but may be reflections of them at a higher level. Thus his conclusion is not too astounding when he declares that the aim of ethnographic analysis is "the reintegration of culture in nature and finally of life within the whole of its physico-chemical conditions [1962/66:247]."

One should see Lévi-Strauss as playing the role of scientific theorist within his own, rather nonscientific discipline. There has been a strong tendency in anthropology (as in sociology) to accumulate facts, without questioning to whom they might be of interest. Lévi-Strauss found his field buried in minutiae, and proposed to integrate this disparate information into a general model. He has done this twice: first with a gigantic synthesis of kinship descriptions in his *Elementary Structures of Kinship*, and more recently with the thousands of myths that anthropologists have collected and that have been gathering dust ever since on library shelves. One cannot deny that Lévi-Strauss has a generalizing, systematic, even scientific intent, however much he hides it in the cloak of faddish antipositivism.

What is most of value in Lévi-Strauss, moreover, is not his later theory of mind, but a structural theory of historical change found in his early works. Lévi-Strauss has been interested in history more often than we realize, especially in the hidden history of eras without records. He even implies, here and there in his later corpus, that the decoding of myths is a way to read this history. The material of *The Raw and the Cooked* (1964/1969), for example, can be read as illustrating universal mental categories, but it is also a record of the fundamental breakthrough of human culture from nature: the invention of cooking as the result of the discovery of fire, the first event in human history.

Lévi-Strauss, in fact, has held varying ideas about what myths might reflect. There are, of course, plenty of occasions where he declares that they reveal universal categories of the human mind. Some of this reflects a politically popular position, defending the tribal Third World as having a logical mentality not inferior to that of scientific western society. At the same time, he admits a difference between the two modes, since he contrasts primitive with modern thought, to the advantage of the former (e.g. 1968/1978:499, 508). However, Lévi-Strauss sometimes uses his methods not to show the universal but the culturally specific. In the mid-1950s, Lévi-Strauss was still interested in kinship, but also in the ecological arrangements of campsites, in tribal art forms, languages, and increasingly in myths (Lévi-Strauss, 1958/63). He suggested that each of these could be deciphered into its code, and that this code would be the same for each item in that specific culture. We find occasional touches of this even in much later works: "Thus we can hope to discover how, in any particular society, cooking is a language through which that society unconsciously reveals its structure [1969/1978:495]." (He goes on, however, in a way that is the bane of sociologists looking for solid, testable generalizations: "unless—just as unconsciously—it resigns itself to using the medium to express its contradictions.") All this is a claim that the code is not universal, and that each society has its own code ruling over all aspects of its social and cultural life.

This idea from Lévi-Strauss' middle period is one that he does not follow up. It would have been hard to do, and perhaps he had intimations that it would not have been successful. But there is a third purpose in Levi-Strauss' decoding activities, and this is specifically aimed at a theory of history. In his wonderfully poetic autobiography, *Tristes Tropiques*, he expresses a different notion about the deep structure of societies. He describes his youthful passion for geology:

I count among my most precious memories not so much some expedition into an unknown region of central Brazil as a hike along the flank of a limestone plateau in Languedoc to determine the line of contact between two geological strata. It was something quite different from a walk or a simple exploration of space. It was a quest, which would have seemed incoherent to some uninitiated observer, but which I look upon as the very image of knowledge, with the difficulties it involves and the delights it affords.

Every landscape appears first of all as a vast chaos, which leaves one free to choose the meaning one wants to give it. But, over and above agricultural consideration, geographical irregularities and the various accidents of history and prehistory, the most majestic meaning of all is surely that which precedes, commands, and to a large extent, explains the others. A pale blurred line, or an often almost imperceptible difference in the shape and consistency of rock fragments, are evidence of the fact that two oceans once succeeded each other where, today, I can see nothing but barren soil. As I follow the traces of their age-old stagnation despite all obstacles—sheer cliff faces, landslides, scrub or cultivated land—and disregarding paths and fences, I seem to be proceeding in meaningless fashion. But the sole aim of this contrariness is to recapture the master-meaning, which may be obscure but of which each of the others is a partial or distorted transposition.

When the miracle occurs, as it sometimes does; when, on one side and the other of a hidden crack, there are suddenly to be found cheek-by-jowl two green plants of different species, each of which has chosen the most favorable soil; and when at the same time, two ammonites with unevenly intricate involutions can be glimpsed in the rock, thus testifying in their own way to a gap of several tens of thousands of years, suddenly space and time become one: the living diversity of the moment juxtaposes and perpetuates the ages. Thought and emotion move into a new dimension where every drop of sweat, every muscular movement, every gasp of breath becomes symbolic of a past history, the development of which is reproduced in my body, at the same time as my thought embraces its significance. I feel myself to be steeped in a more dense intelligibility, within which centuries and distances answer each other and speak at last with one and the same voice [1955/1977:48–49].

He goes on to say that Freud's work impressed him as another version of the method of geology: finding the fault lines in the present that lead down into the underground, and simultaneously back into the past. In my opinion, this passage gives the key to what is most enduring in Lévi-Strauss' work. It is this vein of interpretation that is most prominent in Lévi-Strauss' first, and in my opinion his best book, *The Elementary Structures of Kinship* (1949/1969). To be sure, his later themes are also there in embryo. There is the emphasis upon structures, oppositions, and mediations. This time the language is the kinship system itself, and its utterances are acts of exchanging women. Saussurean linguistics is already present: Women are like words, by which groups can speak to one another. And the message? Social solidarity: exchange, reciprocity, giving and receiving, tying the group together in endless chains. There is also a favorite Lévi-Straussian theme, much developed in his later works, of nature versus culture. Here this is found in his discussion of the incest taboo, which divides humanity from the animals, and also makes larger society possible by forcing outbreeding from the isolated nuclear group.

This argument regarding incest seems at first glance to make no advance over the usual teleological functionalism by which incest taboos are conventionally explained. Lévi-Strauss does add his distinctive note, in that the incest taboo sends the first human cognitive message, and in fact creates symbolic thought: "The emergence of symbolic thought must have required that women, like words, should be things that were exchanged [1949/1969:496]." He is implying that the symbol-using mentality that constitutes the human world first emerged not so much within *individual talk*, but in this first, *externalized* form of communication. Kinship exchanges are where people first learned to think in a human way. Left in this form, though, we seem to have an explanation in reverse causal order, reading backward from consequences to the process itself. The entire work on kinship structures, in the light of Lévi-Strauss' later work, appears as a static set of permutations on a basic logical code.

I think that this reading, however, would be a mistake that

deprives us of what is most valuable in the work. This book, on the contrary, lays out the elements of a theory of very long-term social change. The emphasis is upon conflict and history, and a determinative pattern among them. The argument on the incest taboo is in fact an historical one, explaining the earliest transformation from animal to human society; and the varieties of the elementary forms of kinship give a model of which types of structures lead to purely repetitive changes within the same structural orbit, and which ones can break out into new types. The center of the book is a theory of the structural revolution by which stratified, state society arose. The later chapters of The Elementary Structures thus actually try to reconstruct, if only tentatively, the early kinship histories of archaic India and China, and even touch upon the marriage politics of the medieval European aristocracy. At the end, Lévi-Strauss promises another book on complex kinship systems, encompassing both the apparently less structured kinship markets of many African and North American Indian societies, and the more personally as well as economically and politically based marriage markets of historical societies. This book was never delivered, of course; Lévi-Strauss eventually drifted over to decoding myths, and has been there ever since.

In his first and most fruitful period, Lévi-Strauss was trying to expound ancient history. Better yet, his topic was prehistory: the history of the long centuries before writing was invented. This encompasses all those generations from perhaps half a million or a million years ago, until about 300 B.C. and even more recently in some parts of the world. Obviously one cannot pin down the details of that era, stretching a good 20,000 consecutive lifetimes, compared to the mere 200 generations that have lived since history began to be written down. But this enormous amount of time was by no means eventless. Primitive societies are not static, and they are prehistoric only in the literal sense—there were no historians then, and modern historians do not know what to say about them.

Yet we are not entirely without resources. There are the material artifacts and skeletal remains of those people. Lévi-Strauss has never made an effort to coordinate his own program with that of archaeology, although this could certainly be done. Lévi-Strauss perhaps felt that archaeology gives a rather dead picture—life as seen from the outside, from its dry remains. He has concentrated instead on two precipitates of the human mind from that era. What he has done with myths we have already noted: basically, this strategy has yielded a few flashes of historical insight, although the further he has pursued this investigation, the less history appears in it and the more the allegedly universal mental processes take over attention. This has turned into an endless categorizing, rather like the formal sociologies of Parsons and earlier generations of sociologists, which proved so sterile of genuine explanation or intellectual advance.

The kinship materials, though, are inherently much more dynamic. Lévi-Strauss's most brilliant stroke, I think, is to formulate a strategy by which this material explains the course of unwritten history. One cannot write this history in any detail of course, nor can Lévi-Strauss nail down events to particular people in particular places and times. But the scale of analysis is precisely real people dealing with local events in their own lifetimes, not an abstract image of very long-term social stages succeeding one another mechanically across the millenia. The basic stragegy is this: Certain actions repeat over and over again in daily life. These are the structures of society. For tribal societies, these are the kinship structures, which not only encompass sexual and familial matters but also constitute the core of organization for politics, economics, religion, and the rest of culture. Changes in kinship structure are the basic history of such societies, up to the point where the kinship system itself breaks apart into a new kind of society characterized by economic classes and by the state. This is simultaneously the dawn of written history. The sequences of change can be predicted from certain basic forms, choice points in the kinship organization itself. Some of these can even be shown to produce revolutionary breakdowns, by which the kinship-based society transforms itself into something new.

CONFLICT, ALLIANCE, AND EXCHANGE

The Elementary Structures of Kinship by no means gives an idealized picture of primitive social life. There are struggles for food, warfare and threats of violent death, quarrels, divorces, and all the other ills of human life in an imperfect world. Lévi-Strauss's view on this is as hard-nosed as the most cynical conflict theorist. The very basis of the kinship system is sexual domination. Males exert property rights over the bodies and labor of females, and exchange them with other males. Lévi-Strauss is thus the prime mover of a modern sociology of sexual stratification (cf. Collins, 1971), as well as of alliance theory within modern treatments of kinship. To be sure, Lévi-Strauss states his position without regard for the variations in the degrees and kinds of sexual stratification across the whole range of history. But certainly his theory of alliances, augmented with a consideration of variations in other resources and motives for sexual domination, opens the way toward a more refined theory, which does not take male domination as a universal but as a condition that emerges under specific circumstances.

The purposes for which males dominate females in tribal societies are manifold. Aside from sexual gratification, there is also a struggle for food and livelihood itself; women as food providers are a major source of wealth. In the Australian desert, Lévi-Strauss remarks, the bachelor is a poor thing, a creature who barely eaks out his survival without a woman's help. The major value of women is that they determine alliances among groups. Alliances are necessary because of the constant danger of violence. Lévi-Strauss describes the way in which Australians encounter a stranger: They first ascertain his lineage and his marriage ties, because these divide friends from enemies. The man (the sexism is explicit here) without marriage ties is defenseless, thus marriages are the main means of military defense.

Lévi-Strauss continually emphasizes that exchange brings solidarity, and he distinguishes among various types of kinship exchange systems in terms of the amount of solidarity that they bring. But this is not a naïve pan-functionalist argument based on the society's demand for solidarity. Solidarity is important precisely because of the threat of conflict. It is the solidarity of various groups within the society, not of the total social order itself. It is the solidarity of warfare groups, as Lévi-Strauss explicitly remarks (1949/1969:149). Exchange is a crucial weapon of each group, and hence the object of its explicit strategizing.

Lévi-Strauss's most striking point, though, is that exchange both creates solidarity among groups and structures new conflicts among them. Exchange produces conflict itself, and not just in the obvious sense that the structure produced is a lineup of opposing alliances. Exchange also produces strains and potential conflicts within alliances. Gifts give grounds for grievances, if reciprocity is not properly lived up to. The strains in the marriage alliance system are still apparent even today, in our jokes about in-laws, and these were much more serious in societies in which the whole economic and political organization was based on such marriage connections. Many of the fights within tribal societies break out precisely over the way in which rights and gifts due from previous donations are not properly repaid (1949/1969:261). Part of this very instability is due to the fact that gifts are often used as a means of ending a conflict. A murder or an insult might be repaid by the gift of a woman, just as a truce in a feudal war could best be sealed by a diplomatic marriage (1949/1969:113). Marriage, then, is a way of containing quarrels, of keeping them from becoming more serious. This is one reason why tribal marriage ceremonies often involve competitive games or even mock fights (1949/1969:481). The ceremonial carrying-off of the bride is not a survivor of some bygone era of bride-capture, but an indicator of current realities. Lévi-Strauss quotes with approval the phrase "marriage is a socially regulated act of hostility [1949/1969:261]," and sums up his position with a telling remark: "Exchanges are peacefully resolved wars, and wars are the result of unsuccessful transactions [1949/1969:67]."

This interdependence of conflict and exchange is the structural key to historical change. As we shall see, from the existing structure of alliances, the lines of further conflicts and breakdowns of structure are predictable. History is a series of alliance structures, with their strains and conflictual transformations.

THE INCEST TABOO AS EXTERNALLY IMPOSED

The incest taboo itself, by implication, is explainable in these terms. All would agree that the incest taboo is crucial for establishing the larger, non-nuclear networks of society. But Lévi-Strauss's formulation about exchange does not leave us with the usual teleological functionalist explanation of the taboo in terms of its consequences. The logic of Lévi-Strauss's theme of the interdependence of exchange and conflict provides a sequential hypothesis for the creation of the incest taboo.

Men without daughters or sisters cannot get them within the nuclear group, and hence must go outside it to find women. Such situations must have happened often, due to sheer demographic accident. In the absence of exchange relations, raiding for women must have been a source of much warfare, even when there were no other natural scarcities due to an abundance of land. Although Lévi-Strauss does not mention it, the archaeological evidence certainly suggests that primitive humanoids killed one another quite frequently; many of the proto-human species were apparently made extinct in this way.

On the other hand, demographic change would have produced many groups with more than enough females for the men. Men in such groups would have found it advantageous to use this sexual surplus to gain alliances. Thus a gift-economy of women would have arisen. Perhaps the women were given in a purely defensive spirit: instead of being robbed and perhaps killed, better to give the plunder away. The more initiative in doing this, the more goodwill that could be created, and thus alliances would come into being. Eventually the families carrying out this strategy would become more powerful militarily than isolated nuclear families. The exogamous, alliance-making families would sooner or later drive the more traditional groups out of existence.

The incest taboo, then, is not a psychological phenomenon at all, nor is it merely a latently functional practice that first appeared by accident. The incest taboo is imposed from without: It reflects people's recognition that outsiders demand their women and will not allow them to be kept selfishly within the group. It is fear of other people that enforces the feeling that women must not become sexual property in their own families, and it is precisely conflict situations that enforce this feeling.

The theory has the merit of being testable. The larger the network of family-based alliances, the further the incest taboo–exogamy requirement extends among consanguinal relations. In a modern society with a bureaucratic state and impersonal economy, the family is no longer important for alliances; incest taboos shrink back to the minimum level of enforcement, which still requires women to be available in the general sexual marketplace. The mother–son taboo cannot be established in this way, of course, but it is easily explicable in terms of male domination: the father asserting exclusive sexual property rights over his wife against his most immediate male rival. The other incest taboos—on cousins, whole exogamous lineages and groups, and so forth—have narrowed their scope, and perhaps have also been less enforced even where they exist, as modern societies have moved further away from kinship-based economic and political organization. But the mother–son taboo survives, as the strongest and least violated prohibition, precisely because it is not based on exchange.

IDEAL STRATEGIES AND MATERIAL REALITIES

These conflicts are only the first step in human prehistory. They are followed by many more, whose contours are revealed by Lévi-Strauss. But already in the incest model, we can see a key dynamic of Lévi-Strauss's scheme. The demographic realities shift. Some of the proto-human nuclear families had no daughters, some had many. It is precisely this demographic variability that people must take into account in their social arrangements.

Lévi-Strauss has discussed this point intermittently, both in debates over his general method and throughout his writings on kinship and mythology. Lévi-Strauss has been accused of placing too much emphasis on the ideal side of kin structures. It is said that he has failed to attend to the distinction between preferential and prescriptive rules, and has ignored the empirical data of what marriages actually take place, since this data often show the rules being evaded in practice (cf. Needham, 1969). These criticisms are misplaced.

1. Lévi-Strauss has directly replied that even if only a small percentage of marriages take place according to the kinship rules, this gives a certain tendency to the development of the social structure. Those families that do not or cannot obey the rules act essentially at random, and give rise to no sustained changes; it is those that do obey the rules that make social history (1949/1969:xxx–xxxv).

2. Furthermore, Lévi-Strauss argues that the natives themselves tend to see the rules in the same complex way that he does. Sometimes the rules are ideologies, upheld mainly as claims to prestige, not because they can always be carried out. He even remarks that the formal rules can be a kind of myth. Moreover, the natives can deliberately manipulate and change the rules. Australian tribal elders sit and discuss them at great length, devising possible changes to fit new problems. Lévi-Strauss sees such men as native intellectuals, producing deliberate strategies for coordinating pre-existing structures with new demographic problems and political aims (1949/1969:125). In his later reflections on his kinship theory (1962/1966:251), Lévi-Strauss remarks that he should have given even greater emphasis to this conscious creation of rules and myths.

Native intellectuals, in other words, knew what they were doing when they formulated the kinship rules. One can see this as they reformulate the rules to deal with current problems. One can thus infer that similar conscious decision-making went into formulating the earlier rules. We cannot necessarily recover the reasoning directly in the case of strategies that have been in effect for a long time. Kinship strategies are constantly in motion, contrary to the notion that tribal societies are structurally static. It is these new problems and strategies that occupy people's minds. Because of this, the older strategies that are not practically called into question are taken for granted. To focus on one thing necessarily defocuses everything else. (On the fundamental significance of this for social structure, see "The Microfoundations of Macrosociology," in this volume.) Incest taboos would fall into that category, since they are still the fundamental basis of all other kinship alliances, but the reasoning behind them is no longer of interest. They have been thoroughly routinized for tens of thousands of generations.

3. Lévi-Strauss's accounts of the particular kinship patterns found

at one point in time are frequently set in terms of their adaptations to changing demographic circumstances. From highly complicated structures, he reconstructs the sequence of changes that must have brought a particular pattern to its condition. The hypothesized causes are sometimes conflicts, sometimes demographic accidents. He mentions that some lineages die out, and that this must happen not infrequently; other groups grow large and split. Such changes have structural consequences to which the rest of the system must adjust. Even in his later work on the structure of myths, Lévi-Strauss applies the same analysis. A tribe might have had three clans, for example: bear—turtle—eagle (in this case reflecting a division among three elements: land—water—sky). If the bear clan dies out, the structural organization of the society can be re-established only by subdividing the larger of the remaining clans. The modern observer would thus find: yellow turtle—grey turtle—eagle (1962/1966:67). Lévi-Strauss comments: "Demographic evolution can shatter the structure but. . . . if the structural orientation survives the shock it has, after each upheaval, several means of reestablishing a system, which may not be identical with the earlier one but is at least formally of the same type [1962/1966:68]."

The basic process, then, is an interplay of raw demographic facts of nature with deliberate human attempts to strategically respond to them; it is this interplay that produces human history and culture. It is, in fact, by knowing this interplay that one can read the code of the myths. Lévi-Strauss remarks that it is precisely this emphasis upon material history that sets his position apart from that of Durkheim: "Although there is undoubtedly a dialectical relation between the social structure and systems of categories, the latter are not an effect or result of the former: each, at the cost of laborious mental adjustments, translates certain historical and local modalities of the relations between man and the world, which form their common substratum [1962/1966:214]."

Lévi-Strauss's full view, then, not only takes account of demographic accidents, but also builds this into the center of his model. We should add that such arguments refer not merely to demography in the narrow sense, but to the full range of conditions in which humanity interacts with the material environment, to "wars, epidemics, and famines [1962/1966:71]." Social structure is generally to be explained, as Lévi-Strauss remarks of a particular instance, "by the combined action of two forces, one of demographic origin which pushes it towards disorganization, and the other of speculative inspiration which pushes it towards a reorganization as closely as possible in line with the earlier state of affairs (1962/1966:71)." Lévi-Strauss is thus not merely playing lip-service to Marxism when he declares that the material infrastructure is basic grounds for all human action, while at the same time stating that his purpose is to contribute to the theory of superstructures (1962/1966:130). It is fully consistent with the thrust of this approach that we may broaden it further in this direction than Lévi-Strauss himself has done, to take account of variations in the abundance or scarcity of food and natural resources, and in the geographical dispersion or concentration of populations, and build an alliance theory of kinship upon a fuller treatment of these conditions (cf. Fox, 1967; Harris, 1979:81–100).

Lévi-Strauss, then, is elaborating a Maussian theme. Women are currency in a gift exchange system which is really a system of communications. It is not, as mistakenly interpreted, a group mind talking to itself, even though Lévi-Strauss himself often gives grounds for this impression in his later works. The communications are among specific groups of allies. Mauss (1925/1962) showed that shells passing around a kula ring in symbolic ceremonies make possible mundane economic transactions within the structure of the ring; Lévi-Strauss shows that women passing around a kinship structure make possible political alliances. (One might add that this is an economic structure, too, since not only marriage payments, funeral contributions, and property inheritance pass through this network, but also many other and frequent deliveries of food and goods.) These exchanges are carried out under actual or potential threat of warfare, and its milder conflictual equivalent, the scrambel for prestige. Conflicts not only force exchanges, but exchanges also structure conflicts, as Mauss, too, was well aware (1925/1962). Exchanges can contain conflicts and make them milder, but they also produce them in predictable ways.

From a mass of kinship data from many different societies, Lévi-Strauss has tried to reconstruct the basic logic of such alliances and their transformations. Although this project was left incomplete—and still remains so—it is a powerful and at least partially convincing effort. Let us look at its main outlines.

BASIC ELEMENTS: RESIDENCE AND LINEAGE

There are two basic elements of a kinship system. *Residence:* Where do the husband, the wife, and their children live after their marriage? In the tribal societies with which Lévi-Strauss was concerned, the main choices are patrilocal or matrilocal (with avunculocal—residence with the maternal uncle—as a variant on the latter). *Lineage:*

What group do the children belong to? Again, for these tribes, the major choice is patrilineal or matrilineal. Bilineality is also a possibility, but an unimportant one in the Lévi-Strauss model: not that it doesn't occur, but that nothing of structural significance can come from it. We might note, in addition, that lineages need not be narrow family chains in the modern sense, but can be organized as entire clans or subclans, or subidivded into elaborate sectional systems, as in many Australian societies.

These basic forms are by no means ideal constructs. Both are grossly behavioral and material; both in fact can be looked on as forms of property. This is obvious in the case of lineage: In a matrilineal system, children inherit not only their names but also their material goods from their mother's family, while in a patrilineal system this property is inherited from the father's family. But the children themselves are property as well: they are usable for exchange, and hence for alliances, and matri–patrilineality tells us which family group gets to use them as such.

Locality of residence is also a form of property: secondarily as property over the children, but primarily as property over the wife. In a patrilocal system, the woman goes to live with her husband and his kin. She is lost from her own family and cut off from its support, and even her children are not her own. This is an extreme form of male domination. In matrilocality (or its variant, avunculocality), the woman stays with her own kinfolk, and the male is the one in the midst of an alien group. Such practices take various forms: sometimes the males only visit their wives for intercourse; sometimes they live there for a period but later return home; sometimes the males actually move in, although this is rare and confined to subservient relations, since it prevents a man from being with his own property in his sister's household. Although matrilocal groups are also dominated by men, the position of women within them is much stronger than in patrilocal ones. In terms of property relations, sexual property in the form of erotic access and labor service of married men from their wives is a good deal weaker in matrilocal than patrilocal arrangements.

In general, one might say that locality is sexual property as daily enacted; lineality is the long-term, macroaspect of sexual property.

On can infer from these circumstances something of the conditions under which these systems are likely to arise. Matrilocal residence is empirically rather rare. From a structural viewpoint, its rarity should not be surprising, since it is just barely one step away from an incest situation, in which no sexual trades and alliances are made at all. Matrilineality, too, is a good deal less common than patrilineality. (And in fact, both are less common statistically than bilineality.) These empirical distributions seem not to be widely known. The impression is often given in comparative surveys of social history that all societies of a primitive horticultural type are matrilineal. This is probably because, as Lévi-Strauss points out, matrilineal societies are more spectacular than patrilineal ones. They have been the subjects of some of the most famous anthropological studies, such as those of Malinowski. Why are they so dramatic? Not only because of the reversal of our familiar modern forms of kinship, but also because their atmosphere tends to be psychologically heavy, full of jealousies, divorces, conflicts, and their religious and symbolic expressions. In fact, matrilineal societies indicate a situation in which the women-giving groups do not give up very much: They strike a hard bargain in the marriage market. It is in effect a sellers' market.

If we ask, then, what causes these patterns, the answer is that matrilineal societies (and matrilocal ones as well, to the extent that we find them) are much more likely than patrilineal and patrilocal ones to exist in a situation of a high degree of warfare. More recent empirical comparisons confirm this judgment (Divale, 1975). An ecological factor also enters in: Matrilineal societies are usually ones in which various exogenous groups live very close to each other, so that males are not greatly inconvenienced by their relative separation from their property. Patrilineality and patrilocality, however, fit well with situations where groups are geographically remote: The woman leaves her home once and for all, and there are few occasions for subsequent contact. Lévi-Strauss comments that these systems are best suited to creating long-distance alliances between culturally rather divergent groups (1949/1969:289).

Wars are probably both the cause and the effect of matrilineality, as the structure emerges from a situation of high distrust, and also tends to foster further quarrels. Variations in the scarcity of ecological conditions also enter into these determinations; more recent alliance theories have developed this point (e.g., Harris, 1979:81–84, 96–100).

HARMONIC AND DISHARMONIC SYSTEMS

The key structural difference, in Lévi-Strauss's scheme, is neither lineage nor residence per se, but their combination. Either patrilineal–patrilocal or matrilineal–matrilocal is called harmonic; matrilineal–patrilocal or patrilineal–matrilocal is called disharmonic. (In practice the second of each pair can be dropped as empirically rare or nonexistent.) In effect, this is the difference between a sexual property system dominated either by takers of wives (a buyer's market), or by the givers of wives (a seller's market). These two situations make possible quite different historical sequences.

THREE MARRIAGE STRATEGIES

Given these property situations, the native policymakers must decide on an optimum strategy for achieving family alliances. Strategies are put into practice by formulating marriage rules, be they preferential or prescribed, closely adhered to or widely violated, as discussed previously. There are three elementary sorts of marriage strategies. Most prominently, these involve cross-cousins: marriages that link a man either to his mother's or to his father's family.

Two of these strategies are asymmetrical:

- man marries mother's brother's daughter (matrilateral cross-cousin marriage);
- man marries father's sister's daughter (patrilateral cross-cousin marriage).

There is also a symmetrical form, in which either cross-cousin marriage is permitted. Such symmetrical systems can also work by equivalent rules, which do not specify the actual cross-cousin but someone from an equivalent place in the generational and lineage structure.

Even with the best intentions, of course, such marriages cannot always be made. There may not be any matrilateral cross-cousin in that particular generation, or there may be too many sons or daughters, or too few. All of these are historically specific contingencies through which these systems work themselves out. It is, in fact, these various contingencies, which are bound to come up over and over again across the generations, that prove the relative power of one or another type of marriage strategy.

The core of Lévi-Strauss's model is to work out the logical consequences of these different strategies.

SYMMETRICAL MARRIAGE AND
RESTRICTED EXCHANGE

Symmetrical cross-cousin rules bring about a particular kind of social structure. If the rules are followed out consistently, they link the same two families together continuously, with a marriage in each direction, perhaps as often as several times in the same generation. The society is not linked together as a whole, but braided into independent and parallel strands: $A \leftrightharpoons B\ C \leftrightharpoons D$. The same result follows from other symmetrical rules that do not necessarily involve cross-cousins, such as those found in societies with dual organization, a division of the tribe into halves, quarters, eighths, etc., with specific rules regarding preferred and prohibited marriages among members of these sections.

ASYMMETRICAL MARRIAGE AND GENERALIZED EXCHANGE

If marriage rules specify only one cross-cousin and prohibit the other, the system of exchange does not form braids but a long chain of families. The longest chain occurs if matrilateral cross-cousin marriage is consistently performed; $A \rightarrow B \rightarrow C \rightarrow D \rightarrow$. (Eventually the first in the chain also receives a wife by this system: $\rightarrow A$.) This is the long cycle. It is simultaneously the most risky, in that there are many places in which the chain can be broken, either by conflict or by demographic accident. On the other hand, there is the most to gain; the widest network of alliances can be forged in this way. As we shall see, it is via this route that important historical changes occur. This form results in each lineage being linked to another, which always gives it wives but never takes any in return, and then of course to a second, to which it is wife-giver but not wife-taker. The structure is a system of permanent debts. It is out of this that the stratification of the system arises.

The other form of asymmetrical cross-cousin marriage, patrilateral, also creates chains. But in this case they are not very long ones. If followed out, each alternating generation receives a wife back for its previous gift to that particular family. The patrilateral strategy results in a discontinuous structure, with all accounts settled every second generation. Less is risked, but less is gained. It constitutes a short cycle.

WHY ONE ROUTE RATHER THAN ANOTHER?

The structural determinant of which way a system will go, Lévi-Strauss argues, is whether it is harmonic or disharmonic. *Disharmonic systems* (which are mostly of the matrilineal–patrilocal form) tend to follow the patrilateral cross-cousin strategy: They opt for a short cycle, and cut their risks. They are, of course, already in a high-conflict situation in their local relations, even within family groups themselves. This may seem sufficient reason for their unwillingness to invest in the long run. It is also possible to see a structural consequence of the patrilateral cross-cousin strategy in this situation: A man's grandchildren come back into his own descent group, and hence male lineages can be covertly reestablished even though the official connection passes entirely through females (Harris, 1979:182). This amounts to a strategy for preserving some of the power of husbands over their own property, in a situation in which the wive's families otherwise tend to dominate. The strategy boils down to fighting for power within the family, and giving up on the possibility of long-term investments that would strengthen the position of the family as a whole.

Harmonic systems, on the other hand (mainly patrilineal–local), are much more likely to prefer the matrilateral cross-cousin strategy. For a patrilateral strategy here would not only create no more than a short cycle, but would also pass property to grandchildren back into the female's linage. The structural consequences of a patrilateral marriage strategy in a strongly male-dominated system would, paradoxically, undermine control by males (Harris, 1979:182). The matrilateral strategy, then, is much more widespread in these societies, and hence it is in these societies that long cycles of exchange are constituted. (Many patrilineal–patrilocal societies, however, especially in Africa, do not practice cross-cousin marriage at all, and hence fail to create these long alliance chains. Harmonic systems are a precondition, but not a sufficient determinant of this strategy.)

LONG-TERM CHANGES

Which path a group starts down is fateful for the future of that society. Societies with symmetrical or short cycle exchanges produce restricted alliance patterns. A good deal of change can occur here, of course. But conflicts, demographic accidents, and environmental pressures, when they change such structures, nevertheless leave them within the orbit of restricted exchange. Particular family alliances come and go, and particular lineages or even arrangements of lineages appear and disappear. But the structural peculiarity of these forms is that changes are caught within the walls of a certain social type. Quarrels within a reciprocal exchange system, for example, frequently break out because of what their members think of as breaches of gift obligations. These can result in the groups breaking off contacts or going to war with each other. But the now-isolated groups can only go on to establish new alliances of the same sort with some other group

(1949/1969:78–9). The very number of groups can change. Dual systems can become more complex, subdividing into further categories. Australian elders make quite elaborate policy decisions on such matters, creating new exchange rules and new subsections of their tribes to meet the political exigencies of the day. But the structures always change into another version of a restricted exchange system. Moieties may turn into eight-class systems, or sometimes eight-class systems devolve into four or two classes (1949/1969:152). Alliances are patched up, wars arranged, demographic accidents smoothed out. Much changes, but the scale of social organization—especially its form of stratification and its degree of political decentralization—stays the same.

A truly generalized exchange system, though, is unstable in a different way. Because of demographic accident, some groups will have more daughters than others, and they will be able to make more alliances. The returns on these investments take a longer time to materialize, but they are proportionately greater. A family embarked on a positive cycle as giver of wives puts increasing numbers of clients in its debt. In subsequent generations, it has more women coming in, which in turn allows it to get a demographic jump on its rivals in the next cycle. With excess claims on women, privileged families can become polygymous. Since women work, they are an increasing source of direct wealth, while the alliances that they bring make the family increasingly powerful militarily. On the other side, families that get behind in this cycle are likely to become steadily poorer, both demographically and economically. They have fewer women, and these become less desirable for other families as tokens of alliance. Marriages are made on increasingly unequal terms; poorer men marrying upper-lineage women become servitors of the powerful families, while upper-lineage men confine themselves to alliances with other powerful families. Social classes develop, and some groups may even become slaves.

As the system becomes stratified, its forms eventually break down. Exchanges are no longer substantially equal, and additional economic goods are added on as a kind of immediate recompense, through the institution of brideprice. This further exacerbates the stratifying tendencies of the system, because poorer families are less likely to be able to pay the brideprice, hence less likely to be able to produce more daughters. They fall increasingly further behind. Richer families, on the other hand, can afford to pay those prices, and hence increasingly monopolize the marriage (and the political alliance) market. The returns on this, in more daughters and more brideprices, make them richer still. Perhaps the brideprice was even deliberately instituted as a strategy by dominant families for this purpose, a kind of tax they were enforcing by their commanding position on the market.

Finally, both upper and lower classes are motivated to withdraw from the system. The lower-class families can no longer afford to make a marriage in the traditional way; they begin to withdraw among themselves and set up reciprocal exchanges with some other lineage. This at least gets wives for the men, but it seals the family's fate in the overall stratification picture. Upper-class families, on the other hand, are now embarked on an aristocratic scale of living, and on political alliances of major scope. Some are on their way to outright military and political rule. They begin to find their obligations to their lesser kin a drag on their own ambitions. They begin to make short-term alliances outside the kin network entirely, without using marriage politics. In this way, kings eventually arise. Through the feudal tendencies of an unstable system of generalized exchange, the state finally emerges.

THE STRUCTURALIST THEORY OF PREHISTORY

Lévi-Strauss thus allows us to infer the outlines of human history for the last half-million years or so, from the protohuman condition onwards through the emergence of stratified society and the state. The first major event was the development of a strategy of exogamous wife-giving, which enabled some nuclear groups to make alliances and to take an edge in the hostilities that pervaded this period. The incest taboo, as a strategy imposed by the threat of external raiding, eventually became the basis upon which more complex alliance strategies could emerge.

Subsequent history is full of a variety of kinship forms: bilateral and cognate lineages, the so-called "Crow-Omaha" types of purely negative kinship prohibitions, as well as the unilateral forms that Lévi-Strauss concentrated on. These pure unilateral forms may be statistically a minority, but if Lévi-Strauss is right, they are the ones that have an historical logic built into them. Bilateral marriage strategies, cognatic descent, and so forth all tend either to subdivide property, and hence dissipate it, or in effect to randomize and localize alliance patterns. The purer version of restricted exchange and short-cycle generalized exchange stand out with a greater structural elegance. Their histories are structurally more predictable, in that they fall within a given compass, although they are doomed to go around and around the same set of variations. Ironically, it is these pure forms that were especially locked into a kind of historyless eternity: if not strictly without histories, they made a major part of human prehistory into a sort of cyclical universe.

It is the pure form of patrilineal–patrilocal harmonic systems, then, that are the true makers of linear history. That is, they brought about the transformation of relatively egalitarian and small-scale groups into class-stratified societies and into incipient states. This emergence into modern-style history has an almost Marxian dialectic to it. This particular kind of kinship alliance system not only brought about a new society, but also broke down the very system on which it was formerly based. The long chains of matrilateral cross-cousin marriage were eventually repudiated both from below and above. The one structural path out of the cycles of purely kinship-based societies ended by overturning even the most dynamic type of kinship system itself. The first step was to institute a strategy that turned from a series of balanced exchanges to a set of imbalanced exchanges. The imbalanced system finally undermined kinship exchange itself. In its place emerged nonexchange domination: the state.

Is this the only way the state could, or did, come about? We are not sure. Certainly there are competing theories: conquest, hydraulic economies, incipient priesthoods, big-man redistribution systems. The evidence is not really in yet. The Lévi-Strauss theory has mainly been debated in terms of specialized anthropological interests in kinship, and the requisite cross-societal comparisons have not been produced. On the other hand, the rival theories have so far been formulated in general terms, and have not come to grips with the social realities of daily human interaction, and with human strategizing, the way Lévi-Strauss's model does. Surely conquest was often involved in the rise of the states that we know about. But how did the conquerors become organized into a sufficiently large and permanent group to rule, rather than to raid, and for that matter to win, rather than to chip away piecemeal? Again, how did a community become organized to be able to carry out irrigation projects? How could priesthoods break old bonds of religious allegiance and establish new ones? Where did the big man get the wealth to redistribute? Kinship politics was more than likely involved in all of these, and a full model would certainly have to be built up around a structural theory of alliances.

On the face of it, the Lévi-Strauss argument is supported by the existing distribution of kinship structures, which were founded around the world in historical times. Patrilineal–patrilocal systems are found across the major state-building areas of China, India, the Middle East, and Europe. (Exceptions within these areas may help prove the case: If these are the groups that failed to establish strong stratified structures, they would appear to have been held back by their kinship structure.) On the other side, the weakness of state formation in Africa, North America, and Australia fits the model in that these were the areas of bilateral marriage strategies or restricted or randomized exchange systems.

Certainly we know of societies within these large areas that do not follow the hypothesized kinship–state linkage. There were states in central and west Africa, or example, or the Mexican and Andean states, or the North American Indian confederations, that arose in response to European incursions. But a closer look at these may reveal kinship–alliance patterns that approximate those given in the structuralist model. This may be especially likely if we can break that model into a series of variations, predicting partial and weak stratifying tendencies as well as stronger ones. It is also possible, of course, that we will find evidence for other, nonkinship factors, which must be entered into a theory of the state. We may also have to make variant paths within a kinship–alliance theory that have not yet been envisioned: The patrilateral cross-cousin strategy within a harmonic system may not be the only one which has long-term structural consequences. In any case, this line of analysis can only bring an enrichment of our understanding.

A CONTEMPORARY PAYOFF

Finally, we might ask: Why should sociologists be interested in this? One answer is that sociology and anthropology are really the same discipline, and that all of human history and all types of human societies come into the purview of a science of society. Another answer is that the tide of structuralism now washing over American sociology from the other side of the Atlantic deserve a critical analysis aimed at finding its most valuable elements. But most essentially, I would suggest, there is a theoretical lesson in Lévi-Strauss's effort to explain the long-term patterns of change in "historyless' tribal societies.

Formalized kinship networks are no longer important in modern society, but alliances certainly are. Lévi-Strauss's structuralist version of exchange theory appears a much more promising route to understanding this phenomenon than the individual-level, utilitarian style of exchange theory we have seen so far of the type of Homans, Blau, *et al.* Neoclassical economics shares the same utilitarian assumptions, and ignores the structural–network side of theory, which is precisely the strength of the Durkheim–Mauss–Lévi-Strauss tradition. The merit of

Lévi-Strauss's version is that it concentrates on the structures resulting from exchange, not just the form of bargaining at the individual level, and that it systematically accounts for the histories of various kinds of structures, instead of reducing everything structurally to one ideally open market.

The major elements in Lévi-Strauss, in fact, give us the range of types of economic systems. Restricted exchange is a barter system, in which little is risked, but little gained, while social structure remains fragmented and localized. The generalized exchange strategy works on extending credit, betting on getting it back manyfold in the long run. It is a direct parallel to Schumpeter's definition of capitalism: enterprise carried out with borrowed money. The particular formulations of Lévi-Strauss regarding kinship systems may not be precisely the analogies we need to solve problems in other sociological fields. But Lévi-Strauss's concepts, taken more abstractly, may provide just the right building blocks. We find then in his model, property in both a short-term enacted form and in the long-term form of an exchange strategy for reproducing it. We furthermore understand property as a variable institution, representing varying degrees of compromise among conflicting groups. There are strategies for property-enhancing alliances, which are consciously considered while they are on the forefront of pressing issues, but become taken-for-granted forms of prestige or taboo in their more deeply embedded forms. There are unintended consequences of various strategies as they are carried out over many trials: those that produce merely random shifts, those that lock the structure into endless permutations of a basic pattern, and those that give rise to revolutionary breaks.

These elements, taken more abstractly and reworked as needed, may be just what is wanted for a better theory of the alliances that make up modern politics and international relations, as well as interorganizational ties, business communities, friendship networks, and the intellectual world itself. A tremendous amount of the problems of modern sociology—community and national power structures, business elites, social movements, social mobility—hinge upon a successful theoretical conceptualization of the descriptive materials we have been amassing. Above all, we need to see in general terms the conditions under which these structures appear, give rise to new conflicts, and are transformed either in cyclical or revolutionary directions. Perhaps some Lévi-Strauss of the future will seize on this material and one day give us an elegant model beyond the narrow tribalisms of the ethnographers of modern society.

Three Faces of Cruelty:
Toward a Comparative
Sociology of Violence*

To the comparative sociologist, history shows itself on two levels. For the most part it is the site of puzzles and arabesque causalities fascinating to the mind of a theorist. Yet there is another level that occasionally jolts the scholar out of his thoughts—the sense of historical lives as they were actually lived, day by day, moment by moment. Our theories and concepts compress and abstract; to speak of the transformation of the state or the rise of a religion is to look down the decades, if not the centuries, and necessarily to pass over most of the moments and feelings of most of the people involved. To conceive past societies from their great relics of art and literature draws one ever further from the brutal reality. For to empathize with the human reality of history is to receive a shock, as in the following glimpse of ancient China which brought to an end for me several months of fascinated unravelling of the patterns of Chinese history.

> Once a man of Ch'u named Mr. Ho, having found a piece of jade matrix in the Ch'u Mountains, took it to court and presented it to King Li. King Li instructed the jeweler to examine it, and the jeweler reported, "It is only a stone." The

* Originally published in *Theory and Society* 1975, 1. Copyright 1975 Elsevier Scientific Publishing Company, Amsterdam.

king, supposing that Ho was trying to deceive him, ordered that his left foot be cut off in punishment. In time King Li passed away and King Wu came to the throne, and Ho once more took his matrix and presented it to King Wu. King Wu ordered his jeweler to examine it, and again the jeweler reported, "It is only a stone." The King, supposing that Ho was trying to deceive him as well, ordered that his right foot be cut off. Ho, clasping the matrix to his breast, went to the foot of the Ch'u Mountains, where he wept for three days and nights, and when all his tears were cried out, he wept blood in their place. The King, hearing of this, sent someone to question him. "Many people in the world have had their feet amputated—why do you weep so piteously over it?" the man asked. He replied, "I do not grieve because my feet have been cut off. I grieve because a precious jewel is dubbed a mere stone, and a man of integrity is called a deceiver. This is why I weep." The King then ordered the jeweler to cut and polish the matrix, and when he had done so a precious jewel emerged [Han Fei Tzu, 1964:80].

The existence of punishment by mutilation is no surprise to the reader in Chinese history. What shocked was the blasé question: "Many people in the world have had their feet amputated—why do you weep so piteously over it?" This smug conclusion, redolent with Confucian meritocracy, only underlines the viciousness of the prevailing attitude.[1] Shang bronzes and 800-year cycles lost their charm, and I closed for the time my books on China.

The prevailing reality of world history is violence. "History is a slaughterbench . . . " cried Hegel; and James Joyce declared, "History is a nightmare from which I am trying to awake." And it is not merely the violence of a machine out of control; the disturbing thing is the viciousness, the vindictiveness, the deliberate torture in so much of it. Beneath the sociologist's patterns lies the personal dimension of evil; the patterns of history are the work of demons.

This is an attempt at exorcising those demons. It is not a theodicy; the problem is not to justify evil, but to explain it. Is there a pattern, a meaning to the cruelty itself? For it is only in isolating a causal theory that we are able to deal with cruelty; the point is not to learn to live with the demons, but to take away their power.

VIOLENCE AND GROUP STRUCTURE

A sociology of violence, in fact, already exists. Above all, we find it in the sociological tradition of France, with its emphasis on the logic

---

[1] Han Fei Tzu, of course, is the arch-Legalist and anti-Confusian of his day. This passage nevertheless illustrates both the borrowing of the Legalists from the Confucians, and foreshadows the synthesis of a bureaucratic ideology in the unified state after 221 B.C.

of emotions. Tocqueville, for instance, was struck by the degree of public benevolence in the America of the 1830s, the extent of personal sympathy and aid to strangers. He attributed this to the condition of political equality, which made it possible for individuals to empathize with one another; to prove his point, he presents a comparison with the moral atmosphere of France in the seventeenth century.

> Aux Rochers, October 30, 1675
>
> Your letter from Aix, my daughter, is droll enough.
> At least, read your letters over again before sending them; allow yourself to be surprised by the pretty things that you have put into them and console yourself by this pleasure for the trouble you have had in writing so many. Then you have kissed all of Provence, have you? There would be no satisfaction in kissing all of Brittany, unless one likes to smell of wine . . . Do you wish to hear the news from Rennes? A tax of a hundred thousand crowns has been imposed upon the citizens; and if this sum is not produced within four-and-twenty hours, it is to be doubled and collected by the soldiers. They have cleared the houses and sent away the occupants of the great streets and forbidden anybody to receive them on pain of death; so that the poor wretches (old men, women near their confinement, and children included) may be seen wandering around and crying on their departure from this city, without knowing where to go, and without food or a place to lie in. Day before yesterday a fiddler was broken on the wheel for getting up a dance and stealing some stamped paper. He was quartered after death, and his limbs exposed at the four corners of the city. Sixty citizens have been thrown in prison, and the business of punishing them is to begin tomorrow. This province sets a fine example to the others, teaching them above all that of respecting the governors and their wives, and of never throwing stones into their gardens.
> Yesterday, a delightful day, Madame de Tarenté visited these wilds; there is no question about preparing a chamber or a collation; she comes by the gate, and returns the same way . . .

> It would be a mistake [Tocqueville went on] to suppose that Madame de Sévigné, who wrote these lines, was a selfish or cruel person, she was passionately attached to her children and very ready to sympathize in the sorrows of her friends; nay, her letters show that she treated her vassals and servants with kindness and indulgence. But Madame de Sévigné has no clear notion of suffering in anyone who was not a person of quality [Tocqueville, 1840/1960: 174–175].

It is the group boundaries that determine the extent of human sympathy; within those boundaries, humanity prevails; outside them, torture is inflicted without a qualm.

The same approach to morality is taken by Durkheim. In his work, Tocqueville's observation becomes a systematic theory. Moral ideas reflect social boundaries; ceremonial observances test group membership and moral worth; God represents society, and changes as society changes shape. Thus, in the world of mutually isolated tribal societies, injunctions on killing, stealing, lying and other offenses extend only up to the boundary of each group; with the extension of the mutual links of an elaborate division of labor, the moral sense expands, becomes more abstract and universal, less concrete and particular. This insight was expanded by Weber, who understood that the abstract, philosophical world religions signified a shift in the social structure, from the mutual moral isolation of kin and ethnic groups, to a cosmopolitan society with universal political and economic possibilities.

Reading this convergence, some theorists such as Talcott Parsons (1966, 1967, 1971) have interpreted history as moral progress, a gradual extension of the collective conscience and an upgrading of moral obligations. From the particularisms and ceremonial concerns of membership in primitive tribal societies, there is an extension of the scope of humanity, emerging into a potential universal brotherhood by the rise of Christianity and the other great world religions, and culminating in the superior mildness and pan-empathy of an advanced division of labor.

An evolutionary interpretation of Durkheim and Tocqueville's insights, however, does not seem warranted. Some of the greatest displays of cruelty in history were carried out by the universal religions, especially Christianity and Islam; one has reason to doubt that the group boundaries focused on in this version are at the center of the matter. It is true that a decline in institutionalized ferociousness can be discerned in the past two hundred years, but this only reminds us that cruelty comes in more than one form. The concern with alienation in the modern era points to a peculiarly modern form of brutality. Still a third dimension is suggested by the line of thought opened up by Nietzsche and Freud, and echoed in Weber: the migration of cruelty to the interior of the individual mind in the form of psychic repression.

The Durkheimian mechanism takes us in the right direction; we can find a key to cruelty in the connection between morality and in the boundaries of group inclusion and exclusion. A moral evolutionism, however, is not a reliable guide. Moreover, additional dimensions must be added to the Durkheimian group mechanism, above all, those of stratification within and among groups. Georges Sorel (1908/1970), yet another of the French analysts of the logic of violent emotions, proposes that not all violence is of the same sort: There is "force," used by dominant classes in a vindictive (and secretly terrified) upholding of their power; and there is the "violence" of the rebellious underclass, with its clean moral purity, without viciousness but with the clarity of practical work. It will not do to regard all violence as immoral, in the manner of contemporary pacifists or over-domesticated liberals, for morality not only determines violence in a negative way—in the sense that the boundaries of the group mark the limit outside of which violence is allowed—but also in a positive way. Durkheim saw this clearly enough in his theory of the way in which punishment of transgressors against the group's standards reunifies the group in its righteous indignation. Sorel saw this in the external context as well: The height of morality is in the willingness to endanger oneself in combat for the group against its enemies, and hence violent confrontation is the basis of all the moral virtues.

The key to an understanding of violence, then, is above all the structure of solidary groups and the moralities that reflect their emotional ties. The moral boundaries may set some persons beyond the pale of moral obligation, but they may also organize confrontations that make violence not just morally indifferent but morally motivated. Add to this the internal boundaries of stratification, and we find that moral claims and corresponding forms of violence exist also in the internal struggle for domination or liberation. When we pursue these structures into more complex forms, we find routinized and internalized forms of these moralities and cruelties.

In what follows, an explanation of human cruelty will be sought along three principal dimensions. First ferociousness: *homo lupus homini.* This is the dimension of overt brutality; its explanation leads us along the lines of Tocqueville, Durkheim, and Sorel into a consideration of group boundaries, external and internal. Second, callousness: brutality routinized and bureaucratized, cruelty without passion. Our theoretical leads here extend the Durkheimian model into the themes of Marx and Weber. Third, asceticism: the turning of cruelty against oneself and against others with whom one has solidarity. Here, the leads are provided by Nietzsche and Freud, which we may assimilate into the preceding sociological theory.

I. FEROCIOUSNESS: THE VIOLENCE OF HUMAN AND ANIMAL

Consider the extremes of overt brutality:

Mutilation: punishment not by death, but by life at its lowest level. The amputation of feet or hands, or ears—so common in ancient Rome, China, Mesopotamia, Palestine, and in the Arab societies; the gouging out of eyes. The intent is not merely punishment, but prolonged misery and humiliation. This is especially evident in sexual mutilation, prominent in extremely male oriented societies: the great Han historian, Ssu-ma Ch'ien, castrated for an honest but unfavorable memorandum to the Emperor; the Turkish sultan of Egypt punishing a rebellion in the Sudan by castrating the men and amputating the breasts of the women (Moorehead, 1963: 192). Mutilation might be combined with execution, always in a public form (as in the seventeenth-century European case described by Tocqueville); clearly, public humiliation is at the essence of the phenomenon.

Torture: the deliberate prolongation and refinement of pain, usually dramatized and timed to maximize psychological dread. Torture has been routinely used in many judicial systems as part of the examination of prisoners before trial. Yet as a system for collecting evidence (as has been pointed out by rational humanists since Roman times), it is inefficient, precisely because it usually produces whatever reports or fabrications the victims think their torturers wish to hear. Clearly, the purpose of torture is not on this level; it is not to gather evidence, but to enforce submission. The cruelty is not incidental; it is the main purpose.

Peremptory executions: The awesomeness of the powerful lord was usually demonstrated in his death-dealing powers: Attila the Hun with his piles of skulls, King David with the heads of his enemies displayed on a spike (1 Samuel 17: 51–54; 2 Samuel 4: 7–12). This was the extreme dramatization of arbitrary authority.

Human sacrifices: ritual killing as part of a religious ceremony, with a victim offered to the sacred powers of the other world (Lenski, 1966: 155–159). These are of two types: sacrifices related to periodic fertility celebrations, especially in advanced horticultural societies (e.g., the Aztecs, the Benin of West Africa, the Dionysian sacrifices that entered Greece from Asia Minor); and funerals of aristocrats (e.g., Shang China or the Hindu suttee) in which slaves and wives follow the deal lord to his grave.

Ritual warhunts: warfare as a ritual frenzy, built up by dancing, drinking or drugs, and culminating in killing patterned after the hunt (Lenski, 1970: 225–227). The victim is sometimes ritually consumed; in its extreme—cannibalism—he is actually eaten, just like an animal. Not only are the victims treated as animals, but the hunters themselves also emulate the pack frenzy of carnivorous mammals that hunt their prey in groups.

The explanation of these forms of overt cruelty fits the Durkheim–Tocqueville model. In each case, the violence is practiced by one group against another to dramatize the fact that the human community and its ties extend only to a certain limit, and that persons outside are alien and subordinate. The kinds of group boundaries are not the same in each instance. Ritual warhunts are found almost exclusively in simple horticultural, hunting, or pastoral tribes, where moral ties are very localistic indeed.[2] Human sacrifices, especially in the form of fertility cults, are found primarily in advanced horticultural societies, in which the religion is a divine kingship or a theocracy of priests. The sacrifice supports the gulf between the divine rulers and their subjects; but in fact, the latter are divided into two groups for moral purposes, corresponding to those who are under the protection of the local gods and those who are not. Hence, it is almost always captives or slaves from other societies who are the victims of human sacrifices.

This is also true to a degree of funeral sacrifices; the Shang rulers, the pre-iron age (advanced horticultural) dynasty of China, raided other groups for slaves precisely in order to sacrifice them (and like the slave-owning Greeks made a very strong distinction between civilized, i.e., literate human beings, and barbarians fit for slavery and sacrifice). Slavery, in general, it should be noted, is based on these same ritual barriers between groups, especially bolstered by religious communities; slavery in Northern Europe died out with the conversion of the Slavs to Christianity, and it is clearly the extension of Christian missionary activity and the decline of African religion among black slaves that generated the moral sentiments of the antislavery movements in America and Britain.

The Hindu suttee—the burning of widows on their husbands' funeral pyres—is in a slightly different category, since Indian society in general has been relatively free from overt violence, for reasons to be considered below. The sacrifice is of women only, and women are in the category of a subordinate but omnipresent group within Hindu society. As such, they are appropriate candidates for human sacrifice.

Peremptory executions, torture, and mutilation are all characteristic of iron age (agrarian) societies which are highly stratified around a patrimonial form of government. These, indeed, are the most highly stratified societies in world history (Lenski, 1966: 437), and the stratification largely takes the form of external relations of dominance. These are conquest states, often over ethnically diverse areas; ad-

---

[2] (Lenski, 1966: 122–123; 1970: 139). The five main categories of social organization presented here are based on the predominant technology: hunting-and-gathering (stone implements), simple horticultural (primitive agriculture, digging sticks), advanced horticultural (soft metal tools, possibly irrigation agriculture), agrarian (iron tools, plows, and weapons, animal power), industrial (inanimate energy technology).

ministration is tributary rather than intensive, with the local social structure left intact. Hence the moral boundaries along ethnic–religious lines become translated into boundaries along levels of stratification; extreme punishment of the lower by the higher is not only morally neutral, but is also often exacerbated into a Sorelian frenzy of defense of the integrity of the dominant group. Hence the public dramatic nature of patrimonial mutilations, tortures, executions: the public is to be impressed that the status community of the aristocracy is not to be infringed in any way, without the most heinous punishment. These cruelties are not only deliberate, they are also ceremonially recurrent defenses of the structure of group domination.

In comparing human beings and their activities with those of animals, it appears that the above five types of cruelty constitute a scale. Ritual warhunts are the most animal-like; tortures and mutilations are the most human. That is to say, violence among animals involves a building up of frenzy through an interchange of instinctual gestures. The pack of wolves or rats work each other up into shared ferociousness, which enables them to kill as a team (Lorenz, 1966: 133–158). In this, animals show the same in-group solidarity through arousal against an enemy that Sorel proposed for humans; and indeed their post-kill "celebration" in the form of eating their victim together has its human parallels as well.[3]

The tribal ceremonies designed to stir up the war-frenzy seem to be modeled on those of hunting animals; the fact that these are characteristic of societies with little or no permanent stratification of their own (because of the lack of surplus and permanent wealth) suggests that this democracy of the pack is the only form of group aggression compatible with their usual social organization. It also fits well with the rigid boundaries between tribes often found in this situation; alien tribes may appear as distinct species to each other as do the animals which they often take for their totems.

Compare this relatively direct emotional arousal of the cannibals with the psychology of mutilation or torture. The animal is aroused (the human animal invents ways to do this deliberately), he attacks, he eats. Except for some sense of the fear displayed by his retreating victim, there is no empathy.

---

[3] There is another element of emotional contagion: not only between hunter and hunter, but between hunter and hunted. The dog is set in motion by the frightened running of the rabbit. This kind of aggressor–victim interaction seems to go on in human animals in all of the more refined forms of human cruelty; human symbolic capacities only add to the ways in which these phenomena may become consciously sought after.

The torturer or the mutilator, however, could not even attempt his arts without a capacity for taking the role of the other. The torturer does not kill and eat; he concentrates instead on inflicting pain, and above all, in conveying to his victim his intentions and powers for inflicting this pain. For the animal, terror is only an incident in the combat; for the torturer, it is the prime target. Torture and mutilation, then, are distinctively human acts; they are indeed advanced human acts. The boundaries between groups are involved, making possible the detachment that allows (and motivates) a free use of cruelty; but there is a skill at empathizing across the boundary, enough to be able to gauge the effects of cruelty on its victim. This distinctively human violence becomes symbolic; torture and mutilation are above all forms of communication usable as threats and supports for claims of complete domination.[4] "I can get inside your mind," the torturer boasts. "Do not even think of resistance." Mutilation and other public punishments are above all violence to one's social image, and hence are preeminently usable for upholding intergroup stratification.

In this perspective, cruelty bears a relation to technological and social evolution. The refined reflexivity of mutilation and torture reflects a more subtle development of human cognitive faculties than the direct emotional arousal of the war-hunt; the human sacrifice is in the middle, organized in a self-consciously religious form but with little attention to refining the pains of the victim. This is borne out by the types of societies in which each of these is commonly found. War-hunts are found primarily in unstratified, primitive horticultural, hunting, or pastoral societies; here, external boundaries among groups are very strong, but the external relations are so episodic as to constitute (when they are violent relations) only brief fights, animal-like in their intensity and directness. Human sacrifice is found primarily in advanced horticultural societies, especially around the institution of the divine king or reigning priests, and reflects the gulf between dominant and dominated groups. But such stratification is nevertheless very local in scope; the ruler's power is still very circumscribed by surrounding councils and by the weakness of military technology and administrative organization. Cruelty is now used to uphold the awesomeness of the ruler, but only on limited, highly ceremonial occasions, and without any personal element: A victim is offered to the gods in the name of the society. The extremes of refined cruelty are found in advanced iron age

---

[4] Animals do not torture or mutilate one another; they either fight, or quickly arrive at a situation of token deference.

societies, with their great military powers and their high degree of warfare. Patrimonial administration maintains moral boundaries among groups, but the great territorial extension of such states and the prevailing tone of military conflict brings a great many warrior-contenders into the contest. Domination, unstable as it is under such circumstances, is sought with the refinements that come with a literate mentality; a sharp (if unstable) order of internal stratification appears—indeed, the sharpest in all of history—and ferocious and humiliating extremes of violence are used to maintain it.

If we stop at this point and this level of abstraction, it appears that cruelty actually increases with evolutionary advance (Lenski, 1970: 138–139, 474–475). The trend is even stronger if the negative instances are brought in, the examples of societies which show relatively little cruelty and violence. Hunting-and-gathering societies (as far as we can tell) and simple horticultural societies often are relatively peaceful; only a minority are cannibalistic or otherwise warlike, and their violence is very sporadic, external, and unrefined with respect to deliberate cruelty. Compared to this, the height of ferociousness in world history is found among iron-age, agrarian societies, and indeed, among the highly advanced civilizations of this type: ancient Rome, European Christianity, Islam.

The explanation offered here, however, is not an evolutionary one, or even an inverse (or, as we will see, bell-shaped) evolutionary pattern. The variations in group structure that make up the principal explanatory factors are not distributed in a simple way across technological levels. Hence, it is possible to explore this hypothesis into more refined, horizontal comparisons.

The Altruism of the World Religions

One might suppose that the monotheistic or philosophical world religions, with their universal brotherhood and their explicit ethical concerns, would indicate an historical break away from explicit cruelty and towards altruism. Some of them, such as Christianity, have even been formulated as primarily religions of "love." But in historical fact, this is not the case. The world religions arose with the development of cosmopolitan states, "world empires" transcending the previously localized and self-contained kingdoms and their legitimating local gods. Moreover, the world religions have everywhere played a predominantly political role, especially in their early phases, providing the legitimation as well as the administrative apparatus for the large-scale state. In the case of Islam, religion provided the organizing vehicle for a military coalition. Thus, the world religions, far from indicating a break with violence, represent a new form in its organization. Moreover, that form is the most inegalitarian and efficiently stratified form in world history; the iron-age, agrarian societies in which the universalist churches arose supported some of the cruelest forms of stratification ever seen. The moralities of the world religions, generally speaking, contributed more to the extension of violent cruelty than to its mitigation.

In Islam, the church was identical to political organization. Perhaps this is the reason why Islam contains little in the way of personal standards of morality, apart from those laws and ritual obligations defining the status of the respectable and active member of the political community (Andrae, 1960: 73–79). Islam enjoins charity to widows and orphans, the giving of alms to the poor; but, as we shall see in the case of Christianity, this should not be construed as altruism in any general, empathic sense. The requirement is part of the emphasis on mutual insurance in the community of warriors; moreover, the alms are generally collected by the religious leaders, and hence provide part of their organizational resources. Aside from this alms-giving, Islam emphasized primarily ritual and political obligations, above all wholehearted commitment to the military expansion of Islam.

It should be noted that Christian propaganda has colored our image of the ferociousness of Islam. In fact, forcible conversion was never very widespread, above all, after the Moslem conquerors discovered the disadvantage of admitting all subjects into the tax-exempt fold of the faithful (McNeill, 1963: 465–71). There remains a pervasive level of ferocious violence within the Islamic world itself, directed towards upholding the existing deference relationships. As we shall see, none of this is beyond the ferociousness of ancient and medieval Christianity itself. The example of Islam does serve to dramatize the way in which a universalist religion provides little or no mitigation of ferocious violence. The most extreme cases of such violence—the tortures, mutilations, and peremptory punishments of the Ottomans and the Bedouins—may perhaps be explained by an additional element. That is, the core groups of the original Islamic expansion, and its most powerful later converts (in terms of military prowess) came from pastoral cultures: and these are the most male-dominated, violent, and warlike of any societies. The practice of clitoridectomy among the Bedouin, for example, is a ceremonial form of cruelty designed to enhance male control over female sexual property (Goods, 1963: 147, 211). The pre-universalist religions of such pastoralists are also centered around killing: the act of the sacrifice, which is actually a ceremonial preparation for a group feast. Indeed, it appears that the habitual life of herding, prodding, and killing animals fosters a similar attitude towards people. The introduction of a literate, philosophical, and universalist religion only expands the scope of the possible state that can be built around such a culture; internally and externally, it is sharply stratified and violent.[5]

Christianity, at least in the eyes of its modern interpreters, prides itself as being the religion of love. There is the Sermon on the Mount, the parable of the good Samaritan, the admonition to "turn the other cheek," the tradition of the nonviolent martyrs tortured and fed to the lions. Yet the historical record shows very little altruism outside of the sermons of Jesus, and a great deal of ferocious cruelty practiced by Christians, from the very earliest period up through the eighteenth century.

If one examines the social organization of the earliest band of Christians, it is apparent that universal benevolence played a very small part in its activities. The occasional admonitions of Jesus in favor of non-retribution and passive suffering are contradicted by other admonitions and acts of militancy. The advocacy of nonviolence appears purely tactical, a temporary expedient of the weak and outnumbered. When the force of the crowd favored it, the mood shifted to a violent expulsion of the money-changers from the temple, and later, to the destruction of idols and temples as well as to the enemies of Christ.

In addition to this negative altruism of nonviolence, there is a positive altruism in the form of charity. Some of this, however, was due to the organizational demands of the community upon the individual found in any movement: Tithes to the church (or in more extreme form, giving up all material property to it) are only a way of controlling such goods in centralized form. The only radical injunction of Christianity is that of charity towards strangers, including ethnic outsiders, illustrated by the good Samaritan story. But this didactic anecdote, apart from what effect it may have had in practice, bears a more sociological interpretation in terms of the lesson about group boundaries: it emphasized, in a fashion that was to be the primary organizational innovation of Christianity, that the moral community (and hence the church organization) could extend beyond the ethnic group. This form of altruism represents the effort to expand Church membership to a potentially universal basis.

---

[5] By contrast, as Weber noted, it is among city people, especially those in crafts and commerce who never come in contact with animals, that pacificist moralities have arise (Weber, 1958: 199–200).

Moreover, the particular form of altruism expressed in this story—caring for the sick—has a special significance in the organizing activities of early Christianity. The main proselytizing actions of Jesus and the apostles stressed not philosophical or moral doctrine, but the sense of miraculous powers immediately manifested.[6] Their paramount reality was the invocation of the Holy Spirit, especially as manifested in medical miracles—the curing of the sick, the reviving the dead, the casting out of demons; in addition, there were a number of miraculous escapes from prisons and tombs. Such activities might be interpreted in terms of a doctrine of love, insofar as the medical miracles alleviate suffering, and insofar as the intense emotional solidarity involved in generating the proper mood for faith-healing can be so characterized. But this love is a bond within the community extending to those who are about to be admitted into it; the faith healing must be understood as proselytizing, since the cured (and the amazed onlookers) were expected to join the community of the faithful. Within this community, and as long as no disputes arose over the internal control of it, altruism might hold; to its enemies, however, there remained no barrier to the utmost ferocity.

The persecution of the Christians at the hands of the Roman state illustrates the underlying violence of the situation. For Christianity was persecuted only (with a minor and local exception under Nero) when it had become a major political faction; the persecutions of Diocletian were part of a final struggle for dominance within the empire, and preceded by only 10 years the final ascension of the pro-Christian faction with Constantine in 313 (Chadwick, 1967: 116–124). The Christians in power acted exactly like their former persecutors. Indeed, existing forms of torture, slavery, and mutilation (e.g., eunuchry) were not abolished, but widely used by the Christian emperors.[7] Nor did Christian ferocity come only from the political officials among its sympathizers. From the beginning, there were violent conflicts within the Church over questions of heresy and leadership. The election of the Bishop of Rome in 366 was settled by the murder of several hundreds of one Christian faction by another;[8] struggles over the Bishoprics of

---

[6] See the Gospels of St. Matthew, St. Mark, St. Luke, St. John, and The Acts of the Apostles.

[7] A characteristic utterance of the Empress Theodora: "If you fail in the execution of my commands, I swear by Him who lives forever that your skin shall be flayed from your body." (Gibbon, 1963: 305).

[8] (Chadwick, 1967: 160–161). The origins of the doctrine of papal infallibility date from this incident; the individual who won the Bishopric of Rome in this fashion was so badly discredited personally that he strictly emphasized the sanctity of the office as separate from that of its occupant.

Constantinople and Alexandria were fought out by mobs hurling stones. When the Church felt its strength, its pagan opponents were subject to ferocious violence, as in the case of the philosopher Hypatia:

> in the holy season of Lent, Hypatia was torn from her chariot, stripped naked, dragged to the church, and inhumanly butchered by the hands of Peter the reader and a troop of savage and merciless fanatics; her flesh was scraped from her bones with sharp oystershells, and her quivering limbs were delivered to the flames [Gibbon, 1963: 256–257].

The ferocity of this attack, it should be noted, is ceremonial, combining elements of the tribal war-hunt with the refined torture and mutilation of the iron-age aristocracy defending its status.

Indeed, this was the main consequence of Christianity for social organization: It provided a basis for a universal state, with internal stratification based on a solidary elite. It provided for the first time in the Western world the mass mobilization of groups within the urban, cosmopolitan society of the Mediterranean; such groups were then brought directly into the struggle for political and social domination. If this universalism also contained some philosophical bases for altruism, in practice, this simply meant the potentially universal membership of the church-state; its main effects on the phenomenon of cruelty were not altruistic. It provided a means for mobilizing people for violence in a highly emotional form. Its universalism served only to allow the degree of empathy necessary to understand the depths of torture and humiliation that might be inflicted on one's opponents. Universal religion here extends human empathy in a form that heightens the psychological aspects of the struggle for dominance; ferociousness is heightened, not limited, by the availability of social categories of infidelism and heresy.

Medieval Christianity, with its judicial tortures, crusades, inquisitions, and witch burnings, is not an aberration from the main pattern, but is the pattern itself. Altruism, in its Christian form, is usually characteristic of the medieval church. But this altruism stayed within the mold already set. The papacy's occasional claims to benevolent rule over European society were simply the ideological side of its political claim for dominion (Southern, 1970: 36–41 and *passim*); even its prohibition on internal warfare (which itself was not so much observed as used as an occasion for the sale of indulgences), only saved military forces for the external enemies of an ambitious ruler. The positive acts of medieval Christian charity—visiting the sick, visiting prisons, burying the dead, caring for widows and orphans— continue to be both a form of mutual insurance for those safely within the orthodox community, and an organizing device (not the least, financial) for the church. One might add that this kind of charity is hardly the essence of humanitarian altruism. It does not represent a universal sympathy and a striving towards the spreading of individual happiness; it is rather a negative, organization-oriented altruism. It aims in part to alleviate extreme suffering, but not to remove it; indeed, here we find yet another version of the inner alliance first pointed out by Nietzsche: Christianity battening on suffering. The aim is to support the organization of the benevolent community: the sick, the poor, the lepers, are necessary sufferers in the scheme of things, wretched and blessed at the same time (Foucault, 1965: 17–18). Above all, alms are for the deserving poor, the repenting, obedient, subservient; acts of charity are ceremonial reaffirmations of domination and subordination, in which the extremes of suffering are preserved and affirmed as emblems of the social order that is being upheld.

In his comparative analysis of the world religions (Weber 1915, 1951: 20–29) points out that the Western religions, growing out of the literate civilizations of the Near East, have an especially military tone. The Near East is an area of many heartlands, and hence fosters a number of relatively unstable military states. Their early state gods are strong personalities, above all, gods of arbitrary power, war and domination. Monotheism appears there when the expansion of a few states calls into question the power of particularistic gods. But the monotheisms—Zoroastrianism of the Persians, Jahwehism of the Palestine kingdom, later Christianity, Mithraism, Islam—retain the militaristic, violent tone of their predecessors. By contrast, the religions of the Orient, in regions that either supported only a single heartland state without external rivals (China) or where geographical conditions made a prolonged state power difficult (India), were philosophical transformations of more primitive nature-cults. The ferocity of the West, in a world perspective, is rooted in its especially militaristic history, where the unstable resources for total military domination have enhanced a continual struggle, and supported a particularly ferocious use of violence.

The example of India lends weight to this analysis, and also amplifies the Durkheimian theme with which we began. For Indian society, although never approaching the ideal of nonviolence preached in the highest form of Brahminism and in many of the salvation cults, has nevertheless shown much less ferocious violence than the West. Orthodox Hinduism, in fact, makes a special place for the warrior, the Kshatriya caste; the famous Bhagavadgita's central concern is to justify a battle, even against kinsmen, as part of the ordained karma of that particular station. But this same device also encapsulated and limited the use of the violence, above all since the caste system maintained privileges through the mechanism of group inclusion and exclusion, establishing pervasive ritual barriers in every activity of life. The Kshatriya caste, although fighting within itself for political domination (over rather small kingdoms, at that) was not itself the bulwark of the caste system. Ferociousness is most institutionalized where ritual boundaries are structured within an autonomous state; India had the former without the latter. Hence, the relative lack of mutilation and exemplary punishment in India (at least in the classical period, before the Moslem conquest, and after the rise of the caste system by the end of the Mauyra period); even judicial torture, so widespread everywhere in the pre-industrial world, was not used in medieval India.[9]

Indian society has its own form of cruelty. The caste system can be described as a special form of the cruelty of callousness. The inferior position of women, also supported by the reincarnation doctrine, involves other forms of callousness, including the extreme form of the immolation of widows. Yet all of this is far from the ferocious violence characteristic of other iron-age societies. India, the negative case, supports both the Weberian and the Durkheimian theories. India, the land of the limited, weak state, has a religion emphasizing ritual barriers, not forcible subjugation; passivity and inner experience, not external domination. In terms of group boundaries, one may say that the caste system makes for psychologically impenetrable barriers, the degree of empathy necessary to motivate torture, mutilation, terrorist punishments does not exist; nor does stratification *within* a ceremonial community, which is the structure upheld by symbolic and ferocious uses of violence.

The position of Buddhism is more ambiguous. (de Bary, 1969; McNeill, 1963: 587–190; Oyama, 1965; Spiro, 1970; Suzuki, 1959) As a religion of mystical contemplation and freedom from the illusoriness of the material world, it promotes pacifism; as a religion of universal salvation, it promotes a certain form of altruism. But it is the altruism of mutual escape from misery, not mutual sympathy for individual happiness. Moreover, Buddhism has made the political alliances character-

---

[9] (Dumont, 1970; Kosambi, 1970: 133, 151, 157, 173, 197, and *passim*; Rudolph and Rudolph, 1967: 160–192). Borale (1968: 83–94) shows that the ancient laws of Manu prescribe mutilation as the punishment for various small offenses by Sudras against the dignity of the higher castes: Spitting on a Brahmin called for cutting off the lips, listening to the Vedas called for filling the ears with molten tin. These laws applied only to a portion of the populace, however, and were apparently not much put into practice.

istic of all great world religions, and thus has involved itself in particular forms of violence. In central Asia, above all Tibet (but also the nomadic coalitions such as those of the Mongols), Buddhism provided the literate civilization that made possible military organizations on a large scale; in these areas, it amalgamated with shamanistic religions (and especially the ferocious, death-oriented cults of pastoralists), to produce a rather ferocious military Buddhism. In Southeast Asia, on the other hand, Buddhism adapted itself to relatively pacifist, weak kingships of the advanced horticultural variety. In China, where Confucianism provided (after the end of the warring states period, from which our early quotation from Han Fei Tzu derives) a set of universalist principles for the educated civil servant class, Buddhism entered as an organizing device for rival political factions. Amalgamating with Taoism, its results included quietism, but also at particular times rebellious political movements legitimated by apocalyptic versions of Buddhism (especially Amitabha, the future Buddha). Accordingly, Chinese Buddhism underwent some of the same cycles of favor and official persecution experienced by Christianity in the Roman Empire. With these military ramifications, it is not surprising that Chinese Buddhism developed a more activist form (Ch'an Buddhism, whose emphasis on sudden illumination was compatible with manual work), and even created its distinctive martial art (Kempo, the predessor of karate and kung fu, originating in the Shao-lin-su monastery of the lower Yangtze around 500 A.D.). Literate civilization spread to Korea and Japan through the vehicle of Buddhism; in medieval Japan, Buddhism had become militarized to the extent that armed monasteries held the balance of power for several centuries. After the defeat of this extreme form of militarism, the influence of Buddhism on the military culture of Japan continued through the training of warriors in Zen Buddhist techniques of fighting.[10]

In the degree of ferocity, the history of violence in Japan bears some resemblance to India. The samurai ethic, based on an extreme form of military courage, was hedged round with an elaborate system of courtesies that reduced its ferociousness; to engage in violence was itself a mark of privileged status, never of humiliation. This extended even to the practice of permitting suicide rather than execution. The power of the aristocracy over other ranks of society, supported by con-

---

[10] Japanese Buddhism is noted for other extreme versions of secularization, including the practice of priestly marriage—in a religion in which celibacy was the *sine qua non*—and a distinctively nationalistic doctrine of salvation, Nichiren Buddhism.

stant ritual deference and built into the very structure in the terms of verbal address, seems to have provided the equivalent of the mutual caste isolation of India. Japanese society has been more violent than Indian; but the violence has been largely confined to a gentlemanly game within the aristocracy itself.

Chinese society after the Han dynasty lacked this military aristocratic emphasis; its cultural ideal, instead, has been the rule of an internally pacified empire by literate, cultivated administrators (Weber, 1915/1951). The macho ethic was lacking here; the military forces were concentrated on the borders, and the heartland of the civilization adhered to another ethic. That ethic, expressed most strongly in Confucianism, emphasized traditional loyalties and subordinations within the family and within the structures of government. The power of emperor, mandarin, family head, were indeed upheld by force—above all by beating (even to the point of death) with bamboo sticks. The mutilations and public ferocity of the warring states period seem to have been reduced; torture in judicial proceedings and punishments appear to have had less of the public ceremonial significance of more militarized and conflictful societies, and the Mandarins were given special exemption. Here again one may invoke the Durkheimian dimension: The stratification of Chinese society, built around the centralized state, encompassed and reinforced traditional psychological barriers among groups—in this case, especially kinship groups—that institutionalized ferocity even in the milder Confucian ethos.[11]

The Decline of Ferocious Violence

Modern society has seen an abrupt decline in ferocity. Torture, mutilation, exemplary punishment have disappeared as ideals; while these practices still occur, they do so privately and secretly—in the hidden interrogation rooms of police stations, in the personal interaction between guard and prisoner—rather than as the explicit, ceremonial enactments fundamental to the social order. Executions are now to be humane and relatively painless, and are carried out in private; their justification is generally held to be of a rational, educative, warning

---

[11] There are other aspects of violence in Chinese society that strike one today as unjust, especially the punishment of family members for the transgressions of a kinsman. But this is a general aspect of patrimonial social structure, and should not be confused with ferocity per se.

nature, not passionate vengeance.[12] Ferocity in war becomes atrocity, to be hidden, or even expiated, not gloried in. The heads of malefactors are no longer displayed on spikes but buried from view.

At what point does the transition come about? We have seen that it does not depend on the universal religions per se, least of all historical Christianity. The movement against ferocity, rather, is a secularizing movement, originating perhaps with Erasmus and the tolerant rationalists who opposed the fanaticism of the Reformation period. It gained ground with the antireligious *philosophes* of the French Enlightenment and their British utilitarian counterparts, and began to have a practical effect with the judicial reforms, the antislavery campaigns, and other benevolent movements of the nineteenth century.[13] It is true that a number of liberal (nonritualist, nontraditionalist) Christian reformers were involved in these movements; but in general, it indicates a break with the ritual boundaries of stratification upheld by traditional religion. This is clearest in the case of the most vehement enemies of religion, the socialists and the communist radicals, who perhaps for the first time extended altruism into a positive concern for universal human happiness, rather than merely a token concern for suffering as an ongoing part of an order of privilege and deference.

In terms of our theoretical principles, the explanation seems to be structural shift. Modern industrial society, for the first time, makes for a shift in patterns of interpersonal interaction that destroy the traditional cermonial barriers among groups. Above all, the fortified household, with its support for the moral absolutism of the family community and its internal authority structure, gives way to the community of small private household (Aries, 1962: 365–404; Stone, 1967: 96–134); urbanism, mass transportation, large-scale work and business organizations, mass education, all contribute towards the replacement of older ritual barriers with a new form of ritual comembership. The social conditions for the human community, in general, emerge for the

---

[12] A great deal of popular support for the death penalty, however, seems to come from advocates of a traditionalist group structure (and probably members of such pockets of traditional groups as exist in modern society); although they may argue in the language of deterrence, the tone bespeaks ritual revenge of a strictly Durkheimian sort. The rationalist opponents of the death penalty have failed to grasp this.

[13] The classic advocate of cruelty, the Marquis de Sade, emerges in the transitional period, and his writings capture all the major structural elements of the system then passing out of existence: the hermetically sealed status group of the aristocracy, the awesome terror of traditional Christianity, and the deliberate use of violence for psychological effect. De Sade shared enough of Enlightenment's clarity to express, far better than the *philosophes*, the nature of the society that was passing away.

first time. Along with this, differential resources remain in existence, and the struggle for power, wealth and prestige goes on. But a crucial earlier resource—freely available private violence—is no longer permissible because the monopolization of violence by the modern state and the ritual barriers that both allowed its use and motivated the retention of a specific deference structure have largely disappeared. With the passing of these conditions, the ceremonial ideal of ferocity has disappeared.

In its place, we have two conflicting tendencies. On the one hand, conditions favor universal movements, including those proclaiming extreme forms of altruism. At the same time, the large-scale and remote organizational forms of modern society do not eliminate the tools of violence and manipulation, but only depersonalize them. Turning from the evil of ferocity, modern social structure delivers us into the hands of another evil: callousness. And in the very mobilization of modern groups there emerges still another side of altruism: demands upon the individual in the form of asceticism.

II. CALLOUSNESS AND BUREAUCRATIZATION

Callousness is cruelty without passion: the kind of hardship or violence people may inflict on others without a special intent to hurt. The subject of the violence is simply an instrument or an obstacle, and his suffering is merely an incidental (usually ignored) feature of some other intention. In this sense, the structural conditions for callousness must be very different from those that produce ferocious violence. Torture, mutilation, and exemplary punishment all involve a certain type of empathy between perpetrator and victim; the victim's subjective life is the target, and his total personality is to be deformed. By comparison, callous violence represents a very restricted contact with the victim, and arises from structures that cut off the possibility of personal empathy.

Callousness is found in all societies throughout history, but it is especially characteristic of certain types. In a sense, the extreme mutual isolation of primitive tribes results in a form of callousness towards each other; but the amount of cruelty done is likely to be severely limited by the very sporadic nature of such external contacts. Where social relationships are organized on a regular basis along impersonal lines, however, callous cruelty is maximal. This, of course, is the theme of Marx, especially in terms of the callousness of the wage system in an impersonal market economy.

More generally, callous cruelty is especially characteristic of large-scale, bureaucratic organization—the violence of the modern army and state. Indeed, the structural organization of bureaucracy seems uniquely suited to the perpetration of callous violence. Bureaucracy is typically hierarchic, and hence, routinely enforces relationships of domination and submission. But both the means and the ends of bureaucratic action deal not with the individual person and his subjective feelings, but with segmented elements of individual lives. The fundamental principle of bureaucracy, indeed, is the separation of the individual from the position; instead of the charisma of the individual, there is the charisma of office; instead of personal power and personal domination, there is domination by reference to formalities and specialized functions.

Thus, even the application of violence is carried out segmentally; the bureaucrat does not invest his personality and his subjective status in the dominance relationship that results, and the identity and feelings of the victim are not a concern. Bureaucratic violence is the psychological opposite of the ceremonial ferocity of patrimonial society; however painful and terrifying the consequences, they are epiphenomenal to the more general policy being carried out.

The major atrocities of the twentieth century are of this sort. The Nazi extermination camps were the epitome of bureaucratic organization.[14] What we find so horrifying about them, above all, is their dramatization of the ultimate Kafka-esque possibilities we have always feared lurked in this organizational form. The very methodical, impersonal, and ritually unthreatening character of most stages of the Nazi extermination procedures are features that no doubt were most responsible for the relative lack of resistance and even the degree of active compliance among the Jewish victims. The secrecy of the camps and gas chambers, the nighttime round-ups—all of these stand in sharp contrast to the public, ritual nature of violence in patrimonial societies. For the Nazi participants, the well-known "Eichmann syndrome," the routinized following of orders, eliminated any personal sense of moral

---

[14] Of course the individual face-to-face relationships between guards and prisoners provided scope for personal sadism as well. Political and military torture do not disappear entirely in the modern world; the transition to bureaucratic organization is hardly uniform at all places and all levels. In this sense, we may use the instances in which it occurs as further variations against which to test the model of ferocity proposed above. For modern ferocity seems to occur in precisely those instances where the strong ritual barriers may still be found among stratified groups: above all, sadistic torture seems to occur across ethnic lines, both in prisons and in warfare, as in the pervasive atrocities of the French-Algerian war.

responsibility. And it is this, the turning up of the dark side of the bureaucracy that surrounds us, that makes the Nazis an emblem of the specifically modern horror, a horror that dwarfs the personalized cruelties of the Middle Ages.[15]

One prophetic element of the Nazi extermination camps was their use of technology, not only to enhance the bureaucratic efficiency of their callous violence, but to depersonalize and distance it from human contact. The development of high-altitude bombing in the Second World War represents the same sort of atrocity, perhaps extended to even more depersonalized limits. The atomic bombings of Japan are only the most dramatic (because both technically novel and highly publicized) of the atrocities of the fire-bombings of major cities in Japan, Germany, and Britain, with their heavy concentration of civilian casualties. The atrocities of the Vietnam War, again, stem above all from a long-distance bombing policy (Harvey, 1967). Not only were the more publicized incidents—the My Lai massacre and a few others— minor by comparison to the several million casualties of the indiscriminate bombing campaigns throughout South Vietnam, but they also were uncharacteristic of the fundamental nature of the atrocities.

Janowitz (1960) has argued that modern military organizations have become internally more civilian-like, above all in the air force, because of the emphasis on technological expertise rather than traditional regimentation. But on the external side, the capacity for callous destruction multiplies correspondingly. The traditional deference procedures between officers and men in the military lessen with the modern bureaucratization of their organization, and along with them goes some of the sadism that characterized internal rankings, and perhaps even the personal attitudes characteristic of soldiers towards the outside world. In its place, though, we find an increase in callousness when the men use instruments of unsurpased destructiveness. In guerilla warfare, as in Vietnam, where guerillas are not only mingled with the civilian population, but very often *are* the civilians, including the women and children, it is not surprising that the use of long-distance, bureaucratically administered weapons should produce appalling atrocities. The long chain of information reporting and the very impersonality of communications categories served to keep much of the human consequences from the awareness of not only the American public, but also of the soldiers themselves; but enough leaked through

---

[15] Arendt, 1963. Milgram (1963: 371–378) shows experimentally the degree of impersonal cruelty that benign middle class persons will inflict when given instructions in a bureaucratic setting.

to create the most extreme sense of schizophrenia between the low-key personal relationships within the modern military and their vicious consequences for its victims.

III. ASCETICISM AND ENFORCED COMMUNITY MEMBERSHIP

Ascetism, at its extreme, is a turning inwards of cruelty, directing it towards oneself. In its origins, asceticism was purely personal, a form of self-denial valued for its supposed key mystical experience. Insofar as asceticism became a part of social organization in religions like Buddhism, it was the social organization of voluntary drop-outs from ordinary social experience; hence, violence towards outsiders was shunned as simply one more ordinary social tie to be cut in the interest of entering the Void.

Asceticism becomes organized social cruelty when an ascetic religion becomes part of the ongoing, secular social structure. In this, Christianity is the prime example.[16] The ascetic ideal, the mark of holiness for the religious specialist, takes on wider significance when a church is organized, and its leaders become the exemplars of ordinary life. What Weber called "inner-worldly asceticism" (i.e., asceticism in the world) may be viewed not only as a motivating force for economic activities, but also as the transformation of self-denial, even positive self-cruelty, into a dominant social ideal. Such a status hierarchy in itself generally constitutes an increase in social cruelty by its effect on others through emulation. Moreover, when religion becomes an important administrative and ceremonial adjunct to the state, as well as the basis for community organization, then the influence of ascetic cruelty becomes coercive. Not only is the ascetic individual rewarded with high status (and certain opportunities for power and wealth), but asceticism also becomes a mark of membership in the community, and is enforced upon everyone by external authority.

The first level of cruelty in asceticism is the cruelty of deprivation, especially of those forms of happiness that are most private and individual. These include, above all, sexuality (especially in forms that

---

[16] The manifestations of such asceticism have varied during the history of Christianity, especially as the more patrimonial structure of medieval European society came to the fore. It was above all during periods when the purer Christian ideal has been emphasized (and along with it, the power of the church and its leaders) that asceticism has been most clearly enforced.

have not been ceremonially justified by the group); the focusing of attention on one's own body and on the private moods of one individual or two (or perhaps a small group), is the attitude most to be combatted by an ascetic mode of social organization. Hence the ban on vanity and display in clothes and decor—precisely because they are individualizing, and because they celebrate the particularism of the body.[17] Lighthearted, trivial, individualized games are banned for the same reason; games are acceptable only if they are made serious, contestlike, above all requiring the mobilization of the individual into the collective cause.[18] Alcohol and drugs, one the subject of battles for control by advocates of traditional community structures in the early twentieth century, the other the focus of a similar battle today, are above all privatizing agents, hence anathema to the ascetic representative of group controls and duties (Gusfield, 1963).

Asceticism may be extended to more symbolic manifestations of individualism. The labor camps and insane asylums of the Soviet Union are used to enforce political conformity, even along lines which do not involve real substantive disagreements with the program of socialism but only with the principle of individual discussion of policy matters. These punishments (although perhaps a more extreme example) are representative of the form that ascetic controls take everywhere. The punishment is regarded as a form of purgatory; the offender is not simply the inadvertent victim of callous violence, nor a low-status creature to be humiliated or mutilated. His identity as a deviant is not conceived of as permanent; the punishment, rather, is to change his soul, to strip him of individualist tendencies and to reintegrate him into the ascetic standards of the group.

We can now see the distinctive social organization underlying ascetic violence. It implies a ceremonially united community, and one that places the strongest possible emphasis on individual membership and commitment. It is, moreover, a community which ceremonially emphasizes the equality and equal participation of all members within it. Such an organization is characteristic of universal religions and univer-

---

[17] Compare the practice of head-shaving in monasteries, and the emphasis on short haircuts (e.g. crewcuts in America during the 1950s) in the military and in admiring civilian groups during periods of ascetic group mobilization: long hair and beads thus serve as emblems of individualist revolt. (Cf. Douglas, 1970 for an analysis of this point, and of the properties of group boundaries, generally consonant with the theory of violence advanced here.)

[18] Cf. the fanatic intensity of interest in school *team* sports in the more traditional Christian communities in America.

sal moral reform movements. It should be especially intense during those times when the group makes the greatest demands on its individual members, above all, in times of war or conflict with outside forces. It should reach a maximum during periods of struggle over the very nature of the group's boundaries, which are defined ideologically as periods of struggle against heresies. Thus, we find the height of ascetic atrocities—purgatorial actions—during the Reformation and Counter-Reformation in medieval Christianity (Thomas, 1971; Trevor-Roper, 1967: 90–192); comparable outbreaks of ascetic violence were characteristic of the Sunni–Shi'ite battles in Islam. There are also the milder, less violent upsurges of asceticism found when groups within a society fight to maintain or raise their social status, putting pressure on all individual members to maintain a united front. An example of this defensive sort of asceticism is found at the height of the antialcohol crusade in the U.S.; of the offensive sort, the "Victorian revolution" in sexual mores that accompanied the mobilization of modern women in their first effort to raise their social status (Collins, 1971b).

Ascetic cruelty remains important in the modern secular world because the issues of community membership and individual obligation to the group continue in the struggles of status groups, and political mobilization of any conflict groups in society—including both intellectual factions and larger social classes—is a continual phenomenon. We cannot escape the fact that most of the major humanitarian reform movements of the modern era, above all Marxism, but also to a lesser degree piecemeal reformisms, are especially prone to ascetic cruelty. Their very universalism and their intense mobilization makes it easy; wherever their gaze is turned outward toward their enemies, and not inward toward their own dangers, it becomes all the more likely.

CONCLUSION

In our contemporary society, ferocious cruelty is no longer structurally induced; it is no longer part of the dominant ceremonial order, although we still find individual cases. In this sense, modern society appears more humane. But at the same time, the dangers of callousness increase; and the technological efficiency of modern instruments of destruction makes its consequencess all the more appalling while it hides them from view. Between these opposing trends, ascetic cruelty has had its ups and down, cresting during periods of mobilized conflict.

There is no evolutionary trend towards kindness and happiness. Ferociousness once increased, then declined; callousness and asceticism now oppose each other as defenders and challengers of the status quo. And the institutionalized asceticism of a victorious revolutionary movement easily amalgamates with the callousness of an established bureaucratic regime.

The demons can be exorcised, but only by seeing them for what they are. Those who claim that the demons can be exorcised only by action in the world, not by theorizing about them, seem to be possessed by demons of their own, especially the demon of asceticism; one senses here the communal hostility of the ascetic to the individual luxury of intellectual contemplation. And here is the danger. Those who deny everything for the self deny it as well for others; our altruism, taken too exclusively, is an infinite regress, passing a bucket from hand to hand that never reaches the fire. When we act, we call out the demons to meet us. Be careful: They are ourselves.

III

Sociology of Education: The Cutting Edge

Class, Codes, and Control*

I

The sociology of education has good claim to be the leading edge of sociological research in recent years, just as community studies were in the 1930s, organizational and occupational studies in the 1940s and 1950s, and social mobility surveys in the 1960s. For these have been areas in which research has posed, and helped to answer, theoretical questions of wide significance for the discipline. For the sociology of education, this significance has been on both macro- and microlevels. Not only did the preceding period of intensive mobility studies show education to be the strongest single predictor of careers, but it can also be argued that education comes very close to being the center of the modern stratification system. By unraveling how educational stratification works, we may have the archetype for the other mechanisms of stratification. And on the microlevel, recent theoretical developments

* Originally published in *American Educational Research Journal*, 1978, 15 (Fall). Copyright 1978 American Educational Research Association.

that have agitated the neighboring disciplines of linguistics, philosophy, psychology, and literary theory find their empirical application in the sociology of education as the study of the cultural codes and practices by which stratification is produced and reproduced. Where both macro-and microapproaches to education are pursued together, then, it is not surprising that we find some of the leading sociological work of our times: in France, that of Pierre Bourdieu's group, and in Britain, that of Basil Bernstein.

The three volumes of *Class, Codes and Control* (1971–1975) present Bernstein's collected papers on education. They include research reports written by and with a series of collaborators, and theoretical commentaries by linguists and sociolinguists. There is a good deal of repetition, but the collection does give a historical overview of the development of Bernstein's ideas from the mid-1950s to the present. For Bernstein has grown constantly, expanding the theoretical relevance of his work to link up with other major lines of investigation. The end result stands as a massive empirical and theoretical contribution to the study of order and change in contemporary societies.

Bernstein begins micro, or rather, he begins by attempting to find the microbases of macrostructure. This was his now-famous analysis of social class differences in language use, deriving from tape recordings of children of different social classes and from interviews with their mothers. Bernstein's earliest version described the class difference as between the *formal* language of the middle class and the *public* language of the working class; later this became translated into the difference between *elaborated* and *restricted* linguistic codes. Middle-class language is described as more abstract, complex in construction, self-reflective, more prone to passive voice, and relatively context-free; working-class language as more concrete, particularistic, sociocentric, and confined to familiar persons and relationships and to the here and now. The former is flexible, capable of providing information across situations, while the latter is situationally specific and less able to communicate with persons unfamiliar with the local scene.

Bernstein and his colleagues produce a variety of measures of these differences. They show that the differences are not ones of ability, for they hold independently of I.Q.; it is not simply a matter of amount of vocabulary, nor amount of vocalization (indeed, working-class children, especially girls, may well be more verbal in certain contexts), but of the underlying structure by which language is used. Studies by Bernstein and by Hawkins, for example, show that middle-class children have more hesitation pauses within their speech. These pauses are not so much at the outset of utterances or clauses, where an entire statement is to be planned (and where working-class children tend to pause), but within clauses, where, according to the authors' interpretation, the middle-class child is considering a wider range of alternatives than the working-class child. These differences are apparent already at age 7, as well as in the midteens.

How are these class-based linguistic codes transmitted? Bernstein assumes they have their origins in the occupational situations of different social classes, but they appear so early that they must derive from parents' linguistic practices. Hence, samples of middle-class and working-class mothers were studied, with a variety of fascinating results. We find that mothers' linguistic styles are more closely followed by their daughters in the working class, less closely in the middle class. (No evidence on boys or on fathers was collected.) We find strong differences in children's conceptions of adults' sanctions for misbehavior: working-class children tend more to use blunt imperatives and threats, middle class to use positional appeals ("You're naughty boys") and abstract statements of obligation ("It's not nice." "You mustn't do this sort of thing."). This material has considerable significance for the microtranslation of macrosociological patterns, and I shall return to this point later.

So far, Bernstein's work is devoted to characterizing the linguistic codes children bring to school and how these derive from the class structure via their parents. The inference is that children will be differentially able to make their way in school, for these are dominated by the middle-class linguistic code. But Bernstein has presented no direct evidence on this point; and when he does get around to it, he takes a different tack than one might expect. For we get no direct microanalysis of linguistic behavior of teachers, of interaction in classrooms, or of the code structure of examinations.[1] What Bernstein does, rather, is to characterize schools more globally, as the macroaggregate of situations that make up its overall organizational character. Here again he uses the notion of alternative codes.

The basic choices in organizing a course of education, Bernstein proposes, are two: Subjects are to be kept apart in neatly bounded activities (collection code), or subjects are to be drawn together into a common time and place (integrated code). In different terminology, the former curriculum exemplifies *strong classification,* the latter *weak*

---

[1] Such microanalysis is now becoming available for the United States, as in Cicourel *et al.* (1974) and Mehan *et al.* (1976). It would be useful if this work could be brought more closely into contact with Bernstein's conceptual scheme.

classification. That is the first distinction; the second concerns not the content but the method of teaching, whether teachers have little or much control over what is taught, how it is taught, and at what pace (hence we have *strong* or *weak frames*).

The two distinctions cross-cut each other, so that school systems can be classified into various subtypes; and further subtypes may be added by combining these with further dimensions (whether education is specialized or nonspecialized, organized around courses or subjects, etc.).

The theoretical basis of these classifications, Bernstein says, comes from Durkheim. For codes are not merely structural bases for classifying organizational forms; they are varying modes of social solidarity, and—adding an aspect which Durkheim overlooked—they are stratified modes of solidarity, upholding various modes of domination. Hence Bernstein can call the school a "ritual order," simultaneously the basis of cultural reproduction and of class structure.[2] The Durkheimian model also suggests to Bernstein the place of education and stratification in a large theory of social change. Codes, he argues, are not microphenomena, but macro-, deriving from the division of labor, which is the basis of class subcodes and of the school system by which the structure is reproduced. But although the shift from mechanical to organic solidarity is the prototype for Bernstein's dimension of segmented, tribalistic solidarities within a collection code, versus reciprocally understandable, cosmopolitan solidarities within integrated code systems, Bernstein has shifted the historical referent. Whereas Durkheim found his distinction in the shift between tribal and agrarian societies on one side and industrial societies on the other, Bernstein sees his in the alleged shift from early to late industrialization. In other words, Bernstein finds the shift between two types of organic solidarity: a formalistic division of labor based on iron-clad specializations, characteristic of the object-centered consciousness of

---

[2] In these themes, Bernstein interacts with other important developments in anthropological and sociological theory. The distinction of collection and integrated codes he attributes to the anthropological theorist Mary Douglas in her analysis of *Purity and Danger* (1966) in tribal category systems. She in turn has acknowledged Bernstein's influence in her next major work, *Natural Symbols* (1970), where she adds a stratification dimension and comes out with a classification of class cultures rather like Bernstein's. At about the same time, Bernstein spent a year with Pierre Bourdieu's group in Paris, coming back with an additional emphasis on education as the basis of the reproduction of the entire system of stratification, while Bourdieu seems to have been influenced to incorporate into his scheme of cultural fields and symbolic capital some dimensions of cultural codes similar to Bernstein's.

early industrialization, and reflected in the collection code of the traditional school; and a flexible division of labor based on the integrated
overview of all specialities, characteristic of the person-oriented concerns of late industrial society, and reflected in recent movement
towards integrated codes (weaker classification and frames) in the
schools.

Bernstein's analysis of the macroorganization of education parallels the pattern of his microanalysis of class cultures. In each case, he
begins with the problem of describing the structure of stratification—
the difference between working-class and middle-class cultures on one
level, the organizational forms of domination on the other—and ends
by emphasizing the differences between old and new middle classes. It
is taken for granted that the schools are dominated by middle-class
culture; the working class simply lags passively behind, while structural changes are attributed to shifts, and perhaps conflicts, within the
middle class. Bernstein is wisely skeptical of claims of educational
reformers to produce greater opportunities for working-class children
by shifting to an integrated code in the organization of the curriculum.
The advantage, he suggests, is still to the middle-class children, but to
those within its newer, person-centered sector.

II

What are we to make of Bernstein's work? The effort to make visible the microrealities of class cultures, in my opinion, is extremely
valuable. This is one of the areas where the sophistication made possible by newer research methods, especially audio and (now video) tape
recordings of natural interaction, has great potential for replacing our
reified abstractions about the class system with an x-ray vision of the
way it is produced, in all its variations, within our very modes of interaction and cognition. And this is very useful for showing (rather
than merely inferring) how the school system, on a more macrolevel,
reproduces the career patterns of social stratification; in this sphere,
Bernstein helps us to understand empirically what Bourdieu refers to as
"cultural capital." More generally, independent of the educational
issue, microresearch such as that reported in these volumes has great
potential for showing how the forms of consciousness are produced
that objectify a social structure out of myriad individual interactions
and beliefs.

Yet I am not fully satisfied that Bernstein's formulations have captured the essential points on either micro- or macrolevels. The concept

of the school as a ritual order is an attractive one, but Bernstein does not analyze it in microdetail as it is actually enacted linguistically and emotionally. We get a structural analysis of the relations among microsituations rather than an analysis of the microsituations themselves. The sociolinguistic studies of children's talk form a strong core for his argument, but they are drawn from a relatively narrow base—most of them are recordings of discussions on middle-class types of topics and in middle-class settings, and hence do not fully represent the style of natural conversation, especially for the working-class children. Similarly, we cannot be confident of Bernstein's macrohistorical explanation that linguistic codes shift because of shifts in occupational structures, without studying just what linguistic behavior is like in various occupational settings and just what effects these linguistic behaviors have on people's ability to carry out jobs.

These are the same issues that underlay Bernstein's debate with William Labov, which Bernstein refers to rather sharply in his most recent writings. Labov produced the pioneering linguistic studies of working-class inner-city blacks, and demonstrated that their language is quite subtle, complex, and effective in its natural context, particularly if taken as a form of discourse or speech action in the large. By contrast, Labov argued, middle-class talk is pompous and verbose, and relatively ineffective at making its points and influencing social situations. Labov had taken Bernstein's work as an example of the opposite bias. Bernstein rather vehemently denies this; and indeed he usually can point to passages he has written, especially at the ends of his papers on class language differences, disclaiming any denigration of the working class and pointing out that working-class language "contains its own aesthetic, a simplicity and directness of expression, emotionally virile, pithy and powerful, and a metaphoric range of considerable force and appropriateness [Vol. 1: 54]." He states that the issue is not to eliminate this language, but to supplement it with the middle-class elaborated code. Moreover, Bernstein argues strongly against the cultural deprivation thesis (the title of one of his papers is "A Critique of the Concept of Compensatory Education"). Working-class children are not to be blamed for their failure in school; rather, the schools must recognize where they are culturally and relate to them on that basis.

Nevertheless, there is a real issue here. (a) On the microlevel, Bernstein does interpret (despite occasional disclaimers) working-class language as cognitively limited compared to the middle class, even in research contexts where the opposite interpretation might well be made. (b) Despite rejection of the cultural deficiency argument, Bernstein makes no move to recognize on the organizational level that the structure of schools themselves might be changed to fit working-class culture, or that the entire relationship of schools to society might be changed if one were sufficiently serious about overcoming stratification.

III

Turning first to the microlevel, in the main body of his papers, Bernstein repeatedly refers to the working-class style of talk as having "poor syntactic construction" and "rigid and limited use of adjectives and adverbs [Vol. 1: 42];" "descriptive concepts of a low order of causality [Vol. 1: 52]." It allows the child to use "savage and unfeeling terms quite freely, without a sense of guilt or shame . . . . Respectable figures or institutions may be caricatured, denigrated and slandered quite happily with joyous unconcern. . . . The rhymes and catch-phrases to do with eating, sex, death, and unpopular children are stark and revolting to an adult (Vol. 1: 73]." Later he tries to soften his terminology, but the point remains the same. This comes out most clearly in his treatment of the hesitation phenomenon. Middle-class children have many more pauses within their sentences (false starts, difficulty in choosing the proper words or sequences). But Bernstein avoids the straight-forward interpretation that middle-class children are clumsier speakers and claims instead that the evidence shows just the reverse—middle-class children have more cognitive alternatives at their disposal, and hence hesitation pauses are a sign of their strength. Yet surely this is not a sign of strength in language use per se; such speech comes across as choppier, harder to follow, and more confused. Surely it is less effective *communication*, and all the more so if one considers (as Labov did and Bernstein did not) that social speech is not merely words and ideas but an act of discourse, in which timing, rhythm, and the emphasis provided by emotional flow are crucial components. (Bernstein, in other words, attends only to the locutionary and ignores the illocutionary force of utterances.) Bernstein's evidence, in fact, supports Labov's point that middle class talk is more verbose, pretentious, less competent at getting to the point or at getting an idea across. Similarly, the finding that middle class talk uses the passive voice more often is hardly a sign of its strength; passive constructions are not only a way of avoiding clear causality and responsibility, but also the bane of good style.

The distinction is of no trivial significance. For Marxists arguing in a

Lukacsian vein have proposed that the consciousness of the dominant class is made of up reified abstractions, and hence is further from fundamental material realities than the consciousness of the working class. This is particularly true in regard to the means of domination; middle- and upper-class thought obfuscates the real bases of power with a veil of moralistic, nationalistic, or technocratic ideals, while working-class cynicism sees more clearly that money talks, that who you know is more important than what you know, and that power comes out of the barrel of a gun. Again, Bernstein's evidence shows in concrete detail just how this is done: working-class children and parents see authority (including their own) as based upon direct imperatives and material threats, while middle-class children and parents hide sanctions under appeals to reified positions or by attempts to arouse feelings of guilt. Similarly, Bernstein's evidence on middle-class talk—full of hesitation pauses, abstractions, passive constructions, and hemming and hawing over alternative ways to put a point—shows the veil of middle-class ideological obfuscation being drawn whenever middle-class children open their mouths.

Still, one cannot simply reverse the theme and argue that working-class talk and culture is clearly superior to middle-class talk and culture. Working-class thought may be more direct and aware of the crude actualities of life, but it is limited by the inability to formulate very complex and long-range relationships. The working class is more sophisticated than the middle class about what power is like on the microlevel, but less capable of understanding the large-scale alliances, the organizational structures and financial markets by which macro-domination is exercised.

There are at least two main dimensions of difference among class cultures.[3] There is the difference in horizontal relations *within* a social class. Here the conditions of working-class life, with a limited range of contacts, usually combined with high social density, produce very particularistic and context-bound world views; whereas the greater cosmopolitanism of middle-class life produces more abstract and flexible ideas and the capability of seeing alternatives and long-range consequences. This is the dimension Bernstein has captured. But there is another dimension, the vertical relations *between* classes. Here the working class is on the order-taking side, doing the material work that makes the world go on, and receiving relatively little return for it; while the white-collar class is on the order-giving side,[4] engaged in what

---

[3] For evidence, see Collins (1975 Chapter 2).

[4] I gloss over many complexities here, elaborated in Collins (1975 Chapter 2).

might be called the "political labor" of maintaining domination and bargaining over the disposition of the spoils. Hence the other dimension of difference among class cultures, between the cynical realism of the working class and the obfuscating idealizations of the middle class.

The question for educational reform, then, is more complex than Bernstein sees, although also more complex than his critics see. It is not simply a matter of bringing working-class children up to the middle-class capabilities of macrounderstanding (what old-style Marxists call "consciousness raising," although of course this might as well detach individuals from the working class as mobilize them as members of it). This needs, perhaps, to be done; but the opposite tack should also be pursued: Schools ought to try to build on the *strengths* of the working-class language and to teach these strengths *to middle-class* children as well.[5] That is, contrary to Bernstein's implication, teachers ought to be looking for ways to create more fluid speech among middle-class children, without endless balled-up hesitation pauses, passive constructions, and indecisive reflexivities. Emphasis ought to be placed not merely on verbal content abstracted from its use, nor on ritualistic verbosity and showing off, but on the rhythm of effective communication. With this, the schools might well help not only to clean up the conversational environment, but also to puncture some of the pretensions and verbal obfuscations upholding class domination.

This may not be easy. For we do not know much yet about what makes for elegant and effective social language use (as opposed to abstract and solipsistic speech making), and still less about how to teach it. On the favorable side, there is the whole trend of recent philosophical, literary, and linguistic studies of language use and form, which is achieving good theoretical results and may soon produce practical payoffs of this sort. One of the resources in this area is one to which many teachers have especially favorable access: the presence of natural working-class speech forms from which much might be learned. Even so, we will need not only the technique, but also the will to use it; and there are strong countervailing forces. For if conversation itself (as well as education) is a ritual order, we must recognize that

---

[5] For example, stereotyped utterances on the level of clauses do not necessarily mean cognitive inflexibility if they are combined into well-organized sequences on the level of sentences and topics. In fact, such phrase and clause stereotyping may well be a characteristic of highly effective discourse, as exemplified, say, in Homer or other epic literature. Thus middle-class hesitation pauses indicate an overriding concern for precision at the level of the smaller components of talk and an obliviousness to what this does to the larger organization of the utterance.

middle-class people have vested interests in maintaining verbose and inelegant forms of speech, precisely because these are marks of membership in the political sector of society. In this world of bureaucratic maneuvering over monopolies and sinecures, it may well be perversely effective, in the organizational sense, to have a language that is ineffective as solid, action-oriented communication. In the realm of a class society where little useful work is done, the filling of time with endlessly competing alternatives and abstract schemes may be an effective political weapon. In taking a stand against this, teachers would be committing themselves to the role of an embattled opposition.

IV

Turning next to the macro-, or structural level, we can trace a similar difficulty in Bernstein's argument. He claims that schools should take account of working-class children's special linguistic and cognitive problems in dealing with the middle-class culture. But his admonition does not go beyond a general moral tone of not condemning these children as inferior, and does not envision any structural changes that might be made. He never seriously entertains the possibility of changing the selective culture of the school to build on the strengths of working-class culture rather than middle-class culture. His main analysis in this direction, perceptive though it may be, is to point out that shifts toward the free school type of organization do not mesh with working-class culture but only with the culture of the new middle class. Further alternatives, for reasons mentioned above, do not come into his view.

Nor does Bernstein see the largest structural alternative: that if schools operate as inalterably class-biased selection devices, the opponents of stratification could move to break the link between schools and the occupational structure—by legal deschooling, decredentialing jobs, or otherwise bypassing schools and going directly to reforming control of the occupational structure. This line of analysis is not open to Bernstein because his concept of social causality is ultimately a closed system at the macrolevel. For he regards the cultural code as a fundamental macrocomponent of an integrated social system (somewhat in the fashion of Talcott Parsons or of Claude Lévi-Strauss). Individuals do not create codes but simply fit into them. The dominant code comes directly from the degree of division of labor in society, whether pre-, early, or late industrial; and this in turn produces both the dominating culture of the school system, and the distinction of dominant and subordinant cultural codes among the occupational classes. There is no room for reform at the individual or school level because the macrostructure for that time in history inexorably determines the system into which they must fit.

But this structural theory is not convincing, especially if one takes account of historical and contemporary differences among educational systems. Bernstein himself recognizes, in applying his scheme of strong and weak classification and framing of the curriculum, that British, American, and European schools are not organized alike (one could add Japanese, Russian, Chinese, and others). The differences do not simply correlate with an alleged scale of evolution from early to late industrialization. Moreover, there are other differences in structure—the sheer size, length, and demographic inclusiveness of the educational system, and the pervasiveness of educational credentials throughout the occupational structure—that are not captured in Bernstein's set of curricular differences and that predate any recent shift to late industrial conditions.[6] The existence of these variations implies that school systems are not simply responses to unvarying structural conditions on the most global level but are part of the different political and economic struggles of particular societies. Education credential markets are not all alike; and the struggles that go on in and around the schools themselves have had important effects in shaping the system of stratification.

We need not be as pessimistic as Bernstein is about the possibilities of reform, on either micro- or macro-levels, nor need we be as wedded to traditional middle-class conceptions of what culture is desirable and inevitable. This is not to say we can easily shift to a ready-made oppositional culture. As I have suggested, the means of learning from the linguistic strengths of working-class speech patterns (and in the United States perhaps especially from the strengths of the linguistically rich black cultural variant) have hardly been sought, much less found. But the possibilities are there, on both macro- and micro-levels. We do not yet know what will work on either level, but at least the taken-for-granted frames are beginning to crack, and a space is emerging in which we may discover some alternatives. And in this, Bernstein's work has made a pioneering contribution. If we can go beyond his argument, it is because he has produced a breakthrough of potentially grand proportions. If the sociology of education has become the cutting edge of advance in recent sociology, it is through work of this sort that the field promises even more in the future.

---

[6] For evidence, see Collins (1977).

Cultural Capitalism
and Symbolic Violence

With the writings of Pierre Bourdieu and his collaborators, one finds oneself unmistakably in the midst of the French intellectual ethos. Every page breathes a combination of logical paradox and metaphysical dramatics. It reminds us that France is the land of the all-purpose intellectual, where the gaps between politics and academics, literature and science are less apparent than anywhere else in the world. It does not make for easy reading. The style is formalistic and rhetorical, full of neat antimonies and pounding with the rhythms of philosophical doom. Sentences are often interminable, as Bourdieu self-consciously maneuvers for critical independence among structuralism, Marxism, phenemenology, and other strongholds of the French intellectual field. For all its elaborateness, though, it is the energies of intense passion that carry the argument along. Bourdieu is among the most empirically oriented of French intellectuals, but we must recognize that he is first of all an abstract theorist. We are required to grant him his premises, and the rest of the system will follow. The premises themselves are not proven, but declaimed like an actor opening a classic play. And what premises they are: "All *pedagogic action* is, objectively, symbolic violence insofar as it is the imposition of a cultural arbitrary by an arbitrary power [Bourdieu and Passeron, 1977:5]" thus opens Bourdieu and Passeron's *Reproduction*. It must surely be the most striking introduction ever to a book on the traditionally bland field of the sociology of education.

Bourdieu is more than a sociologist of education. Education is only a strategic site for his argument. His strength is his access to two different sorts of empirical materials. On the one hand he draws upon his antrhopological studies of rural Algerian tribal life (the Kabyle). On the other hand he and the members of the Paris institute which he directs, the Centre de Sociologie Européenne, have studied not only modern French education, but also all aspects of modern French culture, high and low. Museum going, amateur photography, home decor, the competitive field of the high fashion designers or the factional structure of intellectuals—these are the territories that they chart.

Bourdieu operates widely, then, across the realm of culture. His uniqueness is that he sees culture as an arena of stratification and conflict. Culture is itself an economy, and it is also related to the material economy of goods and services. Stratification in the cultural economy and in the material economy are reciprocally related, both as cause and effect. Again, culture is a realm of power struggle, related to the struggle over the means of violence that characterizes the realm of politics. This threefold theme shows that one of Bourdieu's intellectual roots is in Max Weber. His other roots are in the traditions of Marx and Durkheim. Bourdieu's eminence with the modern French intellectual field is very much a result of his capacity to make simultaneous use of all aspects of this grand inheritance.

Among Bourdieu's central concepts is *symbolic violence*. This is defined as "power which manages to impose meanings and to impose them as legitimate by concealing the power relations which are the basis of its force. [Bourdieu and Passeron, 1977:4]." Such power, the authors assert, is very widespread. It makes up the content of formal schooling, but also of childrearing, of public status display, or religion, and the communications media. Their legitimacy, as cultural meanings by which people define the world and each other's place in it, is based upon force. But this force is hidden, and necessarily so. The school teaches a culture authorized by the dominant class, but it must claim to be neutral in all class conflicts, for only by appearing to be neutral can it add any additional power to the dominant side. And one of Bourdieu's main contentions is that culture does have a relative autonomy, adding its own specific force to that of sheer physical and economic coercion. The culture of the school is an arbitrary selection from the universe of possibilities, but it must hide this arbitrariness; it cannot teach cultural relativism without undermining itself.

Bourdieu has a talent for shocking formulations. Nevertheless, he is following here an old and rather conservative sociological tradition. Bourdieu assumes Durkheim's analysis of education as a civic religion, in which moral and intellectual categories are imposed as ever-present representatives of the force of society. Behind this stands the entire Durkheimian tradition. This is easiest to see in Bourdieu's most theoretical work, *Outline of a Theory of Practice*, where he draws heavily upon his Algerian tribal materials. Here, he claims again, the society is based upon *misrecognition*. Durkheim had argued that society is held together by ritually created beliefs in its gods. In Bourdieu's sense, this involves a fundamental misrecognition, since society creates the gods, but must hide this fact from itself because only by believing in the gods as objective can the belief be effective. Marcel Mauss extended this thought to the exchange of gifts, the basis of the primitive economy. For although the giving, receiving, and reciprocating of gifts is strongly hedged with social obligation, one cannot carry out a gift exchange at all in the proper, and obligatory, spirit, unless one denies there is any obligation involved in it.

This is the line Lévi-Strauss took up in his *Elementary Structures of Kinship* (1949/1969), to derive the various structures of tribal society from the political and economic alliances produced by gift exchanges of women. Bourdieu criticizes Lévi-Strauss for failing to see the extent to which matrimonial exchange rules are "officializing strategies," ideologies imposed by the force of the dominant group and subject in practice to considerable maneuvering among the families struggling for advantageous alliances. Bourdieu carries the model of misrecognized exchanges still further, by showing that feuds and vendettas among the Kabyle are a kind of gift economy. Insults and murders must be avenged, in order to keep up a family's honor. At the same time, it is necessary for a strong family to give insults and start fights, for it is only by having enemies that one can show honor, and hence one must carefully choose with whom one will fight. One dishonors oneself, for example, by challenging, or accepting a challenge from, an opponent who is too weak to fight properly. Carrying out fights with proper enemies, then, brings honor to both sides, and constitutes another hidden gift exchange. Bourdieu goes so far as to refer to it as an economy of "throats" "lent" and "returned." It is an economy of honor, carried out under the guise of physical coercion. Here, Bourdieu even manages to show symbolic violence misrecognized as real violence.

For Bourdieu, this case is not an extreme one. "Every exchange," he says, "contains a more or less dissumulated challenge, and the logic of challenge and reposte is but the limit toward which every act of communication tends [Bourdieu, 1977: 14]." This is Mauss's theme again,

for every gift holds the prospect of dishonoring its recipient, or of ruin-
ing him or her in the effort to repay it; it is upon this logic that the
potlatch is played. And a theme of Lévi-Strauss as well: For the
regularities of tribal marriage patterns breed not only alliances, but
also hatreds and wars when expected exchanges are not satisfactorily
carried out. The borderlines from appeasement to alliance, and again
from alliance to rivalry, are thin ones. It is this logic that Bourdieu has
generalized.

The exchange of culture in this misrecognized form is the basis of
the *reproduction* of the entire society. In modern society, schooling
reproduces the distribution of *cultural capital* among social classes.
The content of the dominant schooling is the culture that corresponds
to the interests of the dominant classes. This constitutes cultural
capital, the chief instrument of transforming power relations into
legitimate authority. Each new generation passing through the school
system thus reproduces the structure of legitimation: Those who are
successful in the system acquire legitimate domination, while those
who are unsuccessful acquire a sense of the legitimacy and inevitability of their own subordination.

This constitutes a double reproduction, in that both the structural
relations among the classes are maintained, and particular families
that constitute social classes pass along their advantages from generation to generation. The principal means by which the latter occurs
Bourdieu calls the *habitus*. This means the internalization of an arbitrary cultural standard, at first in the family, later reinforced in the
school. The habitus grows over time, by feeding upon itself; consumption of a certain kind of culture, such as museum going, gradually
develops into a need for more of the same. Hence children from culturally advantaged or disadvantaged homes not only start in the world
with varying cultural dispositions and possessions, but increase their
distances from one another over time. Schooling, in this view, does not
so much increase symbolic capital as develop it into more refined
forms; as in learning one's native language, one begins practically and
customarily, later consciously and systematically. Once finished with
schooling, individuals carry a fund of culture which, if it is worth
enough on the existing cultural market, gives them entree to particular
occupations and social circles. This movement of individuals through a
system of cultural inculcation thus reconstitutes the structure of society.

In tribal societies, symbolic capital consists of honor, of kinship
ties, and of myths such as those which define the dominant and subordinate places of men and women in the order of things. This culture

hides stratification, by defocusing it, and by creating the authorized categories through which group members must talk and think about the world. Culture reproduces the entire structure of society, including its material economy. Here again we find the logic of misrecognition or symbolic violence. The tribal economy seems to eschew strict economic calculations, and seems instead to work on an ethos of alternating penuriousness and extravagance. Kabyle families bankrupt themselves to put on a display of lavish spending at a wedding, or go to any lengths to hold only onto traditional family lands. Yet all of these are moves in the economy of honor. Like the vendetta exchange, these extravagances and refusals of the markets are means of gaining family honor and hence social power. For the family with much prestige, and a wide network of persons obligated by its extravagances, can call upon many helpers when there are collective tasks to be done. Such a family will have many fighters when it engages in warfare, and many workers when there is agricultural work. Thus expenditures on the symbolic market bring their return in power and in renewed material wealth. The various realms flow into and reproduce one another.

This argument, Bourdieu believes, is completely general. Symbolic capital is always credit. In the tribal economy, it consists of obligations accumulated, which can be cashed in the form of a work force or fighters at the times when they are needed. Such symbolic capital circulates, like money, in a market. "Wealth, the ultimate basis of power, can exert power, and exert it durably, only in the form of symbolic capital [Bourdieu 1977: 195]." Wealth can only reproduce itself if it is turned into forms that generate social obligation, and hence the alliances and deferences that make up social power. The same is true in a modern capitalist society, where the forms of cultural domination shift but the principle remains the same. In either case, the cultural market acts as symbolic violence: "the gentle, invisible form of violence, which is never recognized as such, and is not so much undergone as chosen, the violence of credit, confidence, obligation, personal loyalty, hospitality, gifts, gratitude, piety [Bourdieu 1977: 192]." Such a circulation of cultural capital, in fact, is the most economical mode of domination.

Bourdieu's view of history consists of a typology of the two versions of society he has considered: rural Algeria and modern France. These correspond to two modes of domination. There are those that are constantly being made and remade in personal interactions, and those that are mediated by objective and impersonal media. The former consists of the rituals and vendettas of tribal society; the latter of the organizational forms that distribute titles, whether deeds of property or academic degrees. The difference between the two types of society is the "degree of objectification of the accumulated social capital [Bourdieu 1977: 184]." In the tribal society, power is continually negitiated by individuals on their own behalf. Hence such societies strike the modern observer as both more brutal and also more personal and humane than one's own. In the modern society, domination is based upon objective mechanisms—the competitive structures of the school system, the law courts and the money economy—and hence its products appear divorced from people and take on "the opacity and permanence of things [Bourdieu 1977: 184]."

The transition between the two types occurs when the culture is no longer the immediate possession of everyone who uses it, but becomes stored in writing. Then specialists begin to monopolize culture, and to develop it into esoteric forms of religion, art, and specialized knowledge. This primitive accumulation of cultural capital is Bourdieu's counterpart of the Marxian primitive accumulation; it marks the transition to class societies. A further stage in objectification of the system of domination occurs with the elaboration of the educational system. Whereas the personalized society of ritual exchanges is local and fragmented, the educational system unifies all cultural capitals into a single market. Formal educational degrees are to cultural exchanges what money is to the material economy; both create a single standard of value, and guarantee free and universal circulation. Bourdieu goes so far as to say that an educational system producing certified degrees guarantees the convertability of cultural capital into money at a determinate and objectively fixed rate.

Once a society organized in this way comes into being, Bourdieu sees only very limited possibilities for its transformation. Class society continuously and objectively reproduces itself. Political and economic upheavals cannot change its structure (indeed, Bourdieu pays almost no attention to these), precisely because of the relative autonomy of the cultural system. Neither the Marxists nor the Third World nationalists promise any relief, for these are movements formulated by intellectual rebels, who themselves have come to the top by virtue of their superior cultural capital. A Soviet type of society, dominated by the possessors of ideological capital, would constitute no formal change in the structure of domination. Nor can the school system itself be successfully destratified. Every movement in this direction has been a failure. Citing French data in the post-World War II period, Bourdieu shows that the same rank ordering of educational attainment by social class background has held across a large expansion of school attendance. Nor can reforms within the style and content of schooling change the situation.

For the initiative in such reforms is always taken by highly cultivated intellectuals, themselves the products of the system that they are changing. The shift to the free school environment, to soft discipline and an emphasis on autonomy and creativity, remains nevertheless a mode of cultural inculcation and social selection, and one that most favors the children of avant-garde families. The newest, freest culture only adds another level of sophistication to an accumulation of cultural capital. There is no way to escape from the circle: The person who deliberates upon culture is already cultivated.

Bourdieu's system is completely closed. It is totally cynical, totally pessimistic. We are eternally doomed to stratification, and to misrecognition of our bonds. We cannot get outside our own skins; we can only change places inside an iron circle. Bourdieu does not seem perturbed by his own pessimism. Like most modern French intellectuals, pessimism comes naturally to him, and he seems to delight in revealing yet another twist of the chains that enslave us. And why shouldn't he? He is, after all, an intellectual at the apex of the system he describes. If by his own showing, he cannot escape the pyramiding of cultural capital that enables him to produce his ultracritique, he at least reaps the status of being culturally stratified above everyone else. What may be pessimism for the political actor appears to the intellectual competitor in a different light.

Nevertheless, one is entitled to doubt whether the world is really as closed as Bourdieu's system is. His theory, in a number of crucial aspects, is asserted, not demonstrated. Bourdieu et al. do not present career data on the connection of education to occupation, but claim in very general terms that the possession of educational certificates reproduces the class structure. This is true, to a point. Yet it is doubtful, even in France, that education accounts for as much as half of the variance in occupational attainment, and it probably accounts for a good deal less of the distribution of property. Bourdieu ignores the direct forms of economic and organizational struggle that take place, through the world of politics, finance, productive markets, and the manuevers of unions and professional groups. The more abstract claim that system reproduction takes place via education gives an overly closed and overly static view of stratification.

The main data that Bourdieu and Passeron present deal with the determinants of educational attainment itself. Yet even here, their actual evidence tends to undercut their more sweeping abstractions. Bourdieu and Passeron analyze educational outcomes as the result of two factors. One is the distance between the cultural *habitus* or linguistic capital that each student derives from her or his family, and the degree of mastery of scholarly language which is required at a particular school level. It is this factor that accounts for the diminishing proportion of working-class children the farther one proceeds in schooling. But there is a second factor visible in the data: the degree of selectiveness within each social class at each school level. Thus the small numbers of working-class and provincial children who do survive to the higher levels of culture education perform relatively better in grades than the average of their middle- and upper-class and metropolitan compatriots, because they are more highly selected. But selected for what? For ability, for motivation? Bourdieu and Passeron do not pause to dwell on the point. But obviously they have introduced another resource into the general struggle for domination—or it would be obvious if they did not glide past to a different and more abstract point. For here they become structuralist, asserting that the school necessarily has a relative autonomy within the general system. Indeed, it is because it does not simply reproduce the distribution of cultural capital among families that the school is able to fulfill "its ideological function of legitimation [Bourdieu and Passeron, 1977:102]." Thus what at first sight appears to be an empirical weakness in the reproduction argument is made into a support for it.

Yet surely this is a slight of hand. In effect, Bourdieu *et al.* present a theory that cannot be falsified, no matter which way the empirical evidence turns out. Moreover, the argument smacks heavily of functionalist teleology and even anthropomorphic reification. Even though Bourdieu and Passeron attack functionalists and structuralists for describing unreal systems without human agency, they proceed to speak of how "educational systems are nowadays resorting the 'soft approach' to eliminate the classes most distant from school culture (1977:209]," and in other ways personify the system itself as a goal-seeking actor. This rhetoric is not incidental. There is no escape from Bourdieu's system of stratification, no matter what historical changes occur, because "every transformation of the educational system takes place in accordance with a logic in which the structure and function proper to the system continue to be expressed [Bourdieu and Passeron, 1977: 95]." This, on the basis of evidence comparing the educational attainment rankings among social classes in 1961–1962 and 1965–1966.

The weakness is precisely that Bourdieu operates with virtually no historical perspective. His rather evolutionist model of history is really a comparison between two static pictures—rural Algeria and urban France—interpreted in the old Comtean–Durkheimian fashion as universal stages of development. This lack of historical analysis, and also of contemporary comparisons among different educational systems, makes it seem as if there is an inevitable growth and readjustment of a smoothly operating system of domination. Yet industrial societies vary widely in the size and structures of their educational systems; and the long-term historical record shows that they can not only expand but also contract, and not only reproduce the stratification system but also transform it and even at times undermine it (Collins, 1977, and in the chapter, "Crises and Declines in Credential Systems," in this volume). Bourdieu asserts that educational content corresponds to the interests of the dominant classes, but history casts doubt on this as a universal rule. Educational movements, from the ancient Greek sophists through the medieval churchmen, the post-Reformation Jesuits, the American educational entrepreneurs, and others, have often represented their own interests; they have tended to create social classes as much as they have been created by them.

In constructing an overly closed system, Bourdieu and his colleagues tend to hide the real struggles of organizational interest groups that make up both the content of past history and the key to our own times. French metaphysical pessimism, in the guise of the logic of the system, fails to show either the full number of self-interested factions, or the long-term instability of systems of domination. Despite the rhetoric of violence and capital, Bourdieu's model is not a Marxian theory in any classical sense, nor really a conflict theory. It is an abstract picture of invariable domination, without the possibility of contradiction or revolution. In the world of real history, however, the facts that stand out as crucial are just such contradictions and struggles. It is these that determine to what extent education will indeed dominate the stratification system, and in what way.

The strength of Bourdieu's system is his effort to create a truly general economics. At a distance, his analyses of cultural capitalism and symbolic violence look like a Marxism of the superstructure. More precisely, he claims that the distinction between the economic and noneconomic spheres must be abolished. Conventional economics is but "a particular case of a *general science of the economy of practices*, capable of treating all practices, including those purporting to be disinterested or gratuitous, and hence noneconomic, as economic practices directed towards the maximizing of material or symbolic profit [Bourdieu, 1977: 183]." Thus far, the claim works better as a metaphor and as a guide for further reflection than as a closed system. For Bourdieu's economics still lacks precisely what Marx's uniquely supplies, a dynamism for historical change, and a mechanism for internal struggle and revolution. Bourdieu has correctly transposed the issue of economic systems to the level where cultural actions mesh with material ones. It remains to turn his metaphor into a full-fledged explanatory theory, capable of explaining the variations and the crises by which history comes about.

Schooling in Capitalist America*

Recent decades have seen an unprecedented growth in the intellectual popularity of Marxism. From a low point in the 1950s of reaction against Staliniem and disillusionment with predictions of economic collapse, Marxism has moved step by step toward reestablishing its full intellectual claims. At first the counterattack moved cautiously, jettisoning economic and empirical propositions in favor of the neo-Hegelian philosophical abstraction of the Frankfurt School in Germany, and the left-wing existentialism and humanism of Sartre and Garaudy in France. More recently, Marxism has begun to edge toward bolder empirical claims. In the process, the long-standing Marxist dilemma of doctrine versus realism has reemerged to prominence. Clearly, an empirically viable Marxism must be a revised version, but the ideological dangers of revisionism are already visible in the static, even nonrevolutionary, tones of French structuralism. Some of the freest efforts to develop a genuinely critical yet empirically realistic Marxism have

---

* Originally published in *Harvard Educational Review*, 1976, 46 (May).

come in the United States and Canada. Here, even with the recent popularity of philosophical versions of Marxism, the intellectual tone has long been heavily empiricist.

It is here that the major efforts to salvage a genuinely economic Marxism have taken place, above all through the efforts of Paul Sweezey and Paul Baran: here, through the midwifery of Sweezey's *Monthly Review,* that André Gunder Frank's new approach to the development of underdevelopment was begun, extended recently on a world-historical scale by Immanuel Wallerstein; here that a host of empirical researchers have begun to document a number of specific causal principles from the Marxist tradition.

Samuel Bowles and Herbert Gintis stand squarely in the North American Marxist tradition, in an empirical branch that has become the hot center for critical research. In this age of massive tertiary-sector employment, the classical Marxist emphasis on the position of workers in the industrial sector of the economy has given way to an examination of education as a key structure for reproducing and legitimating social and economic inequality. Bowles and Gintis, building upon an indigenous American revolution that has broken down the conventional liberal wisdom regarding the functions of formal education, have arrived at a position that not only completes the European analysis but also carries it to a new level.

Schooling in Capitalist America (1976) begins by presenting the massive accumulation of evidence demonstrating that, despite liberal hopes, education does not serve as a panacea for social inequalities. In the United States the near-universalization of education through the college level has had no effect on the degree of inequality in wealth or the extent of social mobility; educational achievement and educational opportunities have remained highly heritable. The liberal position, then, must be abandoned in either of two directions. Bowles and Gintis reject the conservative alternative—that genetic differences in ability are behind the failure of equalization—and present evidence that social class exerts an overwhelming influence on educational opportunities and achievement, even with I.Q. held constant.

The roots of inequality, Bowles and Gintis hold, are not in the educational system at all but in the capitalist economy; tinkering with the former can have no effect without a massive restructuring of the latter. To bolster their argument that education does not serve as the basis of meritocracy allegedly demanded by modern technology, they present several kinds of evidence.

First, they examine the growth of the modern division of labor and argue that hierarchy and specialization were created above all as control devices to fragment and to some extent co-opt potential working-class opposition to capitalist controls. In this light, technology reinforces job hierarchization and specialization not by its nature, but because capitalist interests frustrate the development of more democratic uses of technology.

Second, turning to contemporary quantitative evidence, Bowles and Gintis show that the association between education and career success for individuals does not stem from cognitive skills that education may develop. When achievement-test scores are held constant, they note, the relationship between education and economic success remains virtually unattenuated. The same is found when I.Q. is held constant. Education's contribution to individual careers must be found elsewhere.

What education *does* accomplish for the economic system, Bowles and Gintis declare, is to reproduce the structure of authority relations in the workplace from one generation to the next. Drawing heavily upon Melvin Kohn's (1969) work, they show that the experience of authority in different types of work creates distinctive class cultures, which in turn affect parents' values in rearing their children. Drawing upon their own group's research, they show that personality factors—above all diligence and submissiveness to authority—are highly associated with school grades and that these factors account for the association between school and economic success. The schools, in short, socialize a compliant labor force for the capitalist economy. Those students who are most completely socialized gain the most from their education in terms of careers.

Bowles and Gintis then turn to an historical overview of three major crisis periods in the development of education in the United States. Their theme is summarized in what they call a correspondence principle: The social relations of work are reflected in the social relations of the school, thus providing an advance socialization of potential workers into the type of compliance expected of them in the labor market. But Bowles and Gintis recognize that the different components of the social structure may get out of phase; hence, there are crisis periods in which education is reformed to catch up with changes in the economy.

Thus, the initial rise of the factory system in the United States in the early nineteenth century led to the movement for mass public education in the 1840s and 1850s. Bowles and Gintis illustrate this with a sketch of Horace Mann's career and with reference to studies like those of Michael Katz on labor control and conflict in the early compulsory-schooling movement. The rise of organized labor and of huge, monopolistic corporations in the late nineteenth century brought about the second major period of reform, the progressive education movement of 1900–1920. Here Bowles and Gintis show the upper- and upper-middle-class domination of this movement, sketch the development of vocational education as an effort to break the power of union apprenticeship programs, and describe the development of I.Q. and other standardized tests. The third crisis period, they suggest, began in the 1960s and continues to the present. Now we have advanced, affluent capitalism, responding to the labor-force incorporation of rural blacks and women, and the loss of autonomy of independent professionals. These circumstances have caused the ferment of campus protest and two types of response: on many campuses, a shift to more subtle controls appropriate for students who will become highly bureaucratized white-collar laborers, and an abandoning of the liberal ideal of universal education in favor of explicit hierarchization and fragmentation of advanced schooling.

Finally, Bowles and Gintis take on various current proposals for educational reform. Somewhat surprisingly, they reject as a *policy* position Jencks's argument that equalizing education cannot lead to economic equality. Instead, they maintain that equal education will engender revolutionary aspirations by reducing cultural fragmentation among different groups of workers and exposing the incongruities between a liberated education and the world of work. The free-school movement, though, bears the brunt of their critique. Bowles and Gintis find in it little more than romantic, backward-looking individualism and argue that school discipline is necessary in any type of society, above all a socialist one. They attack Illich's deschooling even more ardently, both as a political impossibility (because education is so obviously important for careers, as well as legally compulsory) and as a potential source of social chaos.

In short, Bowles and Glintis hold to a consistently Marxist, socialist line, from their insistence on the fundamental causal primacy of the capitalist economy, to the Althusserian analysis of the educational reproduction of the social relations of work, to their concluding attack upon anarchist individualism. Their contribution is in carrying out the analysis—indeed, for the first time—thoroughly, empirically, and without reliance upon philosophical abstractions or rote dogma. Moreover, this *analysis,* as far as it goes, strikes me as true. The primary role of education is not to provide technical work skills but to socialize compliant personalities, and this role accounts for most of the relationship between schooling and economic success, and for the interest of the dominant classes in fostering education in America.

But Bowles and Glintis's evidence, compelling as it is, can support yet another—and, I would contend, sociologically more sophisticated—interpretation. In addition, their neglect of several dimensions of evidence convinces me that we must go beyond them. That is to say, their argument lacks a serious comparative dimension: It does not satisfactorily account for inflation of educational credentials in the United States over the last century, and it does not quite explain struggles for power and wealth within organizations and among social classes and ethnic groups.

Bowles and Glintis's analysis is devoted almost exclusively to the United States. This is not a weakness per se; evidence like that of Bourdieu (1973) for France and Bernstein for England simply reinforces their arguments on the role of education in reproducing the class structure and on the inefficiency of education as a tool for educational reform. Comparisons are revealing, though, for the causal explanation of the use of educational stratification systems. Not all industrial societies or even all capitalist industrial societies have the same type of educational structure. The massive, continually expanding, and comparatively undifferentiated systems of the United States and U.S.S.R., for example, contrast with the small, elitist, and explicitly class-segregated systems of England and Germany. The United States is not a typical capitalist society; the building of the industrial economy in this country gave rise to a series of educational reforms that have few counterparts elsewhere. This suggests that the pressures for building an educational system are not necessarily those of labor-force control; such control might be produced in other ways, and, as the parallel between the United States and the U.S.S.R. suggests, these pressures might actually be of a somewhat different nature.

My own hypothesis is that the solidarity of alien ethnic or cultural groups is the biggest threat to dominant groups. Massive educational systems, then, are control devices favored in conflictful multiethnic societies, like the United States and the U.S.S.R., and relatively ignored in culturally more homogeneous societies like England, Germany, and China. From the early Massachusetts reforms to control the Irish threat, on through the Eastern European immigration crisis of the early twentieth century, and the black–white struggles of the last decade, the evidence Bowles and Gintis present on education in the United States certainly supports this interpretation.

My argument does not substitute a cultural conflict theory for an economic one, but it does put the two on more of an analytic par. It argues for a recognition that *cultural means* (the solidarity of cultural groups, whether based on prior class, ethnic, or sex lines) may be used to achieve *economic ends* (the various rewards in power and material returns of positions); and for a realization that groups in economic conflict can line up in a number of ways, of which the bifurcation between capitalists and workers is only one. The stakes may be the same in all battles in modern society, but the choice of weapons, such as educational systems, through which dominance can be perfected is determined by the nature of the lineups.

A second major point follows from this one. Bowles and Gintis do not see educational reform as very important in promoting the socialist revolution, although perhaps a little inconsistently (or opportunistically), they favor a continuation of efforts to universalize education in some disciplined form. But if my critique is moving in the right direction, one might infer that this route to economic equality could be more counterproductive than the deschooling they reject. Bowles and Gintis see schooling, as presently constituted, as simply providing socialization in compliance with the demands of the capitalists. But the role of culture in the class struggle, I would contend, is at least two-sided. For dominant classes claim education *for themselves* even more than they impose it upon others. Organizational studies of a nonquantitative sort little cited by Bowles and Gintis depict an incessant informal maneuvering among cliques, in which the easy personal relations of cultural peers play a crucial role (e.g., Crozier, 1964; Dalton, 1969). Education is important for elites, and even for privileged specialists in midlevel positions, because it gives them the solidarity of an esoteric in-group culture, which pays off rather nicely in struggles for organizational privilege and income.

The stratification of educational subcultures, then, is not merely a control device imposed from above. It is probably even more often the result of efforts of particular groups to elaborate ethnic or other subcultures into spheres of monopolization—such as those of school teachers, intellectuals, and media professionals—and to elaborate technological jargons and procedures into independent organizational fiefs. Education has had a direct economic payoff for many groups in the middle through higher occupational ranges, less because individuals in those groups successfully meet the demands of their capitalist masters than because education has enabled them to carve out professional and technical monopolies over lucrative services and vulnerable organizational sectors.

In this view, the inflationary expansion of education in the United States over the last century reflects not only the successive control demands of elites in a capitalist economy, but also, even more importantly, the struggles of the working and middle classes for cultural weapons. These struggles have paid off relatively well, at least for the upper-middle sector. Not least among the beneficiaries of educational inflation have been school teachers and administrators themselves. An active inflationary educational market has favored the professional upper-middle class even more than it has favored the capitalist upper class.

Here, I think, is where the Marxist tradition falls short. The need of capitalism for control is only one of two major sources of inequality; the organizational weapons of the members of the propertyless upper-middle class in a bureaucratic, and especially a multicultural, industrial society make them a second major force. The lower classes come out on the short end relative to both.

There is some evidence (Pilcher, 1975) that all major recent historical changes, as well as current differences among nations, in degrees of inequality are due to changes in the relative shares of *upper,* and *upper-middle* classes, not to redistribution from either of these to the middle or the bottom. Liberal and even radical reforms have usually been argued in the name of the masses, but have primarily benefited the upper-middle-class professionals who have advocated and administered them.

We have, then, not one, but two revolutions to concern ourselves with. Educational credentialism, an offshoot of the inflationary tendencies of educational expansion, has been the main contributor to upper-middle-class privilege. To push for a further extension of universal education, as Bowles and Gintis suggest, coud provide yet another opportunity for upper-middle-class self-serving and idealistic self-delusion. But in posing the socialist critique and alternative as clearly and sharply as they do, Bowles and Gintis have elaborated a major part of the problem of education and equality. Any real solution will have to take account of their work.

Crises and Declines in Credential Systems

In recent times, education has become widely recognized as a main basis of economic stratification, and hence a popular policy for producing social justice has been to expand public access to education. This policy has been a failure. Sociologists have assembled a great deal of evidence that the pattern of social-class advantages in education and occupational attainment has not been changed by the expansion of education in most twentieth-century societies. These findings, however, have tempted sociologists to think of the relation between education and stratification as structurally static. It may be true that the relative mobility chances for individuals are not changed as the school system becomes very large and credential requirements pervade the labor force. But in the long run, it is not true that education simply reproduces the social structure. For the record of history shows that educational systems have gone through quite long-term cycles of expansion, crisis, and contraction. Education has been a major part of the dynamics of politics and economics. Far from playing a static role, it has been a key both in the struggle for new forms of stratification and in the crises that bring about their decline.

If we are undergoing a long-term credential inflation today—in the

U.S., in Europe, in Japan—the best way to understand the future may be to look at the cycles of educational growth and decline in the past. I have found a number of such cases: medieval Christendom as a whole from about A.D. 1050–1450, England 1500–1800, Spain 1500–1800, France 1500–1800, Germany 1350–1800, the North American colonies–early United States 1700–1880. I believe there is a basic model, with a number of variants. To illustrate the main process, I will concentrate on the case of the rise and fall of the medieval universities, which is simultaneously the case of the rise and fall of the papacy, and of the medieval economy. This gives us the purest form of the general model; brief comparisons with other cases show that it may reveal a structure of considerable generality.

CULTURAL PRODUCTION AND POLITICAL MOBILIZATION

The main dynamic, I suggest, is in the largest sense political. Schools produce a standardized culture, Bernstein's "elaborated code," which is essential for creating any large-scale and permanent organizations. Historically, such bureaucracies or quasi-bureaucracies first emerge in what I would call the political sector. I mean here politics in the very largest sense, in that any adminstrative organization is political: It is a network of domination and control, and the locus of continuous struggles to expand or evade that control.[1] The political sector has included both state and church, for religious organization was closely connected to, or even an alternative form of, political power under the nineteenth century in most places. The medieval church was a compulsory organization of the community, with discipline and doctrines upheld by military force, owning considerable property, and competing for political supremacy throughout Europe. Such organization was made possible by the administrative skills and the sense of organizational indentity produced by education. In quantitative terms, the more investment in cultural production, the more political organization can be constructed. Schools, then, are politically mobilizing in the widest sense; they enable people to form long-term structural ties and hence to wield power over others.[2]

---

[1] A fuller exposition of this perspective, including the concepts of productive labor, political labor, and the sinecure sector, is given in Collins (1979, Chapter 3).

[2] This means the capacity for organizational politics in any type of setting; by the twentieth century, this becomes important in the private sector of the economy as well (Cf. Meyer, 1977).

Political organization, however, can be turned to many ends. When schooling is successfully linked to the organization of the state, educated persons can use the state to enforce credentialed monopolies over particular occupations. This happens first of all in the specialties most intimately connected with political and religious administration, namely law and theology. Medicine, as a lucrative source of income, has also been quickly monopolized; and as education grows in importance, the practice of teaching is also monopolized by holders of licenses based on formal accreditation.

The interaction between cultural production and political organization tends to be dynamic and unstable for several reasons. Political organization may provide a framework fostering economic growth, which makes it possible to invest in further cultural production and political organization. But political organization is not inherently unified organization; increased political mobilization can mean not only successful domination but also increased conflict, both in outright warfare and in administrative manuevering. Increased political mobilization can lead to the fragmentation of states as well as to their growth, and to revolutions as well as stability. Which of these occurs depends partly on the sheer quantitative relations among cultural and economic production and political investments, and partly on exogeneous political (usually military) factors.

Moreover, cultural production is inherently difficult for an elite to control. Culture is a resource and a form of prestige that is easily detachable, in principle, from family ties; hence it is especially appealing to ambitious members of the population below the ranks of hereditary upper classes. Since the nonprivileged are a large reservoir of the population at any time, the prestige of a formalized culture is likely to mobilize more people than can readily translate this investment into elite occupational positions. Overproduction crises are endemic to culture-producing institutions, especially since culture is intrinsically difficult to monopolize; the effort to do so only tends to make the monopolistic sector seem artificial and formalistic. This encourages intellectuals and cultural consumers alike to desert the formal schools for less controlled means of cultural production, creating an explosion of counter-culture versus formal culture, and increasing cultural competition still further. The resulting overproduction not only affects the organization of schooling, but also tends to spill over into political consequences, challenging or dispersing political power.

Ultimately, both cultural overproduction and political conflict put strains on the basic material economy, making both culture and politics more expensive. The schools, the political sector, and the material economy itself may eventually be diminished by these strains.

The long-term dynamics of credential crises go through four phases.

In the first phase, there are new opportunities for the growth of political organizations. Schools develop to provide personnel for this expanding market. As schools and state–religious organizations become large, both become increasingly formalized. Political authorities license schools; schools develop internal credential sequences; the major professions are monopolized by degree requirements enforced by the state.

In the second phase, cultural production begins to outstrip political consumption of educated personnel. This is especially likely to happen if the economy is expanding and also if rival political–religious organizations are the sites of cultural investment. In the latter case, different jurisdictions tend to promote schools on their own, further increasing cultural overproduction. A vicious cycle is set in motion: cultural production increases political mobilization and hence political conflict and the dispersion of political power; this in turn fuels the competitive expansion of cultural production. The failure rate of educational institutions goes up. Moreover, increased conflict in the political sector tends to make politics both more more expensive for the economy as a whole, and also reduces the chances of people attaining lucrative sinecures. Education becomes more expensive at the same time that its payoffs decline.

In the third phase, cultural production reaches a peak. Positions in church and state and in the major professions available to formal credential holders are filled up. This happens all the more readily to the extent that some of these positions go to noncredential holders, such as members of the hereditary upper classes or those relying entirely on personal connections—at all times, a non-negligible fraction. Formal degree requirements are escalated to their peak; cultural inflation reaches a limit beyond which the cost of producing the currency itself will not allow it to go. Cheaper or nonformalized means of acquiring culture spring up: rival schools with shorter courses or no formal (state-sanctioned) certificates, on-job or apprenticeship training, a direct market for culture in the form of popular preachers, books, or other mass media. The previous expansion of the formal schools themselves helped promote these alternate forms of cultural production; formally educated persons unable to find traditional positions spill over into the new media and challenge the older currency.

This phase is also likely to coincide with the exhaustion of the dominant state–church organization due to strains on its finances, legitimacy, and military power. For the long-term expansion of cultural production fosters accelerating political mobilization; in the up phase, states and churches become increasingly confident and increasingly aggressive militarily and politically. Both military expenditures and the number of political sinecures—positions living off the production economy but not contributing to it—increase. This puts a strain on the economy, increases prices generally, and may even trigger an economic downturn. Moreover, political mobilization is likely to occur simultaneously in rival states or rival political sectors within a given society—and this is all the more likely the more widespread the cultural mobilization, especially through the popular media, which tend to easily cross national and institutional boundaries. Hence extensive external war or internal revolt are especially likely at this point.

The final phase, if a crisis goes all the way through to the end, is a sharp downturn in the cultural sector, especially in formal credential-granting schooling. Educated unemployment, and possibly the political decline of the state or church that had supported the traditional schools, generates a widespread disillusionment with traditional credentials. Loss of control over training in the elite professions tends to follow from these same conditions, especially as the link between traditional schooling and state power is broken, and the state no longer enforces old licensing privileges. School enrollments fall, weak institutions disappear or turn into cheap degree peddlers, further destroying the prestige of credentials. With this decline in the cultural economy, political mobilization may well eventually lessen; whatever form of crisis the state underwent—military or revolutionary—is likely to resolve itself into a lower level of organization, and probably lessened economic production or growth.

THE MEDIEVAL UNIVERSITY CRISIS

This pattern is most clearly illustrated in the rise and fall of medieval Europe. The great European universities date back to the A.D. 1100s or even earlier. The ealiest organizations developed informally and by local initiative; by the early 1200s, the first universities had codified their internal regulations and acquired external legal charters from the pope or the emperor. The 1200s was the great era of the universities. The earlier foundations at Bologna, Salerno, Paris, Montpellier, and Oxford were joined by vigorous new foundations at Padua, Naples, Toulouse, Orleans, Cambridge, Valladolid, and Salamanca, and by a number of smaller universities primarily in Italy and Spain.

This is the period of the expansion of the Papacy as the first large scale administration of this territory. Monastic and cathedral schools, and then universities, sprang up to provide it with personnel. From about 1050 to 1250 or 1300, all components of medieval society expanded. The cultural sector flourished, with the growth of schools and new monastic orders; universities became independent of the cathedrals, developed their own formal structures and internal ranks, and acquired monopolistic licensing over all the major professions. In the political sector, the church grew in wealth and political influence and was able to make a claim for theocratic rule within Europe, and to launch military crusades against its external enemies. Secular states also began to consolidate their powers vis-à-vis the feudal aristocracy by the use of educated administrators and centrally paid armies. Economic production expanded within this framework.

The height of student enrollments at the universities was in the 1200s.[3] Paris in the period 1280–1300 had some 6000–7000 students (and approximately another 2000 students in preliminary Latin studies attached to the university); the number began falling in the 1300s and fell below 3000 by 1450. Thus in 1284, masters of arts degrees were conferred on 400 students, but only 80 M.A.s were given in 1447. Toulouse may have had 2000 students at its height; this fell to 1380 students and teachers in 1387 and below 1000 in the 1400s. Avignon, founded in 1303, had about 1000 students in 1394, virtually all in law; by 1441, there were some 200 law students, and the university was "almost empty" in 1478. Orleans in 1394 had some 800–1000 students, almost all in law; these numbers fell off drastically in the following century. Other French universities, at their height, never had more than a few hundred students, and these institutions tended to disappear entirely as the crisis advanced.

In England, Oxford may have had a maximum of 3000 students in the 1200s; there were an estimated 1500 in 1315 and fewer than 1000 in 1438. By 1500–1510, the yearly average was 124. Cambridge was at first somewhat smaller than Oxford; both were approximately equal in size in the 1500s.

In Italy, Bologna rivaled Paris's size in the early 1200s but fell behind thereafter. Padua in the 1540s, the leading university in Italy, perhaps in all of Europe, had somewhat under 1500 students, and this was in a period of educational revival. Enrollment at other medieval universities in Italy numbered in the hundreds, never in the thousands, and many of these collapsed for lack of students.

---

[3] The following enrollment data are from Rashdall, (1936:Vol. II, 149, 171, 178–181; Vol. III, 324–328); Stone (1974:91); Simon 1966:245).

The German-speaking states had no universities before the mid-1300s. Here, the decline was milder and seemed to come somewhat later. Prague, founded in 1347, had some 1500 students until the early 1400s, when it fell off drastically. Vienna, Leipzig, and Cologne succeeded to the leadership, attracting around 1000 students at various times in the 1400s, although their yearly averages were much lower (Leipzig averaged 504 students from its foundation in 1409 until 1540; Cologne averaged 388 from its foundation in 1388 until 1540). The other German universities were smaller, varying from 80 to 400 students (including the lower grammar students), hitting their peaks around 1450–1480 and declining thereafter.

A similar picture emerges if we consider the financial soundness and failure rate of institutions. Table 1 shows the number of major and minor universities in existence, and the new foundations and failures, for the 1100s through the 1500s. Universities were founded throughout this perid, and at an accelerating rate. The failure rate also went up steadily, reaching a level three or four times as high in the 1400s as in the 1100s. In the 1500s, the failure rate dropped sharply—the beginning of a new educational upturn, whose downswings we will notice below. Moreover, the failure rate for the 1200s is artificially weighted by several stillborn foundations of the 1290s (the two failures listed for France); most of the 1200s is a time of untroubled growth. Again we find it is in the 1300s, 1400s, and early 1500s that the system is in crisis.

To be sure, the total number of universities increases steadily, and especially during this crisis period. But the expansion was primarily in the ranks of the minor universities, those enrolling a few hundred students at best and often barely clinging to the margin of respectability. Some went past the margin: The University of Orange in France was legally suppressed in 1485 for selling degrees in absentia; the University of Bordeaux hung on in the 1500s by selling bogus absentee degrees, as did Ferrara in Italy. Nonuniversity schools also horned in on this underground market; the chancellor of the cathedral school at Geneva sold illegal degrees in the years before 1365 (Rashdall, 1936: Vol. II, 54, 185, 201).

The crisis was worse in some places than in others. A high failure rate began early in Italy, reaching an overwhelming 80% in the 1300s and 1400s; in France, a high failure rate came only in the 1400s (78%). In some parts of Europe, the crisis did not occur. The many states of the German Empire did not begin to acquire universities until the latter half of the 1300s; they then went into a large and sustained expansion of three centuries, producing virtually all of the new major universities in Europe as well as a host of minor ones with considerable staying

Table 1

University Foundations and Failures, 1000–1600 A.D.[a]

	Total	Italy	France	Britain	German Empire, Scandinavia, Low Countries	Iberia
1000s						
	F = 1	F = 1				
	f = 0					
	T = 1M					
1100s						
	F = 6	F = 3	F = 2	F = 1		
	f = 17%	f = 1				
	T = 5M	T = 2M	T = 2M	T = 1M		
	1m	1m				
1200s						
	F = 19	F = 8	F = 5	F = 1		F = 5
	f = 37%	f = 3	f = 2			f = 2
	T = 12M	T = 4M	T = 4M	T = 2M		T = 2M
	6m	4m	1m			1m
1300s						
	F = 34	F = 15	F = 5	F = 1	F = 10	F = 3
	f = 47%	f = 12	f = 1	f = 1	f = 2	
	T = 18M	T = 4M	T = 5M	T = 2M	T = 6M	T = 2M
	14m	7m	4m		2m	3m
1400s						
	F = 41	F = 5	F = 9	F = 3	F = 15	F = 9
	f[b] = 48%	f = 4	f = 7		f = 4	f = 5
	T = 22M	T = 5M	T = 5M	T = 2M	T = 8M	T = 2M
	34m	7m	6m	3m	11m	7m
1500s						
	F = 54	F = 5	F = 4	F = 2	F = 18	F = 25
	f = 31%	f = 2	f = 1		f = 2	f = 12
	T = 23M	T = 4M	T = 4M	T = 3M	T = 9M	T = 3M
	70m	11m	9m	4m	26m	20m
Totals 1000–1600						
	F = 155	F = 37	F = 25	F = 8	F = 43	F = 42
	f = 39%	f = 60%	f = 44%	f = 13%	f = 19%	f = 45%

SOURCES: Rashdall, 1936; Shepherd, 1964: No. 100; *The Cambridge Modern History Atlas* 1912, Map 9; Kagan (in Stone, 1974:355–405).

[a] F = foundations; f = failures; T = total in existence at end of century; M = major universities; m = minor universities.

[b] Includes "paper universities" given legal charters, but which did not actually come into existence. Rashdall (1936, Vol. II:325–331) lists 10 of these, mostly in the 1300s, and notes that his list is probably very incomplete" for the 1400s. Hence this failure rate is probably 10–15% too low.

power. Similarly, Scotland had no universities of its own in the High Middle Ages, but founded three in the 1400s and another in the 1500s, the last of which (Edinburgh) became prosperous and internationally famous. England, on the other hand, remained institutionally stable from early in the 1200s with only two major (Oxford and Cambridge) and no minor universities. There were no British failures during the entire period, except for an abortive colonial venture at Dublin in 1312. The institutions were secure although, as we have seen, their numbers of students fell precipitously.

Not only were universities generally in crisis throughout much of Europe during the later Middle Ages, but the social prestige of their education also declined, as did the occupational value of their degrees. The defining characteristic of a university, as it emerged in the High Middle Ages, was that it offered training in one or more of the higher faculties: civil law, canon (church) law, theology, and medicine. The university degree thus conveyed the legal right, and the legal monopoly, to practice these professions; the significance of the granting of papal (and sometimes imperial) charters beginning in the early 1200s was that it made such monopolies legitimate throughout Christendom. Universities were not the only type of school of the time; schools attached to cathedrals (and especially earlier, to monasteries) taught a course in Latin grammar and argument, from the latter part of which emerged the discipline of philosophy. Such schools, then, existed in every cathedral town (i.e., every church administrative center), only some of them acquired a substantial body of teachers and students, organized themselves along guide lines, and acquired the license to teach the higher professional subjects as well, thus becoming universities.

When this happened, not only were the legal, medical, and higher clerical professions licensed, but teaching also acquired a new form of professional licensing and monopoly. Thus the degree of master of arts, given upon completion of the lower Latin grammar course, not only entitled one to study in the higher faculties for a professional degree; it also licensed one to teach in the lower faculty. For this level of studies, the significance of the legal recognition of one's school as a university meant that one held the *jus ubique docendi*—the right to teach these subjects anywhere. The university degree thus gave a universal license to teach, backed up by the pope or the emperor, which was superior to any local monopolies established by teachers at particular cathedral chapters. Such rights over the licensing of school teachers, including at parish or private schools within the hinterlands of a cathedral town, were jealously guarded by cathedral authorities, who usually acted to exact fees or to restrict teaching even at the lowest levels in their own favor. Hence, the establishment of university rights meant that local teaching monopolies were superseded by members of an international guild (Ariés, 1962:114–152, 287–296; Knowles, 1964:153–176; Powicke, 1971:149–197; Simon, 1966: 19–32).

In this way, the universities held legal rights over the practice of the learned professions. Such licenses operated with varying success, for other corporate organizations and social groups within medieval society also pressed their claims. In this era of monopolistic guilds, university-licensed teachers confronted the legal claims of cathedral chapters as well as competition from the guilds of scriveners (professional copyists and writing masters) and mathematicians. The secular and canon lawyers battled the hereditary aristocracy, and sometimes secularly trained bourgeois laymen, over control of administrative positions in municipalities and governments. Medical doctors had competition from guilds of pharmacists and barber-surgeons (especially since these latter were more likely to hold some technical competence instead of fanciful medical theories). Theologians competed with high-ranking aristocrats over lucrative offices as bishops and archbishops, abbots, and cardinals.

On the whole, the university degree holders appear to have done increasingly well up through the early 1300s. A number of them advanced to the papacy and to high ranks within various royal governments; an educated papal bureaucracy reformed the church on centralized lines of authority and tried to bring secular rulers under its sway. Every major pope from 1159 to 1303 was a university-trained lawyer. Many popes were former university professors; from 1271 to 1287, every pope had previously been a master at the University of Paris (Southern, 1970: 34–44, 91–133).

In the 1300s and 1400s, however, a reversal set in. The Catholic Church, locked in struggle with the German emperor and with various secular princes and undergoing a series of internal schisms, began to lose its international character. The papacy and the papal curia became patronage positions for the French monarchy or for wealthy Italian families. The University theologians began to side with various secular powers, and theology degrees lost their preferentiality in high ecclesiastical appointments. The papacy itself turned away from university education even for its own priests after the Council of Trent (1543–1563). Canon law began to decline as a favored university faculty in many places. Civil law held its own for awhile but also suffered defeats. In England in the 1400s, it became customary to acquire one's legal training by an apprenticeship at the Inns of Court in London, and

the legal faculties disappeared at Oxford and Cambridge. In France as
well, it became customary to study law by home study or by apprenticeship; although the legal faculties enjoyed a last gasp in the educational revival of the late 1500s, by 1650 the university degree in law
was a mere formality, to be settled in a day by a payment of money
(Ariès, 1962:201). In medicine too, the university faculties decayed and
generally disappeared; in England, the Royal College of Physicians was
founded in London in 1518, breaking the Oxbridge monopoly, and in
1553 the Medical Licensing Act gave nonclergy the right to practice
medicine (Carr-Saunders and Wilson, 1933:66–75).

Throughout the old medieval strongholds of the university, above
all in England and France, the higher faculties disappeared. The
universities were transformed almost entirely into collections of colleges teaching younger students, the equivalents of the medieval
cathedral schools of grammar which had not achieved university
status. Such colleges did not even hold a monopoly on education at
their own level; especially in the succeeding period (after 1550), they
were to be joined by a large number of nonuniversity colleges, of an
equivalent level of instruction. The only difference between the two
types was that some of them continued to offer the final degree of M.A.
to those few students who completed the entire course. But this degree
itself had lost certification value, for teaching was no longer very much
influenced by the possession of such degrees. The cathedral chapters,
the secular guilds, the new religious order of Jesuits, and the new
humanist intellectuals became successful rivals for teaching careers.

The most radical challenge to the medieval university culture
came from the humanist—the specialist in the literary styles and
manuscripts of ancient Greece and Rome. Beginning in the late 1300s
and reaching a peak in the early 1500s—in other words, throughout the
period of accelerating decay of the universities—the humanists attacked the university curriculum as barbarous and pedantic. They
satirized the life of professors and students and held up instead an
ideal of poetic grace and humane values which they attributed to the
ancient classics. The humanists worked in favor of new cultural institutions: Many humanists made their living as editors and publishers in
the new printing industry that emerged after 1450; others attempted to
found new forms of school, on the same level as but in opposition to the
university colleges of grammar; others attached themselves to wealthy
aristocrats, clergy, or merchants in the capacity of librarians, entertainers, and discussion leaders in the adult education structures called
academies. Their efforts were often to move education out of the formalized schools and into the leisure routine of adult life. Thus the

humanists acted, at least initially, to break down the occupational credentialling forms of education. Humanist culture nevertheless could also make occupational claims; the writers of the "pure" Latin style of Cicero claimed diplomatic and official positions in the chanceries and courts of Italy as early as 1375 (Ward *et al.* 1907 Vol. I, 544–548). Humanism constituted the counter-culture which seems to emerge in oppositon to the dominant, credentialled culture whenever it goes into crisis.

It is likely that the decline of the medieval universities made education more exclusively the province of the wealthier social classes. The universities of the 1100s and 1200s drew from a wide range of social backgrounds; many of the eminent men of the time who rose through the universities came from modest beginnings. Education in the 1300s and 1400s became progressively more expensive. One result was that an increasing proportion of students were monks, supported by their orders instead of by their own resources, and the monks themselves (especially their privileged, educated sector) tended to come from the higher social classes (Simon, 1964:32–39; Southern, 1970: 296–298). The old channels of educational opportunity were closing up.

The transition point of the medieval cycle was in the 1200s and early 1300s. Cultural production expanded beyond the demands of the papacy. Secular states developed strong organization and tended to gain control over local church organization. Rival cities and kings, especially in Italy and France, established universities to provide loyal personnel. Heresies began to break out, supported by contending political factions. State and religious administration alike grew larger, putting an increasing burden on the productive economy.

The magnitude of the educational boom was quite astounding for these rather small societies with their crude agrarian economies. Oxford at its height in the 1200s had some 1500–3000 students, and together with Cambridge must have totaled 2000–4000; and these *absolute* numbers are never matched by Oxbridge together until after 1900, nor by all of the universities of England, including the newer ones, until the 1870s (Green, 1969:133). If we can draw a parallel between Stone's (1974: 91) calculation of ratios of the age 17 population and the total enrollment and population figures for Elizabethan England, it is likely that medieval England, with a population of about 2 million, had at least *four times as high* a proportion of its youthful population at the universities as it did during the Elizabethan boom around 1600. In other words, some 5% of the young male population of England must have attended a university at the peak period of the

1200s—a substantial figure even by twentieth-century standards (the U.S. did not reach this figure until 1910, England until after 1960). Moreover, I have used the more conservative total of medieval students (2000) in this calculation; if the 4000 total was ever reached, the ratio could have been twice as high! Similar conditions probably existed in the 1200s in France and Italy as well. It is no wonder, then, that the medieval economy would eventually fail to support this level of mobilization. Within the universities themselves educational credential requirements for elite degrees tended to lengthen under this competition. In the 1300s, a total of 20 years' study was required for the doctorate in theology, which provided access to high-level positions within the church.[4] This lengthening made the degrees even more expensive.

In the 1300s and 1400s, the system went into crisis. Cultural investments supported numerous political jurisdictions, which now fought over control of the church. In the late 1300s, the Papacy itself was split among rival organizations. States now had the resources to extract enough wealth from the material economy to field sizeable mercenary armies, and enough cultural legitimacy to make aggressive claims both internally and externally. These states tended to fight each other to mutual financial exhaustion; the Papacy, reduced to being one territorial prince among others, underwent the same financial problems, which it attempted to offset by the sale of certificates of spiritual pardon (indulgences), thereby debasing its own spiritual currency.[5] The numbers of universities continued to increase, fueled by rival jurisdictions, with a resulting competition among themselves that ruined many of their enrollments and the general prestige of university degrees.

Finally, cultural, political, and material sectors were all in crisis. The Reformation of the early 1500s brought an end to the Papacy as a political institution and stripped the church of most of its property. The medieval university system was reduced to a shadow of its former self. Rival forms of cultural production had triumphed even earlier. In place of formalized credentials produced by licensed schools, religious and secular culture alike were most widely distributed by independent media, especially by a mass market first for hand-copied books, and then for printing (Southern, 1970:349–350). (The hand-copying market

---

[4] In 1215 at Paris, 6 years were required for the M.A., 8 more for the doctorate in theology. In the 1300s, the theology course was lengthened to some 13 or 14 years beyond the M.A. (Knowles, 1964:172–175, 224–225).

[5] Southern (1970:133–169) and passim on the economic crisis of the church generally. See also M. M. Postan (1966:Vol. I, 688–700); North and Thomas (1973:33–90); Nef (1952:3–41); Southern (1970:349–350).

prepared the way for the printing market; both were parts of the same sector of counter-culture production.) Inexpensive, do-it-yourself religious practices stressing personal piety and inward experience replaced the religious rituals of expensive priestly specialists. Although these processes culminated with the Reformation, they were actually spread out over the preceding two centuries. The last phase of the crisis was a long one, during which the cultural economy expanded beyond the bounds of its credentialled, high-cost forms, destroying its claims to elite prestige at the same time that it provided the political mobilization that destroyed the hopes of leading political institutions for hegemony. During the height of this struggle, the material economy, under strong pressures from a nonproductive and even destructive political sector, underwent a sizable contraction. The long downturn of the cultural cycle brought political and economic downturn with it.

EDUCATIONAL EXPANSION AND CRISIS IN EARLY MODERN EUROPE

After expanding for some 200 years, the medieval university system went into a period of crisis of at least equal length. Then the cycle began again, but this time on a national basis. The pan-European society of medieval Christendom broke apart as the result of its cultural and political crisis; separate European nations built up on the basis of a new series of educational revolutions in the century between 1550 and 1650. Then came another series of crises, this time along distinctive national lines—in England, Spain, France, Germany—and lasting until the different educational revivals of the 1800s. The North American colonies and the subsequent United States also underwent this cyclical development, although considerably out of phase with the European societies: American education expanded throughout the 1700s, went into crisis in the 1800s, and then began a new cycle around 1880. The characteristics of educational crisis in these cases are summarized in Table 2.[6]

Every case does not show all the symptoms of crisis, but there

---

[6] Sources: Rashdall (1936); Stone (1974); Simon (1966); Knowles (1964); Arès (1962); Weinberg (1967:28–34); Kagan (in Stone, 1974:355–405); Elliot, (1970:310–317); McClelland (1974:146–173); Bruford (1935); Brunschwig (1947); Paulsen (1906); Schnabel, (1959, Vol. I); Schelsky, (1963); Rosenberg (1958); Collins (1979, Chapters 5 and 6); Lipset and Riesman (1975); *Quinquennial Catalogue of the Officers and Graduates of Harvard University, 1636–1910* (1910).

seems to be a general pattern. I suggest that some of the symptoms are mitigated by other factors, and some societies are able to institute reforms that keep the sequence from going through to its end.

The first symptom is credential inflation, occuring in the period of expansion. Within the schools themselves, degree requirements become lengthened as more students compete for higher degrees. At the height of educational expansion, the value of degrees in the external job market begins to fall; the positions for which degree requirements can be established reach their limit, and the number of candidates exceeds the available positions.

The full-fledged crisis comes on as the numbers of students begins to fall. This occurs above all at the universities, and in many instances in secondary schools as well.

At this point, the financial difficulties of weaker institutions tend to bring a high failure rate. Institutional failures are not necessarily a sign of the depth of a crisis, however; failures are most common among newly founded institutions, and the rapid onset of severe crisis may dry up new foundations and reduce the failure rate, as in Spain after 1620. Similarly, a society that never allows a proliferation of new foundations, such as England before the 1800s, may go through virtually all the crisis symptoms except this one. The disappearance of institutions, moreover, may take place at the very end of a cycle, as in Germany around 1790–1820 when many weak institutions were abolished just before new expansion occured.

During the depth of an educational depression, the universities usually lose monopolistic control over the licensed professions. Alternative sources of training appear for medicine, law, and divinity, and for school teachers at nonuniversity levels as well. There are some exceptions: Some university systems hold on partially or totally to training in divinity (England—for Anglican but not dissenting ministers; Germany) or in law (Spain, Germany).

A universal sign of severe crisis consists of widespread attacks on the contents and methods of schooling. The intellectuals desert the academy; altenative popular media spring up as well. This coincides with the pattern within the schools of treating education as perfunctory exercises; degrees become easy to acquire; often the financially weaker institutions are corrupted to the point of selling cheap degrees outright.

Finally, there often seems to be a long-term tendency for the financial costs of schooling to rise drastically for the student, and hence for the social class basis of recruitment to narrow to a segment of the higher classes. This occurs especially in the contracting phase of enrollments, although it may start earlier; it is notable that this ten-

Table 2
Educational Crisis Conditions in Six Historical Cases

	Medieval Europe	England 1500–1860	Spain 1500–1850	France 1500–1850	Germany 1500–1800	U.S. 1700–1880
1. Lengthening credential requirements in universities; educational overcrowding in professions	A.D. 1200	?	?	?	After 1760	?
2. Declining numbers at universities; at secondary levels	1300–1500 Probably same	By 1630 1640–1780 Probable	By 1620 1620–1800 No information	? 1600–1800 Late 1700s, early 1800s	After 1760 1630–1680; 1790–1810 Probably same	? 1850–1860? Rise
3. Institutional failures and financial difficulties	1300–1500; also 1200s in Italy	No failures; financial problems in 1700s	Failures 1500–1620; many poor schools thereafter	Universities abolished 1790s	Some continuous difficulties; many abolished 1790–1820	1800–1870

4. Loss of professional monopolies in medicine and law; in divinity	1400s–early 1500s	Never regained law and medicine	Never lost	1600s	Never lost	1800–1870
	Protestant Reformation 1520–1550	Partial control, challenged by dissenters 1700s	Never lost	1600s lost to seminaries	Never lost	1800–1870
Secondary and elementary teaching	1400s–1500s lost to humanists and secular schools	Challenged by dissenting academies, Sunday schools 1700s	Lost to Jesuits	Lost to Jesuits	Lost to Jesuits, humanists, Ritter-akademie, teacher-seminars	Partially lost to high schools and normal schools
5. Attacks on educational contents	1375–1500	1700s	1600 ff.	1700s, especially 1750 ff.	1700–1810	1840–1870 especially
6. Cheap degrees—mere formalities	1400s especially	1700s	No information	1650 ff.	1700s at many universities	?
7. Rising costs; narrowing class bases of recruitment	1200; and later?	1600–1800s	Probably early	By late 1700s	After 1800	Only in elite professions, after 1880

dency may continue for many decades after a system begins to reform and even expand (as in England, France, and Germany after the mid-1700s and even the early 1800s).

Medieval Europe gives us the classic case of a system that manifests all the crisis symptoms. England, Spain, and France deviate only in minor respects, as in the rate of failures or in the loss of control over particular professions. In each of these later cases, the initial upward phase of the cultural economy occurs as a national state was built upon the ruins of the old international papacy. The first phases of educational expansion are modest in England and France, quite enormous in Spain, with its newly conquered territories and its sizable treasure from its American possessions. Nevertheless, all three systems undergo overexpansion: in England, filling up available positions in the church by the 1630s and creating both a mass of underemployed and increasingly nonconforming clerics, and a highly mobilized gentry class seeking government preferment and resisting royal prerogatives; in Spain, creating an enormous army of unemployed lawyers pressuring the government for sinecures; in France, making the classical culture so widely available in the early 1700s that prestige seekers turned to the new secular media and denounced the old religiously legitimated education.

The apex of the crisis, in each case, involved a political catastrophe for the old regime. The mass cultural mobilization of England in the early 1600s produced both religious dissenters and a well-organized and well-educated body of parliamentary politicians to oppose the crown.[7] It also contributed to the weakness of the crown because the earlier phase of state expansion was carried out in a confident mood that exhausted the state treasury on military expenses and domestic sinecures. In Spain, the incomes were proportionately much greater; so was the expansion of educated office seekers, the largesse distributed in sinecures, and the efforts at foreign military expansion. The collapse in the mid-1600s was even more severe, though it was not a revolutionary one; it simply entailed the destruction of Spain's international position and of its domestic economy. In France, the combination of a mass cultural mobilization via the schools and the reaction against it in the late 1700s contributed in several ways to the revolutionary overthrow of the monarchy at the end of the century. It mobilized a large

---

[7] In 1563, 38% of the members of Parliament had attended a university or an Inn of Court; in the civil war Parliament of 1640–1642, this had increased to 70%; it fell again to 45% during 1734–1761 (Judd, 1955:37; Stone, 1964:63).

portion of the population who put pressure on the state for sinecures and for military expansion and thus contributed to the financial bankruptcy that brought on the Revolution; it also destroyed the prestige of the traditional religious and cultural legitimation of the state. In all three cases, the political denouement went along with the collapse of the cultural institutions that had supported the old regime.

It is clear that the political consequences of cultural overproduction can go in several directions. The political structure built on the original cultural expansion is always shaken, but it does not necessarily fall to a liberalizing revolution. It may fall apart into smaller components, as the medieval papacy disintegrated into national states; it may shift the internal locus of control to a different level of administrators or politicians, as in France and England; it may remain a conservative autocracy but shorn of its military and economic strength, as in Spain. Which direction the crisis will go depends on other factors besides the cultural market itself.

Germany and the early U.S. show yet other alternatives. Germany began its university building much later than other parts of Europe, and evaded the most severe effects of the late medieval crisis. After a boom in the 1400s, there was a decline, but a number of moderately prospering new universities were founded even in the early 1700s. Many other universities languished and other crisis symptoms appeared at that time: credential inflation, loss of university control over secondary schooling, declining intellectual prestige, and the rise of alternative popular cultural media. Control of the major professions of law and divinity was retained, however, providing a basis upon which the reformed educational system could reestablish itself after 1820. In the U.S. as well, the full sequence was not followed out, and some of the principal symptoms were unclear or absent. It is not certain that the total number of students was falling off everywhere in the mid-1800s, although there were clearly problems in many places for a number of decades, if not a longer period. The narrowing of the class basis of recruitment perhaps did not occur throughout the system and there were no signs of spiraling credentials or of educated persons overcompeting for employment. The U.S. did have a very high failure rate for new institutions before 1860, comparable to Italy and France during the worst part of the medieval crisis. During the early 1800s all professional monopolies were lost in the U.S., including university production of high school and elementary teachers. At the same time, the content of traditional education was severely attacked, and alternative cultural media made rapid strides.

In neither case was the educational crisis especially severe. In the

U.S., the crisis was rather short (some 60–80 years, compared to the several centuries of crisis in some of the European cases). There was a very rapid recovery in the late 1800s, spurred by the new cultural challenge of non-Anglo-Protestant immigration, and consisting of a massive bureaucratization of the educational system under the direction of university credentialling (Collins, 1979:Chapter 5). In Germany, the wave of late medieval university foundations was part of an upswing of cultural mobilization that culminated in the victory of the local governments over the Papacy in the Reformation. But the conflicts engendered by this cultural mobilization would not stop with that victory; cultural and military competition continued among rival states in central Europe, culminating in the wars of the 1600s, which wrecked the German economy.

But this political crisis was not as debilitating for the German cultural system as it was for those of most other European societies. The universities retained control of careers in law and divinity, although the latter provided much less lucrative sinecures than it had in the Middle Ages, while the former had to take second place to the expanding military in the struggle for the spoils of government. Nevertheless, the formal culture retained its links to the centers of power. In the 1700s, the cultural system and German political organization grew again, although the state for a long while allotted only a minor portion of its positions to credential bearers. Some sectors of the universities maintained a link to elite positions, while others languished. When military defeat in the Napoleonic era brought a transfer of power, it was a mild revolution, not involving total delegitimation of the state or destruction of the former ruling class, but only a thorough bureaucratization in which the educational system was given a firm link to government positions. This mild revolution also strengthened the university against its educational rivals, subordinating all other schools into a hierarchic sequence and improving the position of the larger universities by eliminating a large number of the weaker ones. On this basis, the German cultural, political, and economic sectors could experience a new round of growth.

EDUCATIONAL CYCLES AND POLITICAL-ECONOMIC UPHEAVALS

The causes of the educational cycle, I have suggested, are within the dynamics of the political economy of culture. It is easy to dispose of certain alternative lines of argument commonly asserted in histories of education. Crises are not caused by the technological obsolescence of education.[8] Educational booms and busts are centered above all in the highest *credential-producing* level of schooling, and to some extent in the secondary schools with a high-prestige intellectual and cultural content. Noncertified technical training, whether in schools or in apprenticeships, has not been subject to the same fluctuations in prestige. The more directly practical the training (as in the writing and arithmetic schools of the Renaissance or the military schools of the 1700s), the more quickly the supply of its skills has adjusted to employment demands, avoiding the long-term swings characteristic of formally credentialled schooling. In the case of professional skills such as law and divinity, formal schooling has lost repute not because of obsolescense of the content of university training, but because of overproduction of credentialled trainees. Nor have the revivals of education that follow crises usually remedied any particular defect in *practical* education. The reforms of the 1500s in England and France were carried out under the banner of ancient Latin and Greek literary style; those of the 1700s and 1800s in Germany and the U.S. under the banner of detached scholarship; the revival of Spanish education in the 1500s was carried out with a largely medieval content. Though the technological rhetoric has come in with the Industrial Revolution, it has by no means displaced the underlying dynamics of educational credential systems, which operate in the realm of certified prestige, not of practical skills.

Another simple explanation is to ascribe rises and falls in education to population shifts. Of our six cases, however, only two give any evidence of this pattern. The educational crisis periods in England, France, Spain, and the U.S. coincided with rising levels of population (Cipolla, 1976; McEvedy and Jones, 1978). German education underwent a decline in the mid-1600s, at the time of population losses connected with the Thirty Years' War, but many aspects of crisis were most severe in the 1700s, when population was rising rapidly. In England, where we have calculations of actual student–population ratios, we have evidence that the crisis occured not only in absolute but also in relative numbers (Stone, 1974:103). Only the late medieval crisis seems to be strongly implicated in a population decline, the Black Plague of 1347–1349, which reduced total population about 25% in much of Europe, with milder recurrences throughout the following centuries. Nevertheless, although the plague must have reduced university

---

[8] The small place of technical skill training in formalized educational institutions is documented in Collins, (1977, and 1979, Chapters 1 and 2).

enrollments, it cannot have been the sole or even major factor in the educational crisis. University enrollments began to decline at least 50 years before the plague began, and enrollments continued to fall in many places through the early 1500s, long after population had returned to thirteenth-century levels.[9] The medieval crisis, moreover, is not just a matter of falling numbers, but exhibits the full range of symptoms and stages found in other cases, and these cannot be attributed to population decline at all. Demographic factors, although they may contribute to crises (and perhaps booms), are not a major cause of them.

Are educational cycles due simply to long-term economic growth and decline? Here there is some relationship, although not a close one (North and Thomas, 1973; Kostow, 1962:349; Wallenstein, 1974: 21–28, 69–75). The late medieval crisis, the Spanish crisis, and part of the German crisis that occurred in the mid-1600s coincided generally with periods of economic decline. But the medieval universities remained depressed for 50 to 80 years after the European economy began to revive in the 1480s; the Spanish educational system expanded during a period of very mixed prosperity, and declined for a century after the economy had reached its trough; the German universities were in crisis in the prosperous latter half of the 1700s. The English, French, and American crisis occurred at times of general economic growth, although the English economy after 1640 did not expand as rapidly as in the previous 80 years, and the height of the American university crisis in the 1850s did correspond to a mild economic depression in that decade. Economic declines, then, may play some part in educational crises, but again they cannot be taken in themselves as the major underlying cause. This is all the more apparent because educational crises have a long-term pattern, which begins within the period of prosperous expansion, and which involves aspects, such as the loss of professional monopolies and the rise of rival cultural institutions, that are not attributable to economic decline.

The most satisfactory perspective is to see educational cycles as rises and falls of cultural currency. When a particular kind of culture generates enthusiasm and acquires social prestige, then organizations can be built and legitimated by drawing upon people who possess that culture. It may be religious, or it may be a secular culture growing out of the counter-culture of a prior round of the cultural production cycle.

---

[9] The plague recurred many times, including during the period of educational revival of 1550–1650. Thus it cannot be taken as a necessary or sufficient cause of long-term educational declines. Moreover, the percentage decline in university attendance during crisis periods was much more than the 25–35% *maximum* attributable to population loss. See Postan (1966: 563–570, 661–677).

Humanism, once the private cultural alternative to medieval educational credentials, became the basis for formal education in its next round of expansion. The rebelliously modernist rationalism and science of the Enlightnment counter-culture eventually moved out of the salons to become the content of a new round of bureaucratic schooling in the 1800s and 1900s. Through a kind of long-term dialectic, each new period builds its schools and its organizational politics on a cultural currency that grew out of opposition to the culture of the previous regime.

Of course, political organization-building does not depend only on such cultural production. Obviously we live in a multicausal world. But this series of causes need not be unpredictably complex. I think that geopolitical factors affecting the warfare of states are a key causal structure that cross-cuts the mobilization produced by internal cultural markets (see the Chapter entitled "Long-term Social Change and the Territorial Power of States," in this volume); it may be because of the different military fates of states that they have had such different political outcomes to their cultural expansion cries. Similarly, although the economic sphere is heavily dependent on political and cultural preconditions, (Collins, 1980), economic dynamics add another independent range of causation to all of these outcomes.

What I do propose is that cultural expansion has a dynamic of its own, and that left on its own it tends to produce cycles that have effects in cultural, political, and even economic realms. At some times in history this cultural dynamic takes a purely religious form, in others it takes the form of educational markets, and in others the form of antiofficial counter-cultures. But in the eras when religion has been the central agency of cultural production, it has simultaneously been the form that education takes in that society, and counter-cultures eventually become formalized into school systems as well. Cultural production is ultimately an extension of the dynamics of school systems. The varieties of history are determined by the ways in which this pure cultural dynamic of educational markets cross-cuts political and economic factors.

I have examined only a few cases from medieval and early modern European societies. There are many others that could be considered. For example, Buddhist and Confucian education in the T'ang and Sung dynasties in China show many of the familiar features of credential inflation, counter-cultural disillusionment, and organizational crisis. Comparative analysis of these and other cases should reveal a regular structure of alternatives emerging from the various combinations of factors.

There is also an application, of course, to our contemporary situation. The U.S., after a century of growth in schooling and credential-ling, now shows many of the classic signs of crisis. Enrollment levels may have passed their peak a decade ago, for both universities and secondary schools; many institutions are in financial crisis. There is a sharp escalation in the cost of schooling, a contraction in the class base of students, grade inflation, a cheapening of degrees, an increase in at-tacks on educational testing and on professional certification, and an atmosphere of dissatisfaction with official educational culture. In Europe, too, there has been somewhat more recently a very rapid ex-pansion of education, and some signs of dissatisfaction with the resulting process of credential inflation. On the basis of the general historical model, I would predict for our own societies that the cycle of educational expansion will once again go into the phase of contraction and crisis. Nevertheless, there are three important points to bear in mind before expecting immanent collapse.

1. Different societies are not all on the same cycle. The U.S. educa-tional system may well be going into a phase of decline, while many European systems are still expanding.

2. As the historical examples show, different kinds of political contexts can push the consequences of educational crisis in quite dif-ferent directions. Some consequences may be politically quite revolu-tionary, while in other scenarios of educational decline may be only a disillusioned fading away, like Spain in the 1700s. Here the range of modern comparisons—such as the future of the massive educational systems of Japan and the U.S.S.R.—should be very interesting to con-template.

3. The processes involved are very long-term. In all the historical cases I have considered, periods of expansion and of contraction were each on the order of 100–200 years (with the exception of one short 60–80 year crisis in the U.S.). This means that the kind of crisis symp-toms that we have seen in the 1970s probably do not signal any very sharp turning point. High levels of formal schooling and occupational credentialling will not suddenly disappear. But the early symptoms of crisis can be seen even farther back in the period of expansion itself; on this basis, I think it is very likely that the U.S. is entering into quite a long period of educational downturn. This would extend through the whole next century, and the worst part of the crisis may be several generations in the future. For European and other modern societies, I am less prepared to predict. For many European societies, in view of their rather recent expansion to mass higher education, even the begin-ning of the downturn may be rather far in the future.

One need not be too pessimistic about any of these developments. For a crisis of the educational system is not necessarily the same as a general collapse of civilization. The counter-cultures of the past that have arisen during these periods of educational crisis have often been very creative in their own right. The one that occured during the decline of the medieval universities, for example, goes by the name of the Renaissance. What other political and economic consequences there may be of our future periods of educational decline should become clearer as more progress is made in the basic theory of cultural production.

IV

Breakthroughs in Microsociology

Three Stages of Erving Goffman*

Erving Goffman is a multileveled writer indeed. The variety of interpretations he has received—no two of them alike—makes us suppose that his analyses, or his capacities for presenting himself, are endlessly varied and not to be categorized. Throughout his work he has toyed with the relativistic gambit of social reality-constructing, although usually in tandem with assertions about the bedrock of social rules and obligations. One is tempted to find the larger frame of endless alternation between these views more compelling than the Durkheimian determinism lodged within.

Is this multileveled complexity on the surface or in the depths? I would say we can capture the main features of Goffman's work under two headings: Goffman's popular side, and his scholarly side. The latter, taken as a whole, has been relatively constant; the work changes, but the principles of transmutation are clear enough. The popular side ought to be given less attention; the scholarly contributions of Goffman are so often overlooked that they deserve the center of the stage. But to

---

* Originally published in Jason Ditton (Ed.), *The View from Goffman*. London: Macmillan, 1979. Copyright 1979 Randall Collins.

miss the popular side would be to miss a secret of Goffman's power, and to miss some key, if unconscious, insights that Goffman's work offers about the historical world we have just been passing through. In what follows, I will briefly (a) sketch Goffman's popular persona; (b) analyze Goffman's scholarly methods and the theoretical traditions to which he contributes; (c) revert to the popular image for some reflections on role distance, intellectuals' reflexivity, and the cultural revolutions of the twentieth century.

I.

For those who like him, Goffman is a kind of hero-anthropologist, donning his pith helmet in the darkest reaches of our own society. He is the man who took the dare of finding out what it's *really* like to be treated as if you are crazy, by having himself committed to a mental hospital with only the secret connivance of the superintendent (well, *almost*—he actually posed as a recreational therapist and blended in with the group); who took a job as a Nevada casino dealer to study the fast action scene; who wrote an eyes-open study of the mutilated and stigmatized, feeling his way into the lives of those suffering what no one would want to have happen to anybody. And having proved his courage, his cool, and his stomach out in the wilds of everyday "real life," he forces us to the line of self-consciousness about the taken-for-granted, at best uneasily-reflected-upon things we all do all the time.

Goffman's most popular territory, then: the things people do not talk about. Embarrassment, flustering, and making a fool of oneself in company: Goffman catches it in his steely gaze. How the hostess behaved when the dog shat on the carpet during her tea party; how we behave toward closed doors, both from the front and from behind; how we put on a social face each morning in the bathroom mirror; how eyes meet and then look away while passing on the street; how making love may be the ultimate performance rather than the ultimate intimacy. Goffman sits back with his psychiatrist's aplomb, letting the patients throw ashtrays past his ear, observing their demeanor (and his own), watching all do deference to the demands of the situation. Reading Goffman in the 1960s, we know we are all uneasy passengers with averted eyes descending in our social elevator like a coffin being lowered into the grave. And we know Goffman knows it, too, when we read at the end of "Where the Action Is" (1967) that the Nevada slot machines give out little mutilated twitches of the self at the barren ends of the earth.

Goffman resonates with the public moods over the years. He treated games and strategies, con men and international espionage amid the nuclear shadows of the CIA-infested 1960s. He conveyed a sense of why people are wary of each other on the public street that went far beyond the violence of crime, protest, and ghetto uprising. And he leapfrogged to a deeper level of reflexivity on the mind-blowing happenings of the psychedelic era.

Goffman at his best is the explorer of our social unconscious. He lets us know why it is unconscious—not because it is buried in our dreams or the dark recesses of the mind, but because it is right on the surface. In fact, it *is* the surface itself, a surface we need to look *through* to keep everything else in focus, and hence a surface that cannot bear much self-consciousness without dire results. Freud occupied a similar territory early in the century, when intellectuals began to point to each others' Freudian slips and claimed to know the unconscious meanings of everyday behavior. Freud reached America most powerfully in the 1930s and 1940s, when Goffman was a student, and there is a sense in which Goffman is the next stage one level over, revealing the underside of everyday life but with the insights of sociology rather than psychology. The theories differ, but Goffman shares several of Freud's ambivalent appeals. Freud's dictum that in civilization we are all neurotic becomes translated by Goffman into the social inevitability of artificial realities, and the deep and ever-present vulnerability of individuals to each other. Yet Goffman, too, opens the way to a therapy—the one-upmanship and black humor of the 1950s crystallizing into a self-consciousness foreshadowing the honesty revolution that flared up at the turn of the 1970s.

Goffman's popular appeal, one might say, comes from his showiness and his topicality—perhaps all the more so because on the surface of it, Goffman's works go out of the way to strike a calm, detached, and scholarly note. It is to this note we should first attend, for here are the treasures of mid-twentieth-century observational sociology—and a good deal of twentieth-century intellectual life as well—sitting around half unobserved because most readers have been mesmerized by the popular themes to which they point. Goffman's self-expressed concerns are virtually the opposite of the image of hipster and iconoclast in which he is often placed. Yet when all is said and done on Goffman's explicit scholarship, it will be worthwhile returning to the popular persona once more. The traditions to which Goffman contributes as a serious theorist, with a little historical development, provide a lens through which to understand the significance of Goffman's popular appeal, and thus perhaps of the energy that drives his work.

II.

Goffman's written self-presentation is the epitome of scholarly correctness. His language is cool and precise. His claims are modest. He suggests his points rather than trumpeting them; he offers his perspective of dramaturgy or impression management as merely one of five alternative social perspectives, along with the technical, political, structural, and cultural (1959:240). Yet his concerns are unyieldingly theoretical, and theoretical in the grand tradition. They always concern the central questions of the conditions of social order. However sensational the material, Goffman transforms it with a classically Durkheimian strategy. Mental hospitals and paranoid breakdowns are important because they tell us, by a process of experimental subtraction, what are the conditions for normal self and normal interaction. Con men and spies reveal the vulnerabilities and the resources upon which all shared realities are built; the theatre and the bizarre newspaper clipping tell us about fundamental human competencies which undergird mundane life.

These are not the canons of narrower academicism, to be sure, and Goffman has been attacked by the proponents of a studiously quantified and scientized sociology as impressionistic and unserious. Goffman never raises his voice in reply; in fact, he scarcely deigns to reply at all. The polemic of academic specialists is not part of Goffman's repertoire.

His writing is very pristine, then, perhaps too much so for the proper packaging of his themes. Goffman organizes his materials in careful analytical sequences, generating comprehensive taxonomies of his own, making and leaving his mark across near-virgin territories of face-to-face sociology. Notice his array of coinages and concepts shaped to his own use:

> face-work, deference and demeanor, impression management and the presentation of self; frontstage and backstage, teams and team-work, discrepant roles; a typology of secrets: dark, strategic, inside, entrusted, and free; moral careers, total institutions, and ways of making out in them; commitment, attachment, embracement, engagement, and role-distance; focused and unfocused interaction, face engagements, accessible engagements, situational proprieties and improprieties, and the tightness and looseness of situation rules; vehicular units and participation units; territories of the self; personal space, use space, turns, information and conversational preserves; territorial violations; markers and tie-signs; supportive interchanges (access rituals) and remedial interchanges (accounts, apologies, body gloss); frames, keyings, fabrications, frame breaking and out-of-frame activity.

And within these, further taxonomies of the subtypes.

Yet oddly, even as many of these concepts pass into wide sociological use, Goffman himself abandons them with the publication of each book, going on to a new set of coinages for the next. This conceptual frontiersmanship is not the result of radical shifts in topic, for Goffman has been faithful to a set of themes throughout—face-to-face interaction, the creation and vulnerabilities of social belief, mental illness in relation to social normalcy. Nor can one say, taking the opposite tack, that Goffman is forced to manufacture new terminology to justify repeating the same old materials. For each of his works, carefully examined, reveals a new body of *empirical* materials that he brings to his themes.

His early interaction ritual papers, the most predominantly theoretical of his works, draw loosely upon a variety of background observations, as befits pathbreaking analysis. *The Presentation of Self in Everyday Life* draws heavily upon the Chicago School's treasury of occupational studies, on linguistic studies of occupational argot, and upon Goffman's dissertation research in a Shetland Island community. *Asylums* covers the results of organizational sociology and insiders' accounts of total institutions, along with some of his field observations in St. Elizabeth's mental hospital (those observations concerning patients' vulnerabilities and defenses in relation to the institution itself). *Behavior in Public Places* uses another set of St. Elizabeth's materials, this time to demonstrate by the Durkheimian norm-violation technique the moral bases of public order, and balances this with primary sources on moral ideals themselves, analyzing an extensive collection of etiquette books. *Encounters* broadens out to the more positive side of interaction, drawing upon observations of merry-go-rounds, horseback riders, and cocktail parties. "Where the Action Is" comes from participant observations as a casino dealer. *Relations in Public* has the benefit of a decade of microstudies of everyday life, of conversation, people passing on the street, and the like, and Goffman can review a burgeoning field that has grown up around him. *Strategic Interaction* and *Frame Analysis* cull yet other sources of data—memoirs of spies, newspaper clippings of cons and put-ons, insiders' accounts of the theatre and the movies.

In short, Goffman's work is that of a theoretically oriented empiricist, be it an empiricist who has broken new grounds in our conception of empirical materials. He has steadily broadened and deepened his empirical bases, while maintaining a theoretical focus that should ensure cumulative development in explanatory power. For this very reason, the noncumulative look of Goffman's work is puzzling, and some of the blame is due to his continual shifts in concepts. Goffman never reuses earlier concepts in later works, manifesting a kind of role-distancing from his own previous work; and he very seldom refers to his earlier work in any respect. Thus one never gets from Goffman himself any overview of his own theory, and one is left to figure out for oneself if one is to expect any theoretical unity or only a string of self-contained virtuoso performances. The same organizational trait is found in each work separately. For although Goffman is a master of the upbeat ending, with a strong theoretical point jumping from the last paragraph—and often the last sentence—of every work, he does not pause to survey the ground that has been conquered. Every book, every paper, lays itself out smoothly before the reader in architectonic symmetry. But the order presented does not invoke the order of the theoretical traditions within which Goffman works. Goffman's systematic quality is a taxonomic frame within which his explanatory ideas show only their surface of immediate relevance, while obscuring their connection with the long-standing theoretical issues that make up the central questions of sociology.

For notwithstanding his other merits, in my opinion, Goffman's contributions are most striking as developments of the major theoretical ideas of the twentieth century. Such theoretical work is necessarily transindividual. It plays up the formulations of famous masters, though these classics are only the emblems of a larger intellectual community of the past whose debates they focused into a striking mnemonic. It situates contemporary empirical and theoretical work in terms of the major long-term questions of the field, and it provides for its own superseding by implying a future in which still more adequate formulations will be found. As I will shortly demonstrate, Goffman is preeminently a team player in the intellectual world, and from the theoretical content of his work one would hardly expect him to slight the social basis of any activity (although he has never written on the sociology of the intellectual world per se). Nevertheless, Goffman does not situate his work as part of a historical development of theory. He does not exactly bury his roots: there are scattered references to Durkheim, Radcliffe-Brown, Simmel, Cooley, Freud, and occasional citations to the more nearly contemporaneous work of Parsons, Sartre, and Kenneth Burke, and in Goffman's later works to Wittgenstein, Austin, Schutz, and Garfinkel. The nature of the references, and of Goffman's theoretical discussions (cryptic at best), though, makes it easy to miss the significance of what Goffman is doing. The citations do not differentiate between important and unimportant traditions, and hence make it easy to take Goffman for a processual reality-constructing symbolic interactionist, or whatever reading one wants to bring to him. Goffman's low-key theoretical note also tends to leave the center of the stage for Goffman's own conceptual innovations, and were it not for Goffman's unwillingness to give any long life to his own coinages, one might wonder whether his stance is one of modesty or the reverse.

Intellectual progress being inherently collective, we need have no qualms about presenting Goffman's work in a different light than he himself does. We need have no modesty on his behalf; modesty is rarely an intellectual virtue in any case, and a straightforward overview of the theoretical themes in Goffman's work, and of the larger theoretical and empirical efforts in which it is historically situated, will show more continuity—and more progress—than he allows either himself or the intellectual field as a whole.

Goffman has gone through several theoretical phases, although it would be misleading to separate them too firmly. More accurately, he has had different strands of theoretical interest, somewhat overlapping in time. His early work is heavily within the tradition of Durkheimian social anthropology, with a slight admixture of symbolic intentionism. To be sure, Goffman's constant interest in the idea of the social self, in the early essays, in the title of *The Presentation of Self in Everyday Life*, and in *Asylums, Stigma,* and *Encounters*, together with a focus on face-to-face situations and a theme of social reality-construction, has given many observers the impression that Goffman is simply a follower of Mead and Cooley. The external facts seem to support this interpretation: Goffman's training at the University of Chicago in its symbolic interactionist heyday under Herbert Blumer, Louis Wirth, and Everett Hughes; his scattering of references to Cooley and to Kenneth Burke (whose symbolic-dramaturgical processualism was much in vogue at Chicago in Goffman's student days); and his heavy use of Chicago-based empirical studies. Yet Goffman equally scatters his pages with references to Durkheim and Radcliffe-Brown, to Simmel and Sartre, and to a host of less theoretical sources. Strikingly enough, one looks almost in vain for references to the classic symbolic interactionist, George Herbert Mead, or to his major contemporary exponent, Blumer. Explicit references count for relatively little in fixing Goffman's theoretical concerns; as we shall see, though, his early theoretical arguements are strongly Durkheimian, but applied in a new empirical direction to the microscopic materials of situational interaction in modern civilized life.

In the works of the 1960s, Goffman became increasingly oriented to an empirical exploration of this new realm. The Durkheimian concern for ritual tended to fade into a reference to functional rules of social order, and the latter was pressed little further than to provide a rationale for an elaborate taxonomy of features of everyday life inter-action. Yet even here the ritual model occasionally reappeared, as in the analysis of supportive and remedial interchanges in *Relations in Public*.

During this period as well, one can discern an interest in game theory. While the economic bargaining aspect of this does not interest Goffman, its mathematical formalization interests him even less. But he does speak highly of the strategic nuclear arms race analyses of Thomas Schelling for separating the informational side of bargaining from the expressive side. Goffman pursues this theme in several works, especially *Strategic Interaction,* and his subsequent two books make use of the rich vein of empirical materials it uncovered for him regard-ing spies, gamblers, and con men. Here Goffman seems to have most nearly yielded to the temptation to be merely entertaining and topical, but an analytical message does come through. The earlier emphasis on a functional coordination among social actors in upholding the fabric of social reality shifts over to a greater concern for the way in which this may be a conflictful situation among rival reality-constructors. At the end of this progression, we find the theme of multiple realities and the maneuvering that is possible to contain one constructed reality within another.

In Goffman's latest major work, Goffman turns explicitly to the issues of social epistemology and social phenomenology. The earlier concern for self and for ritual interaction are gone—the individual hav-ing been declared dissolved, in *Relations in Public,* into a myriad of concepts specific to different analytical tasks, and rituals almost squeezed out of the picture by Goffman's new focus of attention. In *Frame Analysis,* Goffman directly confronts the ethnomethodologists (which is to say, as directly as he ever deals with other theorists, which is relatively little in terms of explicit and sustained discussion). The ethnomethodologists are the theoretically most radical and also em-pirically most thorough of sociologists working on the social construc-tion of realities—on common sense practical reasoning, as they prefer to express it—and on the competencies and contingencies underlying this. Both theoretically and empirically, they challenged Goffman by pushing his themes and his researches onto more radical grounds. Goff-man responds to them somewhat ambivalently, repudiating their more relativistic claims with counter-assertions of the rule-bound and exter-nally constraining qualities of social life. Here he returns to some of his early Durkheimian themes. Yet at the same time, Goffman reem-phasizes the fragility and theatricality of social belief. Goffman does not resolve the issue, but he does advance it by giving an alegant device for dealing with it. His frame model gives us a strong analytical grip on perhaps the key problem uncovered by Garfinkel and stressed by his most radical followers: the potentially infinite regress of levels of analysis and hence of levels of reality itself.

Goffman's theoretical allegiances and associations, then, are mixed and somewhat shifting over time. His classic early work is heavily Durkheimian anthropology, with some mixture of themes from the symbolic interactionists, Kenneth Burke, and situational-processualism generally. Later Goffman has toyed with the more conflictual and utilitarian themes of game theory, and grappled with the epistemological challenges of social phenomenology. In the following sections, I will deal with these three themes, examining Goffman's works and also the larger traditions within which they are situated. My aim throughout is to assess the progress of these fields as a whole and Goffman's contributions to them.

Durkheimian Social Anthropology

The central themes of most of Goffman's early works are Durkheimian. His early papers are collected under the title *Interaction Ritual*. The phrase is exceedingly apt and deserves wider currency (although Goffman, of course, himself neglects it, just as he neglects most of his coinages). For the core of the Durkheimian approach, on the level of empirical field work, is to see people's behavior through the lens of ritual and its group-sustaining functions, to look beneath the usual surface of practical business and see the real dynamics of the crowd and its moral ties beneath.

"On Face-Work" (1955) is Goffman's first important statement. Its title lends some place to pin a symbolic interactionist connection on Goffman, but it is nevertheless subtitled "An Analysis of Ritual Elements in Social Interaction." It very quickly states the key elements of Goffman's early social-anthropological model. How people come on in conversation and in their appearance, their "line," is usually "legitimate" and "institutionalized." Being legitimate means it is normative; one feels it is morally proper "that this should be so" for one to act this way, and *also* for other people to help one sustain one's line. Being institutionalized means it is part of the cultural apparatus of society—people repeat certain lines over and over under some hidden social constraint to do so. Society and its collective conscience, then, is not a big balloon in the sky; it is a deep and complex moral arrangement in our everyday encounters, which helps people stage their personal realities. Reality-construction may be focused on individual selves, but it is carried out collectively; as Goffman states at the end of the paper, under the heading "The Nature of the Ritual Order": "the ritual order seems to be organized basically on accommodative lines [1967:42]."

The conclusion is worth quoting in full:

> societies everywhere, if they are to be societies, must mobilize their members as self-regulating participants in social encounters. One way of mobilizing the individual for this purpose is through ritual; he is taught to be perceptive, to have feeling attached to self and a self expressed through face, to have pride, honor, and dignity, to have considerateness, to have tact and a certain amount of poise. These are some of the elements of behavior which must be built into the person if practical use is to be made of him as an interactant, and it is these elements that are referred to in part when one speaks of universal human nature.
>
> Universal human nature is not a very human thing. By acquiring it, the person becomes a kind of construct, built up not from inner psychic propensities but from moral rules that are impressed upon him from without. These rules, when followed, determine the evaluation he will make of himself and of his fellow-participants in the encounter, the distribution of his feelings, and the kinds of practices he will employ to maintain a specified and obligatory kind of ritual equilibrium. The general capacity to be bound by moral rules may well belong to the individual, but the particular set of rules which transforms him into a human being derives from requirements established in the ritual organization of social encounters [1967:44-45].

Goffman's other major early statement, "The Nature of Deference and Demeanor," (1958) is even more explicitly Durkheimian. It begins:

> Under the influence of Durkheim and Radcliffe-Brown, some students of modern society have learned to look for the symbolic meaning of any given social practice and for the contribution of the practice to the integrity and solidarity of the group that employs it. However, in directing their attention away from the individual to the group, these students seem to have neglected a theme that is presented in Durkheim's chapter on the soul [1915: Book 2, Chapter 8]. There he suggests that the individual's personality can be seen as one apportionment of the collective *mana*, and that (as he implies in later chapters), the rites performed to representations of the social collectivity will sometimes be performed to the individual himself [1967:47].

And it concludes:

> In this paper I have suggested that Durkheimian notions about primitive religion can be translated into concepts of deference and demeanor, and that these concepts help us to grasp some aspects of urban secular living. The im-

plication is that in one sense this secular world is not so irreligious as we might think. Many gods have been done away with, but the individual himself stubbornly remains as a deity of considerable importance. He walks with some dignity and is the recipient of many little offerings. He is jealous of the worship due him, yet, approached in the right spirit, he is ready to forgive those who may have offended him. Because of their status relative to his, some persons will find him contaminating while others will find they contaminate him, in either case finding that they must treat him with ritual care. Perhaps the individual is so viable a god because he can actually understand the ceremonial significance of the way he is treated, and quite on his own can respond dramatically to what is proffered him. In contacts between such deities there is no need for middlemen; each of these gods is able to serve as his own priest [1967:95].

The Presentation of Self in Everyday Life is an elaboration of these two papers. It introduces the mechanics by which face-work is done and ritual deference paid to these little collectively supported realities called selves. The book takes us backstage amidst the stage props, and hence seems to have a more iconoclastic tone than the earlier papers. But the theoretical model is much the same, although references to it are now buried rather more deeply. The dramaturgy of everyday life is explained, not as a Machiavellian conflict of opposing con men, but as a moral and functional process of creating order.

any projected definition of the situation also has a distinctive moral character. It is this moral character of projections that will chiefly concern us in this report. Society is organized on the principle that an individual who possesses certain social characteristics has a moral right to expect that others will value and treat him in an appropriate way. Connected with this principle is a second, namely that an individual who implicitly or explicitly signifies that he has certain social characteristics ought in fact to be what he claims he is. In consequence, when an individual projects a definition of the situation and thereby makes an implicit or explicit claim to be a person of particular kind, he automatically exerts a moral demand upon the others, obliging them to value and treat him in the manner persons of his kind have a right to expect [1959:13].

Later Goffman refers to the ritual distance given to the performer, and quotes Durkheim (the same passage he quoted in "The Nature of Deference and Demeanor"): " 'The human personality is a sacred thing; one does not violate it nor infringe its bounds, while at the same time the greatest good is in communication with others [1959:69].' "

Goffman does add a twist of his own to this Durkheimian model of ritual social order. Society is upheld as a moral entity, not, as symbolic interactionism would have it, merely as a cognitive-informational process of defining situations. All social reality-constructing is constrained by shared moral obligations. Social reality, although constructed, is not constructed in free-flowing processes in which nothing is foreordained or anything can emerge from a new situation, as the followers of Thomas's dictum seem to believe. Yet for all this criticism of symbolic interaction, Goffman does take something from it: a sense of the potential fluidity and hence fragileness of social realities. Social life, under functional constraints for people to uphold consistent definitions of reality both for themselves and for each other, is nevertheless forced into a two-sidedness: a frontstage and a backstage. As Goffman states in very nearly the closing words of the book:

> We come now to the basic dialectic. In their capacity as performers, individuals will be concerned with maintaining the impression that they are living up to the many standards by which they and their products are judged. Because these standards are so numerous and so pervasive, the invididuals who are performers dwell more than we might think in a moral world. But, qua performers, individuals are concerned not with the moral issue of realizing these standards, but with the amoral issue of engineering a convincing impression that these standards are being realized. Our activity, then, is largely concerned with moral matters, but as performers we do not have a moral concern with them. As performers we are merchants of morality. Our day is given over to intimate contact with the goods we display and our minds are filled with intimate understandings of them; but it may well be that the more attention we give to these goods, then the more distant we feel from them and from those who are believing enough to buy them. To use a different imagery, the very obligation and profitability of appearing always in a steady moral light, of being a socialized character, forces one to be the sort of person who is practiced in the ways of the stage [1959:251].

Ultimately, then, we have a functional model, not a moral-cultural one. Unlike Parsons, Goffman does not find social order to be founded on *internalization* of moral obligations; the obligations, rather, come because of the way we encounter pressures from each other in specific situations to help each other construct a consistent definition of reality. In order to live up to this *external* morality, one is forced to have a nonmoral, manipulative self as well.

Goffman is no iconoclast. He does not take the side of the beleaguered individual against falsities of society, but condemns this outlook sarcastically as an effort "to keep a part of the world safe from sociology [1961:52]." Goffman rather takes the standpoint of society as fundamental, for without it nothing else would exist. He brings a sophisticated awareness of the problems society has in protecting itself, and hence the pressures individuals undergo—and make for each other—in order to keep up the society that makes them what they are. Goffman's studies of deviance are made for the same purpose. Embarrassment and alienation from interaction are important in that they show the norm by its violation; and although there are continuous difficulties that make violations always possible, the fundamental importance of the norm creates pressures to bring violators back into line.

The nature of the norm, though, cannot be taken for granted, since the term is a gloss on a set of social processes that empirical analyses like those of Goffman have now opened up for us as issues to explore. Goffman's descriptive rhetoric does not always advance this search. "Conversation," he says, "has a life of its own and makes demands on its own behalf. It is a little social system with its own boundary-maintaining tendencies [1967:113]." Here he echoes the social-system ideas popular in the late 1950s in Parsons, political science theorists, and others. In *Behavior in Public Places*, Goffman claims that social order is based on a set of moral norms, alternately referred to as rules. And later, in *Frame Analysis*, despite a much more relativistic outlook on social reality, he asserts that "frameworks are not merely a matter of mind but correspond in some sense to the way in which an aspect of the activity itself is organized . . . Organizational premises are involved, and these are something cognition somehow arrives at, not something cognition creates or generates [1974:247]." Reality is external, and is generally recognized by individuals consensually. For examples, Goffman falls back on formal games; one can always recognize when someone is playing checkers, whatever transformations of this setting might be added onto it.

Yet it may well be that we recognize games as something artificial, different from ordinary life, precisely because they have explicit rules, while ordinary social life does not. An observer may offer a description of interaction as a set of practices guided by rules, but the question remains: are these rules merely an observer's convenient summary of what goes on, or are they formulations that participants have explicitly in their heads and refer to in order to guide their actions? In fact, just how such social cognition is done is now open for study, in part because of Goffman's encouragement of this area of microresearch. But Goffman does not carry his research in this direction nor to this level of detail. Nor does he give a sustained argument for his perspective and against the alternatives. Despite the smoothness of his appeals, the question should be regarded as still open and still awaiting definitive proof.

In general, Goffman seems to overstate the necessity of a single, strong definition of reality. He seems to regard any retreat from this ideal state as scarcely tolerable to the social fabric, and speaks of "the utter mayhem that would result were the individual to cease to be a gentleman. [1967:170]." This is all the more suspicious when we see that Goffman draws his favorite examples of ritual interaction from the most polite social classes in a very settled period of history. How much order of a given kind may be found is much more of a variable than Goffman would have us believe, and hence his functional claims that such order is produced by inexorable necessity seem empirically very loose.

These problems are endemic to the Durkheimian tradition. Since this tradition includes, in my opinion, the major strengths—and the major weaknesses—of modern sociology in general, it is worth examining its intellectual history a little more broadly.

Durkheim provides the classic "aha!" experience of sociology. He broke through the common-sense surface view of society in a number of ways, showing that society is not merely a utilitarian order of practical business. Indeed, it can operate practically only because it is founded on a prior precontractual, prerational solidarily. He mounted a series of efforts to prove his point. He gave a logical argument to show that there must be an implicit contract to uphold any explicit contracts, and a historical-comparative argument that earlier societies are based on a strong and repressive collective morality. He concluded that the group is prior to the individual; the individual, as a relatively autonomous center of identity and self-reflection, emerges only under particular conditions of social structure, notably a high division of labor. He rounded this off by deducing that group solidarity gives meaning to life, and attempted to show this empirically by examining the conditions for its opposite—suicides that should occur where social bonds are lacking.

Durkheim's insights cut in several directions. On one side, he is a functionalist and an evolutionist, tending to reify society, or at least make its normative demands for order an overriding force. For society is the source of morality; there is no reference point beyond it. Order is both necessary as an ontological property of social existence and the fundamental moral category itself. Hence Durkheim and his followers tend to make no distinction between arguments as to what is good and analyses of the causes of particular forms of social order. This tendency is most notable in the macrolevel followers of Durkheim, especially Talcott Parsons.

To put this point another way: Functionalist Durkheimianism ignores stratification, at least insofar as recognizing stratification as based on any struggle for domination. This, I believe, is the essential weakness of the position. For stratification, and the various resources for conflict and domination that produce it, are the major explanatory tools that can actually be demonstrated empirically to explain the range of social variations and historical changes.

From another angle, the problem is methodological. A purely functional analysis is highly interpretive. It shows a pattern, argues that this must enable society to sustain itself, and then closes its books. Functional analysis is hard to take further because society as a whole is the basic entity under consideration. All forms of order fall under the same rubric, and to seek conditions for *which* form among them is called forth does not easily fall within its purview. To look for such internal comparisons implies that parts of society do not all operate together as a system, and that individuals and their resources may act as independent variables in their own right.

Functionalists seeking stronger empirical support by the method of empirical comparisons have had two options: (*a*) to compare societies in their totalities, usually by establishing evolutionary stages; (*b*) to compare deviance with normalcy. The evolutionary comparison, though, has caused difficulties because in fact historical societies have not followed neat evolutionary patterns. They have not followed the same sequences of change, nor maintained external independence from each other as separate, self-regulating systems. The historical record, in fact, tends to give much more support to the role of conflict, conquest, and domination, and their material means and spoils. The other alternative, to compare deviance with normalcy, runs into a similar problem: risking functional theory by empirical test, it tends to find that pressures for a fuller empirical account begin to point to elements of struggle and domination over who and what is considered deviant, and hence pushes again towards a more pluralistic and conflict-oriented analysis.

Durkheim, though, opened up possibilities for analysis in several directions. Alongside a macro, totalistic, and functional approach, he also developed a very powerful microapproach. Working against the background of the French crowd-psychologists of his day, Durkheim was able to focus on society as actual interaction of human bodies in particular places, and to see that all such interactions have two levels—the cognitive, symbolic level of manifest consciousness; and the emotional, moral level in which common feelings are developed and strengthened by cognitive focus and emotional contagion.

From this come some of Durkheim's most striking insights. One of his most paradoxical formulations—that crime contributes to social solidarity—is based on the insight that punishment of deviants is a ritual occasion that bolsters the norm by creating ceremonial solidarity around it in the very act of punishing its transgressor.

Later, Durkheim showed that religion is fundamentally a set of ceremonial actions, assembling the group, heightening its emotions, and focusing its members on symbols of their common belongingness. Thus Durkheim's most striking formulation: that god is society, and that the type of society determines the type of sacredness it recognizes. And since ceremonies generating and regenerating our sense of the sacred and the profane underlie all possibilities of mundane social cooperation, in effect society is a religious phenomenon.

These analyses, to be sure, can be taken in a purely abstract, macrofunctional sense, and this is the way they have generally been taken. Durkheim's analysis of crime has been applied by Kai Erikson (1966), for example, but only in the macro sense of arguing that every society, as a totality, must produce a given rate of deviance. But taken in a strictly micro sense, the analysis cuts in a very different direction. If a punishment ceremony creates social solidarity, then we might expect, from the perspective of a struggle for domination, that individuals and groups would attempt to make use of such ceremonies to create a solidarity that bolsters their own preferred positions and undermines those of their opponents. Similarly, religious rituals can be used as weapons in the struggle for domination in a particular kind of stratified order. And indeed, an examination of political and religious history shows much of this sort of pattern.

But doesn't this interpretation land us back in the world of individual calculation that Durkheim earlier showed was merely a surface phenomenon, itself dependent on the existence of deeper solidarities and propensities for order? I do not believe so. Durkheim makes a convincing case that our conscious sense of reality is a surface comprised of shared cognitive symbols; hence it makes sense that people do not generally think in terms of blatant calculation of personal advantage. On the contrary, we think—and talk—in terms of moral ideas, convincing ourselves and others that we act because of generally valid principles and that everyone should act as we do, since we act for the good of all as much as for ourselves. But these mental furnishings are not themselves to be taken as ultimate realities; they are themselves products of ritual situations that foster such world views. Hence, it is perfectly consistent to see human beings as animals struggling naturally and without conscious self-reflection for advantages, while at the same time subject to processes of emotional contagion and social cognition. People struggle, but they do not struggle alone, just as they do not do much else of social importance alone either. The rituals of solidarity are major determinants of how alliances in social struggles will line up and who will win what in these struggles.

The key to a more realistic and empirically satisfying analysis, then, is to focus Durkheim's leads on the microlevel, and to see the ritual creation of solidarity as a series of events that add up to a larger set of struggles over domination. The British tradition of social anthropology developed the Durkheimian model at least partially in this direction. With Radcliffe-Brown, Gluckman, and others, the focus was on rituals within tribal societies; funerals, marriages, initiations and the like were shown to contribute to re-creating group solidarity, especially in inevitable periods of transition due to individual life-careers. That the sum total of such interactions might be a structure of domination and conflict, though, was by and large glossed over—although one may find traces of this view in Lévi-Strauss's (1949/1969) continuation of the French line of this tradition.

Durkheim's work offers a good deal for filling out a bare stratification perspective, and later empirical developments have tended in this direction. Durkheim's model of variations in the division of labor, although originally couched in evolutionary terms and applied to entire societies, is capable of being applied analytically as a set of variables within any one society. Basil Bernstein (1971–1975), Mary Douglas (1970), myself (Collins, 1975:67–79) and others have proposed that a major difference among the cultures of social classes is that some of them approximate the conditions for mechanical solidarity, others for organic solidarity, and hence manifest corresponding differences in class outlooks. Bernstein (1971–1975) and Bourdieu (1972, 1977) argue that such cultural differences may be a key basis for maintaining domination, especially when the culture of the higher classes is used as a career selection device through the school system.

The contributions of Durkheimian analysis to our understanding of stratification can be made even tighter if we see that its detailed micro-basis is in the sphere of interaction ritual. Here Goffman's contributions are central. For Goffman's early work, in particular, draws heavily on empirical materials of occupations—social classes at work—and of leisure status groups and their idealized self-presentations. Although Goffman does not raise this dimension to explicit consideration, it is not difficult to do so.

That Goffman should be the one to make this connection is not surprising when we consider his biography. Goffman, a Canadian, was trained at the University of Toronto in the 1940s, notably by C.W.M. Hart, in Radcliffe-Brown-style social anthropology. Goffman then went on to graduate work at the University of Chicago, where his anthropology background and perhaps also his British Commonwealth connection led him to work with W. Lloyd Warner, the Australian anthropologist-sociologist. Warner was a key figure in the development of empirical sociology in America. He began, very much in the Radcliffe-Brown tradition, with a field study of the Murngin bushmen in Australia, but then decided to transfer his anthropological field techniques to virgin territory—a modern civilized community. Thus the 1940s saw a long series of volumes by Warner and his associates on Yankee City (Newburyport, Massachusetts), then on Jonesville (a midwestern town), Bronzeville (black Chicago), Deep South (a segregated southern city), eventually leading to efforts to capture the entire society beyond the community level, by studies of business executives' careers and of the structure of the corporate economy. Warner, in short, set out to map the entire structure of American society in anthropological detail.

In the process, Warner tended to lose much of his earlier Durkheimian analytical refinement, and to concentrate on sheer description. Perhaps it is for this reason that Goffman moved away from explicitly following Warner's concerns with stratification. Goffman's first paper (1951), published while still a graduate student, was on stratification, dealing with material displays of status ranking. But it was a pedestrian effort, staying close to the utilitarian surface, and Goffman must have felt the need to move farther afield for greater analytical punch. The line he chose was a combination of Durkheimian ritual analysis with the empirical materials of banal face-to-face interaction. Yet even here, in a sense, he was following Warner's lead. He took up the challenge to look at his own society with the detachment of an anthropologist in the most unfamiliar place, although on a more micro level than Warner. Nevertheless, a comparison with Warner's last book in the Yankee City series, The Living and the Dead (1959), shows what Warner could do, amidst all his other projects, with a straightforward ritual analysis of such American institutions as parades and cemeteries.

The Chicago tradition helped Goffman find his own empirical focus for his Durkheimian analysis; the symbolic interactionist emphasis on situations and on the social self gave him his early subject matter, although Goffman transformed the explanation of these phenomena in a strongly Durkheimian direction. But situations and selves are highly abstract notions, and with Goffman's drive for empirical grounding, it is not surprising that he emerged with a body of materials that revealed the differences in social situations and social selves of people in different positions in society—which is to say, differences in the class structure. For one of the great empirical strengths of the Chicago School was not only the Park-Thomas-Wirth tradition of studying urban ecology and ethnic relations, but there was also a strong emphasis on the ethnography of professions and occupations. *The Presentation of Self in Everyday Life,* in one respect, may be regarded as a synthesis of this literature.

In it, Goffman cites some 20 Chicago M.A. and Ph.D. theses, along with a number of other dissertations on occupations. We find studies of garbage collectors, shoe salesmen, pharmacists, labor union officials, bureaucrats, and many more; we find the names of Dalton, Wilensky, Blau, Becker, and virtually all the important researchers of the world of work. Everett Hughes, who organized and guided this line of research at Chicago, had already produced some synthesizing ideas (collected in Hughes [1958]), and we find echoes of them in Goffman: How occupations attempt to deal with their dirty work by shunting it off to subordinate occupations; relatedly, how the professions build up an idealized public image, and how all occupations attempt to follow this self-idealizing path.

The result is that when Goffman came to write on the ritual creation of selves, and hence of shared definitions of social reality, he had at his disposal an array of empirical studies showing how people at work maneuver to present an idealized front, and showing as well what stage-setting resources they have to use in this dramaturgy of everyday life. Goffman's reflections remain on a high level of abstraction, covering the commonalities of all occupational experiences (and of analogous processes in the leisure realms of polite sociability); but it is not a large shift to see that he has illuminated as well the major differences among the immediate day-by-day experiences of social classes. Classes differ because of different kinds and amounts of self-presentational experiences. Moreover, solidarity within classes (i.e., their transformation into status *communities*) is to a large degree the solidarity of teams in putting on performances and guarding common backstages. And the overall structure of stratification, in the final analysis—the distribution of wealth, power, and prestige—is the result of the ongoing activities by which some people idealize themselves better than others in the everyday encounters that make up the world of work and hence the organizational structure of society.

Why should rituals be important as a basis of power and material wealth? Because the solid economic and political organizations of society must nevertheless be enacted. Ordinary macrolevel social theory tends to take such organizations for granted, as does everyday discussion, as if they were things, with a permanence that exists apart from the people who perform them; in the same way, we take positions to be entities with an independence and solidity of their own. But these are metaphors, and hyperboles at that. Empirical reality, in the most detailed sense, is made up of a succession of minute-by-minute encounters. Organizations and positions are thing-like in their solidity only because they are continuously and repeatedly enacted in a series of microsituations. They are solid to the extent that they are taken for granted and thus smoothly reenacted, minute by minute and day after day; but without this process of *continual* social definition, they cease to exist. Now we can see the ultimate importance of interaction ritual: Ritual creates sacred, solid-seeming realities, social symbols that are not to be questioned and that have a strong and compelling sense of exteriority. Organizations and stratified postions within them are prime instances of such things, which take on coercive reality because we collectively believe them to be so. Thus well-performed rituals create and re-create the stratified order, and hence underlie the distribution of material, power, and status privileges.

We can go further into this line of analysis. It is possible to consider variations in the resources for producing and controlling rituals of various sorts; Goffman connects the Durkheimian to the Weberian and Marxian universes by showing us some of the crucial means of mental production, and the means of emotional production too. Such analysis would repay consideration of both its vertical and horizontal dimensions (i.e., relations of domination and conflict *among* classes, and relations *within* classes by which solidarity is maintained and a common definitional line upheld). And Goffman's concern for the fragilities and contingencies of reality construction tells us much about the difficulties under which people labor, both to dominate others consistently and to rebel successfully. Goffman does not perform this analysis, and given his propensities for looking at the world from a particular angle, we should not expect him to do so. But his work nevertheless does situate itself in an extremely useful position. In this sense, Goffman fits naturally into the history of Durkheimian analysis in the twentieth century—from Durkheim's own original functionalist themes to its recent twist toward an analysis of stratification ritual and the ritual weapons of conflict.

Neorationalism and Game Theory

Goffman's early works culminate in a burst of publications at the turn of the 1960s. *The Presentation of Self* (1959), *Encounters* (1961), and *Asylums* (1961) appear virtually simultaneously; *Stigma* (1963) and *Behavior in Public Places* (1963) a few years later. All push a

Durkheimian line, emphasizing the primacy of the social over the individual, and the moral and functional nature of social arrangements. Then another note begins to emerge, as Goffman begins to pay more attention to the egoistic and calculative side of interaction.

This note is already present in *The Presentation of Self*, but Goffman plays it down, considering the manipulation of impressions to be a secondary phenomenon produced by the demands of society itself for a clear definition of the situation. *Asylums*, again, takes mainly a functional stance, claiming that the self-destroying pressures on inmates are due to the technical needs of the organization processing masses of people. Ironically, this is the book that gave the sharpest impetus to the labeling theory of deviance—that what happens to one *after* one is apprehended by the authorities is fateful for the self, not what happens before. Yet Goffman himself does not enter this theme as a note of protest, but as an inevitable irony of social order.

But *Asylums* includes another note that pushes explicitly away from Goffman's sociocentric view. His explanation of the behavior of inmates working the "underlife" of a total institution posits a nonsocial self as well, a kind of pure existential will that struggles for a sense of autonomy, most obviously under adverse conditions (especially pp. 319–320). Goffman's essay on "role-distance" could take a similar line but does not. Here the argument is turned the other way, claiming that when one deliberately distances oneself from a social role, it is because that role is too demeaning in the light of some *other* role the individual also holds. Hence role-distance (of which the underlife of a total institution is an instance) does not mean the victory of the self over society, but simply the claim of part of society over another part. "Fun in Games," the companion essay in *Encounters* to "Role-Distance," stresses the positive side of this interpretation: Euphoria, Goffman claims, is when one is fully absorbed into a social role, unselfconscious of any transformative staging rules involved.

Still, the more egotistical image of the self does not go away. "Where the Action Is" recognizes a widespread desire for individuals to show their ability to deal with competitive stress, even to the extent of manufacturing artificial situations in which to show this character. Nevertheless, Goffman proposes that such behavior is at least half socialized, since society can make use of such personal strength, even if it is often used against social routine. And finally, in *Strategic Interaction* (1969), Goffman explicitly takes on conflictual and calculative situations. Although he is critical of game theory, he nevertheless follows out its neorationalist modifications, making little effort to bring conflict back into the fold of functionality and social morality.

This, then, is a legitimate second theme in Goffman, rising from its subsidiary place in the earlier works, while the Durkheimian emphasis recedes in his middle period. There is no sharp break; Goffman's early descriptive works on public interaction all include moves with relatively low levels of trust, just as the Durkheimian themes continue into *Relations in Public* and even later. But Goffman has clearly made an incursion into a different theoretical territory.

This territory, broadly speaking, might be called the utilitarian tradition. Game theory emerged from economics, and gives in explicit form the economic actor as a rational, calculating, egoistic individual, matched against other individuals in competitive and bargaining situations. In a sense, it is surprising that Goffman should have anything to do with this line of thought, for Durkheimian anthropology is explicitly and thoroughly critical of utilitarianism. Durkheim's starting point was his proof that rational economic exchanges could not take place without building upon a more basic precontractual solidarity. And Goffman does follow a version of this line in criticizing game theory.

But intellectual alliance is still possible, for game theory itself has been taken in quite a different direction from its earliest stance by its second generation of theorists. Thomas Schelling (1963), in particular, whom Goffman credits (in a discrete footnote) with creating the field of strategic interaction, reoriented game theory away from the model of independent rational actors with clear knowledge of payoff matrices and toward the question of communications and metacommunications that go on in strategic bargaining, especially in the absence of clear information. This development was part of a larger intellectual shift occurring in the late 1950s. What may be called neorationalism emerged, especially within organizational theory and operations research. Such theorists as Herbert Simon developed a revised and more realistic model of the human actor as information processor, stressing strategies used within cognitive limitations, in the absence of direct sanctions to control others' behavior. And as we shall see in the next section, there is an even wider trend in twentieth-century thought, arising above all in philosophy (although ultimately from mathematics), which points to the different *levels* of activity in which cognition is embedded. All across the board, the narrower model of individual rationality has given way to a more sophisticated version. It is this more sophisticated version to which Goffman brings his sociology.

In *Strategic Interaction*, Goffman takes up game theory and especially its application to conflict situations: spies and counterspies, armed confrontations, and the like. And he argues that this sensational material nevertheless does apply widely to everyday life. "In every

social situation," he says, "we can find a sense in which one participant will be an observer with something to gain from assessing expressions, and another will be a subject with something to gain from manipulating this process [1969:81]." Thus every encounter between buyer
and seller, employer and job applicant, supervisor and worker will
have some quality of strategic conflict; so will relations among friends
and acquaintances, since one is often in the position of having feelings
about another which cannot be admitted. Goffman does not develop
any full-fledged conflict viewpoint, of course, but one can easily
ground these points in a larger view of the processes that produce such
conflicting interests. After all, it is competitive economic markets
based on private property that undergird the maneuvering of buyer and
seller of both commodities and labor; and the varieties of sexual property relations, and the market-like aspects of conversational networks
in general, that underlie much of the pressures for duplicity in personal
relations.

Goffman's major interest, though, is on another level. He is concerned to distinguish between communication—the messages that people explicitly send to each other—and expression—the impressions that
people give off, whether they are aware of them or not. In general, expression is much more basic than communication. For, as Goffman
points out, "as a source of information the individual exudes expression and transmits communications, but . . . in the latter case the party
seeking information will still have to attend to expression lest he will
not know how to take what he is told [1969:9]." A spy may be told certain information by a contact, but still must assess not only (a) if the
contact's statement is correct; but also (b) whether it is believed by its
maker. If the statement is about some future action, there are not only
these questions of correctness and self-belief; but also (c) whether the
actor has the resolve to carry out the action; and (d) whether the actor
has the capabilities to do so. In assessing most of these matters, one
must pay more attention to how and in what context something is said
than to what is said itself.

Goffman goes on to consider the ramifications of strategic games,
as players attempt to manipulate each other's responses to moves and
communications. Since one makes an impression as well as transmits a
message, a skilled interactional strategist attempts to control or
fabricate impressions. The skilled observer tries to penetrate the
"cover" by discovering the opponent's strategy. Here, Goffman points
out, game theory and the symbolic interactionism of George Herbert
Mead converge. The game player takes the role of the other and interprets messages by reading the intent behind them. In classical game

theory, these intentions are transparent; there is no difficulty in placing oneself mentally in the other's place.

But here, Goffman finds both game theory and Meadian social psychology to be naïve. In real life, it is often unclear who the opposing players are, or what their moves can consist in, until after the moves are made. Imputation of social motives to others (and often to onseself as well) is more usually retrospective than prospective—in Garfinkel's term, it is an "account" rather than a cognitive program of action. And even where the Meadian role-taking model does fit better—in open, conflictual, game-like interaction—it is inadequate as a model for the actual performance of social action because it ignores the way in which people manipulate impressions to prevent successful role-taking.

Game theory and symbolic interactionism are both flawed, then, because they apply a single-level model to a two-leveled situation. Neo-rationalist game theory, though, is closer to an appropriate model, especially in Schelling's (1963) version of tacit coordination games. Schelling's argument is that coordination can occur, in the absence of communication, if there is an *obvious* solution—a move that both players will see as much more likely than any other. Goffman tends rather to emphasize the ambiguities that exist, and hence the difficulty of arriving at clearly coordinated activity. Thus he explains that espionage and efforts to maintain secrecy are often failures, partly because information, being nonphysical, is relatively easy to steal, but more importantly because of humans' inability to fundamentally control their *expressive* behavior. People who wish to conceal something, he says, usually appear self-conscious, and "it is this incapacity to inhibit warning signs of self-consciousness that makes an individual relatively safe to be near [1969:33]." In effect, Goffman tells us that the human animal automaticaly gives off expressions in its posture, emotions, gestures, and that these telegraph one's intentions to act. Communication may be added into this process, even in the form of reflexive communications to oneself via internalized others (as in Mead's theory of verbal thought), and one's conscious thinking may be directed toward controlling and manipulating one's nonverbal expressions. Nevertheless, the expressive side remains fundamental and will control interaction whether or not communication takes place. In effect, Goffman is saying that Schelling's tacit coordination is brought about, when it occurs, because the most obvious signals are the unconscious, expressive ones, not the manifestly communicated symbols.

The argument can be made more generally. For problems of mutual assessment of motives are not confined to strategic conflicts. The game may be one of coordinating the members of a social team, yet

the issue still remains of how this is done, especially since overt communications, even when possible, always presuppose some tacit understandings of how these messages are to be taken. Goffman gives the example of ordinary sociable conversation. Friends often engage in the
exchange of joking insults, with an attempt at witty repartée. Here, the
manifest content of communication is *not* to be believed; nevertheless,
the activity tends to be highly controlled, not by communication rules
but by expressive standards. One does not judge such talk first of all in
terms of objective truthfulness, sincerity, and candor, but of suitabil-
ity to the situation and the personal relationships; in many situations,
sincerity and candor would be highly unsuitable. And it is possible to
go beyond Goffman's example to cite many other types of conversation
that fit this scheme—not merely joking statements not to be believed,
but the egotistical self-dramatization or mutually self-indulgent com-
plaints that make up so much of sociable talk, not to mention their
counterparts in serious political talk within organizations and govern-
mental arenas of all kinds; all of the latter tend to be situationally
believed, even though fairly inaccurate. "What is enforced," says Goffman, "is not words but standards of conduct [1969:134]."

Goffman does give communication a place, but it is not on the
level of face-to-face interaction. Where games are loose (i.e., where enforcement of payoffs is in the hands of someone other than the immediately confronting players) communications through organizational
channels become important. Here *communication* itself may be manipulated; here efforts at cheating take the place of efforts at impression
management. Goffman's perspective on this point remains very conflict-oriented. It is apparent that the moral ties that bind people are
fundamentally based only on the face-to-face level where the contingencies of expression are located.

But even here Goffman has become doubtful about how central a
role moral obligations play. For although mutual trust has an obvious
functionality in making social relations possible, trust in people's truthfulness as communicators touches only a relatively small part of what
is involved in successful coordination of actions. As noted, actors must
also assess each other's correctness of judgment, and their resolution
and capacity to carry out promises and threats, as well as other situational factors, that may make outcomes quite different from what any
individual consciously intends.

Goffman in fact proposes several different reasons for the relative
stability of social order, which go rather far afield from moral obligations and trust. There is people's relative inability to control their nonverbal expressions, which makes them more trustworthy than they

themselves might wish. Moreover, the fact that people do not come completely clean with each other, and that yet other persons are aware of these duplicities among their acquaintances, often makes for a "multiplicity of checks—everyone, in effect, is in a position to blackmail everyone else [1969:76]." Hence overt conflict is not the usual state, but not because there is an overriding soildarity to offset the Hobbesian war of egotistical actors, all against all. Overt conflict occurs so seldom, rather, because conflict is a form of interaction as much as cooperation, and a winning strategy involves as many cognitive and coordinative difficulties as other forms of social order. Thus the game model is further circumscribed, primarily by human weakness. Whether because individuals are cowardly or because they are constrained by the difficulties of successful conflict, we find that the actor

> does not use his turn to make a move; he gets by with half-actions. Instead of commitments and enforcements, he provides assurances and resentments. Instead of moves, mere expressions. To frame this gestural realm entirely into strategic equivalents is to violate its regrettable nature; we end by making sustainable imputations of complex play to persons who aren't quite players and aren't quite playing [1969:135].

Goffman's conclusion can be read as an expression of existential cynicism. Not only can we not maintain social order on a firm functional or moral foundation, but we also cannot even maintain a decent and dignified level of conflict. But in a less evaluative vein, the argument may also be read as a striking extension of the arguments of neorationalism. One of the most important formulations is that of March and Simon (1958). In the clasical model, the rational actor optimizes the gains from each move. Realistically, however, in any complex situation this is usually impossible. Even a computer programmed to play chess cannot consider all possible moves and countermoves, as the set quickly becomes unmanageably large. Similarly, the manager of an organization cannot plan for all possible contingencies. Instead, the rational strategy is to replace *optimizing* with *satisficing*—to set minimally satisfactory levels for each area of operation and attempt to optimize only the most salient. The others are left to routine unless they fall below satisfactory levels, in which case one can attend to them for trouble shooting.

This model of limited human cognition in a complex world has several implications. It fits with Simon's theory of organizational power (1947)—which builds in turn on Chester Barnard's classical work (1938), itself frequently cited by Goffman—in which an organization cannot be simply controlled from the top, programming all members' behavior in advance. Rather, delegation of authority is inevitable, whether it is officially recognized or not. Hence real sources of power may be unofficial ones, and these exist wherever the outcomes of activities are most uncertain. In particular, technical advice-givers or trouble-shooters, even if they lack the official power to give orders, have effective power because they deal with the nonroutine areas where choices must be made. What they express focuses nonexperts' sense of the reality of the issue at hand, and this circumscribes what official decisions they can take.

The neorationalist model, then, envisages a world in which open-ended strategies for action are followed rather than iron-clad rules. In aligning himself with this position, Goffman has moved away from an earlier stance (in *Behavior in Public Places*) in which rules govern public behavior. Rather, the position taken in *Strategic Interaction* implies that the simple communication of rules, whether to others or to oneself, rests on a deeper strategy of following certain lines of conduct. In an interactional situation, it is the expressive side—the ways in which people make moves and telegraph them in advance by their physical set—to which one must pay most attention. In effect, both Goffman and Simon converge on a model of human consciousness as figure and ground. It is impossible to attend to everything at once, so one satisfices in most areas and optimizes only a few (Simon); one operates most basically on expressions of real moves and judges the significance of explicit communications in this light (Goffman).

Schelling's (1963:53–118) contribution to neorationalism (which has explicitly influenced Goffman) was to point out what solution can be reached in an interaction in which each side has cognitive limitations and is aware that the other side has the same. Two individuals, trying to meet in a large city on a given day but lacking more specific plans and unable to communicate with each other, will be able to meet if there is a sufficiently obvious landmark to orient to. Upper-middle-class residents of the northeastern U.S. generally can reach a solution for meeting in New York City: Grand Central Station under the clock at noon. Similarly, in an arms race or a military operation where communication is limited by mutual distrust, stability or escalation depends on whether or not an obvious stopping place exists under the circumstances.

The sociological importance of this analysis is that it explains how political power can be simultaneously based upon threat and consensus. The political leader, whether military dictator or party influence broker, is powerful only because others obey the leader's orders; but this in turn depends on whether they believe the leader is powerful and thus able to reward acquiescence and punish defiance. The problem of every political actor, then, is to find where the winning coalition is, and to make sure they are with it rather than against it before a showdown occurs. The cumulative social definition of someone as powerful makes them powerful, and the same holds for powerlessness. Hence the neorationalist explanation of political authority points to the expressive symbols by which this tacit coordination game is resolved. As in Goffman's earlier dramaturgical model, the publicly accepted definition of the situation is all-important, above all in cases of potential conflict; a clear definition of the situation creates an obvious solution to the coordination game, while the disturbance of this clarity can cause power to crumble. The stakes, then, in effective social dramaturgy are not only the general need for cognitive order of which Goffman speaks; they include the entire structure of domination.

The ramifications of this model are considerable, and mostly remain to be worked out. For in moving to a model of stratification, conflictual interaction, and tacit coordination, it is not necessary to abandon the earlier ritual model of the construction of social realities and moral ideals. These are two different perspectives on the same empirical phenomena. The ritual model is especially useful because it can be cast in terms of variables, notably variations in social density, which affect the strength and abstractness of shared moral symbols (cf. Collins, 1975:75–76; 153–155), while the models of strategic interaction and cognitive limits on overt communication point to the distribution of power and the contingencies for its change. Goffman, as usual, has left these lines for others, while his focus has moved on to a consideration of the levels of social reality itself. This is the subject of our final section.

Social Epistemology and Multileveled Realities

From Goffman's various works, we can compile a set of reasons why reality is not hard and simple, but multileveled and fragile. The list grows as he moves along, and by his later book, *Frame Analysis* (1974), it is easy to assimilate Goffman to the hyper-relativism of sociology's epistemological radicals, the ethnomethodologists. Yet Goffman began by stressing the hard external constraints of society upon what individuals can afford to do and believe; and in *Frame Analysis*, along with an explicit social relativism, there is an equally strong stress on why the world, although capable of shifting, nevertheless tends to find a solid resting place. In effect, Goffman wants to have it both ways, and through the notion of frames, he finds an elegant device that comes very near to allowing this. The world is complex and shifting, but it is not infinitely so; Goffman sets out to chart a finite number of levels among which shifts can take place.

Let us look first at the compendium of reasons why reality is multisided. First, the early Durkheimian argument that reality is socially constructed implies—although Goffman barely touches this point—that different social conditions, such as different historical eras, result in different realities. This is especially so since society is so much organized around moral realities and their concrete embodiments in sacred objects, such as the self, or as symbols of society itself. The point Goffman does draw from this is that social realities, as created, are in some sense artificial and arbitrary; yet because they are (allegedly) so beneficial in their consequences, people place great pressures on themselves and each other to maintain these realities, to uphold a single strong definition of the situation. The pressure to do so is so great, and the difficulties that crop up are so common, that people are forced into a second level of reality right there: They are not only participants in a social reality, but also technicians manipulating the stage setting in order to uphold it. Hence the first complexity: that of frontstage and backstage realities.

Second, Goffman recognizes that many sorts of social situations are doubly artificial, as in the case of games, refined social etiquette, and the like. Some of society, then, is a play within a play, and often people's goal is to forget the transformative rules by internalizing them and taking them for granted. This is the source of euphoria, of "fun in games." This is not a primitive social achievement, but a relatively sophisticated one.

Third, persons in complex societies tend to have multiple roles; hence they may manifest displays of ironic or deprecating distance from some of these roles, the better to uphold other ones. Here social complexity (and especially the status differences among various parts of one's role-set) produces yet another lamination of realities.

Fourth, social conflict and efforts at domination create further cognitive multiplicities. This is already implicit in the frontstage–backstage distinction, where it can be seen that different occupations and social classes maintain misleading frontstages and deprecating backstages toward each other. The analysis of strategic interaction shows that one may maneuver to throw off one's opponents or competitors by managing one's expressive behavior. This gives us not only the complexity of what an actor really intends and what impressions the actor gives off, but also the distinction of communication versus expression.

And to all this Goffman adds another subtlety, in the form of human cowardice or incompetence at playing strategic games to the hilt, leaving us in a slushy realm of gestures half-intended and half-retracted.

Finally, conversation itself is analyzed as a realm in which people concern themselves with certain types of conduct and not primarily with the objective truth of what is said. Conversations create little realms of temporary belief all their own, for part of the appropriate standard of conduct is to engross oneself in the world that is narrated. This produces pressures not only to insulate one's conversation from actual states of affairs in the world to which it allegedly refers, but also to perfect and idealize the subject matter, to make it a good story. In a final irony, Goffman can point out that professionally made conversation, such as the stories of commercial dramatists, appear truer than real life precisely because they have a clearness and elegance that ordinary life and our amateur efforts at recounting it seldom reach. Realities are not only multiple but are socially biased so that it is that which has been most transformed that often appears most real.

In *Frame Analysis,* Goffman assembles and formalizes many of these themes. The frame metaphor gives us the image of a picture—the content—and the perspective from which it is viewed—the frame. The metaphor can encompass various such distinctions—Goffman's communication versus expression, Austin's locutionary and illocutionary forces, or the distinction in formal logic between rules within the system and the formalities constituting the system. For Goffman's purposes, it is useful because it can encompass a series of shifts among levels. For if one can look at a picture with its frame around it, one might also draw another picture, which puts the picture and frame in the center and adds the viewer inside another frame. But this in turn raises the possibility of drawing still another picture, including the viewer's perspective, and so on, ad infinitum.

Goffman is not concerned with infinite ramifications, but rather with spelling out the socially relevant number of levels. He suggests two primary frames people recognize—events occurring in the natural world and those within the social world. On these can be done a number of key shifts, to switch to a musical metaphor—transformations of primary settings into make-believe, contests, ceremonials, technical redoings (practice sessions, exhibitions, replayings and the like), and other regroupings. Among these the explanations and accounts, fantasies, intellectual commentaries, and other restructurings of life experience in ordinary conversations ought to be included. Various laminations may be added by keyings of keyings (if one stuck to the earlier metaphor, one could say frames around frames), and possibly even further.

The theme of the potentially infinite regress of self-reflexivity is one that Goffman might seem to have taken from the ethnomethodologists. In a larger perspective, Goffman is only expanding a sociological version of a theme that has spread more and more widely in twentieth-century thought. Its origins might be traced to the paradoxes generated by late nineteenth-century mathematicians dealing with the concept of infinity, which produced the turn-of-the-century battle between mathematical formalists and intuitionists, each with their own program for avoiding such paradoxes. Bertrand Russell's efforts to produce a formal system of mathematical fundamentals, however, produced further paradoxes, and in the 1930s Gödel showed that any axiomatic system like Russell's always involves at least one principle that cannot be proven or refuted within the system; while a larger system containing a proof of this principle could be constructed, it in turn would involve another principle standing outside it, and so on, ad infinitum (see Kramer, 1970:444–462). Moreover, Wittgenstein's revelations of the multileveled nature of language is not only an analogy, but also a cousin to Gödel's incompleteness theorem. For Wittgenstein was a pupil of Russell, and he first attempted to follow his teacher's footsteps, but in another field, by formalizing a theory of language; later Wittgenstein played his own Gödel by turning about to show that language not only involves the level of explicit syntax and reference, but also a metalinguistic level, later christened by Wittgenstein's imitator and rival, John Austin, as *speech acts*. Thus Goffman's expression versus communication is rooted in an understanding that had built up through the first half of the twentieth century, and his concept of frames extends to social cognition—Gödel's recognition of the potentially infinite regress of self-reflexive thought.

Goffman's model, though, is especially satisfying because it combines the Gödel-type recognition of potentially infinite boxes within boxes with the Wittgenstein-Austin recognition of a finite number of incommensurable levels of human language, and it does this in a fuller context than either. For Goffman deals with types of *social* action, among which the purely logical or linguistic patterns of the mathematicians and philosophers might be placed. The activities of intellectuals, or even of ordinary language speakers, were previously given without any context, even though both the mathematicians and the linguistic philosophers point beyond themselves—Gödel in a purely formal sense, Wittgenstein and, especially, Austin coming near enough to see that symbolic communications are embedded in various social actions and indeed *are* a type of social action. The next step would be to a fully sociological perspective, and Goffman takes this step, if only rudimentarily. He takes it via the stepping stones of his previous works; hence we get a typology of frames and keys based on his familiar concerns with the theatre and with social dramatury, with spies and con men, conversationalists and managers of self-expressions. But surely Goffman's frame is the larger one and his social typology implies, somewhere within it, particular keyings of other realities that make up the productions of intellectuals and the expressiveness as well as the content of ordinary speech actions. In effect, Wittgenstein told us that speech acts exist; Austin give the category a name, while Goffman provides the beginning of a systematic mapping of the territory.

In following this train of intellectual development, Goffman moves somewhat parallel to the ethnomethodologists. But whereas Garfinkel and his followers have tended to emphasize the paradoxical side of multileveled realities and their potential for infinite regress in the search for the ultimate ground, Goffman asserts that solid ground does exist in the contours of the levels themselves. Natural and social worlds may be transformed by various keyings, and social actors may explicitly play on these transformations in order to capture someone else in a constructed reality. Nevertheless, Goffman emphasizes, there *are* real cops and real robbers (or real innocent suspects), and real military enemies with their espionage agents. And although they may play mutual containment games on each other, with the infinite ramifications of drawing the trickster into a trick, discovering the trick and containing it with a further trick, nevertheless these matters are reduced back to ground zero when someone is shot, caught, or escapes with the goods. Goffman himself notes that resolution of cognitive ambiguities often comes out of the barrel of a gun (1974:316).

Thus, Goffman points to real sanctions in the material world as the ultimate grounding, and all transformations of it as secondary. More generally, he stresses that although the social world contains complex levels, people nevertheless usually know, or could know, what level they are on. One is practicing for a game (a keying of a keying); one is reminiscing conversationally about work experiences (another transformative keying of the natural and social world), and so forth. Goffman probably overstates the point, reiterating his earlier, functionalist-period position that the *rules* of any level of activity are sufficiently clear to most people most of the time. The point is undermined by Goffman's own arguments that expressions of conduct are more fundamental than explicit communications (among which rules are surely included), as well as Garfinkel's (1967) demonstration of a similar point, which he refers to as the "indexicality" of all social communications and rules. But Goffman at least manages to capture both sides: not only the complexities and dynamics of the world, but also the ability of people (and of a sufficiently sophisticated sociologist) to settle on a clear reality much of the time.

Regrettably, Goffman once again misses the implications of his analysis for a theory of stratification and hence a link to the mainstream of macrosociology. For the police and the con artist, with their defense of or attack on property, the military and their spies, with their search for territorial power: These are ultimate realities indeed in the sense of controlling the sanctions before which all else will bow. In one sense, all the social game-playing is only superstructure to political and economic fundamentals. But Goffman himself, were he to follow his own assertions in this vein, might be ready to point out that the superstructure acts back upon the material base. For the police and the military, like economic and any other human organizations, are made up of physical bodies of persons *coordinated* for mutually supporting actions. And such coordination requires coordination games, dependent on human communicative and above all expressive maneuverings. Out of the shifting cognitions of the superstructure are determined the alliances that make up basic social structure, and the shifts and breaks that make up the dynamics of human history. In this sense, Goffman's middle and early periods of theorizing complement his later themes nicely. A synthesis of all three, reaching out to their surrounding intellectual traditions, would come very close to providing the skeleton of a very powerful general sociology.

III.

Such a synthesis would not be very much in keeping with Goffman's own intellectual habits. We have seen that he has continually drawn upon powerful intellectual traditions and upon wide-ranging empirical research—both of his own rather innovative procurement and of the best of his contemporaries. But Goffman hides his intellectual elitism behind a theory-deprecating manner, producing a kind of underground, hermetic theorizing beneath a popularistic-seeming surface. Yet even the surface is paradoxical and misleading; for although, as noted, Goffman's actual wording is restrained and judicious and his actual contents scholarly in a very elevated sense, his works have almost always been received as an iconoclasm that is virtually the opposite of his manifest messages. Yet the impression of iconoclasm is not exactly accidental. Goffman himself has warned us that manifest communicative content is less important than the expressive style in which it is presented. It is the frames through which Goffman's work has been presented that have attracted the attention, as, following his theories closely, we might have expected. The Durkheimian content of *The Presentation of Self* has taken back seat to the dramatic, if allegedly superficial, imagery of frontstage and backstage maneuvers, and the functionalism of *Asylums* to the implicit irony of a labeling theory in which mental illness is produced by the very processes that are supposed to cure it. And the relativism of the frame metaphor popularly overrides the conservative assertions studded through the contents of *Frame Analysis.*

One must suspect that Goffman, whether motivated consciously or unconsciously, has pursued a multileveled strategy of intellectual self-presentation. For he has not only kept up with the major intellectual action of the esoteric world of fundamental theory, but he has also had a keen sense for where popular movements were going. His covert sponsorship of labeling theory predated the popularity of Thomas Szasz and R. D. Laing and the whole outburst of encounter grouping and other efforts to break through the conventional institutional frameworks of psychotherapy. *The Presentation of Self,* in its popularistic interpretation, foreshadowed the 1960s critique of the mindless conformity and social phoniness of the 1950s, just as *Frame Analysis* seems to reflect the living theatre of the hippie era.

Goffman even hit on a formulation of a phenomenon, that, if read correctly, could well have predicted the whole trend of onslaught upon traditional deference and demeanor patterns that made its sharpest cut in the casualness revolution of the hippie period. For Goffman's essay on role-distance, published in 1961, pointed directly to the trend, prominent even then among American youth, of ironic coolness or flippancy toward conventional social roles. Goffman was almost alone in bringing this to theoretical attention, while most sociologists described in boring detail the "straight" roles of the conventional world, missing with textbook blandness the most salient feature for most young Americans—the distinction between the "cool" and the "finky," between the "hip" and the "square," between those confining themselves within the bland and blind world of traditionally proper conventionality, and those with enough energy and self-possession to distance themselves and eventually to catch a glimpse of the arbitrary and enacted nature of the whole social order.

Goffman, it must be said, seems to have captured the point more unconsciously than consciously. His explicit analysis of role-distance sees no historical significance in the phenomenon, and he explains it in all-too-conventional fashion. The cause of this failure is not unlike the cause of his failure to push on through to full possession of the theoretical territories he has reconnoitered. Goffman seems hyper-reflexive; he himself manifests an extreme form of role-distance, separating himself from any clear, straightforward position, be it theoretical or popular. In this sense, he appears as the epitome of the 1950s intellectual—hip to the point of unwillingness to take any strong stance, even the stance of his own hipness.

In a larger perspective, Goffman represents a kind of extreme point in the moral career of the twentieth-century intellectual. The modernism and self-glorification of the creative intellectual early in the century had long since given way to unbridled experimentalism and to an esotericness that left the intellectual entirely free from popular pressures, and at the same time progressively more and more nihilistic about having a meaningful social role. Goffman's intellectual youth coincides with existentialism and the theater of the absurd, with idolization of the ultra-cool, heroin-fed jazz musician and the nihilistic cynicism of the beatnik painter. Goffman, I think, is their sociologist counterpart, like a good many of his sociological generation who expressed their own hipness by confining their research to the backstages of society, to pool halls, jazz musicians, con men, and "deviants" generally. Where Goffman stands out is in his intellectual superiority, his ability to use links with the elite intellectual mainstreams—with the Durkheimians and the game theorists, philosophers and organizational researchers—to provide an extra measure of role-distance from his hip exposé role itself. And, one might add, unfortunately, vice versa, as far as the systematic advancement of theory goes.

But that would be to judge Goffman by a type of engagé standard that is more characteristic of another intellectual generation. In his own terms, Goffman has been eminently successful. That he might prove to be even more successful on terms alien to his own would be an appropriately Goffmanian irony.

The Language-Game of Power*

Sometimes intellectual fields undergo revolutions that spill outward and influence other fields, perhaps even more strongly than their original home. This happened with both Freudian and behaviorist psychologies in their day; it has happened more recently in linguistics (some of the ramifications of which are evident in the topic at hand). But the revolution that we are now feeling the brunt of in the social sciences is the revolution that began in the early twentith century in philosophy. There are a number of versions of it: the British, beginning with Moore and Russell and reaching its full force with Wittgenstein and Austin; the German phenomenological version, beginning with Husserl and extending into sociology via Schutz and Garfinkel; the existialist, drawing also on Husserl and others and exerting its more recent influence through Heidegger, Sartre, and Merleau-Ponty; and even an American version stemming from Pierce and having some echoes in the recent popularity of Kuhn. What we have experienced in the last few decades has been a kind of philosophical imperialism, extending

* Originally published in *Administrative Science Quarterly, 1976, 21* (September). Copyright 1976 *Administrative Science Quarterly.*

into political science, the sociology of knowledge, of deviance, of cognition, and of everyday life.

With the work of Stewart Clegg (1975), and the related studies by David Silverman, we find the wave washing over the sociology of organizations. The first half of Clegg's *Power, Rule, and Domination* comprises a general philosophical and theoretical discussion. He begins by criticizing the "picture theory" of words—the doctrine that words are images of things—and argues instead for a grammar of word use. Sociological writing itself is not only *about* something; it also, and above all, *does* something. It is a way of seeing the world, of constructing a reality, of carrying on an argument. Clegg illustrates this with theorizing about the word power. "Power" is not a thing, he argues, but a mode of doing, and especially of doing in the community of players in a language-game. But Clegg wishes to avoid the nihilism of an endless regress of examining one's own statements (about statements about statements about statements ad infinitum). Avoiding the sheer conventionalist interpretations of Wittgenstein, on whom he primarily draws, he proposes instead the interpretation of language-games as a form of life, and hence an empirically researchable topic.

Before we get to this research, though, we are given several chapters examining theories of power that derive from other empirical work. Focusing on the community power debate, Clegg carries on the point made by Bachrach and Baratz, that community power involves not merely decision-making per se, but the *grounds* that determine what becomes considered as an issue. Behavioral models, exchange theories, and the like are criticized because they stay on the surface, and ignore the deep structure, what ethnomethodologists call the "background assumptions" or the "taken-for-granted." Similarly, Clegg criticizes the theory of power as control over areas of environmental uncertainty, since such uncertainty must depend upon a prior, unexplicated sense of what can be taken as certain because it is taken for granted.

This background against which uncertainties arise Clegg interprets, with a reverential bow to Max Weber, as an unexplicated but potent set of *rules*. He interprets Weber as showing two levels of power; *authority*—the taken-for-granted grounds of whatever can be legitimately done; and *domination*—the realm of carrying out one's will against others' opposition on particular concrete issues. Again, Clegg translates this into the language of ethnomethodology, using Cicourel's linguistic model (adapted from Chomsky) of society as a deep structure plus surface rules. Clegg criticizes Cicourel for what he perceives as an undue attachment to the social order perspective, since

Cicourel allegedly infers the deep structure from the surface, instead of vice versa; a criticism that strikes me as somewhat frivolous, since Clegg himself lets his analysis come all too readily to rest with having formulated some deep "rules," sometimes even referring to them as dominant "icons" (such as the icon of capitalism, which he believes somehow controls the material arrangements of western organizations).

Having thus made his bows and his growls in various directions, Clegg finally arrives at his empirical study, an investigation of a construction site in the north of England. His focus is on management work, which is a form of talk—characterized, in the Marxist tones that float occasionally into earshot, as "linguistic labor."

What is most novel about Clegg's research is not simply his perspective, however, but his research techniques. In fact, I believe that he has introduced the first new research technique into the study of organizations since the use of questionnaires (which became prominent in the field in the 1960s, though not wholly displacing the earlier emphasis on a less formal participant observation, actually made up by a mixture of open-ended interviewing and visual inspection). Clegg, like the new wave of ethnomethodologists, went armed with a cassette tape recorder, and collected the actual conversations that made up the order-giving, advising, negotiating, and informal socializing of the organization's managers. The results of this, however, are not entirely as novel as Clegg would have us believe. What he was able to do was to demonstrate certain processes, with a great deal more empirical documentation, that the earlier tradition of participant observation, above all such conflict-oriented researchers as Dalton and Crozier, had referred to more loosely. We find nice depictions of informal maneuvering to produce formally required reports and legal documents, as in Clegg's description of "cooking the books." We see a good example of the bargaining strategies by which the contractors get back at the contracting agency for taking a narrow and penurious interpretation of one facet of the works contract. And more in Clegg's own chosen line of analysis, we have examples of how the formal structure is taken for granted, especially among the workers within the organization, while attention is concentrated on the surface of particular issues.

How successful is this approach? The shift from the long philosophical–theoretical introduction to the research is a bit incongruous, but no doubt inevitably so, given the nature of this effort to combine the hitherto uncombinable. There is a certain element of sophistry at times, which is virtually the hallmark of certain versions of ethnomethodology, but Clegg usually overcomes this because he has a strong sense of having analytical work to do. As a reflexively open-ended style of work, there is plenty of room to throw in side issues as the author feels fit, and humanistic and Marxist themes sometimes break up the main line of argument in a way that makes this book rather hard to follow. There is some tendency to belabor the obvious with the empirical materials, to the extent that, from the point of view of a sociology of science, one is tempted to see ethnomethodology as yet another stage of hyperempiricism. Organizations are one of the best studied, and in my opinion, theoretically most advanced, areas in social science; after having done most of the more important studies, we are left with the necessity for young researchers to make their own mark, to search for closer and closer documentation, and for finer and finer subtleties of interpretation.

But while this is one side of the process, I believe that there is a much more powerful contribution being formulated. Clegg's methods put us on the brink of understanding, through empirical study, the actual mechanisms that produce power and legitimacy: the manipulation of emotional tones, the cognitive resources that go into negotiations both of the taken-for-granted and the up-for-grabs. The conception of management as linguistic work, and of all work (and all formal and informal structure) as empirically observable sequences in time and space, is an important tool for seeing the mechanisms underlying our more macrolevel generalizations (on the effects of various kinds of controls, on the actual influence-making procedures of experts, etc.), and for resolving some of the outstanding issues (such as finding out just how much productive work is actually done in our allegedly technocratic societies, and how much work is really time-killing or organizational politiking).

These issues take us rather far afield from the philosophical center from which Clegg starts. But the newer method and outlook does have promise, even as it presents a peculiar mixture of tediousness (which is by no means absent from most standard organizational research) and of freshness. Of the latter, one could ask no better example than Clegg's comments on bringing his rather short data analysis to a close:

> My analysis stops at this juncture. It could be elaborated almost indefinitely—but what would be the point of that? To overwhelm you with evidence? And would surfeit be proof? I would rather you took my analysis as a point of departure for your own, rather than as a substitute. The possibilities of your reading have been an ever-present feature of my writing. While I have read myself [my tradition] in others, others will read themselves [their tradition] in me. And thus my conclusions must be interpreted not as a closure but as an opening—an opportunity for us [thought] to find our way [pp. 152–153].

Or, to sum it up another way, there is the striking front cover of the dust jacket, displaying an Escher woodcut of a construction organization viewed from God's-eye perspective, half hard at work building the unfinished—and unfinishable—Tower of Babel.

The Microfoundations of
Macrosociology*

Microsociology is the detailed analysis of what people do, say, and think in the actual flow of momentary experience. *Macrosociology* is the analysis of large-scale and long-term social processes, often treated as self-subsistent entities, such as "state," "organization," "class," "economy," "culture," and "society." In recent years there has been an upsurge of radical microsociology, that is to say, empirically detailed and/or phenomenologically sophisticated microsociology. Radical microsociology (Cicourel, 1973; Garfinkel, 1967), as the detailed study of everyday life, emerged partly from the influx of phenomenology into empirical sociology, and partly from the application of new research techniques—audio and video recordings—which have made it possible to study real-life interaction in second-by-second detail. This has led to the close analysis of conversation (Sacks, Schegloff and Jefferson, 1974), of nonverbal interactions (Goffman, 1971:3–61), and of the construction and use of organizational records (Cicourel, 1968; Clegg, 1975), and hence to a view of how larger social patterns are constructed out of micro materials.

* Originally published in *American Journal of Sociology*, 1981, *86* (March). Copyright 1981 University of Chicago Press, Chicago.

This radical microsociology, under such labels as "ethnomethodology," "cognitive sociology," "social phenomenology," and others, cuts in a number of different directions. The direction that I would argue is most promising for the advance of sociology as an empirical science is not the phenomenological analysis of concepts, but the emphasis upon ultradetailed empirical research. This detailed microanalysis offers several contributions for the field of sociology in general. One is to give a strong impetus toward translating all macrophenomena into combinations of microevents. A microtranslation strategy reveals the empirical realities of social structures as patterns of repetitive microinteraction. Microtranslation thus gives us a picture of the complex levels of abstraction involved in causal explanations.

Another contribution of radical microsociology is its discovery that actual everyday life microbehavior does not follow rationalistic models of cognition and decision-making. Instead, social interaction depends on tacit understandings and agreements not to attempt to explicate what is taken for granted. This implies that explanations in terms of norms, rules, and role taking should be abandoned, and that any model of social exchange must be considerably modified. These are large departures from accepted sociological traditions. But these traditions have not been very successful in advancing explanatory principles. I would contend this is because they have an incorrect model of the actor. What we need, instead, is a micromechanism which can explain the repetitive actions that make up social structure such that interactions and their accompanying cognitions rest upon noncognitive bases.

Such a mechanism, I will attempt to show, is provided by *interaction ritual chains.* Such chains of microencounters generate the central features of social organization—authority, property, and group membership—by creating and recreating mythical cultural symbols and emotional energies. The result of microtranslating all social structure into such interaction ritual chains should be to make microsociology an important tool in explaining both the inertia and the dynamics of macrostructure.

THE TIME-SPACE TABLE

It is useful to visualize the empirical basis of micro and macro categories by a time–space table (see Table 1). On one dimension are laid out the amounts of time considered by the sociologist, ranging from a few seconds, through minutes, hours, days, weeks, months, and

Table 1

Time and Space as Levels of Sociological Analysis

Space scale (sq. ft.)	Time Scale					
	Seconds (10^0–10^1 sec)	Minutes–hours (10^2–10^4 sec)	Days (10^5 sec)	Weeks–months (10^6 sec)	Years (10^7–10^8 sec)	Centuries (10^9 sec)
One Person (1–3)	Cognitive–emotional processes	Meaningful events; work; repetitive and intermittent behaviors			Careers; life histories	(Genealogies)
Small Group (3–10^2)	Eye-contact studies; microconversational analyses	Rituals, group dynamics, exchanges, bargaining				
Crowd–Organization (10^3–10^6)		Crowd behavior		Organizations: informal; formal	Organizational structures and histories	
Community (10^7–10^{10})				Social movements	Communities	
Territorial Society (10^{11}–10^{14})					Political, economic, demographic, and stratification patterns (mobility rates etc.) "cultures"	Long-term social changes

up to years and centuries. On the other axis are the number of people in physical space one might focus on: beginning with one person in their local bodily space, through small groups, large groups and aggregates, and up to an overview of all the people across a large territory. I have filled in the cells of the table with the kinds of analyses that sociologists make of that particular slice of time and space.

It is clear that the distinction between micro and macro is one of degree, and admits of at least two dimensions. All levels of analysis in this table are more micro than those below and to the right of them, and all levels are more macro than those above and to the left. Micro and macro are relative terms, in both time and space, and the distinction itself may be regarded as a pair of continuous variables. Moreover, one can see that microanalysis in sociology has recently shifted its level: symbolic interactionism, for example, has traditionally been concerned with situations (although sometimes with more long-term processes—e.g., Becker, 1963; Bucher and Strauss, 1961; Dalton, 1959) located generally on the minutes-to-hours level. Radical microsociologies such as ethnomethodological analysis of conversation, or micro-ethological studies of eye movements, have shifted the focus to the seconds level (e.g. Schegloff, 1967); and phenomenological sociology, in its extreme formulations, verges on Platonism or mysticism because of its focus on the instantaneous "now" at the left edge of the table.

The strict meaning of "empirical" refers to the upper-left corner of the table. You, the reader, sitting at your desk or in your car, or standing by your mailbox, etc., are in that microsituation (or possibly also slightly further down the left column), and it is impossible for anyone to ever be in any empirical situation other than this sort. All macroevidence, then, is aggregated from such microexperiences. Moreover, although one can say that all the vertical cells in the far-left column are empirical in the (slightly different) sense that they all exist in the physical world of the present, the cells horizontally to the right must be regarded as analysts' constructs. In the few seconds it takes to read this passage, you the reader are constructing the reality of all those macrocategories, insofar as you think of them. This is not to say that they do not also have some empirical referent, but that it is a more complex and inferential one that direct microexperience.

Everyone's life, experientially, is a sequence of microsituations, and the sum total of all sequences of individual experience in the world would constitute all the possible sociological data there is. Thus the recent introduction of audio- and videotapes by radical microsociologists is a move toward this primary data.

MICROTRANSLATION AS A STRATEGY

There are several advantages in translating all sociological concepts into aggregates of microphenomena.

The first point is epistemological. Strictly speaking, there is no such thing as a "state," an "economy," a "culture," a "social class." There are only collections of individual people, acting in particular kinds of microsituations, which are characterized thus by a kind of shorthand. This can be easily seen if one examines empirically how researchers go about studying macrosubjects. Researchers themselves never leave their own microsituations; what they do is compile summaries by a series of coding and translating procedures, until a text is produced that is taken as representing a macroreality, standing above all the microsituations that produced it (Cicourel, 1975; Garfinkel, 1967). This is true whether the researcher is relying on conversation with informants or upon closed-item questionnaires, or even upon direct personal observation. In each case there are a series of tacit summaries between the actual life experiences and the way in which these are finally reported. The same is true to an even larger degree where historical materials are used; these are usually constructed from previous written accounts, which even in their original form contain numerous glosses upon the actual flow of minute-by-minute experience.

It is strategically impossible for sociology to do without this kind of macrosummary. It would take too much time to recount all the microevents that make up any large scale pattern, and a total recounting in any case would be tedious and unrewarding. Nevertheless, we need not reconcile ourselves to the complete loss of information of the truly empirical level, satisfying ourselves with remote abstractions. For if macrophenomena are made up of aggregations and repetitions of many similar microevents, then we can sample these essential microcomponents, and use them as the empirical basis of all other sociological constructions.

The significance of the first point, then, is: *sociological concepts can be made fully empirical only by grounding them in a sample of the typical microevents that make them up.*

The implication is that the ultimate empirical validation of sociological statements depends on their microtranslation. By this standard, virtually all sociological evidence as yet presented is only tentative. This of course does not mean that it may not be a useful approximation, although this is not always the case. Success at some degree of microtranslation, I would suggest, is the test of whether the macro statement is a good approximation or a misleading reification.[1]

A second implication is that the *active* agents in any sociological explanation must by microsituational. Social patterns, institutions, and organizations are only abstractions from the behavior of individuals, and summaries of the distribution of different microbehaviors in time and space. These abstractions and summaries do not *do* anything; if they seem to indicate a continuous reality it is because the individuals that make them up repeat their microbehaviors many times, and if the structures change it is because the individuals who enact them change their microbehaviors.

This is not to say that a causal explanation is totally micro-situational. In another paper (Collins, forthcoming), I have attempted to show that the microtranslation of a large body of causal principles leaves, in addition to a number of pure microprinciples, a residue of several types of macroreferences. Individuals within microsituations themselves make macroreferences to other situations, as well as to abstract or reified social entities; the effects of microsituations upon individuals themselves are often cumulative, resulting from repetition of microexperiences; outside analysts cannot establish microprinciples without comparing across microsituations. There are also three pure macrovariables: the dispersion of individuals in physical *space;* the amount of *time* that social processes take (including temporal patterns of intermittent and repeated behaviors); and the *numbers* of in-

---

[1] To cite a recent example: The controversy over the reputational and decision-making models of community power is a debate between the merits of a more macro and a more micro model. Decision-making focuses on particular microevents and claims greater empirical realism; the reputational model is criticized, as loose macrotheories often are, for taking the hypostatizations and illusions of commonsense discourse as if they were reliable pictures of social realities. Advocates of the reputational method, on the other hand, criticize the microfocus of decision-making for missing the larger pattern, and especially that part of it that is hidden by focusing only on actual decisions, ignoring what decisions are never raised, including institutional arrangements that are never challenged but are implicitly defended by being taken for granted (Bachrach and Baratz, 1962). The macrotheory here promises a greater range of explanatory power but is empirically weaker. Yet it is salvageable by translating it into an aggregate of microterms. A move in this direction has been accomplished by Laumann *et al.* (1977), who show a key link between the crude macrosummary of actions involved in reputational power and the actual exercise of that power, by demonstrating that there are networks of reputed influentials who actually discuss political matters informally among themselves, and thus tend to arrive at a general line of behavior that presumably includes taken-for-granted routines as well as the raising of explicit decisions.

dividuals involved. In other words, there are some irreducible macro-factors, but there is only a limited set of them. All varieties of macrostructures or macroevents can be translated into these kinds of aggregations of microevents.

If causality involves stating the conditions under which particular social processes happen, then it is apparent that both the independent and dependent variables, "the conditions" and "the social processes that happen," are composite terms. Both, at a minimum, refer to an analyst's selection of repetitive microevents. Both IV and DV may be further composite in the sense of comprising a spatial–temporal arrangement of a number of different microactors. Yet further macrosamples (control variables) must be compared by the analyst to establish any given causal statement.

In any empirical instance, then, to fully account for the behavior observed involves the analyst in comparisons with a wide range of non-present situations, and with statements linking behavior in one situation with behavior in other situations. For example, an individual's situational behavior is conditional upon the overall distribution of behaviors in other times and places that can be referred to metaphorically as an organizational network. But to show such a pattern—and I believe we have shown a number of such patterns, cryptically summarized under such statements as "social class background affects attitudes about x" [e.g., Collins 1975:73–75]—is not yet to show its dynamics; it is only to refer to an observed correlation between behavior in certain kinds of repeated situations and behavior in other situations. We still need to produce the mechanism by which conditions—certain arrangements of microsituations—motivate human actors to behave in certain ways. This mechanism should explain both why they behave as they do in specific situations, and why they maintain certain dispersions of microbehaviors among themselves, across time and space, thereby making up the macropatterns of social structure. Such a mechanism, moreover, should be able to produce, by different states of its variables, both repetitive behaviors—static or regularly reproduced social structure—and structural changes.

The second implication, then, comes down to this: *The dynamics as well as the inertia in any causal explanation of social structure must be microsituational; all macroconditions have their effects by impinging on actors' situational motivations.* Macroaggregates of microsituations can provide the context and make up the results of such processes, but the actual energy must be microsituational.

It remains to produce such a micromechanism. Here, the substantive research of radical microsociology provides further leads.

THE MICROCRITIQUE OF RATIONALISTIC COGNITIVE AND EXCHANGE MODELS

Much of the classic ethnomethodological research was oriented toward showing that the basic everyday life stance is to take it for granted that meaningful activities are going on. Garfinkel's (1967) breaching experiments indicate that to question or violate the usually tacit aspects of behavior makes people upset. They assume there are aspects of life that they should not have to explain. There is a deeper reason for this reaction: It is in fact impossible to explicate all the tacitly understood grounds of any social convention, and the effort to do so quickly shows people the prospects of an infinite regress of discussion. Cicourel (1973) has shown some of the bases of the "indexicality" of social communications. Many elements of communication involve nonverbal modes, which cannot be completely translated into words; and *activity* of talking itself (as opposed to the content of talk) has a structure that results in verbalizations but is not itself verbalizable. These materials imply that meaningful cognitions do not ultimately *guide* social behavior, but rather that cognitive meaning is usually given to events *retrospectively*, when some difficulty has arisen which is to be remedied by offering an "account" (Scott and Lyman, 1968).

This perspective undercuts a number of conventional explanations of social behavior. Values and norms become dubious constructions. Ethnomethodological research indicates that people are rarely able to verbalize many social rules guiding their behavior. This is especially true at the deeper levels of tacit understanding, such as of the circumstances under which particular kinds of surface rules are appropriate (Cicourel, 1973). Normative concepts, rather, are observed mainly in retrospective accounts, or an analysts' constructs; there is no first-hand evidence that they guide actors' spontaneous behavior (cf. Cancian, 1975; Deutscher, 1973). Nor is it possible for individuals to operate cognitively by simply matching external situations to mentally formulated rules.[2]

---

[2] Of course, one may rescue the concepts of norms or rules as nonverbalizable or unconscious patterns that people manifest in their behavior. But such norms are simply *observer's* constructs. It is a common, but erroneous, sleight of hand to then assume that the *actors* also know and orient their behavior to these rules. The reason that normative sociologies have made so little progress in the last half-century is because they assume that a description of behavior is an explanation of it, whereas in fact the explanatory mechanism is still to be found. It is because of their potential for this kind of abuse that I believe that the terminology of norms ought to be dropped from sociological theory.

Similar considerations cast doubt on the adequacy of assuming that behavior is guided by definition of the situation or by role taking. These concepts imply that behavior is determined cognitively by well-defined verbal ideas. But if the most common stance is to *assume* normalcy as much as possible, even in the absence of discernable meaning, and if meanings are mainly imputed retrospectively as part of some other conversational situation, then immediate situations do not have to be explicitly defined in order for people to act in them. Moreover, if there is an irreducibly tacit element in cognition and communication, situations and roles never *can* be fully defined. What guides interaction, then, must be found on another level.

These difficulties arise again in the case of exchange theories. For the microevidence does not show that the usual cognitive stance is one in which actors calculate possible returns; on the contrary, most people most of the time operate on the basis of an assumed normalcy which is not subject to conscious reflection. Comprehensive samplings of conversations in work settings, for example, show that the prevailing tone of most interactions is to take organizational routine for granted; bargaining relations are largely confined to external contacts, as between business heads and clients (Clegg, 1975). More fundamentally, the ethnomethodological findings imply the even where exchanges do take place, they must occur against a background of tacit understandings which are not challenged, or even raised to consciousness. Durkheim (1947/1893) made a similar point in criticizing social contract theories. Any contract, he pointed out, involves one in further obligations not bargained for, such as an implicit obligation to uphold the contract.

Analogous difficulties have arisen within exchange theory itself (Heath, 1976). There are certain kinds of calculations that actors cannot make on a purely rational basis. They cannot rationally choose among amounts of two or more alternative goods, if there is no common metric; and this is frequently the case in everyday life, as is dealing with such goods as status, comfort, or affection, which have no simple monetary equivalent. The problem is even more acute when one must calculate the expected value of different courses of action, which involves multiplying the probability of attaining a good times its relative desirability; here there are two incommensurable scales to be combined. Yet another difficulty is that probabilities of attaining one's ends are impossible to calculate for a particular situation, in the absence of knowledge of the objective distribution of outcomes. There are further limitations on the applicability of an exchange model. Many exchanges, such as those among members of organizational positions, or among persons who have established a bond of repeated gift exchanges, leave no room for bargaining, having excluded alternative partners after a once-and-for-all agreement. The applicability of a model of exchange, then, seems very restricted.

The findings of empirical microsociology and the self-critiques of exchange theories are equivalent, and point to the same underlying conditions. If cognition is limited to a few relatively uncomplex operations, then people cannot follow a chain of thought very many steps, neither into its future consequences, nor into questionings of its premises. Most courses of action must be taken for granted. In March and Simon's (1958) neorationalist reformulation, the only feasible strategy for an actor monitoring a number of complex actions (as in managing an organization), is to "satisfice" in most areas (i.e., ignore most chains of actions as long as they meet a certain routine level of satisfaction, and concentrate instead on troubleshooting the most unpredictable and irregular area). This is essentially the same procedure that ethnomethodologists find in people's conversational practices. People do not question the truthfulness or pursue the full meaning of most utterances, unless severe misunderstandings or conflicts occur, and then they troubleshoot by offering retrospective accounts.

Williamson (1975) has drawn some of the consequences for economic theory. Like the ethnomethodologists, he proposes that human rationality is limited, and hence that any complex or potentially conflictual negotiations can become exceedingly long and costly—conceivably even interminable—unless there is some tacit or non-negotiable basis for agreement. Hence, in many circumstances open markets for labor and for goods give way to organizations (i.e. to repeated exchanges at conditions negotiated on a once-only basis). These are economically more efficient than continually renegotiating relations among workers, or among suppliers and manufacturers, when there are tasks of any degree of complexity to be carried out. This argument is tantamount to saying that the structural consequence of the cognitive features documented by microsociologists is to replace open-market exchanges with taken-for-granted routines in organizational networks.

Nevertheless, substituting organizations for markets does not eliminate the problem of showing the microfoundations of social structure. Granted that limited rationality makes people rely on routine rather than on bargaining in many areas of life, the question still remains: Why does any *particular* form of organizational routine exist, and to what extent will it be stable? Any organization involves authority, the power of certain people to give and enforce orders which others carry out. The basis of authority is a chain of communications. The ultimte sanction of a lower-level manager over a worker is to communicate to others in the management hierarchy to withold the worker's pay; the sanction of a military organization is to communicate orders to apply coercion against any disobedient soldier. The civilian case is founded on the military one; control chains based on pay or other access to property are ultimately backed up by the coercive power of the state. Thus the microbehaviors that make up any organizational routine must involve some sense of the chains of command that can bring sanctions to bear for violating the routine.

Carrying out a routine, then, cannot be a matter of complete obliviousness to possible contingencies. Moreover, there is a good deal of evidence from observational studies of organizations that struggles to exercise or evade control go on among workers and managers, customers and salespersons; that managers negotiate coalitions among themselves; that staff and line officials struggle over influence; that promotions and career lines are the subject of considerable maneuvering. (Dalton, 1958; Glaser, 1968; Lombard, 1955; Roy, 1952). Given the nature of power, this is not surprising. Sanctions tend to be remote, and take time to apply; and the very conditions of limited cognitive capacities in situations calling for complex coordination or involving uncertainly leave room in the routine for negotiation. Routine may be cognitively desirable, but it is not always forthcoming. When breakdown points occur, the prior routine itself cannot prevent individual actors from negotiating *which* further routines are to be established.

Even when ultimate sanctions actually are applied, the negotiable nature of power itself again becomes apparent. The ultimate basis of property and of private authority is political authority, backed up by the power of the military. Political and military authority, however, are based on a self-reinforcing process of producing loyalty or disloyalty. A political leader, even of dictatorial power, relies on others to carry out orders; this includes using subordinates to enforce discipline upon other subordinates. Hence a leader is powerful to the extent that the leader is widely believed to be powerful, most essentially among those *within* the organizational chain of command (cf. Schelling, 1963:58–118). For less dictatorial leaders, and for informal negotiations at lower levels within organizations, power is even more obviously dependent on the accumulated confidence of others (Banfield, 1961).

Organizational authority, then, is based on shared orientations among the members of a group, directed toward the extent of shared orientation itself. Organizational members monitor what each is feeling toward the other, and especially toward those in authority. The ultimate basis of routine is another level of implicit negotiation.

Here we come to the crux of the issue. Both neorationalist self-criticisms and microsociological evidence agree that complex contingencies cannot be calculated rationally, and hence that actors must largely rely on tacit assumptions and organizational routine. But the actual structures of the social world, especially as centered around the networks upholding property and authority, involve continuous monitoring by individuals of each other's group loyalties. Since the social world can involve quite a few lines of authority and sets of coalitions, the task of monitoring them can be extremely complex. How is this possible, given people's inherently limited cognitive capacities?

The solution must be that negotiations are carried out implicitly, on a different level than the use of consciously manipulated verbal symbols. I propose that the mechanism is *emotional* rather than cognitive. Individuals monitor others' attitudes toward social coalitions, and hence toward the degree of support for routines, by feeling the amount of confidence and enthusiasm there is toward certain leaders and activities, or the amount of fear of being attacked by a strong coalition, or the amount of contempt for a weak one. These emotional energies are transmitted by contagion among members of a group, in flows that operate very much like the set of negotiations which produce prices within a market. In this sense, I will attempt to show that the strengths of a market model for linking microinteractions to macrostructures can be salvaged, without incorporating the weaknesses of traditional exchange theories.

SOCIAL STRUCTURE AS MICROREPETITION IN THE PHYSICAL WORLD

From a microviewpoint, what is the social structure? In microtranslation, it refers to people's repeated behavior in particular places, using particular physical objects, and communicating by using many of the same symbolic expressions repeatedly with certain other people. The most easily identifiable part of this repetition, moreover, is physical. The most enduring repetitions are those around particular places and objects. Most of the repetitive structure of economic organization takes place in particular factories, office buildings, trucks, etc. The most repetitive behaviors that make up the family structure are the facts that certain people inhabit the same dwelling places day after day, that the same men and women sleep in the same beds and touch the same bodies, that the same children are kissed, spanked, and fed. The state exists by virtue of there being courtrooms where judges repeatedly sit, police who leave the same headquarters building and ride in the same squad cars, troops that stack their weapons in a common barracks, assembly halls where congresses of politicians repeatedly gather.

Of course, there is also symbolic communication that goes on among these people, and this bears some relation to the structuredness of society. But what I am contending is that the repetitiveness is not primarily to be explained by the *content* of this symbolic communication. The social structure is not a set of meanings that people carry in their heads. I believe that this is borne out by the findings of the empirical microsociology of cognition. The structure is in the repeated *actions* of communicating, not in the contents of what is said; those contents are frequently ambiguous or erroneous; not always mutually understood, nor fully explicated. People do not always (or even usually) have a very accurate idea of the political state to which they defer, the organization in which they work, or the family or circle of friends with which they associate. But if the structuredness of society is physical, not cognitive, then these disabilities do not prevent us from carrying out a great deal of orderly repetition. No one needs to have a cognitive map of the whole social structure, nor even of any organization; all they need is to negotiate a fairly limited routine in a few physical places and with the particular people that they usually encounter there.

The limitations on human cognition documented by the ethnomethodologists show why social order must necessarily be physical and local for all participants. Although this may seem paradoxical, in view of the philosophical and antimaterialist themes associated with this intellectual tradition, it is consonant with the main examples of indexical statements that ethnomethodologists have cited (Garfinkel, 1067): terms such as "you," "me," "here," "this" are irremediably bound to the specific context, because people's activities always occur at a *particular* physical *location* and at a *particular point* in time. The inexpressible context on which everybody depends, and on which all tacit understandings rest, is the physical world, including everyone's own body, as seen from a particular place within it.[3]

---

[3] A phenomenologist would object that individual persons and particular situations cannot simply be seen as physical moments in time and space, because they are always *defined* by a cognitive structure that transcends the immediate situation. In other words, we do not know who the individual is or what the situation is without using some situation-transcending concept. Nevertheless, here again I believe we encounter a confusion of the theorist-observer's viewpoint and the actor's viewpoint (as in Footnote 2). It is the outside theorist who wants to characterize the individual as a citizen or husband, or

Again, it is plain that this *physical* social world is not static. People do come and go; homes are formed and dissolved; workers move to new factories and offices; politicians are replaced by others; new friends meet while others cease to see one another. Nor are the patterns historically constant; indeed, much of what we mean by structural change in history is shifting patterns of physical organization: separation of work places and armaments places from homes, shifting numbers and shifting rates of turnover of people in political places, and so on. My point here is simply that the microreality of any social structure is some pattern of repetitive associations among people in relation to particular physical objects and places, and that this must be so because human cognitive capacities do not allow them to organize in any other way.

These cognitive capacities do not prevent them from systematically misperceiving the nature of their social order to make claims about it on a symbolic plane. How this is done will be suggested below.

The question now arises: Why is it that people repeatedly inhabit the same buildings, use the same tools, talk to the same people? Part of the answer has already been given. Routine occurs because the world is too complex for us to have to renegotiate all of it (or even very much of it) all the time. It is easier to stay where one is familiar most of the time. But this is only the beginning of an answer. We still need to know why those particular people occupy those particular places. And since they do not stay there forever, we need to know why they move when they do, and where they will go. Moreover, the answer to this question, the mechanism that explains when they will move (and by the same token, when they will stay), should also be the mechanism that explains just what they will do, both in action and in communication, with the people they repeatedly encounter in their usual places.

From a macroviewpoint, one way to gloss these microrepetitions is to refer to them as property or authority. This brings in the notion of possible sanctions against violating a particular pattern of repetitive behavior. The person who goes into someone else's factory or takes someone else's car stands the risk of being arrested and jailed; the person who fails to carry out a boss's orders risks being fired. Never-

---

the situation as a home or a workplace. What I am contending is that most of the time actors do not think about such concepts at all; they simply are physically in certain places, carrying out certain actions, including the action of talking to other people. It is only when this physical and emotional routine is disrupted that people rise to the level imputed to them by phenomenological theorists, and begin to offer macroconceptual accounts of themselves and their settings.

theless, from the viewpoint of strict microtranslation, we must ask: to what extent do people actually think of these contingencies from moment to moment in their lives as they act either to respect property and authority, or to violate it? The reality of sanctions upholding property and authority cannot by doubted, as microevents that *sometimes* occur; but they do not occur very often, in relation to the sheer number of microevents that actually take place. Moreover, the general model of human cognition suggested previously is that people do not calculate contingencies or refer to explicit rules most of the time; they act tacitly, and only consciously think of these formalities when an issue arises. Not that people cannot formulate rules or calculate contingencies; but there is no conscious rule as to *when* people must bring up the rules, and no conscious calculation of when one should calculate and when not (cf. Cicourel, 1973).

What we have instead, I suggest, is a pattern in which people act toward physical objects and toward each other in ways that mostly constitute routines. They do not *ordinarily* think of these routines as upholding property and authority, although an analytically minded outside *observer* could describe them as fulfilling that pattern. They follow those routines because they *feel* natural or appropriate. Moreover, these routines may be quite variable, with respect to what an observer may describe as property and authority; people can rigidly avoid stepping on someone else's front lawn, or they may take the office stationery home—in both cases, without consciously thinking about it; they may nervously jump to a boss's every request, or sluff it off behind the boss's back—again, without consciously invoking any general formulations of rules or roles. This variation may, of course, also extend to instances where peole *do* become property-conscious, rules-conscious, authority-conscious; what I am arguing is that we need an explanation of why this symbolic consciousness occurs when it does. That explanation is again in the realm of feeling. People invoke conscious social concepts at particular times because the emotional dynamics of their lives motivates them to do so.

The underlying emotional dynamic, I propose, centers on feelings of *membership in coalitions.* Briefly put: Property (access to and exclusions from particular physical places and things) is based on a sense of what kinds of persons do and do not belong where. This is based, in turn, on a sense of what groups are powerful enough to punish violators of their claims. Authority is similarly organized: It rests on a sense of which people are connected to which groups, to coalitions of what extensiveness and what capacity to enforce the demands of their members upon others. Both of these are variables. There is no inherent, objective entity called "property" or "authority," but only the varying senses that people feel at particular places and times of how strong these enforcing coalitions are. There may also be memberships groups who make little or no claims to property or authority: purely informal or horizontal groups such as friends and acquaintances, whose solidarity is an end in itself as far as its members are concerned.

The most general explanation of human social behavior encompasses all of these. It should specify: What makes someone a member of a coalition? What determines the extensiveness of a coalition, and the intensity of bonds within it? How do people judge the power of coalitions? The answer to these questions, I am suggesting, determines the way in which groups of friends and other status groups are formed; the degree to which authority and property routines are upheld; and who will dominate others within these patterns. The basic mechanism is a process of emotional group identification that may be described as a set of interaction ritual chains.

A THEORY OF INTERACTION RITUAL CHAINS

From a microtranslation viewpoint, all processes of forming and judging coalition memberships must take place in interaction situations. The main activity in such situations is conversation. But no one situation stands alone. Every individual goes through many situations: indeed, a lifetime is, strictly speaking, a chain of interaction situations. (One might also call it a chain of conversations.) The people one talks to also have talked to other people in the past, and will talk to others in the future. Hence an appropriate image of the social world is a bundle of individual chains of interactional experience, criss-crossing each other in space as they flow along in time. The dynamics of coalition membership are produced by the emotional sense individuals have at any one point in time, due to the tone of the situation they are currently in (or last remember, or shortly anticipate), which in turn is influenced by the previous chains of situations of all participants.

The *manifest* content of an interaction is usually not the emotions it involves. Any conversation, to the extent that it is taken seriously by its participants, focuses their attention upon the reality of its contents, the things that are talked about (Goffman, 1967:113–116). This may include a focus on practical work that is being done. What is significant about any conversation from the point of view of social membership, however, is not the content, but the extent to which the participants can actually maintain a common activity of focusing on that content.

The content is a vehicle for establishing membership. From this viewpoint, any conversation may be looked on as a ritual. It invokes a common reality, which from a ritual viewpoint may be called a myth: in this case, whether the conversational myth is true or not is irrelevant. The myth or content is a Durkheimian sacred object. It signifies membership in a common group, for those who truly respect it. The person who can successfully become engrossed in a conversational reality becomes accepted as a member of the group of those who believe in that conversational entitiy. In terms of the Durkheimian model of religious ritual. (Durkheim, 1954/1912; cf. Goffman, 1967), a conversation is a cult in which all believers share a moral solidarity. In fact, it *creates* the reference point of moral solidarity: those who believe are the good; defense of the belief and hence of the group is righteousness; evil is disbelief in, and even more so attack upon, the cognitive symbols that hold the group together. The cognitive symbols—however banal, particularized, or esoteric the conversational content may be—are important to the group, and defended by it, because they are the vehicle by means of which the group is able to unify itself.

Not all conversations, however, are equally successful rituals. Some bind individuals together more permanently and tightly than others; some conversations do not come off at all. Among those conversations that do succeed in evoking a common reality, some of these produce a feeling of egalitarian membership among the conversationalists, while others produce feelings of rank differences, including feelings of authority and subordination. These types of variability, in fact, are essential for producing and reproducing stratified social order. Conversational interaction ritual, then, is a mechanism producing varying amounts of solidarity, varying degrees of personal identification with coalitions of varying degrees of impressiveness.

What, then, makes a conversational ritual succeed or not, and what kinds of coalitions does it invoke?

I suggest the following ingredients. (a) Participants in a successful conversational ritual must be able to invoke a common cognitive reality. Hence they must have similar *conversational* or *cultural resources*.[4] A successful conversation may also be inegalitarian in that one person does most of the cultural reality-invoking, the others acting as an au-

---

[4] Bourdieu (1977) and Bourdieu and Passeron (1977) propose a similar concept, "cultural capital," although this refers more specifically to the culture legitimated by the dominant class in a society.

dience; in these case we have a domination-and-subordination-producing ritual. (b) Participants must also be able to sustain a common emotional tone. At a minimum, they must all want to produce at least momentary solidarity. Again, the emotional participation may be stratified, dividing the group into emotional leaders and followers.

These two ingredients—cultural resources and emotional energies—come from individuals' chains of previous interactional experience, and serve to reproduce or change the pattern of interpersonal relations. Among the most important of the things reproduced or changed are feelings about persons' relationships to physical property, and to the coercive coalitions of authority. How individuals are tied to these is the crucial determinant of which coalitions are dominant or subordinate.

Conversational Resources

Particular styles and topics of conversation imply memberships in different groups. At any point in time, the previous chain of interaction rituals that have been successfully negotiated have made certain conversational contents into symbols of solidarity. The range of these has been discussed elsewhere (Collins 1975:114–131). For example, shop talk invokes membership in occupational groups, political and other ideological talk invokes contending political coalitions, entertainment talk invokes groups with various tastes, general discussion invokes different intellectual and nonintellectual strata, while gossip and personal talk invoke specific and sometimes quite intimate memberships. Again, it is not important whether what is said is true or not, but that it can be said and accepted as a common reality for that moment, that makes it an emblem of group membership.

Conversational topics have two different types of implications for reproducing the social structure. Some conversational topics are *generalized:* they refer to events and entitites on some level of abstraction from the immediate and local situation. Talk about techniques, politics, religion, entertainment are of this sort. Their social effects, I would suggest, are to reproduce a sense of what may be called status group membership: common participation in a horizontally organized cultural community which shares these outlooks and a belief in their importance. Ethnic groups, classes to the extent that they are cultural communities, and many more specialized cultural groups are of this type. Successful conversation on these topics brings about a generalized sense of common membership, then, although it invokes no specific or personal ties to particular organizations, authority, or property.

Other conversational topics are *particularized:* They refer to

specific persons, places, and things. Such talk can include practical instructions (asking someone to do something for someone at a specific
time and place), as well as political planning about specific strategies
(as in organizational politics), and gossip and personal narration. Some
of this particularized talk serves to produce and reproduce informal
relations among people (i.e. friendships). But particularized talk,
paradoxically enough, also is crucial in reproducing property and
authority, and hence organizations.[5] For, as argued above, property
and authority structure exist as physical routines, whose microreality
consists of people taking for granted particular people's rights to be in
particular buildings, giving orders to particular other people, and so
on. In this sense, property and authority are re-enacted whenever people refer to *someone's* house, *someone's* office, *someone's* car, as well
as whenever someone gives an order to do a particular thing, and the
listener acknowledges the reality, at least for that moment, of that
order. Again, it is worth pointing out that orders are not always carried
out; but it is the situation in which the *communicative* ritual occurs
that is crucial for maintaining the structure, as a real social pattern, not
the actual consequences for practical action.[6]

Of course, as indicated, even the degree of *ritual* compliance is a
variable, and we must inquire into the conditions which make people
respect and enact organizational communications less and more en-
thusiastically, or even rebel against them. This brings us to the second
ingredient of rituals, emotional energies.

Emotional Energies[7]

Emotions affect ritual membership in several ways. There must be
at least a minimal degree of common mood among interactants if a con-

---

[5] This is contrary to the emphasis in Bernstein's (1971, 1973, 1975) theory of
linguistic codes, in which restricted (particularized) codes are seen as the communication
mode of the lower classes, while the middle and upper classes primarily use an
elaborated (generalized) code. This theory focusses only on class cultures, and misses the
role that particularized talk plays in enacting specific organizations. The higher classes
do engage in more generalized talk than the lower classes, but they also engage in particularized talk that is, in fact, crucial for enacting the organizations they control.

[6] This, I believe, is the significance of Goffman's (1959) concept of frontstage
behavior in organizations. Enunciation of *rules*, then, is a special type of frontstage
enactment; its significance is not that the organizational rules directly cause behavior,
but that rules are *conversational topics* that are sometimes invoked as crucial tests of
feelings of members toward authority coalitions in organizations.

[7] Some alternative theories of emotion are given in Kemper (1978), Schott (1979),
and Hochschild (1979).

versational ritual is to succeed in invoking a shared reality. The stronger the common emotional tone, the more real the invoked topic will seem to be, and the more solidarity will exist in the group (cf. Collins, 1975:94–95, 153–154). Emotional propensities are thus a prerequisite for a successful interaction. But the interaction also serves as a machine for intensifying emotion, and for generating new emotional tones and solidarities. Thus emotional energies are important results of interactions at any point in the ritual chain. The emotional solidarity, I would suggest, is the payoff that favorable conversational resources can produce for an individual.

If successful interactional rituals (IRs) produce feelings of solidarity, stratification both within and among coalitions is a further outcome of emotional flows along IR chains. As noted, conversational rituals can be either egalitarian or asymmetrical. Both types have stratifying implications. Egalitarian rituals are nevertheless stratifying in that insiders are accepted and outsiders are rejected; here stratification exists in the form of a coalition against excluded individuals, or possibly the domination of one coalition over another. Asymetrical conversations, in which one individual sets the energy tones (and invokes the cultural reality), while the others are an audience, are internally stratified.

The most basic emotional ingredient in interactions, I would suggest, is a minimal tone of positive sentiment toward the other. The solidarity sentiments range from a minimal display of nonhostility to warm mutal liking and enthusiastic common activity. Where do such emotions come from? From previous experiences in IR chains. An individual who is successfully accepted into an interaction acquires an increment of positive emotional energy. This energy is manifested as what we commonly call confidence, warmth, and enthusiasm. Acquiring this in one situation, an individual has more emotional resources for successfully negotiating solidarity in the next interaction. Such chains, both positive and negative, extend throughout every person's lifetime.[8]

Let us consider the variations possible within this basic model. The main conditions which produce emotional energy are these:

1. Increased emotional confidence is produced by every experience of successfully negotiating a membership ritual. Decreased emotional confidence results from rejection or lack of success.

---

[8] This does not imply an infinite regress in the past; it points to the important fact that human children are born into an *emotional* interaction, and that successive emotional states build upon the initial one.

2. The more powerful the group within which one successfully negotiates ritual solidarity, the greater the emotional confidence one receives from it. The power of a group here means the amount of physical property it successfully claims access to, the sheer size of its adherents, and the amount of physical force (numbers of fighters, instruments of violence) it has access to.

3. The more intense the emotional arousal within an IR, the more emotional energy an individual receives from participating in it. A group situation within a high degree of enthusiasm thus generates large emotional increments for individuals. High degrees of emotional arousal are created especially by IRs that include an element of conflict against outsiders: either an actual fight, a ritual punishment of offenders, or, on a lower level of intensity, symbolic denunciation of enemies (including conversational griping).

4. Taking a dominant position within an IR increases one's emotional energies. Taking a subordinate positions within an IR reduces one's emotional energies; the more extreme the subordination, the greater the energy reduction.

INTERACTIONS AS MARKETPLACES FOR CULTURAL AND EMOTIONAL RESOURCES

Why will a particular person, in any given interactional situation, achieve or fail to achieve ritual membership? And why will particular persons dominate or be subordinated in an IR? These result from a combination of the emotional and cultural resources of all the participants in any encounter. These in turn result from the IR chains that each individual has previously experienced. Each encounter is like a marketplace, in which these resources are implicitly compared, and conversational rituals of various degrees of solidarity and stratification are negotiated. Each individual's market position depends on the emotional cultural resources they have acquired from their previous interactions.

The several kinds of emotional and cultural resources interact. Since emotional energies result from success or failure in previous IRs, having high or low cultural resources also contributes to high or low emotional energies. To a lesser extent there is an effect in the opposite direction: the more emotional energy (confidence, social warmth) one has, the more one is able to gain new cultural resources by successfully entering into new conversations; at the opposite extreme, a person with low emotional confidence may be "tongue-tied," unable to use even what cultural resources they have.

Both cultural and emotional resources change over time. But they change in different rhythms. Generally speaking, I would suggest that emotional energies are much more volatile than cultural resources, and that they can change in both positive and negative directions. If one encounters a series of situations in which one is highly accepted or even dominating, or in which the emotions are very intense, one's emotional energy can build up very rapidly. The rhythms of mass political and religious movements are based upon just such dynamics. On the contrary, if one goes through a series of ritual rejections or subordinations, one's energies can drop fairly rapidly.

Cultural resources, on the other hand, are fairly stable, and they change largely in a positive direction. But here we must pay attention to the distinction between generalized and particularized cultural resources. Generalized resources usually grow over time, and at a slow rate. Individuals may forget some of the generalized information they possess, but since it is often reproduced as common conversational topics are repeated in their usual encounters with other people, loss of generalized cultural capital is probably confined to those occasions in which someone leaves their habitual milieux of conversational partners for a long time. And even so, there is a considerble lag; the power of memory makes generalized cultural resources a stabilizing force in social relations.

Particularized cultural resources, on the other hand, are potentially more discontinuous. Particularized conversational actions (giving a specific order, asking practical advice, negotiating a strategy regarding a particular issue in organizational politics, joking with friends, etc.) are evanescent. The particular bonds that they enact are permanent only to the extent that those particularized actions are frequently reproduced. Particularized cultural resources are especially important as the microbasis of organization, authority, and property, as well as of close personal ties. The relationship of people to particular physical objects that constitute property is enacted, over and over again, in ordinary and taken-for-granted encounters, in IRs that have a particularized content. The same is true of the microreproduction of authority and of organizations.

Particularized conversational resources differ from generalized conversational resources, and from emotional resources as well, in that they are not only acquired in one's *own* conversations but they also circulate independently of oneself. When other people talk particularistically about some individual, they are constituting the person's reputation. One's reputation, then, is a particularized conversational resource that circulates in *other people's conversations*. For the microtranslation of macrostructures, the most important kind of reputations that circulate are simply the parts of talk that identify someone by a particular title (the chairman, his wife) or organizational membership (he is with G.E.), or that tacitly give someone a reputation for certain property and authority ("I went into his office." "She sent out a memo directing them to . . . . "). Particularized conversation, both as enacted and as circulated secondarily as reputations of other people, is what principally constitutes the social structure of property and authority.

Compared to generalized conversation, particularized conversation is potentially quite volatile, although much of the time it simply reproduces itself and hence reproduces social routines. Most of the time the same people are placed into organizational and property-maintaining routines, by both the particularized conversational rituals in which they take part, and those in which they are conversational subjects. But this flow of particularistic cultural resources *can* shift quite abruptly, especially on the reputational side. On a small and local scale, this happens quite frequently. A new person enters a job, a familiar one leaves a place—the old round of particularized conversational enactments and reputations suddenly stops, and a new particular social reality is promulgated. Most of the time these particularized items of conversation reinforce the bedrock of physical routine, which human cognitive capacities require us to rely on to such a great extent. But by the same token, the particular structure of organizational behavior, including very large organizational aggregates such as the state, is potentially very volatile. It is not upheld by generalized rules or generalized culture of any kind, but by short-term, particularized interaction rituals, and these can abruptly take on a new content. This microbasis of property and authority, then, implies that these routines alternate between long periods of relatively stable microreproduction, and changes in dramatic episodes of upheaval or revolution.

If we ask, then, what causes the variations in this pattern—when will particular individuals move in or out, and when will the whole pattern of property and authority be stable or shift—we find a market-like dynamic. Particular individuals enact the property and authority structure because their previous IR chains give them certain emotional energies and cultural resouces, including the resource of reputation for belonging in certain authority rituals and particular physical places. The relative value of these resources may shift from encounter to encounter, as the combinations of different individuals varies. If one begins to encounter persons whose emotional and cultural (including reputational) resources differ as greater or less than what one is used to, one's own capacity to generate ritual membership and conversational dominance will shift up or down. Hence one's emotional energies will undergo an increase or decrease. If these energy shifts reach the point at which one is motivated to, and capable of, shifting one's physical and ritual position in the pattern of property and organizational authority, then one's reputation and other particularized conversational resources will abruptly shift. Generalized cultural resources, finally, may build up across a long series of interactions, but this occurs relatively slowly.

IR situations are market-like, but it is worth stressing that the mechanism by which individuals are motivated by their market positions is not one of rational calculation. As noted above, a fundamental difficulty in rationalistic social exchange models is that there is no way for individuals to compare disparate goods that have no common metric, nor is it possible to multiply these values times the different metric of a scale of probabilities of attaining them. But if individuals are motivated by their emotional energies as these shift from situation to situation, then the sheer amount of emotional energy is the common denominator deciding the attractiveness of various alternatives, as well as a predictor of whether an individual will actually attain any of them. Individuals thus do not have to calculate probabilities in order to feel varying degrees of confidence in different outcomes. Disparate goods do not have to be directly compared, but only the emotional tone of situations in which they are available.[9] Nor do actors have to calculate the value of their various cultural resources (generalized and particularized) in each situation. These resources have an automatic effect on the conversational interaction, and the outcomes are automatically transformed into increments or decrements of emotional energy.

The fundamental mechanism, then, is not a conscious one. Rather consciousness, in the form of cultural resources, is a series of inputs into each situation that affects one's *sense* of group memberships available to varying degrees of attractiveness. It is possible, of course, for individuals sometimes to consciously reflect on their social choices, perhaps even to become aware of their own cultural and emotional resources vis-à-vis those of their fellows. But choices consciously made,

---

[9] There may be occasions, of course, in which individuals find disparate sources of attraction or repulsion, among which they are evenly balanced. In those cases, the IR chain theory predicts that their behavior will in fact be immobilized—they will remain in whatever physical routine they are in at that time, until the flow of IR energy combinations with other actors motivates them to leave that routine.

I would contend, would be the same as choices made without reflection.[10] One's sense of choice or will nevertheless rests on the accretion of energies—one's degree of self-confidence—which is the product of a larger dynamic.

Another long-standing difficulty of social exchange theories is answered by the IR chain model: Why do people repay a gift? Self-interest is not a sufficient explanation, as an exchange is only rewarding to the extent that individuals *already* know there will be reciprocity. Hence theorists have felt it necessary to fall back on such claims as "what is customary becomes obligatory [Blau, 1964]" or to invoke an alleged "norm of reciprocity" [Gouldner, 1960; cf. Heath, 1975]. Both these formulations beg the explanatory question. In both cases, the customariness of the behavior is just what remains to be explained, and to call this customariness a norm is only a description of it. The IR chain model, instead, proposes that feelings of solidarity within a social coalition are fundamental. If two individuals feel a common membership, then they will feel a desire to reciprocate gifts, because the gift and its reciprocation are emblems of continuing their common membership. This model has the advantage of making gift-giving and reciprocation into a variable instead of a constant: individuals will reciprocate to the extent that a particular coalition membership is attractive to them in terms of its emotional dynamics. Similarly, they will feel like giving gifts or not because of the same range of circumstances. Hence the variables described above should account for the degree to which reciprocity is actually practiced.

The aggregate of IRs, then, may be described as market-like. What happens in each encounter is affected by what has happened in the recent series of encounters in each participant's IR chain; and what happened in those encounters, in turn, was affected by the recent experiences of *their* participants, and so on. This larger aggregate of encounters produces what may be described as a series of cultural and emotional prices at which individuals can negotiate IRs of different

---

[10] Hochschild (1979) shows that people in fact do sometimes reflect on their emotions, and try to make themselves feel in particular ways that are appropriate to the situation. The fact that they do *not* automatically feel the "right" way is explainable, I would argue, by the market attraction or repulsion of various alternative situations in their own IR chains. What Hochschild is describing, then, may be situations in which individuals are torn between two different forms of resources, or are getting very mixed payoffs from their immediate interactions. Such situations may arise when, as argued below, an individual's market position is shifting away from a previous equilibrium point, and a new equilibrium has not been established.

degrees of solidarity and domination with one another. I say a *series* of prices because only certain combinations of individuals can successfully create a ritual, and different combinations will settle on deals at different prices.

There are several different markets of this kind operating simultaneously. At one level, there is a relatively slow-moving market for organizational ritual repetitions (positions), and for other property enactments. There is a great deal of repetition in the microrituals that make up the reproduction of such structures; yet individuals do try to move in or out of positions. Their motivations to stay put or to move, and the chances of being accepted when they attempt these actions, are determined by the aggregate of IR chains with which their own lives physically intersect. Informal shifts within organizational relations are similarly determined—shifts in which bosses gain or lose influence, informal allies win or lose, workers show greater or lesser enthusiasm and compliance. At another level, there are markets for personal friendships, for horizontal coalitions among different organizational executives, etc., which are not tied to the direct enactment of property and authority relations between the participants. These markets are capable of moving much more quickly and continuously than those in which organizational structures are enacted, because informal conversational partners do not have to change the more complex and particularity-embedded ties of property and organizational position.

Both types of markets, however, operate by a similar mechanism. In the organizational position market, individuals will be motivated to press for more domination within the organizational routine, or to leave that routine to find a better one, to the extent that their aggregate of experiences in IR chains is emotionally positive. Similarly, in markets for horizontal alliances (whether personal or business–political), individuals who experience relative surplus of emotional energy over those in their usual encounters will be motivated to seek either more domination or to move to a different set of encounters. But such individuals will eventually tend to reach the limiting situations to which their resources will take them: situations in which their partners are equal or higher in resources, hence stabilizing or reversing their emotional surplus.

From a very abstract viewpoint, one can imagine an equilibrium point in such markets, at which all individuals have settled on the particular people to ritually interact with, so that all emotional and cultural resources are statically reproduced. Such an equilibrium point may be a useful concept, but only if we see it as *one tendency* of aggregate interactional markets, which is modified by a number of other processes. The situation is constantly being destabilized, whenever any individuals anywhere experience new increments (or decrements) of cultural resources and emotional energies. A particular boss who is losing emotional energies (through ill-health, let us say, or a shift in family interactions) will bring about small increments in energies among the workers they routinely dominate, which in turn may raise their influence in other encounters. Such effects will cause at least local destabilization of microinteractional equilibrium. The equilibrium point is a pattern towards which interactions will tend again and again, subject to these disturbances.

Many of these disturbances will be local and temporary; their outcomes do not change the pattern of macroorganization. Others, however, may be large-scale and pervasive in their consequences. In the following section, we consider what kinds of aggregate microprocesses can cause either gross reproduction or gross change in macrostructures.

MACROSTRUCTURAL EFFECTS

The preceding model suggests that large-scale social changes are based on micromechanisms of one or more of the following kinds: large-scale changes in the amount or distribution of (a) generalized cultural resources; (b) particularized cultural resources; (c) emotional energies.

The generalized cultural resources across a large population can shift due to the introduction of new technologies of communication, or by more individuals specializing in the production and dissemination of generalized culture. Writing implements, mass media, and educational and religious organizations of varying size, have introduced new cultural resources, or increased their distribution, in societies at various times in history. One can picture at least two kinds of structural effects of this. The distribution of the expanded culture may be concentrated in particular populations; hence these will be able to raise their level of success in IRs at the expense of the others, forming new organizational ties and thereby eventually developing emotional and reputational advantages over others. A second kind of effect occurs when the whole population uniformly receives an increase in generalized cultural resources; the sheer degree of mobilization, of efforts to negotiate new IR connections, should increase throughout the society. Although no one gains relative to others, the overall process should increase the amount of organization-building generally in that society. It can be suggested that early phases of this process contribute to economic booms, and to the growth of political and/or religious movements; the later phases, however, if generalized cultural currency becomes continuously expanded, may involve a devaluation of the cultural currency, with ensuing contraction of political and economic activity (see the chapter entitled "Crises and Declines in Credential Systems" in this volume).

Particularized cultural resources define individuals relative to particular physical properties and authority coalitions. What can change the whole structure of these resources? The volatile aspect of particularized culture, I would suggest, is especially important in the reputations of the individuals who ritually enact the most powerful coalitions. Most reputational talk, as indicated, is local and repetitive. But rapid upheavals in personal reputations characterize important shifts in political and religious power. A person becomes powerful (or charismatic) when a dramatic event, usually involving success in a conflict, makes large numbers of people focus upon the individual. The widespread and rapid circulation of their new reputation gives them the self-reinforcing power of commanding the largest, and therefore dominant, coalition in that society. Conversely, powerful persons fall usually because of dramatic events—scandals or defeats in conflicts—which suddenly circulate their *negative* reputation.

The movement of such particularized cultural resources, then, suggests several implications for the dynamics of social change. Such changes are discontinuous, and alternate with periods of routine. They depend on dramatic events that are highly visible to many people. The most dramatic events, I would contend, are conflicts, and especially violent ones. It is for this reason that wars are so important in mobilizing revolutions and other rapid social changes (cf. Skocpol, 1979). Politics itself is a master determinant of the property system and so many other routine aspects of social life, because politics consists of continuously organized coalitions mobilized to engage in conflicts. These coalitions gain their power from broadcasting the dramatics of their own conflicts in ways favorable to themselves, thereby creating particularized reputations for various individuals as powerful, villainous, or impotent. Politics, as the struggle over reputation, rests upon control of the means of reputation management.

Emotional energies are the most crucial mechanism in all of these processes. Shifts in both generalized and particularized cultural resources have effects upon people's actions in microsituations because they affect their emotional energies. The reputation shift of a political leader, for example, is truly effective only when the rumours carry an emotional impact, a contagion of feelings throughout the society as to where the dominant coalition now resides. Hence the market attractiveness of that coalition increases, all the more so to the extent that it spreads fear of the danger to those people who remain outside of it. Conflict, war, and politics, in the preceding account, can be regarded as quintessentially emotion-producing situations. The stronger the conflict, the more emotional energy that flows through the networks of microinteraction constituting the macrostructure. Periods of rapidly changing reputational resources become particularly important for the organization of social networks to the extent that they are vehicles for strong emotional contagion.

There are also conditions that change the entire level of emotional energy in a society. Parallel to the introduction of new communications technology and generalized culture-producing specialists, one can think of the historical introduction of new emotion-producing technologies, including shifts in the numbers of emotion-producing specialists. From this viewpoint, changes in material conditions are most important because they change the numbers of people who can assemble for ritual purposes, or because they change people's capacities for impression management or dramatization (Collins 1975:161–216; 364–380). Such technologies of dramatization have ranged from the massive architecture and lavish religious and political ceremony of the Pharoahs through the various styles of political display of today. The history of religions can be seen similarly as a series of inventions of new social devices for generating emotions, ranging from the shaman's magic ritual, to congregational worship, to individual meditation and prayer. In this perspective, shifts among tribal, patrimonial-feudal, and bureau-cratic forms of organization are shifts among diverse sources of emotional impression-management. The various combinations of these emotional technologies available at any given time, and their degree of concentration or dispersion among the populace, are crucial factors in the struggle for power in any particular historical society.

An overall picture of the statics and dynamics of macrostructures emerges, at least in general outline. There are relatively slow processes of macrochange, fueled by new emotional technologies or by stepped-up production of either generalized cultural currency or of emotional energies. There are also episodic shifts in particularized cultural resources—especially the reputations of persons who ritually enact the most powerful political, military, and religious coalitions—which occur at times of dramatic conflicts. The slow processes, which may spread either to certain privileged groups, or more uniformly throughout the society, bring about long periods of organization-building and personal mobilization, which alter both the structure of the society and its degree of fluidity and conflict. The rapid, episodic processes bring about revolutionary shifts, in which dramatic conflicts focusing attention on a new dominant coalition can bring about massive changes in the patterns of property and organization, and in the particular distribution of persons in them.

CONCLUSION

The preceding model has been presented in very abstract form. It does not attempt to describe the detailed variants of ritual interaction, nor the complexities of conversational negotiations and emotional energies. Integrating these variants into the general model should greatly improve its explanatory power. On the macrolevel, as well, there are many ramifications to be worked out in translating all macropatterns into microinteractional markets of generalized and particularized cultural resources and emotional energies.

Even at this degree of imprecision, I hope that the model conveys some of the advantages of integrating micro- and macrodescriptions into a common explanatory framework. It suggests, for example, that entities that have been located in individuals, such as "personality" or "attitudes," are rather *situational* ways of acting in conversational encounters, and that personalities and attitudes are stable only to the extent that individuals undergo the same kinds of repeated interactions. Charismatic personalities, by this account, are simply individuals who have become the focal center of an emotion-producing ritual that links together a large coalition; their charisma waxes and wanes according to the degree that the aggregate conditions are met for the dramatic predomination of that coalition. On a smaller scale, one may hypothesize that upwardly mobile individuals are those whose cultural resources lead them through a sequence of IR experiences that builds up their emotional energies, hence their confidence and drive; when they reach IR matchups which no longer give a favorable emotional balance, this advantage disappears, and they cease to move further upward. To mention one more area of application, the growth of a productive economy as well as its cycles of boom and depression, should be to an important degree determined by shifts in emotional energies throughout the working population in general, or possibly among entrepreneurs in particular.

Such explanations of specific phenomena need to be elaborated from both the micro and macro sides. I would also suggest that the connection between the two levels can be made empirical by a new form of research. Generalized and particularized conversational resources exist simply as things people say in conversations; emotional energies exist in the rhythms and tones with which people say them. Accordingly, one may take a macrosample of the distribution of microresources by sampling conversations across a large number of different social groups, and by repeated conversational samples over time. Such a method moves away from the predominant emphasis of contemporary conversational research, which performs detailed analyses of single conversations taken in isolation. The proposed method resembles sample surveys, but instead of tapping attitudes or self-reports by interviewer questions, it would sample natural conversations by audio or video recordings. Technical devices may make it possible to characterize the emotional energies of conversational tone and rhythm from tape recording or by expressive postures in video recordings. Generalized and particularized conversational resources may be characterized by the same data, by classifying verbal contents. With this kind of data, it should be possible to show the actual operation of IR chains, their effects upon individuals' situational behavior, and their aggregate effects on social stability and social change.

SUMMARY

The following principles have been suggested to construct an explanatory theory of macrostructures from aggregates of microsituations:

1. Sociological concepts can be made fully empirical only by translating them into a sample of the typical microevents that make them up.
2. The dynamics as well as the inertia in any causal explanation of social structure must be microsituational; all macroconditions have their effects by impinging on actors' situational motivations.
3. Human cognitive capacity is limited, hence actors facing complex contingencies of social coordination rely largely on tacit assumptions and routine.
4. Any individual's routine is organized around particular physical places and objects, including the physical bodies of other persons. The sum of these physical routines, at any moment in time, makes up the microreality of property.

5. Authority is a type of routine in which particular individuals dominate microinteractions with other individuals.

6. What particular routines are to be adhered to is subject to self-interested manuever and conflict. Both adherence to routines and changes in them are determined by individuals' tacit monitoring of the power of social coalitions.

7. Conversations are rituals creating beliefs in common realities, which becomes symbols of group solidarity. Individual chains of conversational experiences over time (IR chains) thus recreate both social coalitions and people's cognitive beliefs about social structure.

8. Conversational topics imply group membership. Generalized conversational resources (impersonal topics) reproduce horizontal status group ties. Particularized conversation enacts individuals' property and organizational positions, and further reinforces this concrete social structure by circulating beliefs about it, including the reputations of particular individuals.

9. An encounter is a "marketplace" in which individuals tacitly match conversational and emotional resources they acquired from their previous encounters. Individuals are motivated to enact or reject conversational rituals with particular persons to the extent that they experience favorable or unfavorable emotional energies from that interaction, as compared to other IRs they remember in their recent experiences.

10. An individual's acceptance or rejection in an IR respectively raises or lowers their emotional energies (social confidence). Similar effects are produced by experiencing domination or subordination within an IR. These emotional results are weighted by the intensity of emotional arousal in each IR, and by the power of the membership coalition it invokes (its control over property and force).

11. Several different ritual markets operate simultaneously: a slow-moving market of persons shifting in and out of particular property and organizational positions; more rapidly changing markets for informal solidarity within organizations and among individuals outside organizational relations; and very long-term markets for the growth and decline of organizations as a whole.

12. In each market, individuals sense their personal opportunities via their degree of emotional energies. They move toward more advantageous ritual exchanges, until they reach personal equilibrium points at which their cultural and emotional

resources are matched by equal or greater resources of their partners.

13. Social structure is constantly changing on the microlevel, but tends to an aggregate stability if individual fluctuations of emotional and cultural resources are local and temporary.

14. Large-scale changes in social structure occur via changes in any of the three types of microresources:

   a. Increases in generalized cultural resources, produced by new communications media or increased activity of religious and educational specialists, increase the size of group coalitions that can be formed, and hense the scope of organizational structure.

   b. Particularized cultural resources change, for a whole society, when dramatic (usually conflictual) events focus many people's attention on particular individuals, thereby creating rapid shifts in their reputations and shifting the organizational center of power coalitions.

   c. New "ritual technologies," including shifts in the materials of impressions management and in the typical density and focus of encounters, change the quality of emotions throughout a society. Such shifts bring about changes in the nature of social movements and in the dynamics of political and economic action.

15. Conversational resources and emotional energies may be directly measured by sampling conversation through time and across populations; the cultural resources are found in conversational topics, and the energy levels in the tone and rhythm of talk.

V

The Old Guard
and the New

Merton's Functionalism*

Robert Merton was no doubt the best-known figure in professional American sociology during the middle of the twentieth century. This is not to say he was the most famous in the outside world: that would probably be David Riesman. Nor the one with the greatest political impact: that would certainly be C. Wright Mills. Nor the major comprehensive theorist, which would be Talcott Parsons. And none of these, in my opinion is the figure who contributed most to intellectual progress: that honor might well go to Erving Goffman, and also collectively to a number of theory-oriented empirical researchers in various fields. But citation studies of the sociological literature prove what we would tend to take for granted: Merton had the greatest visibility and impact in the discipline for the period that began some time around the Second World War and lasted until about 1965.

Why was he so eminent? Partly because of the sheer number of areas in which he worked, the research traditions that he began or contributed to, and the modes of analysis he labelled and popularized. In

* Originally published in *Contemporary Sociology, 1977,* **6** (March). Copyright 1977 American Sociological Association.

other words, Merton was the formulator of a considerable number of miniparadigms. Or was he? Coser and Nisbet's Festschrift volume (1975) is rather a good place to piece this out, for it contains not only a great many biographical encomiums, but also a long section of essays "on the shoulders of Merton," which generally review the various fields in which he worked, and a couple of detailed sociology of science studies of the growth of two areas in which he made especially famous contributions. Not everything can be taken at face value, of course, since this volume consists of the Merton camp extolling their own leader. But the material is there, both in form and content, for a fairly comprehensive assessment of Merton's work and of the process that made it eminent.

The work falls by and large into five areas:

1. anomie and deviance;
2. the sociology of science;
3. various aspects of role theory, including cosmopolitans and locals, reference groups, and role sets;
4. structural ironies and dilemmas;
5. bureaucracy, and especially the bureaucratic personality.

There are also his methodological essays, which add up to the reminder, once badly needed and still very pertinent, that theory and empirical research develop best in mutual interaction. This is something not specifically treated in this volume, perhaps because it is an overall strategy of analysis rather than a contribution to a particular field. It is the strategy that put him in the running for sociological eminence, though; Merton situated himself at the crossroad of a discipline of almost mutually oblivious approaches, and thereby managed to come as near as anyone to directing traffic.

Merton's paper "Social Structure and Anomie" is apparently the most cited paper in all of American sociology. According to Stephen Cole, it was the dominant theory in the area of deviance from the early 1950s until about 1970, when symbolic interactionist/labelling theory came to the fore. It proposes that deviance is engendered by the social system as a way for individuals to react to a disparity between society-wide goals (monetary success) and institutionalized means (mobility opportunities). If one interprets (as Cole does) Albert K. Cohen's delinquency theory as a version of Merton's then one can make out a strong case for influence on a major line of empirical research, and one with a fair amount of explanatory power.

Yet certain questions arise. As Cole himself notes, relatively few of the papers citing Merton attempted to test the theory; even fewer presented contradicting evidence. Most simply referred to it as part of the review of the literature, or as a legitimation for the author's theories and interpretations. Cole takes this as supporting a Kuhnian view of paradigms as rising and falling not by empirical proof or disproof, but by some larger social factors. Thus labelling theory came on strong a few years ago, not because Merton was disproved, but because the fashion had shifted. If we look backwards in time, we find a similar phenomenon: A paper first published in 1938 sat dormant for about 15 years, before enjoying a rise to phenomenal popularity in the literature. Why? Perhaps it was really Albert K. Cohen who made Merton famous in this area, and not vice versa. Or more fundamentally in the background, the great juvenile delinquency scare arose in the 1950s, which Martin Trow has nicely shown elsewhere was related to the shift to mass secondary schooling, filling up the high schools with recalcitrant working class students.

So Merton's theory rode a wave which came along at the right time for it to make legitimate sociology out of topical social-problems investigations. Yet this is not entirely accidental; after all, in this rather parochial and theoryless area, he invoked the high intellectual shades of Emile Durkheim; and his typological category-constructing resonated with the contemporary grand typologizing of Talcott Parsons. And perhaps most importantly, it was a basically All-American theory; the great American creed of social mobility occupies the center of the stage, and lack of mobility opportunities (not the more fundamental structure of inequalities of distribution) is the villain of this structural drama.

The sociology of science is an area which is even more uniquely Merton's own. His Ph.D. thesis was in this area, and most of his publications of the later years as well as his current work are here. Here we find Merton's application of the so-called "Weber thesis" to science, claiming that the Puritan ethos affected the scientific revolution of the seventeenth century. We find also his analysis of multiple discoveries in science, leading up to the argument that virtually all discoveries are really multiples, produced by the social structure of science rather than by individuals. There is his analysis of the norms of science, which include not only disinterestedness and intellectual communism, but also the recognition of priority in scientific discoveries—Merton's claim that a disinterested element normatively governs the priority disputes that rage through the history of science. There is his fairly recent formulation of the "Matthew Effect," by which already famous scientists are more easily recognized for their contributions than new and obscure individuals, and which serves to integrate a science around a central focus of attention. And there is a considerable group of Merton's students, especially those of the last decade, who have developed the sociology of science as an empirical field.

As Jonathan Cole and Harriet Zuckerman (two of these students) show, Merton is far and away the most cited individual in this field since the mid-1950s. Nevertheless, one can question just what this really means. Substantively, I would suggest, Merton has done more for the sociology of science by drawing attention to the area, than in actual theoretical or empirical contributions. For the "Merton thesis" on Puritanism has almost no supporters among historians and historical sociologists of science; there were far too many Catholic scientists in the seventeenth century (an overwhelming number, outside of England), and in England itself it turns out that most of the Royal Society members, and its most eminent figures, were not real Puritans at all, but latitudinarians and back sliders. The model of multiple discoveries (put forward a good deal earlier than Merton by William F. Ogburn, among others) has turned out to go nowhere. The analysis of "norms" simply leads to a glorification of science as a perfectly tuned system, and has had little empirical application or explanatory development; in effect, it says that scientists are really disinterested, good people, and that everything happens pretty much for the best in that world. I would say that priority disputes show, much more importantly than disinterestedness, that scientists are competitive and contentious; they force other scientists to recognize yet a third scientist's priority, not because they are so disinterested, but in order to put down the pretensions of the second party with whom they are arguing. (Examine the conversations you have with your intellectual acquaintances and see if this is not so.) Ths kind of analysis would lead off to another direction, of course; it would point to the variations in resources that individuals have for producing intellectual work and commanding agreement, and thence to a more content-oriented explanation of what gets produced and when it gets accepted, instead of a bare formal argument that social systems are controlled by ideal norms. The same could be said about the Matthew Effect, which really says that stratification does exist in science, but that it is basically a good thing, or at worst, an inevitable irony; it does not go on to make this an explanatory and testable model of what produces variations in stratification and hence in the types of science produced.

Looking at Merton's work in the sociology of science externally, rather than internally as I have done in the previous paragraphs, it seems apparent that his eminence in the field is not due to his having organized a workable paradigm. Again we find the lag: His Puritanism theory comes from the 1930s, republished in the late 1940s; his norms and priorities papers in the 1940s and 50s. But the literature of the field only begins to take off in the 1960s; and indeed, it is only after that that Merton himself begins to have an active research group working closely on his ideas. What happened in the early 1960s to set off the field, I would suggest, was a couple of inputs from quite different directions: Derek de Solla Price, who set off the quantitative study of scientists and citations, and above all Thomas Kuhn, with his iconoclastic theory of paradigms and paradigm-revolutions. (Ironically, one can even find evidence for this among Merton's own students; the two by and large excellent papers in this volume by the two Coles and Zuckerman reflect much more the influence of Kuhn and Price in their methodology and theoretical reflections than they do that of Merton.) One could even say that it was the appearance of several rival approaches that sparked Merton's revival of his own sociology of science in the later part of the decade. In other words, one cannot explain what happens in a science by a bare analysis of some hypostatized systemic norms; or even by the career of a particular individual or group. Rather, the conflict among rival groups may well by the feature that most strongly influences work in a given field. But this leads to a type of conflict analysis that Merton was at pains to avoid.

Merton's solidest contributions, in my opinion, are in the area of role theory. I have never been overly fond of the theory of role sets; like so much of this analysis, it takes phenomena that are basically matters of stratification and disinfects them by passing them through a bath of abstractions, substituting horizontal categories for hierarchical ones. Yet Rose Laub Coser, in a fine paper entitled "The Complexity of Roles as a Seedbed of Individual Autonomy," uses this idea to bring together the work of Melvin Kohn and of Basil Bernstein, around the theme that differences in class cultures can be explained as products of more and less complicated role sets in people's daily encounters. Reference group theory brings us back to Merton's old favorite idea of the centrality of social mobility; Herbert Hyman's paper here gives us some potentially interesting survey data on "reference idols," but doesn't manage to bring off any theoretical interpretations. This serves to remind us that when C. Wright Mills attacked "abstracted empiricism," he had the Columbia department in mind; Merton had an alliance with empiricists that tended to give them concepts to label their findings, but didn't necessarily generate explanations.

The theory of cosmopolitan and local roles, on the other hand, managed to set itself free from the social mobility theme. Some of the biographical materials in this volume point out that Merton initially attempted to categorize community influentials by their mobility patterns, but eventually hit on a more fruitful categorization, in terms of their structural positions. Gouldner fleshed this out empirically, and this research tradition shows up in the volume in a closely reasoned and empirically supported paper by Peter Blau which shows a number of countervailing attitudinal effects of cosmopolitan and local orientations among university faculty. Blau's main advance, interestingly enough, is to introduce the hierarchical status dimension back into role sets, and thus greatly increase the number of individual and aggregate phenomena it can explain. Here Merton has plainly engendered a considerable tradition of empirical analysis, and one that has made steady progress in explanatory refinement.

Under the category of "structural ironies and dilemmas," one would include Merton's papers on manifest and latent functions; on self-fulfilling prophecies; and on the dilemmas of applied social researchers. This style of analysis has certainly had considerable appeal. But it is not an appeal to actual explanatory power: it does not tell us what sort of conditions produce various outcomes, and hence it does not lend itself to test. What it gives instead is a kind of imagery of the world, and one with a strongly implied (but nicely disguised) political resonance. "Manifest and latent functions," after all, was a very abstract way of talking about corrupt political machines and why they survive. But it distracts from the struggle for power and privelege, and tells us instead that the system distributes these things, and that if our ideals seem not to be fulfilled in reality, one should look beneath the surface to where some aspect of the great self-equilibrating system does get its way. "Self-fulfilling prophesies" are introduced via the example of race relations; Merton's perspective is a liberal one, pointing out that prejudice and discrimination end up producing their own empirical justifications. But again, this ends up distracting attention from either an explanatory theory of variations in racial domination, or even from a practical effort to change the situation. Instead, the self-equilibrating image rolls gradually but inexorably into the center of attention; that's the way society is (is it really?) and the height of sociological intellect is to capture the pattern and appreciate the irony.

Finally, there was the involvement of Merton in the upsurge of interest in bureaucracies as of the 1940s and 1950s. He was early into the area, and his paper on the bureaucratic personality is a fine exposition of a major idea whose origin was in Mannheim's distinction between substantive and functional rationality. Whatever impetus he gave to the organizational studies that came out of Columbia was certainly salutary, for these included major works of Blau and Gouldner (and perhaps more remotely, Selznick). But it is clear that the field owed much more of its growth to the Harvard Business School (institutional base for Mayo and Barnard), and to the Chicago school. What is apparent, though, was Merton's eye for where the action was, even though this was not a field that he entered, or legitimated, in a big way.

If there is a central theme that underlies virtually all of Merton's work, I would say it is the effort to defuse stratification issues. In good American style, structural inequalities are simply settings for the drama of social mobility. Instances of conflict, whether in the form of juvenile crime or scientific priority disputes, are refocused onto the claim that they really are evidence for some common values that people are upholding or striving to attain. Relationships of authority and subordination are transformed into abstract collections of roles; political conflicts and racial domination become instances of self-equilibrating systems. This kind of intellectual sleight of hand makes a fine stage for virtuoso performances; and given the probability that Merton's liberal biases were shared by most of his sociological audience they drew quite a crowd.

What was weak about American sociology in the years in which Merton worked was its attempt to defuse stratification. In the process it ended up turning away from the very variables that are most fundamental to consider in any real explanatory theory. Those were, after all, the years of the great anti-Communist scare. Intellectuals probably did magnify the extent of the threat to themselves from the radical right, but it is clear enough that they turned against each other, conducting their own internal witch hunts to avoid being hunted themselves. Marxism was thus driven as far away from mainstream sociology as possible. Yet it has been precisely in the times in which Marxism, and radicalism generally, has been strong that the intellectual dialogue has had to focus on the crucial materials. In cutting off that dialogue, midcentury American sociology cut off its mainspring of development.

Merton rose to prominence in the political dark ages of American sociology, the cold war years of the 1940s and 1950s. He helped guide sociology across those mindless and repressive years, even as he helped perpetuate the darkness.

Postindustrialism and Technocracy*

The Coming of Post-Industrial Society (1973) is a compendium of Daniel Bell's productions over the last decade, pulled together around the idea of the new evolutionary stage now upon us. The argument has a rather familiar ring. We have made the shift from the production of goods to the production of services; technology is the major driving force of social change, and has produced a new stratification based on education and expertise; the business corporations have become socialized, regulated, and socially responsible; the university has become the new center of power; needless to say, economic class conflict has disappeared. These processes are worldwide, but are most visible in America, the forward edge of evolutionary advance. What is novel in Bell's presentation is mainly his discussion of the dilemmas that social planners will have to work out: dissension between idealists and pragmatists within the scientific elite; the paradoxes of meritocracy, given biological and social determinants of I.Q.; new inequal-

---

* Originally published in Journal of Political and Military Sociology, 1975, **3** (Spring). Copyright 1975 Journal of Political and Military Sociology.

ities in knowledge and time arising in place of the old inequalities of
material wealth; the perplexing upsurge of participatory, antitechno-
cratic culture at the very time that Bell's technocrats should be insti-
tuting their utopia; and the recalcitrance of politicians in handing over
power to his heroes.

Bell states that his theory is drawn from Saint-Simon, Durkheim,
Weber, and Colin Clark. But there is no sophisticated Weberian sociology in here: none of Weber's historicism, his antievolutionism, his
understanding of the material and ideal interests and resources that
make up the varieties of stratification; none of his analysis of organizational conflicts, or his concern for the long-term institutionalization of
diverse religions that make up the stuff of world history. Nor is there
any evidence of the more powerful Durkheimian sociology, the theory
of nonrational rituals and emotional ties underlying social groupings.
Bell is only referring to a vulgarized version of the Parsonian Weber
and Durkheim, and that comes down to nothing but its bare evolutionary idealogy. Bell is telling the truth about drawing on Saint-Simon
and Colin Clark, though: indeed, that is all the theory he is drawing on,
and that tells all one needs to know about the basic intellectual quality
of this book.

Saint-Simon was up to much of the same game as Bell; he eked out
a living in the 1820s writing glowing descriptions of the new rationally
organized, socially responsible, industrial society, in publications supported entirely on subscriptions of businessmen pressing for government favors. Both polemicized against the institutions and ideas of the
old order, now passing from view; both ethnocentrically declared their
own country the peak of human evolution; both evaded empirical problems by locating their ideal new stage in a vague future just coming into
existence. Both illustrate the way in which the evolutionary fallacy is
invoked by popularistic thinkers to distort the evidence of past history
and obscure the contemporary conflicts producing the actual shape of
things to come. The currently fashionable notion of *post* industrial
society seems to have been produced as a defense against a growing
awareness of how modern societies actually work. Saint-Simon has
been demolished as an image of what industrial societies are really
like; post industrial theories rescue the evolutionary utopia by adding
another stage, not quite upon us, in which the failures of current reality
to live up to its simplistic theories are finally remedied.

Bell, in polemicizing against a vulgar version of Marxism with the
aid of his already-vulgar Saint-Simonism, remains an outsider to the
more sophisticated sociology of interests, resources, and organizations.
He swallows whole the conception that education is the provision of

technical skills, even though a close look at the evidence shows that there is very little technical skill imparted in schools, but rather membership in a particular status culture; he thinks that the increase in school attendance and in educational requirements for employment is determined by technology, oblivious to the far stronger pattern by which America's decentralized school system has produced a spiral of popular demands for educational credentials that have become progressively devaluated as they have become more widespread. He has no conception of the organizational and political processes that go into producing what Bensman and Vidich call the "sinecure society," the creation of all sorts of white-collar featherbedding through Keynesian economic policies, fat defense contracts, and the internal maneuvering of organizational factions within oligopolistic corporations. He does not seem to know the organizational research that shows that power still goes to organizational politicians, and above all to the external "contact men"—in Wilensky's terminology—who connect with the realms of finance and politics; or that technicians are self-serving interest groups just like any other, concerned about their own jobs and paychecks under the legitimating ideology of "technical requisites" and "services."

Most of Bell's dilemmas for the social planner, in other words, are the trouble spots whose real causes his ideology will not allow him to see. He has no solutions to the inequalities of the school system, because an attack on its credentialism is the one path not open to him; he is troubled by the inequalities involved in startification by I.Q. but cannot understand just how artificial a selecting device is this test for conformity within a school system, and how irrelevent it is to real job performance. He can't even begin to attack problems of economic inequality and the way they are manipulated through the network of government–corporation ties, through the dynamics of inflation, and by the structure of educational credentials, because he has already defined material inequality out of existence as a problem, and the structures that produce it as already socialized into a functional altruism.

One wonders how long we can go along resurrecting the failures of outmoded theory by pushing them into the mode of social forecasting. We have been living in the Buck Rogers era for several decades now. The atom bombs are here, so are the spaceships and the astronauts, the giant computers and the mind-expanding drugs, the deadly lasers and the tiny transistors—*and nothing really fundamental has changed.* I think we have been misled by science fiction movies, which pick out a few idealized settings for scientists and pilots and act as if they were typical of the main social structure. It should be apparent that, even with the most extraordinary technology, it is likely to be used in a very stratified fashion, subject to old-fashioned resources of property and power; the slums are still here even if they have television sets in them, and organizational politicians still line up their coalitions even if they wear white lab coats.

The internal intellectual world of serious sociology has been making progress, putting aside ideological delusions and getting at the causal mechanisms that account for variations of power, reward and outlook within organizations of all types. The externally oriented sociologists continue, obviously, bringing out new versions of the same ideology they have been selling for 150 years. For writers of this sort, it is unlikely that things will ever change; a truly informed policy science awaits a better-trained generation of policy thinkers. The ideas of Saint-Simon have long since been exhausted; it is time to move on to the task of exhausting the far more sophisticated ideas of Marx and Tocqueville, Durkheim and Weber.

Touraine's System*

Alain Touraine is noted for a number of works on industrial organization, industrial society, the Third World, on the May uprising of 1968 and on postindustrial society. In *Production de la société* (1973), he has produced his general systematic theory.

This work is, in fact, comparable in many ways to Talcott Parsons's *The Social System*. Touraine has assimilated American sociology as of approximately the late 1950s, and he weaves a critique of Parsons, Rostow, Merton, and others into his sparring against more recent French intellectual factions. Touraine's stance is, on one side, a thoroughgoing conflict position. He defines society as the product of action—of productive work—while attacking the position of Althusser and Bourdieu as representing society merely as the reproduction of a dominant order, without equal emphasis on the conflictually creative production of society by itself. Touraine rejects as well any sociology of values, arguing that these pertain only to individuals, not to a system,

---

* Originally published in *American Journal of Sociology*, 1978, **81** (May). Copyright 1976 University of Chicago Press, Chicago.

and that they are ideologies of the dominant class. But he is equally opposed to individualistic or phenomenological sociologies; these he
declares utopian because they ignore the system of domination that
determines conflicts, movements, and ideologies. Thus, although he attacks functionalism for its idealizations, its ethnocentrism, and its
obliviousness to class conflict, he regards the notion of system as its
positive contribution: for society is a system producing the orientations
in individuals that make up its functioning.

The basic elements in Touraine's explanatory apparatus are *historicity* (the techniques of production of all aspects of society, including
its operations on the material environment), *the system of historical action* (the complex of cultural orientations through which historicity
operates), and *class relations* (the conflicts between dominating and
dominated groups over control of the system of historical action
[S.H.A.]). The crucial determining variations are under the rubric of
historicity. Its basic components are a type of knowledge, an associated
system of accumulation, and the resulting cultural model of each type
of society. The greater the accumulation, the greater the distance between the production and the reproduction of labor (here the influence
of Althusser's fashionable reading of Marx becomes apparent) and
hence the greater the capacity of the society to act upon itself. Touraine
distinguishes accordingly four ideal types of societies: (a) ones in which
the units of production coincide with those of consumption; (b) ones
with separate means of exchange; (c) ones organized around industrial
capital; and (d) ones organized around the specialized production of
scientific knowledge. The first are agrarian societies, in which the cultural system and its conflicts center on religion; the second are mer-
chant societies (like those of the European Renaissance), whose culture
and conflicts revolve around the state (and around such *étatiste* doc-
trrines as those of Machiavelli and Bodin); the third are industrial
societies, whose culture and conflicts center on economic progress; the
fourth are postindustrial or programmed societies, which turn consciously on the production of themselves and hence have a center of
conflict that is self-consciously cultural. Touraine recognizes all four as
ideal types rather than evolutionary stages, and points out that any
specific historical society may be a mixture of types.

If Touraine's emphasis on the primacy of this cultural level of
analysis bears a resemblance to Parsons,' there is a further resemblance in the way the analysis is elaborated. For Touraine goes on to
cross-classify a whole series of abstract dichotomies—orientations versus resources, culture versus society, movement versus order, and
others—giving names to the boxes of the resulting grids and thereby

typologizing every subject as it comes along, whether it be types of sociological analysis, the component elements of the S.H.A., types of societies, class relations, or political situations. Touraine rather pointedly distinguishes himself formally from Parsons by labeling half the slots in his boxes as counterelements to the others, representing the divisions of class conflict. Furthermore, different kinds of social crises are described according to which axes of the basic grid of eight boxes might be ruptured.

Touraine's analysis of class relations is also fundamentally cultural. The dominant class is that which controls the S.H.A., and its ideology is its claim to speak on behalf of it, as the productive and progressive technical agent of that era. The popular class, in turn, has two faces, one negatively defensive against the ideology in the name of which it is dominated, the other positively contesting control of the S.H.A. and thus producing its own ideology and its own utopia. Touraine sees classes not as directly observable entities but as ideal types. He recognizes the existence of conflicting interests among ethnic, local, national, age, family, sex, religious, and other groups; but he recognizes them not in order to incorporate them into an explanatory model but only to set them neatly to the side of his theory of class conflict. Much of this theory turns out to be more cross-classification (of such distinctions as dominating class versus directing class, the defensive and contestatory orientations of the popular class, etc.), but occasionally more concrete propositions emerge. For example, there is the hypothesis that the more heterogeneous a society is in its mixture of historical types, the more the upper class dominates instead of directing, the more it uses mechanisms of class reproduction as weapons of control, and the more class conflict is directed toward political or organizational levels instead of ideological confrontations over the core culture itself.

Touraine considers other levels of analysis as well: those of institutions, organizations, social movements, and social change. The chapter on institutions is devoted primarily to the state, which he is careful to argue has relative autonomy, being neither completely reducible to class relations nor completely independent of them; he goes on to cross-classify varying degrees of these with various class situations. In the chapter on organizations, Touraine uses a typology borrowed (but with a new terminology) from Etzioni's coercive, remunerative, and normative control types. Here the levels of abstraction take on a reality of their own, as the author argues that on the organizational level per se, roles are based on norms accepted as legitimate because of a strictly technical determination; this is not to say that class conflict is absent from the factory, but that it belongs to a more inclusive level of analysis, that of the S.H.A. In the same vein, Touraine asserts that power, which by its very nature divides people into dominators and dominated, is not on the technical level of organizations but part of the more general conflict system.

Social movements, similarly, are distinguished from social change: the former are class conflicts over control of the S.H.A., while the latter is the result of yet another overlay of forces, which may include external forces like war, conquest, and colonization, or mutation in the basic cultural techniques. Touraine is at pains to dissociate himself from evolutionism of both Marxist and non-Marxist varieties. Societies of different types not only exist simultaneously but also, through conquest and colonization, incorporate elements of each other, a process that fosters interdependently different modes of change: not only does underdevelopment depend on advanced development, but also vice versa, and the revolutionary ruptures of a situation of extreme heterogeneity in underdeveloped societies occur in symbiosis with the smoother accretions of technical modification in advanced ones. But if this argument resonates with the dependency theories of the Left, Touraine is nevertheless highly critical of the Marxist tradition that the dominated class of one era is the agent of transformation into the next. Every society has its own classes, it own conflicts, and hence (by Touraine's definition) its own social movements; as part of each system, classes, conflicts, and movements have no resolutions but merely disappear to make for a new system of conflict when change does come about. Touraine wisely remarks that one should not confuse the conflict between dominant and dominated classes with that between the directing elites of old and new technical systems. Nor should one be led astray by ideological claims of particular classes to represent the future: both dominant and dominated classes carry on two-way ideological battles, each claiming to represent the best ideals of the past and the coming possibilities of the future.

Touraine, in fact, has virtually stood the Marxian scheme of class relations on its head. For him, it is not the dominated class of each era, the workers, who make the productive contribution, but the dominant class. In postindustrial society, it is the technicians, the scientific innovators, who control the core of the S.H.A. Here Touraine speaks the language of the Saint-Simonian tradition; he departs from it into an unidealized realism by recognizing that every form of domination, even a productive one, nevertheless generates conflict with the have-nots. In the postindustrial type, the have-not class is not the workers but those who are excluded entirely: the youthful and the aged, who are outside the realm of work. Economic issues are nowhere part of Touraine's scheme. Like Durkheim, he asserts the absolute autonomy of social explanation from any metasocial forces; what takes their place is a pure cultural conflict, in which the cultural system of every era always offers the possibilities of rival interpretations, and the possession of this cultural instrument of production ensures that there will be forces attached to a positive and a negative side.

Touraine's is indeed a general systematic theory, but I would not call it a very successful one in explanatory terms. He has produced a realistic and nonutopian left-wing functionalism, cleverly playing off against each other the philosophical debates of the French intelligentsia and the concept-classifying techniques of Parsonianism. Neither of these styles has come very near to actual causal explanations; it is perhaps a measure of sociology's progress that Touraine should be able to push through at least occasionally into suggesting some conditions under which empirical differences actually do occur. Much of what he says about political conflicts and social movements in different types of societies moves in a promising direction through the conceptual haze.

But there is also a fundamental weakness in the substantive scheme itself. Touraine relies on an unexamined faith that what are called "techniques of production" are rightly named; from this follows the redefinition of class struggle in terms of the dominating possessors versus the dominated nonpossessors of productive power and the identification of social movements and their debates with classes struggling over the productive techniques. But recent empirical sociology, I would say, is becoming more skeptical about so-called technological skills and more attuned to the actual maneuvers over the control of ideas and emotions that make up so much of the power of professionals, technicians, and other "experts." It is probably because student movements (especially French ones) of the 1960s attacked the domination of technology that Touraine infers that a postindustrial type of domination really exists; one need not take so seriously the rhetoric either of the protesters or of the mouthpieces of authority. In a sense, then, for all his conflict-oriented realism, Touraine falls into yet another variety of the old sociological pitfall—taking ideologies for more than they really are.

Gouldner's Dialectics*

Alvin Gouldner's *The Coming Crisis of Western Sociology* (1970) is in the line of descent of C. Wright Mills's *The Sociological Imagination* (1959). Gouldner's is a larger, more ambitious and more scholarly work, resembling its predecessor most closely in its critical aims and its pungent prose. Both represent a rejection of the dominant versions of positivist social science in favor of a critical sociology of the European type, a turn away from Cambridge and towards Frankfurt.

Gouldner's themes come out of his earlier work. The critique of functionalism was developed already in "Reciprocity and Autonomy in Functional Theory" (1959) and "The Norm of Reciprocity" (1960). The exposé of the pretense of value-freedom in American sociology was published already in the Millsian *Sociology on Trial* (1963). The examination of the roots of Western social thought begins in *Enter Plato* (1963). Most directly, Gouldner here broadens his earlier attack (1968)

* Portions originally published in *American Political Science Review*, 1973, **67** (March), and in *Theory and Society*, 1978, **5** (January). Copyright 1973 by American Political Science Association and 1978 by Elsevier Scientific Publishing Company, Amsterdam.

on Howard Becker's "underdog" approach to social problems, which Gouldner declares is a mere adjunct to the paternalistic meddling of the welfare state.

The Coming Crisis has a dual program. On one level, it is an exercise in the historical sociology of knowledge of the sort practiced in Germany since the 1920s, but with an American-style emphasis on concrete empirical rather than abstract philosophical interpretations. The general approach is to look for the social infrastructure shaping successful theories—the audiences of students, colleagues,and funding agencies and their practical and political concerns. The primary target is the positivist tradition of theoretical system-builders from Comte to Parsons. Parsonian functionalism is interpreted as a distinctively modern version of the complacent bourgeois world view, developed in the 1930s and 1940s in direct response to contemporary events: the rise of the centrally controlled welfare state and the threat of a Marxist alternative in that period of economic and political upheaval. Representing the liberal, university-based (and therefore at least indirectly state supported) segment of the middle class, Parsons' system is both a sociological justification of the New Deal against older laissez-faire ideologies, and a critique of materialist sociology.

A crisis emerged, however, becaue of shifts in the infrastructure. A student revolt broke out in the universities of the 1960s. From Berkeley and New York to Paris and Berlin, the revolts were usually led by sociology students. This constitutes a shift in political conditions, although Gouldner does not exactly put his finger on the reasons for it, and according to his sociology of knowledge, this is a sign of impending intellectual changes.

This diagnosis is bolstered by a second level of analysis, a theoretical critique of positivist sociology in terms of its own claims for logical and empirical adequacy. The main target here is Talcott Parsons (in a section taking up one third of the book), with shorter sections given to Homans, Goffman, and Garfinkel, and a quick survey of sociology in the Eastern bloc. Gouldner's conclusions are that the dominant systematic theory cannot stand on its own when examined purely on its scientific merits, apart from the protective shield of a favorable political climate. The smaller-scale theories are criticized more cursorily: Goffman and Homans as reflecting the commercialism and atomization of today's apolitical affluence; Garfinkel and the ethnomethodologists as reflecting the ethos of psychedelic anarchism.

The work does not quite live up to its aims. The sociology of knowledge is applied mainly to the functionalist version of positivism, as is the theoretical critique. What is left out is the main body of empirically based explanatory sociology, with its considerable advances in such areas as the study of organizations (to which Gouldner himself significantly contributed in his early works), comparative politics, and historical change. Sociology is a more powerful science than Gouldner depicts it in concentrating on the parts that rise least above ideology. Similarly, the treatment of the phenomenological sociologies picks up only their political resonances, missing what they can contribute to grounding explanatory sociology in the real contingencies of face-to-face interaction. Like the Hegelian Marxists prominent in recent years, Gouldner has a tendency to treat scholarship primarily for its political relevance, and to dismiss scientific objectivity as technocratic ideology. The shift from Marx's day is interesting: then scientific objectivity could be identified with revolution because conservative powers relied on religious legitimation; today, a vulgar practical interpretation of science becomes the new opiate of the masses. The task now, it would seem, is to take science back from the opportunists.

Gouldner's version of the infrastructure of intellectual life is too limited to account for those segments of the intellectual community who do pursue the development of knowledge in its own right and for its own sake. Yet scholarly advances do occur apart from political trends; intellectual communities have an internal social structure as well as an externally linked one. Perhaps Parsons received fullest treatment in this work because functionalism is the theory that can be most adequately comprehended in its political biasis.

The shortcomings of *The Coming Crisis of Western Sociology* are contained in its title. "Western sociology" is too broad; it is primarily about functionalist sociology, not about empirical research, neo-Marxist and neo-Weberian conflict theory, phenomenological sociology, or even the European idealist-historicist tradition on which Gouldner himself draws here. And the "coming crisis" is too late: Functionalist sociology has been in crisis for at least a decade, during which the vital front of intellectual advances has passed to the phenomenologists, the historical-comparativists, and the conflict theorists. A more literal title might have been "The Crisis of Functionalist Sociology."

In his conclusion, Gouldner proposes a reflexive sociology in which critical thought corrects itself by reflecting back on its social base. In his subsequent works, he becomes concerned with just those social bases that make for the critical autonomy of intellectuals. In *The Dialectic of Ideology and Technology* (1976), Gouldner focuses on the question of ideology. The sophistication of the new sociolinguistics, hermeneutics and its near relative, Frankfurt-style critical sociology, the revelations of social and intellectual historiography, some elements of traditional social science—along with reflections on the experiences and moods of the world of the Movement, the counterculture, and the Watergate scandal—all these find their places in the book. Some of it, I think, is a product of too much closeness to the particular situation of the late 1960s and early 1970s. Other parts make a general contribution to the analysis of ideology that marks a major intellectual advance. For just how much of an advance, one need only compare it with the work of Mannheim a full generation ago.

Gouldner's major claim is that sociology and ideology, usually name-calling competitors, are close relatives under the skin. Sociology is more ideological and less purely scientific than it claims; ideology is more rational than its opponents give it credit for. Both are forms of the new mode of discourse of the posttraditional era. Both contain commands and reports. To concentrate only on reports, as the social sciences claim to do, is merely to be silent about their command implications, for reports are always relevant to what might be done. Thus the social sciences' claim to superiority over ideology is really a weakness, for their silences make them less rational in the sense of less open to discourse.

Gouldner also explores the "dark" side of ideology. It permits ruthlessness by political leaders in the name of high values, who can mask themselves in an allegedly selfless ambition. Ideology assumes the power of ideas to change the world, and assumes this not usually within the content of ideology, but tacitly, in the seriousness of this speech practice itself. Moving beyond the facade of Mannheim's unattached intellectuals, Gouldner discovers a *generic ideology,* the interest of intellectuals in the power of ideas, and idealisms, per se. This is a dark side that must be explored in order for ideology, as an historically developing rational speech practice, to be true to itself.

For if ideology has its defects, it also has its correctives. Dogmatism is a speech mistake, from the point of view of a grammar of proper ideological usage. Dogmatism is an inflexibility, a blindness to the force of differing contexts for the appropriateness of speech. This limit is not peculiar to ideology, but a danger besetting all versions of rationality. Similarly, Gouldner argues that utopianism is a pathology of ideology, not its normal condition.

Ideology is part of the rationalism of modern life, arising with Destutt de Tracy's explicit creation in 1797 of a science of ideas that would change the world, and successively broadened by Hegel, Marx, and others in an ongoing and continuously self-critical progression. Ideology is based in the communications revolution around the turn of the nineteenth century, when paper-making became cheap and newspapers and magazines proliferated. It is this written form that constitutes modern rationality, for it decontextualizes discourse, forcing it to generalize beyond the taken-for-granted specifics of the face-to-face discourse that made up mass communications in the markets and holiday gatherings of traditional societies. Hence the nineteenth century was the golden age of ideological rationality. It became undermined somewhat in the twentieth century by the emphasis on mass entertainment, intruding into the newspapers in the form of "human interest" and other nonpolitical departments. Yet the form persists, for as long as the print media present information that requires interpretation, it fosters discussion and rational dialogue.

The future of ideology depends on writing, whose unimodality and linearity are a basis of modern ideological rationality. Television is a new modality, which eliminates critical distance and creates a sense of immediate participation. Television creates a version of McLuhan's global village, but in the special sense of returning us to the old context-embedded qualities of the traditional era. It is for this reason, Gouldner argues, that we have undergone a cultural revolution, the reversion from digital to analogue, from the impersonality of rationality to the new personalism and occultism. But ideological rationality does not disappear today, though it is restricted to a smaller elite. And this elite, for Gouldner, has especially great responsibilities.

There is, of course, a dark side of the news. News itself is a dramatic departure from the regularities of life, and hence it defocalizes these regularities, rendering them unworthy of attention and impervious to criticism. Rationality today requires a media-critical politics, specialized watch-dog agencies and social movements to monitor reality-defining media and institutions. This is especially important in the face of the present danger of the fusion of media accounts of reality, and those of the managers, especially the political managers of the state. The "long march through the institutions," then, should begin with the media institutions. But nationalization of the mass media would hardly be a step in the right direction. More generally, for Gouldner, a state-based socialism is really state bureaucratic capitalism; emancipatory socialism requires not a narrowing, but a widening of people's ownership and control.

Gouldner argues that the stability of modern capitalism is increasingly precarious, because it depends on periodic plebiscitarian mobilization (i.e. the ritual of elections), and the old ideological equilibrium has been undermined. Similarly, the Soviet elites are in a precarious position, for their own minority rule must be clandestine, unsupported by ideology. The "end-of-ideology" thesis is a reflection of the ideological incapacity of the hegemonic classes, but a thesis that mistakes this weakness for a strength—since only ideology can bridge interests and create solidarity. The end-of-ideology thesis is really the ideology of the new technocratic sector of the intelligentsia, not of the hegemonic elites they hope to serve, for the latter need a broader legitimation.

There is a sense in which the end-of-ideology thesis is true, however. There is an emerging technocratic mode of organization of the modern state, circumscribing the older rationality of public discourse, and hence the older ideologies. But the rational public is still there, although concentrated now mainly in the universities. An effective modern politics depends on the discourse of technicians and ideologists, and the university is the best site for this, since both sides are found there. Gouldner is mildly optimistic, especially since the experiences of the late civil rights movement and of the Watergate scandal show that an alliance of intellectuals and media technicians is possible, and both have a common structural enemy in the pressures of state censorship. With favorable demographic trends, Gouldner expects the university to remain central, and the fruitful possibilities of critical-media alliance loom large in the future.

Yet on this last point, as on several others, Gouldner seems to be overstating the general significance of events and structures that may be historically specific to the late 1960s and early 1970s. That period was the *height* of university attendance in America, and the tide has turned since then. The crowding of the universities was not due to any technological demand from the allegedly post industrial economy, but simply the optimistic phase of the scramble for educational status-credentials. With increasing availability of the credentials has come a deflation in their value, and the universities have since been contracting as disillusionment has spread. To be sure, some other forms of education are expanding into the gap (and undergoing sky-rocketing credential inflation of their own), but these are in the areas of business and trade schools, where the technocratic consciousness is strongest and ideological rationality is excluded.

More generally, I think, Gouldner overstates the importance of the media, and especially the news-print media, in politics. It does not seem to me that newspapers generate much more motivation to go out and *do* anything about what they report than television does. Both seem to be forms of entertainment, even if the content of news is allegedly reality; people tend to read newspapers as a form of transition, whether from sleep to the morning world of work, or from work on into the private life of the evening—cognitive equivalents and accompaniments of coffee or cocktails, rather than agents of political mobilization.

The media, I would contend, are followers rather than leaders. They come into play only when the balance of contending social forces—real interest groups, real economic processes and military events—moves groups into action. The media defocalize most of these ground swells until they are too large to ignore, and then the media jump on the bandwagon, not without self-congratulatory claims as to their own leadership. But this is just media hype. Real social forces will always dominate the media; without such forces, they are nothing but foam on the surface.

The Dialetic of Ideology and Technology is the best book yet in defense of ideology. It shows ideology's rationality as well as its dark side, and in such a way as to allow some rationally planned ideological praxis. It is a refreshing change from the polemical rallying cries that make up so much of the Left's recent relativism. It is also, in my opinion, Gouldner's best-written book, and also perhaps his best substantive contribution yet.

The writing, in fact, is so strong, so pungent and clear, phrase by phrase, that one can say, and imply, almost anything in it. And here, perhaps, is the weakness of the book, and one of its "dark" strengths. As Gouldner says in his preface: "One must lay one's cards on the table, but there is no obligation to read them out loud. In a serious game, the convention is always the same: it is the cards, not the player, who speaks. But one should never forget, this is a convention."

Blau's Macrotheory*

Peter Blau is perhaps our most productive American sociologist. He has a sharp sense for where the intellectual action is. In the 1950s he turned out *The Dynamics of Bureaucracy* (1955), one of the classics of that golden age of organizational studies. At the turn of the 1960s, when various theorists (March and Simon, Etzioni, Caplow) were pulling together the field of organizations into the most systematically explained area of empirically based sociology, Blau and Scott turned out their comprehensive *Formal Organizations* (1962). When Homans's individual-reductionist social behaviorism began to make a surge, Blau leap-frogged it to a full-fledged nonreductionist exchange theory, with *Exchange and Power in Social Life* (1964). As empirical attention in the 1960s focused increasingly on social mobility surveys, Blau and Duncan turned out the most comprehensive and most methodologically advanced of such studies (partly because it was based on the largest sample and the most extensive questionnaire schedule), *The American*

---

* Originally published in *Social Forces*, 1979, **58** (December). Copyright 1979 *Social Forces*.

Occupational Structure (1967). Since then, Blau has produced a mathematical theory of organizational structure, based on a sample of all the public unemployment agencies in the U.S. (Blau and Schoenherr, *The Structure of Organizations*, 1971), the first really comprehensive comparative study of universities (*The Organization of Academic Work*, 1973), and another general theory of organizations (*On the Nature of Organizations*, 1974). Finally, after all these years of preparation, we have *Inequality and Heterogeneity*, (1977) Blau's most ambitious effort, a general theory of social structure.

Blau's work is very much within the camp that Nicholas Mullins *Theories and Theory Groups in American Sociology* (1973) calls "Standard American Sociology" (SAS). As such, it represents the strengths and weaknesses of that school, and also its shifting moods. SAS at one time was a combination of positivism and functionalism, with a strong dose of Cold War liberalism setting its underlying concerns. Blau is still very positivist (indeed, more than ever), but he explicitly claims to leave behind the functionalism of his early works, at least for the purpose of this book. In fact, he repudiates functional, cultural, and psychological explanations alike, in favor of a macro-structuralism which he likens to that of Harrison White, Edward Laumann, and Bruce Mayhew. This shift bears out Mullins's view that the structuralist group is one of the strong contenders now superceding SAS. (Oddly enough, it also suggests that Blau has transferred his allegiance from Mullins's other new positivist leader, the path-coefficient group, even though Blau and Duncan [1967] is its paradigm-setter).

Even more of a sign of the times is Blau's newfound attitude towards Marxism. Not that he goes very deeply into this position. But formerly taboo terms such as "capitalism" and "dialectical" are found here and there on his pages, and he takes a decidedly pessimistic and critical view of many aspects of modern America that were once polemically defended: discerning a trend of increasing concentration of organizational power, giving a theoretical explanation for the coalescence of a power elite, suggesting that democracy only works well on issues people care little about, and calling for some way to increase participatory democracy in the organizations that surround us. It is a far cry from the panglossian functional interpretations of SAS in the anti-Communist 1950s. Much of Blau's newfound critical stance is on the surface, for the core of his theory is still very much in keeping with traditional American liberal beliefs. But is is striking to see him claim that Marx, the old arch-bogey man of American sociology, actually converges on a theoretical level with his own theory that cpaitalist democracy depends on the existence of cross-cutting status dimensions, and falls to revolutionary pressures when these dimensions converge.

The essence of Blau's theory is actually quite traditional. He is principally concerned with the determinants of social integration, which he considers to be a structural matter of personal associations linking people together, not a cultural matter of common values. Blau couches his argument in very general terms, dealing with social integration in Durkheim's sense; but what he often seems to have in mind is integration in the narrower and more topical sense—the problems between blacks, whites, and other minorities in the U.S. Integration, in Blau's view, is determined by the sheer number of social categories into which the population is divided, and especially by cross-cutting dimensions. The first part of this argument is based on the inference that smaller groups must have relatively more outgroup associations than large groups; hence if larger groups are broken up into smaller groups (in Blau's terminology, as heterogeneity advances), they must necessarily have more outgroup contacts, and social integration will improve. The second part of the argument is the old pluralist theme, so popular in the 1950s as a counter to radical criticisms that inequalities undermine democracy—inequalities, on the contrary, were considered good for social stability if their different dimensions intersected, preventing polarization. Blau avoids the term "pluralist" (I find it only once in the book, on the next to the last page), substituting a variety of neologisms ("intersecting parameters," "multiform heterogeneity"). Whether this is a matter of disguising an unfashionable term, or simply part of the positivist style of writing as densely and abstractly as possible, I could not say.

The core of the theory, by Blau's own reckoning, is the point that segregation in space is far worse for social integration than inequalities within communities and work organizations. (I have translated this into my own terms; Blau's are a good deal more polysyllabic, and take a good deal longer to explain the point.) Blau claims that this is a startling paradox, and perhaps it is, from the abstract way he introduces the topic. More conventionally put, though, it is part of the traditional liberal belief that integrating neighborhoods, schools, and jobs will solve all our problems. Blau goes on to talk about "penetrating differentiation," meaning that the real integrating effects go on only if people are brought together not just within the same city or organization, but right down to the block and work room, and expresses some pessimism that much of this has come about yet.

What causes this cross-cutting pluralism? Blau appeals to an implicitly evolutionary scheme. The growth of population density and of the sheer size of communities (i.e., principally urbanization) leads to more interpersonal contacts, and especially contacts among heterogeneous groups. The sheer volume of contacts requires people to react to others differentially; hence, intersecting dimensions of categorization are elaborated by which individuals may be cross-classified and picked out for differentiated responses. Mere concentric categories (local group memberships nested within larger groups) decline, hence territorial and extended kinship categories decline as societies grow large.

Further, the division of labor advances from little to much occupational specialization: The number of different occupations increases, and so does the dispersion of the population among them. Although at one point, in early industrialization, the division of labor produces increased *routine specialization*, the advanced division of labor involves a shift towards increasingly *expert specialization*. The division of labor, in turn, is determined by urbanization, population density, and industrialization; by a high degree of communications and associations; and by a high level of education of the labor force. Blau takes issue with Durkheim's theory that the advancing division of labor produces organic solidarity—social integration through a form of consciousness arising from exchanges among differentiated roles. Blau rejects this form of explanation of social integration by cultural or psychological factors.[1] More concretely, he also points out that with a high degree of occupational specialization, most exchanges are among organizations, not among the different specialists within them; hence most interpersonal exchanges in the economic realm are relatively superficial ones, between salesperson and customer, or boss and worker. Nevertheless, Durkheim's theory can be salvaged by a structural interpretation: a high division of labor, as high occupational diversity, is a form of heterogeneity of social categories, and hence, results in a high level of intergroup contacts, especially if stratified dimensions cross-cut pluralistically with nominal categories. Thus the progress of the division of labor itself produces social integration.

Blau also states that social mobility is the cause of most social change. From his formalized structural perspective, changes must involve shifts in the numbers of people among categories, or changes in

---

[1] Though not entirely consistently. Page 105 defines stratified dimensions as "differences in comparable social resources of *generally accepted validity* in social exchange" [italics added], and Blau's exchange model, worked into his structural theory at least sketchily in Chapter 6, still makes use of the claim that exchange rests on normative obligations of reciprocity.

the numbers of categories; and both of these involve movement of individuals, therefore social mobility. Again, pluralism is a crucial determining condition. Mobility is facilitated by contacts among groups, and hence is especially likely if people share common characteristics in other dimensions across class lines. Blau lists two other determinants of social change: differential fertility and immigration. But Blau thinks both of these are larger in the lower classes, and hence both tend to enlarge the lower strata and enhance inequality (though immigration into the very bottom pushes up the previous lower classes). Hence the whole weight of social change that diminishes inequality (i.e. of excess upward mobility) rests on pluralism.

Blau does enter a pessimistic note at the end of this argument. Mobility is promoted by pluralism, but once mobility takes place, pluralism declines. Mobility involves individuals who are like people in other social classes in some nonclass dimensions, moving and thus making their class ranking match that of their co-religionists, ethnic brethren, or what have you; those who are already congruent on nonclass dimensions with most of their class compatriots tend not to move. Hence classes become more homogeneous as mobility occurs. This in turn reduces the possibility of mobility. The general paradox, Blau argues, is that change destroys the very conditions that made it possible.

Blau is pessimistic in another respect as well. The advance of the division of labor involves increasingly larger organizations. These in turn result in a larger concentration of power, which Blau measures by the number of employees directly or indirectly under a person's control. Thus, irrespective of how one argues the question of the separation of ownership and control, there *is* a small elite that has most of the organizational power. Furthermore, Blau thinks that this means the consolidation of the elites of power and wealth, and hence declining mobility and (by definition) declining social change. Such blockages, if severe, he warns, presage a revolutionary situation, which he fears would destroy pluralist democracy.

In my view, Blau has not produced a truly primitive theory of social structure, at least not in the sense of having isolated the principles of greatest general applicability. Take his principal dependent variable, social integration. On the face of it, this seems to be a very fundamental category, the answer to the problem of order, the same issue that Durkheim concerned himself with throughout his works. Blau argues that one should see social integration as a matter of concrete interpersonal interactions. This is empirically realistic. But Blau does not mean just *any* interactions; he means sociable, by and large friendly, contacts of a personal nature. Okay, if that's how one wants to *define* social integration. But it is only conceptual sleight of hand to assume that societies cannot exist without widespread social integration in this sense. In fact, there have been societies throughout history with all sorts of degrees and patterns of social ties and social barriers, highly stratified societies with near perfect correlation of wealth, power, ethnicity, and all the rest, as well as many other forms, with and without intergroup friendships. *All* are equally societies, and in fact, they represent the empirical range of structures that a truly general theory should account for. To say that some societies, according to Blau's criterion, are fragmented is a tautology, if it is not backed up by further indications that they are *literally* falling apart into separate economies, undergong political secession, or the like. But Blau does not show this, or even seem to think it is necesary. He does think that a fragmented society will undergo a revolutionary crisis, which he does not like, but there is no reason not to call this a form of social interaction as well. In short, Blau's social integration and fragmentation are no more than value-judgments, conditions that are regarded as desirable or undesirable in themselves. Blau is merely continuing the typical belief of midcentury liberal American sociologists that ethnic integration is a good thing, and that segregation is bad. It may well be so, but it doesn't add up to a general theory of social structure.

Blau's theory of social change is also in the traditional mold. The dependent variable does not give us the range of types of governments, forms of property, systems of stratification, or organizational structures that have existed in world history. Instead, we get an evolutionary stage model, in which sheer population size, density, and urbanization are the principal determinants, and social differentiation, mainly indexed by the complexity of the division of labor, is the outcome. Change is assumed to move in a straight line (maybe with intermittant stops and explosions when too much social mobility undermines its own bases). The United States, as usual, is always the example of an advanced society, and European societies are assumed to be lagging behind in bucolic undifferentiatedness.

This is a pretty naïve picture of historical change, both on the range of causes and effects. Much of it may be due to the American sociological tradition of ethnocentrism, which sees little else in history than a shift towards what exists in the modern U.S. For example, Blau's way of putting the traditional argument about the shift from ascription to achievement is to state that extended kinship must decline with increasing size and density of populations. But in fact (see Blumberg and Winch, 1972) kinship systems become *more* elaborate and extended for a considerable part of that continuum, ranging from hunting-and-gathering societies through advanced horticultural societies, and only decline with increasing size thereafter, most notably in the shift from agrarian to industrial societies.

Blau's criterion for an "advanced" division of labor is an increase in occupational specializations to a very large number. This may be all right as a formal definition, but if so, one cannot bootleg in the implication that advanced division of labor in this sense means highly efficient economic production, or the idea that there is a necessary historical trend in this direction. That occupational heterogeneity and high productivity may be related in a particular case of recent history does not make a convincing argument that *the* trend of history is towards ever more "advanced" divisions of labor (or even that the natural-resource-rich U.S. is a *typical* industrial society). It is particularly dubious (although well within the evolutionary tradition) to see the most recent phase of industrialization as based upon the specialized expert skills produced by mass education. This is the usual uncritical interpretation of rising educational levels, and of the correlation of education and occupational attainment. Yet detailed analyses of what actually goes on in schools and in job placement (Bowles and Gintis, 1976; Collins, 1971 and 1974) show virtually *no* relations between education and actual work output, and considerable evidence that education is implicated in the struggle for occupational position primarily as a device for control and an arbitrary (and inflatable) currency of cultural status. Blau buys the technocratic argument as part of the traditional explanatory package; he is working within a paradigm which, although it may occasionally now admit conflict and domination as outcomes of social processes, never sees them as causes.

Finally, I must say that I found Blau's arguments about social mobility to be rather empty. He states that social mobility is the cause of social change, but one could just as well argue the other way around. Better yet, social mobility *is* social change; it is a different way of describing the same phenomena. As such, it is not an autonomous explanation of change. Nor does Blau give us any concrete theory of the causes of mobility rates. He does drag in a couple of the old standard statements about mobility—that it is affected by class differences in fertility and immigration. Even this is not highly convincing. Blau seems unaware of the fact that it was the *upper* classes in all nonindustrial societies that had the higher fertility, and world history is full of examples of immigrants coming in at the top, especially as military conquerors. Reflection on such variations ought to be included in a truly general theory of mobility and social change. For such historical examples point up very clearly that the number of positions of different kinds change because certain people have the resources—the weapons, strong group solidarity, means of ritual impressiveness, wealth—to create forms of domination over others. We miss this by thinking only of powerless people coming in (or being born) at the bottom, fitting into positions that have been created and defined for them by someone else. A position after all, is only a metaphor; empirically, it unpacks into repetitive behaviors, established and given a social definition by those who have the power to do so. (Incidentally, Blau perpetuates another traditional error about upward mobility in America: for there is no theoretical reason why there should be an automatic escalator effect by which people coming in at the bottom must displace the previous lower class *upward*. If the old lower class had no resources, they could just as well be displaced further down, e.g., into unemployment if a newer, cheaper form of labor were found).

As a general theory, then, Blau's model does not come off. Social integration as a dependent variable does not mean anything empirically useful; pluralism as a cause of all good things strikes me as silly, and certainly not the only or even the major cause of interpersonal associations, political tranquility, etc.; social mobility as a cause of change is really a tautology; the inevitable evolutionary advance of the division of labor can be established only by an empty definition; and the recent development of "expert specializations" needs a realistic explanation instead of a technocratic glossing.

The main contributions of this book, rather, are the thorough working out of some more limited principles of *some* of the causes and consequences of interpersonal associations, and other structural phenomena of a relatively diffuse sort. The most striking contributions, in my opinion, are several technical points regarding inequality. Blau develops a quantitative measure of power, and presents us, for the first time, with some evidence on its distribution. Like all pioneering efforts, it has its flaws. I think Blau overstates the concentration of effective power; most detailed studies of what actually goes on in organizations (including Blau's own 1955 study) show that actual control over what policies are carried out, how much work gets done, how positions and definitions of organizational reality are shaped, are very considerably influenced by organizational participants who do not have formal line authority. Blau's index, based only on cumulative numbers of employees nominally under one's control, misses this, and he flatly denies that organizational decentralization affects the distribution of power by his calculations. Clearly, there are many complexities to be worked out here. But Blau has done us a service by giving us at least an initial measure that can now be used in interorganizational and intersocietal comparisons.

Blau's other major contribution is the one of his paradoxes that I really did find striking. This is the "paradox of inequality:" that increases in the concentration of some good (power, wealth, whatever), beyond a certain point, actually lead to decreases in overall inequality. For as most of the wealth, say, comes into the hands of fewer and fewer people, differences among the mass of population become less. Thus very great inequality turns out to approach near total equality. This does suggests a reason why, at certain points in history, power can shift very rapidly (although I'm not convinced this is the usual cause of revolutions, which have more to do with military and financial exhaustion of rulers due to foreign affairs). But at least theoretically Blau has succeeded in resuscitating one of the connotations of another old conceptual scheme, the dialectic.

Blau's latest work, then, shows that SAS is certainly not dead. Indeed, it is using many of the same old arguments, although in a much more technical form, and with a new terminology. Functionalism seems to be gone, though its underlying bias lingers on; structuralism, with its own biases, comes near to the center of the stage, and Marxism (which can be easily put in the structuralist camp as well) is making inroads that, however superficial, would not have been believable 15 years ago. And in the midst of all this, some genuine advances occur here and there. Mainstream American sociology is creeping onward.

Sociology Past and Future*

The sociology of science has received a great deal of attention in recent years, especially in terms of social epistemology and critical analysis of prevailing paradigms. What has been less noticeable is that empirical research in the sociology of science has also proceeded, and some of the results are beginning to develop into explanatory theories of some sophistication. Certainly we have come a fair distance from Merton's multiple discoveries, Price's initial studies of the growth of scientific literature, and Kuhn's first formulation of the existence of paradigms and paradigm crises. Nicholas Mullins, one of the sociologists directing the sociology of science along this path, enables us in *Theories and Theory Groups* (1973) to survey how far it has come.

Mullins has developed a theoretical model deriving from Kuhn and from the structuralism of Harrison White (itself, in turn, an elaboration of Lévi-Strauss), and applied it to an empirical approach developed by Ben-David and Collins (1966) on the origins of experimental psychology. That research located individuals in networks of intellectual ap-

*Originally published in *Theory and Society*; 1975, 2 (Winter). Copyright 1975 Elsevier Scientific Publishing Company, Amsterdam.

prenticeship (i.e., who was a student of whom). Mullins has expanded the technique by investigating the horizontal networks constituted by communications (who discusses ideas and sends preprints to whom), colleagueship (who serves in the same department or research organization with whom), and coauthorship. Mullins has assembled this kind of data for a number of different sciences (including the molecular biologists responsible for the DNA revolution); in this book, he develops his theory for American sociologists from 1930 through 1970. Upon this, he builds a theoretical model which takes Kuhn's "normal science" as one stage through which a research groups progresses, but adds three further stages.

Normal stage: This is the period in which intellectual founding fathers produce their first intellectual innovations, but remain isolated among the mass of routine puzzle-solving work within the prevailing paradigm. As yet the new paradigm is not supported by a research and training center; there is only a small informal group around the intellectual leader.

Network stage: Alongside the intellectual leader appears an organizational leader, who develops a research and training center to propagate the new paradigm as its intellectual success attracts new collaborators and students. The intellectual work now comes to include a program statement of the new position. If this is a revolutionary movement (and there can also be nonrevolutionary movements), the group produces critiques of rival positions at this time. The group remains informal, and grows to perhaps 40 members.

Cluster stage: Intellectual founders now have students who produce further work of their own; the organizational leader broadens his activities to arrange for jobs, publications, and meetings; more research centers appear; the program statement of the previous stage becomes a dogma, especially in revolutionary groups; secondary material begins to appear reflecting on the new paradigm, including critical attacks by rivals (if this is a revolutionary group). Relations within the network become more formal, and it divides into a core cluster of 7–25 members and a larger periphery.

Specialty stage: Finally, the intellectual founder may leave his own paradigm, although the organizational leader stays on; research outgrows any specific research center; intellectual successes no longer attract special attention; work becomes routine; a textbook appears. Group size ranges from 20 to over 100.

Mullins conceives this as a structural development in every intellectual network that supports a scientific paradigm. He estimates from his data that the network stage takes from four to fourteen years, the cluster stage four to eight years; the initial and final stages, being more diffusely organized, are less determinate in length.

For American sociology, Mullins illustrates the process with eight cases, three of which have already been completed, while the rest are contemporary and still in progress.

Among the earlier examples, the most prominent Mullins calls "Standard American Sociology" (SAS). Its intellectual leaders were Merton and Parsons: its organizational leader Parsons; its research centers BASR at Columbia and NORC at Chicago; its principal training centers Harvard, Columbia, and Chicago; its first intellectual success Parsons's *Structure of Social Action* in 1937, followed by Merton's *Social Theory and Social Structure* and Stouffer's *The American Soldier,* 1949. The program statements for this group were made by Parsons in the "general theory of action" period around 1950, and the representative textbook is by Broom and Selznick. Treating its development in stages, we find that the normal stage occurred before 1935, with the informal group creating the new paradigm in Henderson's Pareto seminar at Harvard. The network stage was 1935–1945, during which the first generation of Harvard students trained in the new paradigm appeared (Merton, Kingsley Davis, Robin Williams and others), and the *American Sociological Review* displaced the old *American Journal of Sociology* as the official journal of the A.S.A. The cluster stage took place in 1945–1951, with the reorganization of Harvard sociology into the Social Relations department, the appearance of a second generation of Harvard students, and the emergence of Columbia as a second training center. The specialty stage came after 1951, with SAS spreading to Chicago and to many other places, and research becoming routinized into empirical specializations.

The other major group of this period, symbolic interactionism (SI), Mullins calls "the loyal opposition." Its intellectual leaders were Mead and Blumer; its organizational leader, Blumer; its centers Chicago and later Berkeley. This group proceeded through the normal stage up to 1931; the network stage in 1931–1945 (the ascendancy of Blumer and the appearance of Mead's posthumous books); the cluster stage in 1945–1952, with Iowa and Minnesota added to Chicago as centers, and works such as Lindesmith's *Opiate Addiction* providing further intellectual payoff in the new generation. The specialty stage occurred after 1953, with the proliferation of centers and third generation successes such as those of Melville Dalson and Erving Goffman in the late 1950s.

Mullins argues that by the 1960s, SAS and SI had become mori-

bund, and that new paradigms were emerging within their final nor-
malcies. One of the strongest of these has been ethnomethodology, with
Garfinkel and Cicourel as its intellectual and organizational leaders.
The network in ethnomethodology took place in 1957–1966, the cluster
stage in 1966–1971, and it is already in its specialty stage. Another important paradigm is "new causal theory," the correlational analysis
developed by O. D. Duncan and Blalock, which went throught the network stage in 1962–1966 and the cluster stage in 1966–1970. Mullins
also distinguishes a smaller paradigm group of "structuralists" deriving
from Harrison White at Harvard, which was just passing into the network stage as of 1970.

All of these fit Mullins's stage model, with some differences due to
the revolutionary stance of ethnomethodology and the nonrevolutionary stance of the others. But some other paradigm groups, he points
out, do not fit the model: In the earlier period, there was the small-
group theory growing out of the work of Kurt Lewin, which gave rise to
a flurry of works around 1950 (Bales; Festinger; Homans; Lewinn, Lip-
pitt, and White) but failed to develop an organizational leader or a unifying theory, never issued a text and thus gradually disintegrated as a
network by the late 1950s. Similarly, the "social forecasters" of the
1960s, centered around the Hudson Institute and various study groups
(e.g., the Commission on the Year 2000), seem to lack a training center
for students and clear-cut intellectual and organizational leaders;
Mullins doubts that they will survive the network stage. And finally
there is the radical–critical theory group emerging from the activism of
the 1960s which Mullins believes does not fit the developmental model
because it does not publish within the internal realm of American
sociology.

Mullins's model has the merit of pointing up some recurrent patterns in the social networks underlying new theoretical paradigms, and
above all in their common sequence of development. However, certain
questions are left dangling. As a structuralist model, it is content with a
formal characterization and a statement of its sequential transformations; what is misssing is a set of variables that explain whether a group
will indeed go through all four stages, or whether it will fail, like the
small–group theory and (apparently) the social forecasters. And
although this model distinguishes between revolutionary and nonrevolutionary theory groups, it does not give any conditions for the
emergence of either.

What is needed is to integrate Mullins' work with some other
developments in the sociology of science, especially those concerned
with the structure of competition within and among groups, and with

the different kinds of organizational bases from which intellectuals draw their support. Bridges to this kind of analysis are not hard to find in Mullins' own work. Thus, although Mullins treats SAS, SI, and small-group theory as independent contemporaries (and the later five groups also as independent of each other), it is apparent that much of their development was a response to the rivalry between groups. If Mullins had taken his analysis of the Chicago school back before the 1930s SI phase, he would have found the dominant paradigm, especially represented by Thomas and Park, concentrated on research oriented towards social problems. Parsons' new resource was his importation of the European theoretical tradition (in however partial a form) and his ability to train a new group of students to exploit this material in a direction other than social problems. I suspect it was the challenge of this movement that provoked Blumer and his embattled Chicago school to put forward Mead as a countertheory (the battle in 1936 to displace the Chicago-based AJS—subsequently edited by Blumer—with the Ivy League-based ASR was one of the things that probably brought this to a head). What Mullins misses by his abstract level of analysis is the way in which this competition went on for 30 years, during which there was considerable maneuvering among subfactions and even some external alliances. The link between Parsonian grand theory and detailed empirical work had to be negotiated, and Merton at Columbia and Stouffer at Harvard were the key negotiators. (In a sense, Merton's role theory was also an effort to create a grand alliance with the symbolic interactionists, but failed to win them over.) SAS itself tended increasingly to break apart between the functionalist (especially Durkheimian) and historicist–conflict theory (especially Weberian) wings of its European heritage. When Blumer gave up the Chicago citadel to SAS in the 1950s and migrated to the new Berkeley department, he forged a new alliance between the Weberians and the symbolic interactionists.

In general, new departures seem to come from these rivalries and combinations: The ethnomethodologists, for example, derived from a mixture of Parsonian training and European phenomenology in Garfinkel, and a further influx of Goffman- and Blumer-influenced students from Berkeley; Gerth and Mills combined symbolic interactionism with the Weberian side of the classical European tradition; and the Duncan–Blalock style of quantitative empiricism is very much like a breaking away of the old empiricist social-problems analysis from subsequent theoretical accretions.

Mullins's own data do suggest some determinants of whether a group will proceed succesfully through all the stages. It seems to be crucial to gain control of an organizational center where new students can be trained, where a sense of group unity is maintained and career possibilities arranged for. The "social forecasters" lack such a center. This lack parallels other cases in the history of science in which too-close ties with the purely practical bases of funding obviate the formation of an academic training center, and hence cripple the further development of a coherent theory by new generations of students. Apparently Mullins's thinking about radical–critical theory is influenced by the belief that the radicals communicate only with external activist audiences, and thus lack an internal organization that will generate intellectual successors. On the matter of the facts here, I think he is mistaken. Radical–critical theory had its original institutional base at the Frankfurt *Institut für Sozialforschung*, which migrated to New York during World War II (where Mills and Gouldner were drawn into the network), and later sent offshoots to Berkeley (producing *The Authoritarian Personality* research, and leaving Lowenthal as a permanent member of the faculty). Continuing beachheads thus were established for a while at Columbia, Berkeley, Washington University in St. Louis, and Wisconsin, from which much of the radical–critical sociology in America has developed.

One might also profitably analyze why the small-group theory fell apart organizationally. I suspect that rivalry among the successors of Lewin (Bales, Festinger, Homans) and the successful organizing activity of Parsons at Harvard for SAS exerted pressure that eventually pushed them into alliance with the psychologists, and thence out of the main intellectual field of sociology (as exemplified by the reductionist manifestos of Homans in his Skinnerian period). Program statements, after all, are political proposals for group unity within the intellectual field; the failure to develop a theory around which group can unite may be the result of alliances that take one out of the arena entirely.

Mullins's analysis of American sociology is too abstract to capture all of these dynamics, or indeed all of the important paradigm groups at work today. I doubt, for example, that SAS was as unified as Mullins makes it out to have been; and what is happening now is not so much its disappearance as the emergence of several of its components as groups in their own right. This would not surprise Mullins, for he suggests that others might apply his methods to investigating other groups. However, his structuralism still needs supplementing with a causal analysis of the conditions that move groups differentially through the stages, and attention to the rivalries through which groups mutually influence one another.

But these are signs of a research tradition in progress, and it seems likely that one could find a structure (or set of group structures) in the sociology of science that promises just such a further development of Mullins's model. It is precisely this sort of capacity for turning sociological tools on one's own past, present, *and future* that constitutes the appeal of this book. For all its flaws, it gives one the bizarre feeling that what we are doing intellectually right now is part of a larger field of forces, the laws of which are being clarified before our very eyes. What will it be like to experience the even more acute sociological reflexivity of the future?

References

Althusser, L.
  1971 *Lenin and Philosophy and Other Essays*. London: New Left Books.
Anderson, P.
  1974 *Lineages of the Absolutist State*. London: New Left Books.
Andrae, T.
  1960 *Mohammed, the Man and His faith*. New York: Harper and Row.
Arendt, H.
  1963 *Eichmann in Jerusalem: A Report on the Banality of Evil*. New York: Random House.
Ariès, P.
  1962 *Centuries of Childhood*. New York: Random House.
Bachrach, P., and Baratz, M. S.
  1962 "Two faces of power." *American Political Science Review* **56**:947–952.
Banfield, E. C.
  1961 *Political Influence*. New York: Free Press.
Barnard, C. I.
  1938 *The Functions of the Executive*. Cambridge, Massachusetts: Harvard University Press.
Bartholomew, J.
  1954 *Physical World Atlas*. 6th ed. New York: American Map Company.
Becker, H. S.
  1963 *Outsiders*. New York: Free Press.
Bell, D.
  1973 *The Coming of Post-Industrial Society*. New York: Basic Books.

341

Ben-David, J.
   1960   "Scientific productivity and academic organization in nineteenth century
          medicine." *American Sociological Review* **25**:828–843.
Ben-David, J., and Collins, R.
   1966   "Social factors in the origins of a new science: The case of psychology."
          American Sociological Review **31**:451–463.
Bendix, R.
   1964   *Nation-Building and Citizenship.* New York: Wiley.
   1978   *Kings or People: Power and the Mandate to Rule.* Berkeley: University of
          California Press.
Bernstein, B.
   1971– *Class, Codes, and Control.* 3 Volumes. London: Routledge and Kegan Paul.
   1975
Blau, P. M.
   1955   *The Dynamics of Bureaucracy.* Chicago: University of Chicago Press.
   1964   *Exchange and Power in Social Life.* New York: Wiley.
   1973   *The Organization of Academic Work.* New York: Wiley.
   1974   *On the Nature of Organizations.* New York: Wiley.
   1977   *Inequality and Heterogeneity: a Primitive Theory of Social Structure.* New
          York: Free Press.
Blau, P. M., and Duncan, O. D.
   1967   *The American Occupational Structure.* New York: Wiley.
Blau, P. M., and Schoenherr, R. A.
   1971   *The Structure of Organizations.* New York: Basic Books.
Blau, P. M., and Scott, W. R.
   1962   *Formal Organizations.* San Francisco: Chandler.
Blumberg, R. L., and Winch, R. F.
   1972   "Societal complexity and family complexity: Evidence for the curvilinear hy-
          pothesis." *American Journal of Sociology* **77**:898–920.
Bonacich, E.
   1972   "A theory of ethnic antagonism: The split labor market." *American Socio-
          logical Review* **37**:547–559.
   1973   "A Theory of middleman minorities." *American Sociological Review*
          38:583–594.
Borale, P. T.
   1968   *Segregation and Desegregation in India.* Bombay: Manaktalas.
Bourdieu, P.
   1972– *Outline of a Theory of Practice.* Cambridge, England: Cambridge University
   1977   Press.
Bourdieu, P., and Passeron, J. C.
   1964   *Les Héritiers: les étudiants et la culture.* Paris: Editions de Minuit.
   1970/ *Reproduction; In Education, Society, and Culture.* Beverly Hills: Sage Publi-
   1977   cations.
Bowles, S., and Gintis, H.
   1976   *Schooling in Capitalist America.* New York: Basic Books.
Braudel, F.
   1949– *The Mediterranean and the Mediterranean World in the Age of Philip II.* New
   1972   York: Harper and Row.
Breed, W.
   1955   "Social control in the newsroom." *Social Forces* **33**:326–335.

Bruford, W. H.
  1935 *Germany in the Eighteenth Century.* Cambridge, England: Cambridge University Press.
Brunschwig, H.
  1947 *La Crise de L'État Prussien.* Paris: Presses Universitaires de France.
Bucher, R., and Struass, A.
  1961 "Professions in process." *American Journal of Sociology* **66**:325–334.
Burstein, P.
  1972 "Social structure and individual political participation in five countries." *American Journal of Sociology* **77**:1087–1110.
Cancian, F.
  1975 *What are Norms?* London: Cambridge University Press.
Carey, A.
  1967 "The Hawthorne studies: A radical criticism." *American Sociological Review* **32**:403–417.
Carr-Saunders, A. M., and Wilson, P. A.
  1933 *The Professions.* London: Oxford University Press.
Chadwick, H.
  1967 *The Early Church.* Baltimore: Penguin.
Cicourel, A. V.
  1968 *The Social Organization of Juvenile Justice.* New York: Wiley.
  1973 *Cognitive Sociology.* Baltimore: Penguin.
  1975 "Discourse and text: Cognitive and linguistic processes in studies of social structure." *Versus* **12**:33–83.
Cicourel, A. V., et al.
  1974 *Language Use and School Performance.* New York: Academic Press.
Cipolla, C.
  1976 *Before the Industrial Revolution.* London: Methuen.
Clegg, S.
  1975 *Power, Rule, and Domination. A Critical and Empirical Understanding of Power in Sociological Theory and Everyday Life.* London: Routledge and Kegan Paul.
Collins, R.
  1971a "Functional and conflict theories of educational stratification." *American Sociological Review* **36**:1002–1019.
  1971b A conflict theory of sexual stratification." *Social Problems* **19**:2–21.
  1975 *Conflict Sociology: Toward an Explanatory Science.* New York: Academic Press.
  1977 "Some comparative principles of educational stratification." *Harvard Educational Review* **47**:1–27.
  1978 "Some principles of long-term social change: The territorial power of states." In L. Kriesberg (Ed.), *Research in Social Movements, Conflicts, and Change.* Greenwich, Conn.: JAI Press. pp. 1–34.
  1979 *The Credential Society. A Historical Sociology of Education and Stratification.* New York: Academic Press.
  1980 Weber's last theory of capitalism: A systematization." *American Sociological Review* **45**:925–942.
  1982 Forthcoming "Micro-translation as a Theory-building Strategy." In K. Knorr and A. Cicourel (Eds.), *Advance in Social Theory and Methodology: Toward an Integration of Micro- and Macro-Sociology.* London: Routledge and Kegan Paul.

Coser, L., and Nisbet, R. (ed.)
  1975   The Idea of Social Structure, Papers in Honor of Robert K. Merton. New York:
          Harcourt, Brace, Jovanovich.
Crozier, M.
  1964   The Bureaucratic Phenomenon. Chicago: University of Chicago Press.
Cutright, P.
  1967   "Inequality: A cross-national analysis." American Sociological Review
          32:562–578.
Dahendorf, R.
  1959   Class and Class Conflict in Industrial Society. Stanford: Stanford University
          Press.
Dalton, M.
  1959   Men Who Manage. New York: Wiley.
De Bary, W. T.
  1969   The Buddhist Tradition. New York: Random House.
Deutscher, I.
  1973   What We Say, What We Do: Sentiments and Acts. Glenville, Illinois: Scott,
          Foresman.
Divale, W.
  1975   "An explanation for matrilocal residence." In D. Raphael (Ed.), Being Female:
          Reproduction, Power, and Change. The Hague: Mouton. pp. 99–108.
Domhoff, G. W.
  1967   Who Rules America? Englewood Cliffs, N.J.: Prentice-Hall.
Douglas, M.
  1966   Purity and Danger. London: Routledge and Kegan Paul.
  1970   Natural Symbols. London: Routledge and Kegan Paul.
Dumont, L.
  1970   Homo Hierarchicus: The Caste System and Its Implications. Chicago: University
          of Chicago Press.
Durkheim, E.
  1912/
  1954   The Elementary Forms of the Religious Life. New York: Free Press.
  1893/
  1947   The Division of Labor in Society. New York: Free Press.
Eberhard, W.
  1969   A History of China. Berkeley: University of California Press.
Elliot, J. H.
  1970   Imperial Spain, 1469–1716. Baltimore: Penguin.
Erikson, K. T.
  1966   Wayward Puritans. New York: Wiley.
Etzioni, A.
  1961   A Comparative Analysis of Complex Organizations. New York: Free Press.
Foucault, M.
  1965   Madness and Civilization. New York: Random House.
Fox, R.
  1967   Kinship and Marriage. Baltimore: Penguin.
Frank, A. G.
  1967   Capitalism and Underdevelopment in Latin America. New York: Monthly
          Review Press.

Freidson, E.
1970   *Profession of Medicine: A Study of the Sociology of Applied Knowledge.* New York: Dodd, Mead.
Gans, H. J.
1962   *The Urban Villagers.* New York: Free Press.
Garfinkel, H.
1967   *Studies in Ethnomethodology.* Englewood Cliffs, N.J.: Prentice-Hall.
Gibbon, E.
1776–
1787/
1963   *The Decline and Fall of the Roman Empire.* New York: Washington Square Press.
Glen, N. D., and Alston, J. P.
1968   "Cultural distances among occupational categories." *American Sociological Review* **33**:365–382.
Goffman, E.
1951   "Symbols of class status." *British Journal of Sociology* **2**:294–304.
1955   "On face-work: An analysis of ritual elements in social interaction." *Psychiatry* **18**:213–231.
1956   "The nature of deference and demeanor." *American Anthropologist* **58**: 473–502.
1959   *The Presentation of Self in Everyday Life.* New York: Doubleday.
1961a   *Encounters.* Indianapolis: Bobbs-Merrill.
1961b   *Asylums.* New York: Doubleday.
1963a   *Stigma.* Englewood Cliffs, N.J.: Prentice-Hall.
1963b   *Behavior in Public Places.* New York: Free Press.
1967   *Interaction Ritual.* New York: Doubleday.
1969   *Strategic Interaction.* Philadelphia: University of Pennsylvania Press.
1971   *Relations in Public.* New York: Basic Books.
1974   *Frame Analysis.* New York: Harper and Row.
Goode, W. J.
1963   *World Revolution and Family Patterns.* New York: Free Press.
Gouldner, A.
1954   *Patterns of Industrial Bureaucracy.* New York: Free Press.
1959   "Reciprocity and autonomy in functional theory." In L. Z. Gross (Ed.), *Symposium on Sociological Theory,* N.Y.: Row, Peterson.
1960   "The norm of reciprocity: A preliminary statement." *American Sociological Review* **25**:161–178.
1963   *Enter Plato.* New York: Basic Books.
1968   "Sociologist as partisan: Sociology and the welfare state." *American Sociologist* **3** (August).
1970   *The Coming Crisis of Western Sociology.* New York: Basic Books.
1976   *The Dialectic of Ideology and Technology.* New York: Seabury Press.
Green, V.H.H.
1969   *The Universities.* Baltimore: Penguin.
Gusfield, J. R.
1963   *Symbolic Crusade.* Urbana: University of Illinois Press.
Hagstrom, W. O.
1965   *The Scientific Community.* New York: Basic Books.

Han Fei Tzu
  1964   *Basic Writings.* New York: Columbia University Press. Original ca. 235 B.C.
Harris, M.
  1979   *Cultural Materialism.* New York: Random House.
Harvey, F.
  1967   *Air War: Vietnam.* New York: Bantam Books.
Hegel, G. W. F.
  1957   "Introduction to the philosophy of history." In *Hegel Selections.* New York: Scribners.
Hermann, A.
  1966   *An Historical Atlas of China.* Chicago: Aldine.
Hochschild, A. R.
  1979   "Emotion work, feeling rules, and social structure." *American Journal of Sociology* **85**:551–574.
Hughes, E. C.
  1958   *Men and Their Work.* New York: Free Press.
Janowitz, M.
  1960   *The Professional Soldier.* New York: Free Press.
Judd, G.
  1955   *Members of Parliament, 1734–1832.* New Haven: Yale University Press.
Kahl, J. A.
  1957   *The American Class Structure.* New York: Rinehart.
Kohn, M.
  1969   *Class and Conformity.* Homewood, Ill.: Dorsey Press.
Kohn, M., and Schooler, C.
  1969   "Class, occupation, and orientation." *American Sociological Review* **34**: 659–678.
Korpi, W.
  1971   "Working class communism in western Europe: Rational or nonrational." *American Sociological Review* **36**:971–984.
Kosambi, D. D.
  1970   *The Culture and Civilization of Ancient India.* Delhi: Vikas Publications.
Kramer, E. E.
  1970   *The Nature and Growth of Modern Mathematics.* Volume 2. New York: Fawcett Books.
Laumann, E. O., Marsden, P. V., and Galaskiewicz, J.
  1977   "Community-elite influence structures: Extension of a network approach." *American Journal of Sociology* **83**:594–631.
Lenski, G. E.
  1966   *Power and Privilege: a Theory of Social Stratification.* New York: McGraw Hill.
  1970   *Human Societies.* New York: McGraw-Hill.
Lévi-Strauss, C.
  1949/
  1969   *The Elementary Structures of Kinship.* Boston: Beacon Press.
  1955/
  1977   *Tristes Tropiques.* New York: Pocket Books.
  1958/
  1963   *Structural Anthropology.* New York: Basic Books, Doubleday.
  1962/
  1966   *The Savage Mind.* Chicago: University of Chicago Press.

1964/
1969 *The Raw and the Cooked.* New York: Harper and Row.
1968/
1978 *The Origin of Table Manners.* New York:
Liddell-Hart, B. H.
1971 *History of the Second World War.* New York: Putnam.
Lieberson, S. E.
1971 "An empirical study of military-industrial linkages." *Americn Journal of Sociology.* **76**:562–584.
Lipset, S. M.
1960 *Political Man.* New York: Doubleday.
Lipset, S. M., Trow, M. A., and Coleman, J. S.
1956 *Union Democracy.* New York: Doubleday.
Lipset, S. M., and Riesman, D.
1975 *Education and Politics at Harvard.* New York: McGraw-Hill.
Lombard, G. F.
1955 *Behavior in a Selling Group.* Cambridge: Harvard University Press.
Lorenz, K.
1966 *On Aggression.* New York: Harcourt, Brace.
Mann, M.
1970 "The social cohesion of liberal democracy." *American Sociological Review* **35**:423–439.
March, J. G., and Simon, H. A.
1958 *Organizations.* New York: Wiley.
Marx, K.
1963 *The Eighteenth Brumaire of Louis Bonaparte.* New York: International Publishers.
Mauss, M.
1925/1962 *The Gift.* New York: Norton.
McClelland, C.
1974 "The aristocracy and university reform in 18th century Germany." In L. Stone (Ed.), *The University of Society.* Princeton: Princeton University Press. Pp. 146–173.
McEvedy, C.
1961 *The Penguin Atlas of Medieval History.* Baltimore: Penguin.
1967 *The Penguin Atlas of Ancient History.* Baltimore: Penguin.
1972 *The Penguin Atlas of Modern History.* Baltimore: Penguin.
McEvedy, C., and Jones, R.
1978 *Atlas of World Population History.* Baltimore: Penguin.
McNeill, W.
1963 *The Rise of the West.* Chicago: University of Chicago Press.
1964 *Europe's Steppe Frontier.* Chicago: University of Chicago Press.
Mehan, H., et al.
1976 *The Social Organization of Classroom Lessons.* La Jolla, California: Center for Human Information Processing.
Meyer, J.
1977 "The effects of education as an institution." *American Journal of Sociology* **83**:455–477.
Milgram, S.
1963 "Behavior study of obedience." *Journal of Abnormal and Social Psychology* **67**:371–378.

Mills, C. W.
    1959   *The Sociological Imagination.* New York: Oxford University Press.
Moore, Jr., B.
    1966   *Social Origins of Dictatorship and Democracy.* Boston: Beacon Press.
Moorehead, A.
    1963   *The Blue Nile.* New York: Harper and Row.
Mullins, N. C.
    1973   *Theories and Theory Groups in Contemporary American Sociology.* New York: Harper and Row.
Needham, R.
    1971   *Rethinking Kinship and Marriage.* London: Tavistock.
Nef, J. U.
    1952   *War and Human Progress.* Cambridge: Harvard University Press.
North, D. C., and Thomas, R. P.
    1973   *The Rise of the Western World, a New Economic History.* Cambridge, England: Cambridge University Press.
Parsons, T.
    1966   *Societies, Evolutionary and Comparative Perspectives.* Englewood Cliffs, N.J.: Prentice-Hall.
    1967   Evolutionary universals in society. In *Sociological Theory and Modern Society.* New York: Free Press.
    1971   *The System of Modern Societies.* Englewood Cliffs, N.J.: Prentice-Hall.
Paulsen, F.
    1906   *The German Universities and University Study.* New York: Longmans Green.
Perrucci, R., and Pilisuk, I.
    1970   "Leaders and ruling elites: The interorganizational bases of community power." *American Sociological Review* **35**:1040–1056.
Piaget, J.
    1970   *Structuralism.* New York: Basic Books.
Pilcher, D.
    1975   "The sociology of income distribution." Unpublished dissertation: University of California, San Diego.
Pinard, M.
    1968   "Mass society and political movements: A new formulation." *American Journal of Sociology* **73**:682–690.
Portes, A.
    1971   "Political primitivism, differential socialization, and lower-class leftist radicalism." *American Sociological Review* **36**:820–834.
Postan, M. M. (Ed.)
    1966   *The Cambridge Economic History of Europe.* Cambridge, England: Cambridge University Press. Volume 1.
Powicke, F. M.
    1971   *Ways of Medieval Life and Thought.* New York: Crowell.
Quinney, R.
    1970   *The Social Reality of Crime.* Boston: Little, Brown.
Quinquennial Catalogue of the Officers and Graduates of Harvard University,
    1910   1636–1910. Cambridge: Harvard University Press.
Rashdall, H.
    1936   *The Universities of Europe in the Middle Ages.* Oxford: Oxford University Press.

Research Working Group on Cyclical Rhythms and Secular Trends
  1979   "Cyclical rhythms and secular trends of the capitalist world-economy: Some premises, hypotheses, and questions." *Review* **2**:483–500.
Rosenberg, H.
  1958   *Bureaucracy, Aristocracy, and Autocracy.* Cambridge: Harvard University Press.
Rostow, W. W.
  1962   *The Process of Economic Growth.* New York: Norton.
Roth, G.
  1968   Personal rulership, patrimonialism, and empire-building in the new states. In R. Bendix (Ed.), *State and Society,* Boston: Little, Brown.
Roy, D.
  1952   Quota restriction and goldbricking in a machine shop. *American Journal of Sociology* **57**:427–442.
Rudolph, L. I., and Rudolph, S.
  1967   *The Modernity of Tradition.* Chicago: University of Chicago Press.
Sacks, H., Schegloff, E. and Jefferson, G.
  1974   "A simplest systematics for the organization of turn-taking in conversation." *Language* **50**:696–735.
Schegloff, E.
  1967   "The first five seconds." Unpublished dissertation. University of California, Berkeley.
Schelling, T. C.
  1963   *The Strategy of Conflict.* Cambridge, Massachusetts: Harvard University Press.
Schelsky, H.
  1963   *Einsamkeit und Freiheit, Idee und Gestalt der deutschen Universitatx und ihrer Reformen.* Reinbek bei Hamburg: Rowohlt.
Schnabel, F.
  1959   *Deutsche Geschichte in Neunzehnten Jahrhundert.* Volume 1. Freiberg: Verlag Herder.
Schott, S.
  1979   "Emotion and social life: A symbolic interactionist analysis." *American Journal of Sociology* **84**:1317–1334
Scott, M. B., and Lyman, S. M.
  1969   "Accounts." *American Sociological Review* **33**:46–62
Selznick, P.
  1949   *TVA and the Grass Roots.* Berkeley: University of California Press.
  1952   *The Organizational Weapon.* New York: McGraw-Hill.
Shepard, W. R.
  1964   *Historical Atlas.* Ninth edition. New York: Barnes and Noble.
Simon, H. A.
  1947   *Administrative Behavior.* New York: Macmillan.
Simon, J.
  1966   *Education in Tudor England.* Cambridge, England: Cambridge University Press.
Skocpol, T.
  1979   *States and Social Revolutions.* New York: Cambridge University Press.
Sorel, G.
  1908/ *Reflections on Violence.* New York: Free Press.
  1970
Southern, R. W.
  1970   *Western Society and the Church in the Middle Ages.* Baltimore: Penguin.

Spiro, M. E.
  1970 *Buddhism and Society.* New York: Harper and Row.
Stinchcombe, A. L.
  1961 "Agricultural enterprise and rural class relations." *American Journal of Sociology* **67**:165–176.
  1965 "Social structure and organization." In J. G. March (Ed.), *Handbook of Organizations.* Chicago: Rand McNally.
  1968 *Constructing Social Theories.* New York: Harcourt, Brace.
Stone, L.
  1967 *The Crisis of the Aristocracy.* New York: Oxford University Press.
  1974 "The size and composition of the Oxford student body, 1500–1900. "In L. Stone (Ed.), *The University in Society.* Princeton: Princeton University Press.
Suzuki, D. T.
  1959 *Zen and Japanese Culture.* New York: Pantheon.
Thomas, K.
  1971 *Religion and the Decline of Magic.* New York: Scribners.
Thomas, L.
  1956 *The Occupational Structure and Education.* Englewood Cliffs, N.J.: Prentice-Hall.
Tilly, C.
  1967 *The Vendée: A Sociological Analysis of the Counterrevolution of 1793.* New York: Wiley.
  1978 *From Mobilization to Revolution.* Reading, Mass.: Addison-Wesley.
Tilly, C., Tilley, L., and Tilley, R.
  1975 *The Rebellious Century: 1830–1930.* Cambridge, Massachusetts: Harvard University Press.
Tocqueville, A. de
  1840/
  1960 *Democracy in America.* Volume 2. New York: Vintage Books.
Touraine, A.
  1973 *Production de la Société.* Paris: Éditions du Seuil.
Toynbee, A. J.
  1954 *A Study of History.* Volume 9. London: Oxford University Press.
Toynbee, A. J., and Meyers, E. D.
  1959 *Historical Atlas and Gazeteer.* Volume 11. In *A Study of History.* London: Oxford University Press.
Trevor-Roper, H. R.
  1967 *Religion, Reformation, and Social Change.* London: Macmillan.
Tuchman, G.
  1972 "Objectivity as strategic ritual." *American Journal of Sociology* **77**:660–679.
Wallerstein, I.
  1974 *The Modern World-System.* Volume 1. In *Capitalist Agriculture and the Origins of the European World-Economy in the Sixteenth Century.* New York: Academic Press.
  1979 *The Capitalist World-Economy.* New York: Cambridge University Press.
  1980 *The Modern World-System.* Volume 2. In *Mercantilism and the Consolidation of the European World-Economy, 1600–1750.* New York: Academic Press.
Ward, A. W., Prothero, G. W., and Leathes, S. (eds.)
  1907 *The Cambridge Modern History.* Volume 1. Cambridge, England: Cambridge University Press.
Warner, W. L.
  1959 *The Living and the Dead.* New Haven: Yale University Press.

Weber, M.
1915/ *The Religion of China.* New York: Free Press.
1951
1916– *The Religion of India.* New York: Free Press.
1917/
1958
1922/ *Economy and Society.* New York: Bedminster Press.
1968

Weinberg, I.
1967 *The English Public Schools.* New York: Atherton Press.

Wertheim, W. F.
1968 "Sociological aspects of corruption in southeast Asia." In R. Bendix (Ed.),
State and Society. Boston: Little, Brown.

Wilensky, H. L.
1956 *Intellectuals in Labor Unions.* New York: Free Press.
1964 "The professionalization of everyone?" *American Journal of Sociology*
70:137–158.

Wiley, N.
1967 "America's unique class politics: The interplay of the labor, credit, and commodity markets." *American Sociological Review* **32**:529–540.

Williamson, O. E.
1975 *Markets and Hierarchies. A Study of the Economics of Internal Organization.*
New York: Free Press.

Index